Highways and Byways
in the
WEST HIGHLANDS

Castle Stalker.

Highways and Byways

in the

WEST HIGHLANDS

Seton Gordon

Introduction by
Raymond Eagle

Illustrations by
Sir D. Y. Cameron, R.A.

*Foreword and a glossary of place-name elements
with aids to pronunciation by*
W. J. Watson

ublished in 1995
.td,
Street,
h

First published in 1935 by MacMillan and Co., Limited.

ISBN: 1 874744 32 7

British Library Cataloguing-in-Publication Data
A Catalogue record for this book is available
from the British Library.

Cover photograph of
Ardtreck Point and Oronsay, Isle of Skye
by Colin Baxter

Designed by Gourlay Graphics Glasgow

Printed and bound in Great Britain
by Cromwell Press Limited

PREFACE

When I was asked by the friendly publishing firm of Macmillan whether I would undertake, as a work of one volume, the vast area of the western seaboard and islands of Scotland lying between Cape Wrath in the north and Arran in the south, I hesitated. I felt that not one, but at least half a dozen books could be written about that part of Scotland and that a single volume must have the disadvantage of describing only superficially certain parts of that area. For example, a book might be written about Skye, another book about Arran, a large volume on the county of Argyll, and so on. Of certain districts at all events I have written fully, and all through the work I have endeavoured to give as accurate information as possible.

The area described is the Outer and Inner Hebrides and the western mainland of the Highlands of Scotland. This western mainland area of which I have written is bounded roughly by a line joining the heads of the long sea lochs. Loch Lomond is included because it may be said to be the natural route of the traveller from Glasgow to the West Highlands.

The interest of the book grew as I progressed with it, and now that it is completed I can say that it has been the means of my meeting new friends and of reviving old friendships, and it has also taken me over what is to my mind the most delightful part of Scotland and indeed of the British Isles. In whatever district I happened to be I found the people of that district, one and all, anxious to help me, offer me hospitality and place valuable information at my disposal. The number of my helpers has accordingly been so large that I am unable to thank them individually by name, but this does not lessen my feeling of thankfulness to them all.

The proofs of the book have been revised by sea, and on moorland and hill. One evening of June of the present year (1934)

I sat up to midnight correcting proofs beside the summit of Bruach na Frìthe, one of the Cuillin of Skye. I sat here at a height of over 3,300 feet above the Atlantic and facing north, and at midnight the glow of the sunset was still so strong that I had no difficulty in reading print

In writing the volume I have consulted, among many works, such classics as the following :

> Martin's *Western Islands of Scotland* (1703).
> Pennant's *Tour in Scotland* (1772).
> Gregory's *History of the Western Highlands and Islands*.
> Skene's *Celtic Scotland*.
> MacFarlane's *Geographical Collections*.
> *Origines Parochiales Scotiæ*.
> The new and old *Statistical Accounts*.
> Professor Watson's *Celtic Place-Names of Scotland*.
> The *History of the Clan MacLean*.
> Hill's *MacDonnells of the Glens and Antrim*.

My special thanks are due to Professor W. J. Watson of Edinburgh University for his great assistance to me throughout the writing of the book. This scholar has placed his deep knowledge of Celtic matters most generously at my disposal at all times when I had occasion to ask his advice, and he has also kindly read through the proofs for me. His " Glossary of Place-Name Elements," which he has written specially for the book, could perhaps have been compiled by no other Gaelic scholar with the same authority; it contains new, and very valuable information.

I also owe much to the encouragement and helpful suggestions of my wife, who has been my companion by sea and land over the greater part of the area I have described.

SETON GORDON.

Upper Duntuilm,
Isle of Skye,
August 1934.

CONTENTS

CONTENTS

CHAPTER XXXVI

CHAPTER XXXVII

CHAPTER XXXVIII

CHAPTER XXXIX

CHAPTER XL

CHAPTER XLI

CHAPTER XLII

CHAPTER XLIII

CHAPTER XLIV

CHAPTER XLV

CHAPTER XLVI

CHAPTER XLVII

LIST OF ILLUSTRATIONS

xiii

INTRODUCTION

THE POPULAR *Highways and Byways* series, with their familiar blue covers and gold lettering, embraced Scotland, England and Wales. Most were of individual counties while others, particularly for Scotland, covered larger geographic regions.

In selecting Seton Gordon to write two of the major titles, on the *West and Central Highlands*, the Publisher made a wise choice. A trained field naturalist and foremost authority on the golden eagle, he had lived in both areas; his early days on Deeside where he spent many hours in all seasons exploring the Cairngorms or neighbouring Speyside. Later he moved to the Isle of Skye from where he regularly spent days or weeks in various locations from Kintyre to the Outer Hebrides. These two volumes are enhanced by the pen and ink drawings of artist Sir David Young (D.Y.) Cameron who, in 1930 was appointed King's Painter and Limner in Scotland.

Seton Gordon published twenty-five books and hundreds of articles on the Highlands and Islands. He was unique in many ways, not the least that he wore the kilt as his everyday dress, summer and winter. The uniqueness of his writing lay in his ability to transport the reader so that they saw the world through his all-discerning eyes; eyes that were still strong and unaided when he died aged ninety-one in 1977.

Whatever the time of day or time of year, he retained an impression and made it come alive in one of his narratives. Every sunrise, every sunset, every cloud formation and nuance of light he witnessed was as though he saw them for the first time. His writing captured the magic of the Highlands, where light and distance lend an ethereal quality found in few places on Earth and the cloud effects belong to some other dimension.

From the western shore of Kintyre, Seton Gordon tells of watching the sinking sun. In all the times that he watched the sun set, he never penned a repetitive description. On this occasion he wrote; "From a sky overspread by soft cloud a shaft of glowing light shone on sea and land, suffusing the long Atlantic combers that broke upon the shore. Faintly across the sea was Gigha, mysterious across the drowsy waters, and as darkness settled on the coast the tremulous uncompleted autumn songs of wandering curlews mingled with the low murmuring of advancing seas."

Even while editing and correcting proofs he could be found, not at his desk but sitting by a peak in Skye's Cuillin Hills, or within sound of the breaking waves on some western shore. The area covered by this volume, though not immense to someone from outside of the British Isles, is diverse in both scenery and historical events. Because of his wide knowledge there are comments on people and places that others would most certainly have missed. These are just as likely to tell of some ancient piece of folklore as of historical detail.

The years have not been kind to many of the ruins that Seton Gordon describes and Duntulm Castle, near his home on Skye's dramatic north end is no exception. Though still distinctive, most of the keep has disappeared onto the rocks, but it is a significant place in the history of Clan MacDonald and he tells many stories of its place in the clan history. In clear weather the long line of the Outer Hebrides, capped with shimmering cumulus cloud makes a wonderful sight from the castle knoll.

The value of this book and its companion *Central Highlands* is that though several years have passed since they were first published the information is still valid. The roads are busier and there are more people at places of interest, but most come avid for knowledge. Wherever you visit, whether it is Glenfinnan to see where the Jacobite Standard was raised in 1745; or to Dunvegan Castle in Skye to view the Clan Macleod treasures; or perhaps to the Standing Stones at Callernish on Lewis, you will find a wealth of information told in a pleasing anecdotal style.

There has been in recent years a resurgence of the Gaelic language and there is now a Gaelic business college in Skye near Armadale. Gaelic signs are prominent in the Hebrides. You will find in the people a natural friendliness and courtesy that has not been lost despite the number of visitors.

It is still possible to get off the beaten track but it may be necessary to explore by foot occasionally. West of Glenfinnan is Ardnamurchan where, after journeying through some of the finest scenery in the Highlands the road ends at the lighthouse built on the most westerly promontory of the Scottish mainland. En route is Tioram Castle, once the home of the MacDonalds of Clanranald. It has been a ruin since 1715 but so complete is the keep that at first glance the castle appears whole.

Along the coast from Arisaig to Mallaig the smaller isles of Eigg, Rhum, Canna and Muick will appear. The most easily recognised is Eigg, with its distinctive sloping ridge, or Scurr. It was one of Seton Gordon's favourite islands and to sail there is to enter into tranquillity and timelessness. All of these places he knew well and writes of them in these pages.

No matter what weather is encountered, no matter along which of his highways or byways your itinerary might take you, you will be blessed with days that will leave a memory like no other. It is a rare visitor who does not leave regretfully and with a determination, even a longing, to one day return.

RAYMOND EAGLE, F.S.A. Scot.,
West Vancouver, B.C., Canada, 1995

HIGHWAYS AND BYWAYS IN THE WEST HIGHLANDS

CHAPTER I

CAPE WRATH TO SCOURIE

IF you travel north-west from Lairg through the heart of the Reay Country—by Loch Shin, Ben Clibreck and Loch Loyal —you come at length, after many a weary mile, to the open Atlantic. That north-west seaboard of the Scottish Highlands is wild and primitive. Never—not even in the outermost Isles of the Hebrides—have I been so impressed by the loneliness of the shore. Lonely it is, yet with a charm of its own. Inland, the Reay Country is sometimes dreary, but on the coast one is beneath the spell of the beneficent ocean, and one's eyes feast upon ever-changing beauties. A country of sea lochs, wild capes, promontories and pink rock walls and, here and there, set like oases in the desert, delightful bays with sands of burnished gold— that is the north-west coast of Scotland in the Reay Country of brave men and fair women.

When, in 1263, King Haco of Norway sailed south with his splendid fleet to right the wrongs of the isles-folk of Skye he rounded Cape Wrath and, according to the Saga which bears his name, anchored his fleet at Asleifarvīk (now corruptly written as Oldshore Beg) near the northern entrance to Loch Inchard, some twenty-five miles south of Cape Wrath. There is a tradition among the old people of the district that a ship of the Norse fleet was lost on a wild part of the coast a mile or two south of Cape Wrath and that her crew, all except two, were lost with her. These two men with great daring climbed the

B   E

face of the precipitous cliff and reached the open country of Parbh (then a haunt of wolves) beyond the rocks. One of the vikings had in his belt a hatchet, and when he was half-way up the cliff, finding the hatchet a hindrance to him, he left it on a ledge, and there, the old people say, can yet be seen the rusty remains of what was once, almost seven hundred years ago, a keen-edged axe. There is a narrow road to Cape Wrath from the farther shore of the Kyle of Durness, but it is not possible to take one's car across the ferry, and the seven miles must be travelled on foot. It is gratifying to find one road in the highlands which the walker has to himself.

It is inspiring to stand upon Cape Wrath (the name is derived from the Norse word Hvarf, a turning-point) [1] on a sunny day of spring when the north wind urges toward the Minch the blue, crested waves, and to visualise the passing of that great and well-disciplined fleet of fair-haired Norse giants, dauntless and unwearying. The course of that fleet had doubtless been the course of the gannets which flew south, all that April day, five hundred feet below me as I stood upon the Cape. These strong-winged fishermen had come in small companies from the direction of the Pentland Firth. A little way offshore they flew, and when they had rounded the Cape they steered before the wind with gliding, undulating flight west toward the distant Lewis coast. They were perhaps the birds of an Orkney nesting stack ranging far in search of fish, or far-travelled gannets of St. Kilda on passage from some northern fishing ground to St. Kilda rocks, which lay one hundred and sixty miles to the south-west.

From Cape Wrath on a clear day the low land of northern Lewis is visible on the far western horizon, with the lighthouse upon the Butt of Lewis rising, needle-like, to grey skies. In very clear weather the remote island of North Rona may be seen, and the Orkney group of islands, with their gannet stack gleaming white in distant sunshine. More often than not the view west and north is of dun-coloured seas which show no trace of land.

[1] Sometimes to-day written in the Gaelic form of Parbh.

Beside Cape Wrath are two low rocks, over which the Atlantic swells stream in white waterfalls. Am Bodach (the Old Man) and A' Chailleach (the Old Woman) are the names of these rocks, where lobster fishermen set their creels and the fulmar petrel sails in swift flight when the increasing gale brings exultation to its tireless spirit. As one sits high above the sea, among the small crimson buds of the thrift, one looks south to a towering, slender stack which rises some eight miles down the coast. Am Buachaille (the Herdsman) is the name of this lonely rock, and it is more easily approached from Gualainn Lodge, midway between Durness and Rhiconich, than from Cape Wrath.

The north wind was chill and the hill ran water after a night of rain when I crossed westward from Gualainn to Am Buachaille of the Atlantic. The moorlands were silent and deserted, until six ravens appeared overhead and with incessant croakings— whether in ardent discussion or unbridled rage I know not— mounted to a height so vast that at last they were seen in the sky as small black specks. Except for the early draw-moss with its pale yellow flower heads and four violets upon a south-leaning grassy bank, the hill was as lifeless as at mid-winter, and so it was with pleasure that I reached the watershed and looked north-west to the horizon where a line of distant waves broke white upon a shore of pure sand. Sandwood Bay is the name of that very lonely shore, and when at length I had left behind me the last of the delaying peat hags and was now approaching the shore I saw that it had been well named by the Norsemen of old.

Sandwood is from Sand-vatn or Sand-water. There is a small loch beside this shore, and a small river leading from it to the sea. I doubt not that there are salmon and sea trout here in abundance in the season of summer, but when I passed that way it was too early for them to leave their ocean home. I was astonished at the number of wrecks which lie on the fine sand of this bay. All of them are old tragedies : since the placing of a lighthouse on Cape Wrath just over a hundred years ago no vessel has been lost here. Some of the wrecks lie almost buried in the sand far above the reach of the highest tide. Perhaps viking ships are here and the galleys of highland chiefs are buried deep beneath the blown sand. It is evident that the ocean is receding on this part of the coast.

Sandwood Bay and its loch are singularly beautiful, singularly aloof and lonely. As I stood on the damp glistening sands where the Atlantic combers broke eagerly in white foam I could imagine myself in some uninhabited land. Never, either before or since, have I felt in Scotland this sense of loneliness so strongly. Perhaps it is haunted by the spirits of the past—as Magdalena Bay in Northern Spitsbergen is haunted. In that bay I have felt the same curious sense of lonely beauty. There blue glacier walls rose sheer from the ocean towards the dark peaks and airy spires. There, too, were relics of man—bleached lidless coffins, no more than half buried, near the shore, and ancient inscriptions telling of the fate of the daring seamen of old.

I believe that Sandwood Bay is the most beautiful place on all the west coast of the Scottish mainland—the Isles I except. The beauty of its sand dunes, its green *machair*, its dark rocks that guard it, is the greater because of the dreary inland bogs. That April day on which I visited Sandwood Bay the white waves surged in upon the shore in a confused, impetuous company. A faint breeze from the north-west drifted in, ice-cold, from the ocean. At length the delaying sun broke through the thin cloud canopy and shone brilliantly upon the cheerful *machair*, where many rabbits fed, and upon the wreck-strewn shore. High overhead drifted rather than flew some wandering common gulls. A little company of ringed plover tripped gallantly over the *machair*. On the northern horizon rose Cape Wrath lighthouse, and a telescope showed its storm-torn flag flying five hundred feet above the sea. On the cape that bounds the bay toward the south rose Am Buachaille, the Herdsman, whose feet were washed by the spume that, even on this calm spring day, broke incessantly about them. A great steamship passed slowly west from behind Cape Wrath, bound for some transatlantic port. A trawler, deep-laden with her catch of fish for the English market, steered south.

There is a very delightful walk along the coast from Sandwood Bay south to Sheigra, a small township whose men-folk work at the lobster fishing, summer and winter. As I began this walk, along an ancient byway, and climbed from Sandwood Bay to the cape that overlooks Am Buachaille, fulmar petrels glided past me. In the green ocean far below an old shag was diving for his dinner. The water was shallow, and he could be seen making his way to the bottom, reminding me of those insects known as " water boatmen " which are found in moorland lochs and moorland streams. I noticed that he was careful to time his appearance on the surface during a lull between the breaking waves. Rather less than two miles out into the ocean rose a rocky island where many sea-birds had arrived for the season of their nesting. Through my telescope I watched the quaint behaviour of a green cormorant [1] on the crown of the island. She (for I presume by her antics that she must have been a female) was running about the grass with an absurd mincing gait and now and again tugged hard at the fronds of the stunted bracken growing on the island. She was evidently house-building, and when she had stuffed her bill full of bracken and dried grass she flew a little way out to sea, then soared gracefully in and alighted on a ledge of rock. A peregrine falcon sailed along the cliff beside me and a little later a gannet passed north, flying at its utmost speed. Perhaps its thoughts were of its mate on that distant stack beside the Orkneys. A well-worn sheep track led south along the edge of the high rocks, and here Alpine plants were awakening from their winter sleep. Young green shoots appeared upon the cushions of *dryas octopetala* and *silene acaulis*. The track crossed a burn which flows down from a small loch marked on the map as Loch a' Mhuilinn—the Loch of the Mill. There are old ruins where the burn enters the ocean through a

---

[1] Another name for the shag.

small narrow glen. Perhaps they are the remains of the mill from which the burn was long ago named. One can see traces of the old "lazy beds" or *feannaigan* on the hillside here, but it is long since folk lived their hard life in this tiny glen, entirely cut off from the outside world. They lived near to the heart of nature, and the roar of the eager waves fell as solemn music on their ears—that music which calls the wanderer back to the ocean from the silence of the inland country.

From Allt a' Mhuilinn one climbs again to high ground, and looks south over a wide expanse of hill and sea. On the horizon stands Rudha Storr, and in the middle distance the isle of Handa rises. Inland Ben Stack shows its shapely peak and the great bulk of Foinne Bheinn rises to the clouds. There is solitude upon the shore : there is solitude upon the hill. Surely in all this country there is to-day no human habitation ! But one climbs that last *cnocan*, or little hill, and sees, immediately beneath one, the clustered houses of Sheigra with the thin blue smoke of peat fires rising into the evening air, while beyond the village the swell breaks white beside Asleifarvik, where King Haco's fleet anchored that August evening of the year 1263.

At Sheigra one finds a road which is passable for motor-cars. This road, running south-east, passes the populous crofting township of Oldshore, then leads to Kinloch Bervie and joins the main road from Durness to Scourie at Rhiconich, where there is a hotel. From Kinloch Bervie the road rises and falls beside Loch Inchard, through fine wild scenery. Loch Inchard is the most northerly of all the sea lochs on the west coast of Scotland, and at one time was celebrated for its winter herring fishing. From Rhiconich the main road leads to Laxford Bridge, where it joins the main road to Lairg and the east coast. But the wayfarer who wishes to keep to the western highways and byways finds a road which continues south, through a country of many lochs and lochans, and brings him soon to the village of Scourie, where there is a comfortable hotel on a small bay looking west to the Atlantic.

CHAPTER II

HANDA

NORTH-WEST from Scourie a long, high island rises from the ocean. Its name is Handa (the Sandy Isle) and its green *machair* and white sands contrast restfully with the deep blue of the sea. In summer, Handa is a pleasant isle. From the high ground of Scourie the sun is seen, of a June evening, to sink tardily behind its cliffs and tinge with a rosy flush the swell that breaks with irresistible might across the sunken rock known as the Bogha Mór, where great lythe [1] have their home. At midnight, when the afterglow creeps round to the northern horizon and the young moon shines serenely in the west, red-throated divers fly down from the hill lochs for their night's sea fishing, and make weird music as the flood tide creeps slowly across the sands of Scourie. On Handa a hundred years ago seven crofting families lived. The light sandy soil of their island produced excellent potatoes, and they subsisted on these, and on the fish which they caught. There was a Queen of Handa, as there was until 1930 a Queen of St. Kilda, and like the St. Kildans, the men of Handa perhaps held a " parliament " each morning to decide on the affairs of the day. A hundred years ago strangers rarely set foot on Handa, and the people of the isle spoke the Gaelic tongue and had little or no knowledge of English. Then came the disastrous potato famine of 1845, and the people of Handa were in sorry plight. Since starvation faced them, they unwillingly emigrated to America. Picture the scene as the people of the Sandy Isle boarded the vessel which had come for them and had cast anchor in Loch Laxford. Their hearts were heavy with

[1] Pollack.

sorrow as their ship steered west. The old folk knew that never again would they see their beloved isle. They gazed upon it, crowding the stern of the ship, until the highest point of Handa had sunk below the waves, and only the cone of Ben Stack and the long ridge of Foinne-Bheinn remained in their vision.

Handa to-day is uninhabited by man, but is still the home of myriads of sea-fowl. It is a memorable experience to sail round Handa in fine summer weather. The sea is literally alive with guillemots, razorbills, puffins, and kittiwake gulls. With a flick of their wings the guillemots and razorbills dive as the boat nears them, or rise excitedly from the water and circle about the boat, steering themselves with their large webbed feet which, rather than the short stumpy tail, serve as rudder. The 400-feet sheer rocks are black with nesting guillemots, and among them are colonies of kittiwakes. It is on an isolated rock almost touching the main island—the Stack of Handa—that the nesting sea-fowl are most numerous, and their cries almost drown the roar of the Atlantic swell which throws white spray high on the grim rocks which have withstood the buffeting of the ocean for an eternity.

The landing-places are on the east and south-east of Handa. Here are sands that gleam in the summer sun, and an emerald *machair* or stretch of short green turf, small and delightful. On the sands oyster catchers hold their parliaments, and ringed plover flit across the short grass, flying above the old, unenclosed, burying-ground where lie the mortal remains of the sons and daughters of Handa. The *machair* soon gives place to rocks, where silent fulmar petrels glide and wheel above their mates who brood in some crevice of the rock. In the niches of the dark cliffs sea thrift blossoms, pale rose or crimson, and in the air is the pleasant scent given off by crowberry plants under the summer sun. On one of the rocks a colony of greater blackbacked gulls nest by themselves. They are marauders and murderers : they kill the puffins, and they suck the eider ducks' eggs.

On the broad heathery crown of Handa are several lochans. The day on which I visited the island I watched for a time as beautiful a bird picture as I have ever seen. A white cloud of kittiwakes circled low above the loch. A continuous stream of these graceful birds was arriving at the lochan from their nesting quarters far down the face of the cliff. There was a second stream of returning birds, orderly and narrow. The arrivals from the cliff glided down to the peaty water of the lochan, delighted in a long and thorough bath, and when they rose, shaking the water from their snowy plumage, they alighted at the margin of the loch and stood there in rows, diligently pulling up moss and grass. As each kittiwake filled its bill it rose with its burden and flew across to the great sea cliff where its nest was, dropping out of sight when it reached the edge of the precipice. There was a sudden short-lived panic when a peregrine falcon sailed overhead, the birds rising in a white cloud and each one dropping oceanward like a stone when the edge of the cliff was reached. Later in the day I noticed that the kittiwakes had changed their bathing-place and were disporting themselves in a small loch about half a mile distant from where I had watched them in the morning.

Not the least interesting feature of the island of Handa is its Stack. The Stack of Handa rests upon three great pillars. At its nearest point it is only a few yards from the parent isle, but it is fifty years and more since that narrow abyss of five hundred feet was crossed and human feet last trod the crown of the Stack. The last people to cross to the Stack were a fearless crew from Lewis—men who were doubtless skilled in fowling upon the cliffs of Sùla-Sgeir and North Rona—and by means of a rope they traversed those giddy yards with the roaring surf five hundred feet beneath them. Taking with them a bountiful harvest of birds and their young from the Stack, they returned across the stormy Minch to their distant homes on Lewis. It is interesting that no sea-birds now nest upon the top of the Stack of Handa; it seems that the tradition has been handed down to them that there is danger here.   Yet, did they know it, they are now very safe on the Stack.   Wooden stakes, bleached by many winter storms, may be seen to-day on the top of the Stack of Handa, where they were placed by the men of Lewis one summer day more than half a century ago.

The old " Statistical Account " tells of a celebrated native of Handa.   The name of this small man was Iain Beag mac Dhomh-nall mhic Huisdein, and he was one of the MacLeods of Assynt. Iain Beag (Little John) although small in stature, was of great strength and skilled in the use of arms.   He kept his *birlinn* or galley of twelve oars on Handa ready for any daring enter-prise.   His greatest deed was the killing of a hated judge, Judge Morrison of Lewis, the representative of James VI in the Western Isles.   When he had killed this man Iain Beag married his widow.

Handa is an island of contrasts.   It is a curious experience to leave suddenly the sound of the Atlantic surf and to cross quiet moorlands leading to a green *machair* and white sands on the sheltered side of the island where no wave breaks on a summer day.

One day a lover of old pipe tunes visited the *machair*.   Near to the ancient burial-ground he tuned his pipes and I heard him play a composition by one of the hereditary pipers of a highland chief.   The tune that wandering piper played on Handa was the Lament for Donald the Dauntless, Lord of the Reay Country, and in the playing of the tune I heard a lament, not for the chief alone, but for the old people borne in exile across the sea, and the old language of the Gael.

CHAPTER III

THERE is no wilder or more magnificent part of the coast of the Scottish mainland than Wester Sutherland. The land here is deeply indented by the Atlantic. Loch Inchard, Loch Laxford, Loch Carn Bàn, Loch Inver, are a few of these sea lochs, where silver birches stoop to the tidal streams and the bloom of the heather mingles its purple tones with rock gardens of rosy sea anemones which open their tenuous feelers at the coming of the flood-tide.

Here is a land where the place names—Laxford, Handa, Storr—tell of the time when the Norse ruled the western fringe of Scotland, and the Celtic peoples were temporarily eclipsed. With the defeat of King Haco at Largs in 1263 the viking influence came to an end, and during the following centuries Gaelic was the universal language in Wester Sutherland. But now the language of the Gael is passing with startling swiftness from the Sutherland seaboard. So recently as twenty-five years ago little but Gaelic was heard here. Now English is the spoken language, and indeed few of the children have a word of Gaelic, while the old people speak it but seldom. The railway is often blamed for the disappearance of the highland tongue, but in Wester Sutherland the blame must lie elsewhere, for the sea is still the highroad here, and the old Highland Railway is many miles distant over the hills.

From Lairg in Easter Sutherland (where the railway approaches nearest to the western seaboard) a road strikes westward along the shore of Loch Shin, and after crossing mile upon mile of moorland where no house is seen, reaches the watershed at Loch

Merkland and leads north-west through the Duke of West-minster's beautiful forest of Loch More. This loch is separated from Loch Stack by a short river, and from Loch Stack rises a steep and noble hill that was named of old by Norsemen the Stack, that is, the Sharp Hill.

From Loch Stack (where the ruins of a hunting residence of the MacKays, Lords of the Reay Country, stand on one of the islands) the road leads north-west to Laxford Bridge, and then branches—one fork going to Rhiconich, the other to Scourie of the white sands. To climb Ben Stack on a clear day of summer is to realise the loneliness of Wester Sutherland. Far beneath the climber, in every direction, but especially to the north-west, lie an incredible number of fresh-water lochs. They are of all sizes, and each one reflects the blue of the summer sky. A dozen, a score, two score, three score, four score, are counted, and still they stretch away in apparently endless succession. Rising from these lochs, their summits often lost in the idly-drifting clouds that form at noontide heat, are splendid hills—Arcuill, Foinne Bheinn, Beinn Leoid (named perhaps after MacLeod of Assynt)—while some fifteen miles to the south the massive Ben More Assynt is the cradle of snow even at midsummer. Bird life is scarce on these great hills. From the cairn which marks the summit of Ben Stack the golden eagle suns himself, scanning with proud glance the innumerable lochs which lie beneath him. On the breeze from time to time is heard the croak of a wandering raven, or the snorting cry of a cock ptarmigan, surveying his more limited world from his favourite rock. The buzzard (perhaps because the golden eagle is unfriendly to him) is rarely seen here, and the red grouse makes way for the red deer. Scourie—in Gaelic the name is Sgobhairigh, from the Norse skógr, a copse, and Norse-Gaelic erg, a shieling, that is, the Shieling by the Little Wood—stands looking across the Atlantic to the distant coast of Lewis. Scourie was the home of a noted highlander, Evander MacIver, and in his *Reminiscences* he writes an interesting description of the highland life of a past generation.

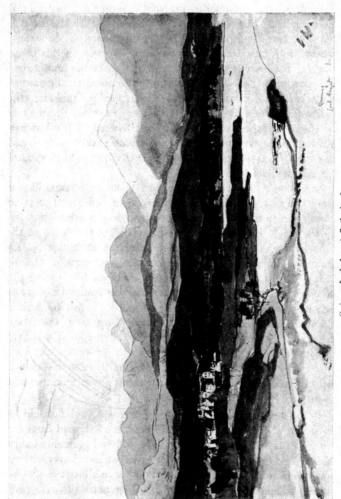

Quinag, Loch Assynt, Sutherland.

From Scourie the road to the south skirts the broad bay of Eddrachillis. This word in Gaelic is Eadar da Chaolas, the Bay between two Kyles, and many isles lie upon its wide waters, where the Atlantic swell roams at will. Because of this broad bay the road winds south-eastward to Kylestrome and crosses the narrows of Loch Carn Bàn at a spot marked on the map as Kylesku, a bad mutilation of the Gaelic Caolas Cumhang (the Narrow Strait). The motor ferry here must for its distance be the most expensive in Scotland, as it is only a few hundred yards across. East of Kylesku the sea loch again broadens, and in two channels—Loch Glen Dhu and Loch Glen Coul—penetrates far into the hills.

It was on a summer day, with much cloud and a strong breeze from the east, that I sailed up these lochs which call to mind Norwegian fjords. Here dark rocks and deep heather approach to the tide. Eider drakes were perturbed at the speed of the launch on which I travelled, and red-throated divers flew swiftly from the approaching craft. Upon the great bulk of Quinag (2653 feet) fast-moving clouds rested. From far beyond the confines of Sutherland Quinag is a prominent landmark, and can be seen from the Isle of Skye. The name of the hill in Gaelic is Cuinneag, which means a milk stoup. Glen Dhu, the Black Glen, was true to its name, for darkness rested upon it, but here and there the sombre tones of its smooth ice-worn rocks were relieved by water dropping from the heights above to the sea loch beneath in a white cascade that appeared light as a feather and as intangible as air.

If the motorist who ferries his car across Kylesku should be in search of adventure he should take the coast road from the ferry to Loch Inver. On this road he will find gradients to try his car, and he will be fortunate if he reaches Loch Inver with no unexpected halt by the way. My own car in all its twenty-two years had met no gradient that it had been unable to overcome, and so (despite gloomy warnings) my wife and I with our heavy camping and photographing outfit set out along the coast road.

Ardvreck Castle, Loch Assynt.

At first the road was very narrow, but the gradients were not alarming. Then we descended what appeared to be a sheer precipice, crossed a narrow bridge, and found barring our way a great hill the gradient of which must have been at least one in three. At the first attempt the ancient Wolseley faltered at the steepest corner. A cautious descent in reverse was made to the foot of the hill, and a second gallant effort met—but only just— with the success it deserved. During the journey along this road we saw no car, but a roadman with whom we conversed told us that many cars used it during the summer tourist season.

The more cautious motorist will probably avoid the coast road and will journey south along the road that leads across the *bealach* or hill pass from Kylesku to the head of Loch Assynt. When he arrives at this beautiful loch he will see, beside the road, one of the most interesting old ruins in the highlands. Ardvreck Castle is the name of this ancient dwelling, which for long was the fortress home of the MacLeods of Assynt. It is believed that so long ago as the Battle of Bannockburn the last of the MacNicols (who had held Assynt from time immemorial) married a MacLeod of Lewis, and that from this marriage came the MacLeods of Assynt.

It was Neil MacLeod of Assynt who is said to have betrayed the great Marquess of Montrose and sold him to Leslie for £20,000 Scots and 400 bols of meal, " and that sour." A few years before that betrayal (in May 1646) Ardvreck Castle was besieged by the MacKenzies. Domhnall Bàn was Laird of Assynt at the time, and he successfully defended the castle against the invaders. But whether or no Neil of Assynt really had a hand in the betrayal of Montrose, from that time the family fortunes steadily declined. In 1654 " Seaforth made great depredations at Assint, destroyed a very great quantity of wine and Brandy which the Laird of Assint had bought, besides other commodities, to the value of 50,000 merks, out of a ship then on the coast, carryed of 2,400 cows, 1,500 horses, about 6,000 sheep and goats, besides that he burnt and destroyed many familys." In July 1672 Neil was denounced as rebel, and commission of fire and sword was obtained against him and his people. The Seaforth MacKenzies then took possession of Assynt and held it for the next hundred years.

In 1760 or thereabouts Hugh MacLeod, second of Geanies, attempted to buy back the estate of Assynt, but was outbid by the Sutherland family, who held the property until about thirty years ago, when it was bought by Major-General Stewart, the present owner. Near the old castle stand the ruins of Calda House which was built by the MacKenzies when they took over the estate. The house is now merely a shell, and the tradition is that it was destroyed by fire at the hands of the MacRaes of Kintail when the estate was sold to the Sutherland family, for the MacRaes vowed that no Earl of Sutherland should occupy it. To-day the ruins of the castle and the old house stand side by side upon the lonely shore of Loch Assynt.

On the shingle beneath the castle oyster catchers nest and divers glide past in their courtship as they doubtless did in the days when Assynt's piper played a *fàilte* or welcome when MacLeod of MacLeod, the chief of the clan, sailing over the sea in his *birlinn* from Dunvegan in Skye, landed at Loch Inver and steered up Loch Assynt in the lesser galley put at his disposal by the chieftain of Assynt.

At Kirkton, near the head of Loch Assynt, is the site of the first church built in the district. Angus MacLeod, laird of Assynt about 1440, travelled widely in France and Italy. He received favours from the Pope, and vowed that in return he would build and endow a church. At the end of the eighteenth century there remained of the original building an arched vault, the burying-place of the MacLeods of Assynt.

From Ardvreck Castle to the village of Loch Inver is a run of rather more than half an hour by car, first along the loch (where the present mansion house of Assynt is seen standing nobly amongst birch trees), then by way of the River Inver, where salmon are plentiful.

C

CHAPTER IV

FROM Handa or Scourie to Rudha Storr is a distance of not more than ten miles by sea, but by land it is three times that length, for the coast-line is deeply indented. The road, too, is hilly and uneven, and it is necessary to travel slowly. There are few places on the mainland of Scotland more remote than Rudha Storr. It is the best part of half a day's journey from Loch Inver, and Loch Inver is half a day's journey from the nearest railway stations at Lairg or Invershin.

Rudha Storr takes its name from the stake-like rock or pinnacle which rises from the deep water of the sea close to the headland. This pinnacle the Norsemen named Staurr, the Stake, and afterwards the Gaelic population of the district added the word Rudha, the Headland. The place-name is thus half Norse, half Gaelic, but this combination is not infrequent in the west; witness Rudha Hunish in northern Skye.

Much of the country of the Sutherland coast is rough and uncultivated—wide moors with hills behind them rising bleak and wind-swept to the clouds. It is pleasant, therefore, to arrive at the peninsula of Storr, and to find here a more fertile country and a more hospitable coast. It is as though the traveller had been transported suddenly from the mainland of Scotland to the Outer Hebrides. Here is the same comparatively level land and the same boggy ground above which the *canach* or bog cotton on June days spreads a white covering. Here are the same small crofts, the same wide horizons, the same feeling of great space that is a gift of the Outer Isles.

Approaching Storr from Loch Inver one enters what I may call

the atmosphere of the Isles near the little bay of Clach-toll. Here
a picturesque township stands beside a green, closely-grazed
machair that leads to a shore of golden sand. Travelling north-
west, one passes in turn the clachans of Balechladdich and
Raffin and then, as one walks along a lonely track, as it were on
the fringe of the world, one comes suddenly and unexpectedly
upon the lighthouse of Rudha Storr.

I reached the lighthouse on a fine June evening. The wind
blew strongly in from the sea. Westward one might have been
looking out over the boundless Atlantic, for a haze in that
direction hid the Outer Hebrides. Eastward were wide acres of
rough grass land, not unlike the " white lands " of the Border
country. The ground beneath this tussocky grass is peaty, and
although the nearest houses are out of sight, the people cut their
peats on these windy acres, and when the peats are dry they are
carted with much labour over rough tracks to the road that leads
to the townships. In Sutherland the peats are cut large, and are
almost as broad as they are long. When dry they are so firm
and hard that it is almost impossible to break them, and they do
not, like the peats of some mosses, absorb water once they are
dry. There is, too, an almost complete absence of *smurach* or
peat dust, so common in the peat stacks of most districts.

It was late in the evening when I crossed the peat grounds of
Storr and the people had returned to their homes, but here and
there thin columns of blue peat smoke were hurried seaward on
the wind. Kettles had been boiled and tea made upon those
smouldering fires. The peat-cutters had set their faces homeward with no thought of extinguishing the embers, for they knew
that the fires were safe amongst those damp peat hags, the home
of meadow pipits and cheery wheatears.

At the edge of this country of peats and white grass lands
pastured by herds of horses the sturdy lighthouse of Rudha Storr
stands. The sea cliff here is high and the north-west swell,
rolling in from the Atlantic deeps beyond the Butt of Lewis,
breaks with muffled roar upon the rocks.

A short distance to the south of the lighthouse is a curious rock, resembling the head of a bearded giant. Perhaps one of the Fingalians keeps unsleeping watch here, gazing toward the distant coast of Skye and the hills of Lewis and awaiting the day when the clear notes of the magic horn shall arouse him from his spell. At dusk Rudha Storr is a place that might well be peopled by spirits of the past. The sea wind eddies and moans about the rocks. Seagulls call complainingly. A grey seal thrusts its sleek head above the frothy tide. The waves ceaselessly beat against the cliff foot. Oceanward the lights of passing vessels sway and dip. Flooding the night with its white rays the lighthouse on Rudha Storr seems a part of the rock itself. The rays shine upon the dark tidal streams; they illumine a passing yacht so that it glides like a phantom through the gloom. They wander far across the lonely country to the east, and shine on the groups of ponies which feed on the short wiry grass, moistened by the sea spray.

The lighthouse of Rudha Storr stands a hundred feet above the sea. To the north the sea cliff rises higher, and at its most northerly point Rudha Storr is more than three hundred feet high. It is here that Storr, the Stake, rises dripping from the sea close to the foot of the cliff. It is from a distance that the Old Man of Storr (for thus he is sometimes named) is seen at his best. From Handa and the coast beside Scourie he appears to tower from ocean deeps, with the blueness of distance upon his ancient head. Above him the clouds of summer drift. In a mirage he may be lifted clear of the water so that he floats magically in air. Perhaps he holds converse with his kinsman Storr of Skye, who rises, tapering and inaccessible even to the most skilled rock climbers, from the shoulder of Beinn Storr to a height of one hundred and sixty feet, and calls down the first snows of autumn upon his hoary head. But Storr of Skye is almost a landsman; Storr of Sutherland is sea-wet as Manannan himself and from the edge of the rocks wandering sheep peer timidly down upon him in his foam-girdled dwelling. The fulmar petrels, wheeling and gliding in buoyant flight, know the Old Man of Storr, just as the eagle and the raven know his brother of northern Skye.

It is where the cliffs of Rudha Storr are highest that the fulmars nest. Their homes are upon giddy ledges where primrose and roseroot blossom together in the long June days, so that the sea wind above the rocks is laden with their perfume. They are not alone, for the *lychnis* throws a red wave of blossom across the fragrant precipices. Near the top of these great cliffs the bladder campion opens white petals, and the sturdy juniper thrusts its strong roots deep into the cracks of the rocks.

Let us leave awhile the sounding seas and the silent-flying fulmars, and walk east to the gently-sloping hill that rises from the top of the cliff. It is an easy walk of a few minutes to the highest part of the hill, and is well worth while because of the splendid view that is seen from here. Away beyond Loch Inver the eye rests upon many hills. Suilven, Canisp, An Stac, and, further to the north, the great bulk of Quinag (or more correctly Cuinneag, since there is no letter Q in the Gaelic language) form a splendid company. Suilven is sometimes known as the Sugar Loaf. This modern name has nothing to recommend it. Súlr is Norse for Pillar, and so Suilven is really Pillar Fell or Pillar Hill.

Far away to the east are the higher slopes and summit of a hill on which the snows of winter gleam white until late in the summer. The old people of the Storr country say that this is Ben Wyvis, the highest peak of Easter Ross-shire. The laird of Ben Wyvis holds his lands on the condition that he is able to present the King with a bucket of snow at any time during the summer, the inference being that snow lies always on the ben. Northward one looks across the islands in Eddrachillis Bay to where the surf breaks white upon the rocks of Handa. Far to the west is Lewis, and the lighthouse keepers told me that in clear weather they could see the rays of the lighthouse on Tiumpan Head, near Stornoway.

During the Great War an important coastguard station on

Rudha Storr kept constant watch day and night for enemy submarines and floating mines, and more than one vessel owed her safety to the vigilance of the men at this lonely look-out station. The coastguard station is now in ruins, and the watch on the coast and on the seas is entrusted to the fulmar petrels and the gulls, and to the Old Man of Storr who saw the passing of Haco's fleet in the days when men fought with chivalry, and war had not been reduced to a science of murder.

CHAPTER V

AT Loch Inver the owner of a car who wishes to travel south along the western seaboard must for a time turn inland and rejoin the sea at Loch Broom. He journeys first along the Invershin road to Loch Assynt, traverses that loch, and proceeds south to Ledmore. Here he leaves the main road and turns south-west, crossing high moorlands between the Cromalt Hills and Drumrunie Forest. At Strath Kanaird he descends, and reaches the sea at the mouth of Loch Broom. But he may, if he should wish to explore the western seaboard thoroughly, take the coast road from Loch Inver by way of Inverkirkaig to Achiltibuie and Culnacraig below Ben Mór Coigeach, where the coast road ends and there is no more than a rough foot track connecting that district with Loch Broom. From Achiltibuie he looks across the water to the fair Summer Isles, where is a safe anchorage for yachts in bad southerly weather.

From Loch Broom the road leads up the loch, past the pleasant village of Ullapool and Leckmelm, where in spring and early summer the rhododendrons are remarkable for their beauty. A short distance inland from the head of the loch the traveller leaves the main road, which leads away eastward to Dingwall and Inverness. He crosses the river Broom at Braemore, bears away to the right, and, passing through the great Dundonnell deer forest, drops swiftly to the sea once more at Little Loch Broom. Before he has left the high grounds he has a glorious view of one of the most inspiring of Scottish mountains—An Teallach.

I had often looked upon An Teallach. From Skye and the

Strathmore and Loch Broom.

Outer Hebrides I had seen it rise to the clouds that so often drift above the high mainland hills when the islands are bathed in sunshine. From the Cairngorms I had looked, times without number, across the intervening bens to its rocky spires, and from the high ground of Sutherland I had seen it guarding the gateway of ocean. From whatever quarter it was viewed An Teallach had always been graceful, always distinctive, so that I was hopeful of exploring it more closely.

At length came a spring afternoon when I was on the Diridh Mór (the Great Ascent) which climbs away eastward

Ullapool, Ross-shire.

from Dundonnell to Garve, and, standing on the road in the setting sun, looked over brown moorlands to where the snowy corries and majestic peaks of An Teallach rose to the silver-edged clouds that idly drifted above its summit. As I was spying the hill-top, a full six miles away, through my telescope, I saw a golden eagle sail across the ice-plastered cairn and soar magnificently, with careless grace, out over the great precipices of Loch Toll an Lochain.

The sun was shining and the air was clear and calm when I left the hospitable inn at Dundonnell on the shore of Little Loch Broom the next morning. The first thousand feet of the

Gruinard.

ascent are steep, but a good path makes walking easy. As I climbed I looked back from time to time to admire the view. Across Little Loch Broom rose shapely Beinn Ghobhlach, the Forked Hill, well named because of its two peaks, and as I mounted higher Ben Mór Coigeach appeared to the north beyond it, with its long and inviting summit ridge holding, here and there, a field of snow. To the east of me was the high hill known as Sgùrr Eideadh nan Clach Geala—the Peak of the

Little Loch Broom.

Garment of White Stones, but on this April morning of strong sunshine these white stones were deeply hidden beneath an unbroken covering of virgin snow. For the first thousand feet of the climb I had been out of sight of the main peak of An Teallach, but now I came suddenly in sight of it. Stately and aloof, it rose to the deep blue of the sky. Upon its dark rocks snow lay thickly, and the mounting sun shone so dazzlingly upon these spotless snow-fields that, even at a distance, it pained the eye to look upon them.

Yet, did one look west, one seemed on the instant to be transported from winter to summer. Eilean a' Chléirich (Priest's Isle) and the Summer Isles rose from a blue serene sea, and beyond them, faint and hazy in the far distance, was the coast of Lewis. At a height of 1,500 feet above sea level I reached the snow. None but those who have actually walked on newly-fallen snow in late spring or early summer have any idea of the intensity of its reflected light. The violet rays of the sun are thrown back from the snow, and the eyes of the climber, unless they are protected by snow glasses, suffer acute discomfort. A long walk over this type of snow may produce snow blindness. I remember on one occasion walking on the Brae Riach plateau on the Cairngorms in late May. The previous day there had been a heavy snowfall, and the sun, shining with almost mid-summer power, rendered the unbroken snowy surface so dazzling that my friend and I, after stumbling forward half blinded for a time, were compelled to sit down beside a few rocks from which the snow had melted. Here we had some slight relief from the glare, and waited until a cloud had obscured the sun before returning to snow-free ground. Snow blindness is a painful thing. It may render the sufferer totally blind, and may compel him to remain for weeks in a darkened room while his sight slowly returns.

I was fortunate to find areas of snow-free ground on my climb up An Teallach. There were sun-warmed terraces of red sandstone on which cushions of sea thrift were stirring into life. It is a peculiarity of this plant that it is equally at home beside the tide or on the high hills. On An Teallach it is more plentiful than on any other Scottish hill I have climbed, and takes the place of the cushion pink, which is the usual flowering plant of the high tops.

The summit of An Teallach is marked on the map as Bidein a' Ghlas Thuill, the Peak of the Green Hollow. It is 3,483 feet above sea level. The last few hundred feet of the peak are steep and stony, and frozen snow made climbing more arduous.

As I neared the hill-top the weather was changing. Gathering clouds hid the sun, and from An Teallach rose vaporous mists like smoke from some giant forge. An Teallach indeed means the Forge, and the old Gaelic name may have been given to the crowded summits which form its *massif* because of the mists that so often eddy about them. A wandering whirlwind caught up a column of frozen snow and carried it over the hill-side just beneath me. The breath of the north wind was keen. Across the snow led the track of a fox. A golden eagle, perhaps the same bird that I had seen from a distance the previous day, sailed across the hill in the teeth of the breeze, a dark, determined form. It was early afternoon when I stood on the hill-top beside the ice-encrusted cairn and looked over the vast precipices to where dark Loch Toll an Lochain lies in the heart of this mighty hill. Across the abyss, where the eagle soars and the ptarmigan at times flies like a drifting snowflake, rose the awe-inspiring turrets and slender spire of Sgùrr Fìona, just nine feet lower than the hill-top where I stood. From Sgùrr Fìona the slopes of an t-Sàil Liath, the Grey Heel, led down to Strath na Sealg, home of swamps and rushes and resinous bog fir. Loch na Sealg, the Loch of the Hunts, lay invisible in its deep glen. East and south storms of snow and hail had formed, and the Cairngorm Hills, which I had hoped to see, were invisible. West was fine weather, but low clouds floating near me obscured the view in that direction. The island of South Rona, over against Skye, was faintly pencilled on the horizon. Nearer at hand, across Gruinard Bay, I could see Rudha Mór, where lies Loch na Béiste, the Loch of the Monster. The supernatural creature was often visible. It appeared even to some elders of the church of a Sunday morning. This audacity so terrified the people of the district that they persuaded the landowner to drain the loch in order that the beast might be destroyed. But the loch could not be dried, and after long months of fruitless efforts it was decided that the monster must be killed in his lair—a deep hole in the middle of the loch. To this end fourteen barrels of lime were emptied into the hole—it must be confessed with much trepidation. The creature evidently submitted tamely to being limed in, for to-day it is seen no more !

The clouds thinned, and overhead the sky once more was blue. Northward the clouds rested lightly on Cuinneag, and the slopes of Ben Mór Coigeach took on that deep blue which so often foretells a change of weather. Away on the north-east horizon rose the great bulk of Ben More Assynt, a remote hill that is the mother of the Oykell River. The dazzling glare had left the snow-fields near me; An Teallach was now bathed in soft lights. A pair of ptarmigan and a wandering deer had the hill to themselves, but when I had descended below the snow-line and walked again by the shore of Little Loch Broom many birds were calling in the quiet of evening. Here was warm sunshine, but looking back I watched a great storm gather on An Teallach. Inky clouds, bearing in their depths both snow and hail, dropped lower and yet lower upon the snowy cones of the mountain group, and I thought of the eagle grasping some rocky pinnacle with his strong talons as he awaited the storm, and the ptarmigan crouching in the shelter of some protecting rock, and the hind hastening with whitened coat to the lower corries.

Loch Ewe.

CHAPTER VI

THE LOCH EWE COUNTRY

From Dundonnell the road winds south along, though considerably above, the shore of Little Loch Broom, then crosses the shoulder of the hill and reaches the sea again at the pleasant bay of Gruinard with its large green island. Gruinard House, standing beside the tumultuous Gruinard River, must surely be in one of the most sheltered and one of the most delightful situations in the west highlands. Larch woods keep off most winds, yet the sun is not hidden by them; it is not surprising that the trees come early into leaf here. There is a grass-grown track leading up the Gruinard River to Loch na Sealg, five or six miles distant, through beautiful scenery.

The main road, continuing along the shore of the bay, crosses the Little Gruinard River, then, leaving the sea, climbs a very steep brae which proved too much for many cars in the early days of motoring. On a small loch near the Little Gruinard River (Loch an Iasgair by name) the osprey formerly nested, but this fine bird has become extinct in all parts of the highlands. The golden eagle survives, though in reduced numbers. It is remarkable that it has not shared the fate of the osprey, as the following account, written a century ago, will show : " Our game-killer, Watson, had a good day once with eagles, producing three splendid birds from a day's shooting, besides two young birds also killed. A pair nested on the west side of Bus Bheinn, and another pair on its east side, both out of reach, even by rope, although the nests were visible from the top about eighty to one hundred yards away. Watson, by daybreak, was on the top of Bus Bheinn, with swan-shot in one barrel and a ball in the other. Peering over the rock, away sailed one of the eagles, but the swan-shot dropped him in the heather below the rock. Another eagle at the nest at the other side of the hill came to the same end. Then hiding himself among the rocks, near where a wounded eagle flapped his wings, a third eagle, coming to see what this meant, was invited down by a shot, making a brace and a half of old eagles before breakfast ! Then, to shorten matters with the two chicken eagles, he climbed the hill again, and ere his bullets were all used up, both of them were dead, and their remains were visible on the nest for many a year after, having got more lead to breakfast than they could digest." (Dixon's *Gairloch*, p. 229.)

At Laide, on the south shore of the Bay of Gruinard, is the little ruined chapel of Sand. The tradition in Gairloch is that the chapel was built by Columba or one of his followers in the seventh century. It stands beside the shore, with a fine view over hill and sea. At Laide the road leaves the coast and crosses the moors to Loch Ewe and its village and hotel at Aultbea. Aultbea during the war was a place of considerable activity, for it was a coaling base of the Tenth Cruiser Squadron. This squadron consisted mostly of converted liners, which patrolled the seas in all weathers as far north as the Polar ice. When one of the Tenth Cruiser Squadron came into Loch Ewe to coal there was considerable stir at the Naval Base, for there was always the possibility that a hostile submarine might torpedo or mine her as she steamed into the loch, or left it. On the rough hill pastures north of Aultbea white-fronted geese have their winter home, and I have seen them feeding on the shores of a small loch here in the grey light of a December day. The white-front is a much rarer bird on the western seaboard than either the barnacle goose or the greylag goose and is a great traveller, for it nests in the far north, beyond the Arctic Circle.

Loch Ewe during the winter months sometimes gives excellent catches of herrings and haddocks, but for long the tragedy of Loch Ewe made small boats unwilling to venture far into the loch. On a calm day in the year 1809 a small boat was fishing haddock in the loch when a whale caused it to sink, with the loss of three lives. According to the old account the whale deliberately attacked the boat and made a great hole in her bow.

At Turnaig, near the head of Loch Ewe (the home of the late Osgood MacKenzie of Inverewe after the burning of Inverewe House), rare and semi-tropical plants and creepers grow. The climate is mild, and there is comparative shelter here from the gales off the sea. Osgood MacKenzie, a charming man of courtly and distinguished appearance and a great Gaelic scholar, was a genius at gardening. In his plantations I have seen eucalyptus trees as high as the well-grown Scots firs which surrounded them, and I remember, when I was stationed at Aultbea during the third winter of the Great War, seeing a mimosa tree in full blossom at Christmas. In Osgood Mac-Kenzie's book, *A Hundred Years in the Highlands*, we are told something of his successful gardening. Shortly after the book was published a spring gale of great severity swept the west of Scotland, and in a very short time blew down almost all the trees which he had so lovingly tended.

At the head of Loch Ewe is the village of Poolewe, built beside the fine salmon river which flows from Loch Maree. Here Finlay Mackinnon, the highland artist, had his home. From Poolewe the road rises steeply, and crosses some high

D

country of moorland and bog, descending again to the sea at
Loch Gairloch. Near the loch is the old home of the
MacKenzies of Gairloch, An Tigh Dìge—now usually called
Flowerdale House. Osgood MacKenzie would never speak
of Flowerdale House, for he said that An Tigh Dìge, the
Moat House, was a simple Gaelic name, and good enough
for him. The original Tigh Dìge was built on a field below

Flowerdale, Ross-shire.

where the present Flowerdale House stands. It was a " black
house," built of turf, roofed with large thin turfs, and surrounded by a moat or ditch as a protection against sudden
hostile attacks. The MacLeods of Gairloch originally lived here,
and how they lost the property and the MacKenzies gained it is
told graphically in Dixon's *Gairloch*. It appears that about
1480 Allan MacLeod was laird of Gairloch. His wife was a
daughter of the laird of Kintail and a sister of Hector Roy
MacKenzie. They had two little boys. One summer day Allan

MacLeod was fishing the river Ewe, and as the sun was hot he lay down on the river bank and fell asleep. Allan had two brothers. These men had such a hatred against the MacKenzies that they were determined that no taint of MacKenzie blood should ever run in the family of the MacLeods of Gairloch. They therefore planned to murder their brother and his two small sons. On the day in question the two miscreants found Allan asleep on the knoll that is called to this day Cnoc na Mìochomhairle, the Mound of Evil Council. They killed the sleeping man, and cut off his head. They then proceeded to the island on Loch Tollie, where they dragged away the two children from their mother, and slew them also. They then stripped the shirts from the bodies, once more rowed across to the island on Loch Tollie, and showed the blood-stained shirts to the mother. The poor lady succeeded in getting possession of the shirts, and hurried with them to Brahan Castle, where she showed them to her father, MacKenzie of Seaforth. The old man could scarcely credit her tale, but the shirts convinced him, and he sent his brother Hector Roy to Edinburgh to the king. The king gave Hector Roy a commission of fire and sword against the MacLeods, and in the year 1494 he received a grant of the lands of Gairloch by charter from the Crown. His descendants still own the old property.

CHAPTER VII

RUDHA RÉIDH : THE SMOOTH PROMONTORY

LOCH GAIRLOCH is bounded to the north by Rudha Réidh and to the south by Rudha Ruadh, the Red Point.

To many persons Rudha Réidh must be familiar because of its lighthouse. Travellers crossing the Minch between Kyle and Stornoway have seen those friendly flashes of brilliant light, perhaps in the gathering dusk of a winter afternoon, perhaps in the still dawn which heralds a summer day. But few of those who have looked upon Rudha Réidh, the Level or Smooth Promontory, have stood on its wind-swept heather and short rough grass, for it is a lonely country, with no dwelling upon it but the lighthouse with its three families.

It was on a quiet spring day that I crossed from Aultbea by way of Poolewe, where the first run of salmon were entering the river, to Gairloch of the pleasant sands. From Gairloch I passed through Erradale and Altgreshan to Melvaig, where the road ends. In the townships of the coast spring work was in full swing. Out on the small wind-harried fields men were covering by means of the *cas chrom* (the wooden hand plough formerly used throughout the highlands, but now seldom seen) the potatoes which their women-folk were planting. The oats had not yet been sown here, yet at Turnaig I had that morning passed an oat-field already green with the young vigorous braird.

There can be few more delightful places on the western sea-board than the Gairloch shore of Wester Ross. The rocky coast is here replaced by sands which seem to hold within themselves a glow of hidden sun-fire. Over the sea is Skye. One looks upon the Cuillin—always hills of distinction from whatever

36

quarter they may be viewed. That day there was snow upon the Fionn Choire with the summit rocks of Bruach na Frithe gleaming in cold beauty at its head and the narrow crest of Sgùrr nan Gillean, in sun-flood beyond a shower that drew a thin misty curtain above the sea. North-west across the Minch rose the Harris hills, the snow-fields on the Clisham gleaming in sunlight. At Melvaig I found a track leading the last four miles to Rudha Réidh and its lighthouse. I had thought to meet no one on this lonely track, but I passed sad-eyed women walking wearily homeward with heavy creels of peats on their backs. Perhaps they envied the ravens that sailed above them on strong wings, care-free birds dipping and somersaulting joyously, or the solans, those keen-eyed fishermen who have no fires to tend, or the dapper wheatears, recently arrived from African winter quarters.

Now the last of the cheerful sandy bays was left behind, and I walked beside a rock-bound coast with a view across the sea to the Shiant Isles, and the coast of Lewis beyond them. The sun was shining warmly as I reached the lighthouse, and as I sat on a warm heathery bank above the smiling sea the long northerly swell leaped ponderously upon the dark rocks below me. Across the blue, foam-flecked sea fulmar petrels sailed, borne upon unperceived aerial currents.

Here, or near this place, sat Fionnlagh Dubh na Saighead (Black Finlay of the Arrows) on that day long ago when young MacLeod of Assynt in his sixteen-oared galley passed north, discouraged and down-hearted. He had sailed down from Assynt to Gairloch to seek the hand of the daughter of Colin Roy MacKenzie in marriage, and had met with a rebuff. As the galley passed him, Black Finlay asked of the rowers whence they had come, and the nature of their errand. When they called out to him that young Assynt's suit had been unsuccessful, Finlay shouted back an expression so insulting that the young laird vowed to be revenged upon him sooner or later. A short time afterwards he returned with a galley of his best clansmen, fully armed, and landed below Black Finlay's house with the intention of taking him, alive or dead. But the intrepid bowman, with the assistance of one other warrior, fired his arrows with such deadly effect that several of the invaders were killed and the remainder put to flight. In still earlier days Norse galleys must have passed Rudha Réidh and on rounding it must have looked southward upon an unknown country. Perhaps a colony of black cormorants lived on the stacks of Rudha Réidh even in those remote times. On this spring day of sunshine it was pleasant to see them in their courting dress, silver-headed, crested, white-thighed, and deliberate. They crowded the tops of the two stacks, while far below them, compelled to take humble quarters, were a few of the smaller green cormorants. The black cormorants had not begun to lay; the green cormorants, early in the spring though it was, already had eggs on which they brooded closely. Around the stacks fulmar petrels glided, like aerial spirits of quiet grace.

It is only when the point of Rudha Réidh has been reached that the hills to the east and north-east are seen. On this April day distant Foinne Bheinn in the Ray country was draped in snow. On Cuinneag the mist rose and fell. An Teallach, in unrelieved white, was beautiful in bright sunshine. Rudha Storr just topped the horizon, its white lighthouse at this great distance appearing like a small snow-field left by departing winter beside the tide. Westward across the sea rose the isles of Fladday Chuain, set in the Minch between Skye and Harris. Bord Cruinn (the Round Table), Guala Mhór (the Great Shoulder), the low parent isle of Fladday—all were clear and distinct, whereas from the north of Skye they are seen as a confused group. When the trusted servant of Sir Donald MacDonald guarded his master's title-deeds on Bord Cruinn during the absence of the Chief of Sleat at the rising of 1715, he must have looked often across the sea to Rudha Réidh (in those days known as Seanna Rudha) and must have quickly extinguished his peat fire at the approach of any craft of doubtful appearance.

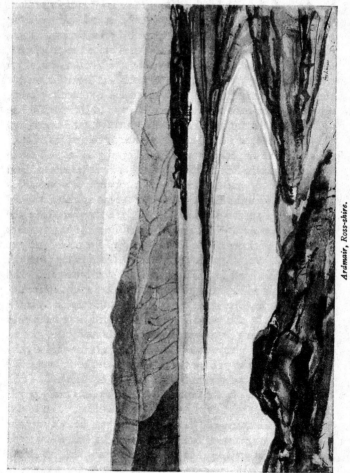

Ardmair, Ross-shire.

East of the point of Rudha Réidh is a wide sandy bay where the far-travelled seas break white. Here great rocks rise from the shore, and it was necessary to strike inland and cross the hill on my way to the Feadan Mór and Locha Druing. These places are beside an old track, little used since the people left the north side of the promontory. In the Feadan Mór, if an old tradition be credited, a keg of gold sent from France for the use of Prince Charlie, and concealed by occult powers, appears to view once in seven years. It was to Duncan MacRae of Isle Ewe that the keg of gold was entrusted, for Duncan had the gift of *sian*, and could render people, or things, invisible at will. He and two friends buried the keg of gold in the Feadan Mór, and since the Prince did not come that way the keg remained hidden. Nearly one hundred years afterwards a woman was herding cattle in the Feadan Mór. As she sat spinning worsted she saw of a sudden the head of the cask showing above the ground at her feet. Sticking her distaff into the keg to mark the spot, she hurried to the township to tell her neighbours the great news. But when she returned with them to the place the keg and the distaff had disappeared, for the brief period had passed during which, at long intervals, the keg might be seen.

Beside Locha Druing are birch woods, with here and there a few larches. In this wood lived a dark-haired fairy lad named Gille Dubh, whose dress was of green leaves and green mosses. He was seen by many, and on one occasion befriended a child who had lost her way in the wood. But since the day when five armed men of note searched high and low for him Gille Dubh has disappeared. In the time of that friendly fairy many people were living in the district around Locha Druing. But to-day no family lives there, and the spirit of the past broods over the place, which is now more lonely than the high hills. I saw many ruins, some of great age, beside the old track, and at Druim Carn Néill I passed near the old cairn built to the memory of one Niall MacLeod who came by his death in the following manner. Black Finlay of the Arrows had a grudge against this man, perhaps because he was of the hated race of the MacLeods of Gairloch, and one day when Niall was near his house Finlay fired at him. On this occasion his aim was slightly at fault, and Niall, although wounded, was doing his best to escape across the moss when Finlay loosed his fierce *leth chu* or lurcher at him. The lurcher chased the fugitive over the hill that is called to this day Bac an Leth Choin, the Lurcher's Bend, and coming up with him at the place which since that day has been called Druim Carn Néill, held him at bay until his master arrived and killed the fugitive. Poor Niall was buried where he fell, and a cairn of stones was raised over his grave.

The fine weather was drifting northward as I reached the township of Inverasdale beside Loch Ewe that evening. Clouds had already hidden the snows of An Teallach; the soft lights of evening were descending upon Beinn Airigh Charr. Over land and sea storm clouds were forming, and as the moon rose that night a freshening wind made music on Loch Ewe.

Loch Maree.

CHAPTER VIII

LOCH MAREE

WHERE the warm west wind of ocean drifts eastward beyond the sands of Gairloch a long and rather narrow loch lies deep among the hills. The loch is Loch Maree, and it received its name more than a thousand years ago in commemoration of Maol Rubha or Maol Ruibhe, an Irish saint whose mortal dust lies in the old churchyard of Applecross over against Skye. The surface of Loch Maree is no more than twenty-nine feet above the western ocean and its winter climate is unusually mild. At Letter Ewe in mid-April the horse-chestnuts were in almost full leaf, and rosebuds on the wall of the house were already tinged with red. On sunny banks primrose and violet were blossoming, and here and there an early birch was tinged with green above the clean sandy shore of the loch.

Loch Maree is a loch of many islands. One of the smallest is Eilean Ma-Ruibhe (Isle Maree), which has been the Mecca of innumerable pilgrims since the time when Maol Ruibhe of blessed memory had his cell here and sanctified the small isle. On the island is a burying-ground with many old recumbent stones, their history unknown. Two very old stones standing close to one another with a simple cross incised upon each mark the tragic ending of the earthly careers of two lovers.

This is the old tradition :—In the days when the Norsemen ruled the west a maiden of high rank who lived on the island was betrothed to a prince of Norway. During the absence of her lover on some warlike expedition, the girl in her anxiety came to persuade herself that the prince did not really return her affection, and she resolved to put his love to a severe test. When his galley was seen to sail up Loch Ewe she was taken out to meet it lying apparently lifeless in her own boat, her maidens, who had been carefully instructed in the part they were to play, grieving over the body. The prince, happy and eager to meet his beloved, saw her lying apparently without life. Beside himself with grief the unfortunate man called wildly to the rowers of the boat, asking them what had happened. The maiden was happy, for on hearing the grief in his voice she realised that she was indeed loved. But at the moment when she was about to rise to her feet her lover, frantic with despair, plunged his dagger into his heart. Here was tragedy indeed. For a few moments the girl was stunned with grief and remorse, then, snatching the dirk from the body of her betrothed, she ended her own life. Side by side on Eilean Ma-Ruibhe the two were buried, and to this day the two stones remain to tell of that sorrowful happening of centuries ago.

On Eilean Ma-Ruibhe is a very old tree trunk. This is the sacred tree which grew beside the sacred well of wishing. The tree is now lifeless, and the well has either dried up or been filled in. The old tree trunk was, I believe, carried away from the island during the Great War, but a lover of old things, hearing of this, had the tree recovered and brought back to the place where it grew, and where it now stands, like some gaunt skeleton of the past. In its furrowed wood, without bark and bleached by summer sun and winter storm, are hundreds of coins. Most of them have been driven so far into the wood that they are likely to remain until the tree crumbles away. But other coins which were less securely fixed have fallen to the foot of the tree. Here scores of them lie amongst the dead leaves and earth. These coins are the offerings of pilgrims who visited the island and, according to the prescribed ritual, attached their offering to the tree, then wished their wish as they looked upon the clear waters of the sacred well.

It is said that Queen Victoria visited Eilean Ma-Ruibhe and made her offering there. Because of its sanctity this island was believed to have a miraculous influence for good on those afflicted by insanity. The sufferer was rowed several times round the island, and was plunged three times into the water of Loch Maree. The sick person was then taken on to the island and knelt before the old altar, subsequently drinking a draught of healing water from the well, and affixing an offering to the tree. Even before the days of Saint Ma-Ruibhe this little isle was sacred. Here the Druids sacrificed bulls, and it is believed that the saint permitted this custom to be continued, just as Columba on Iona did not stamp out all the old observances, but caused them to be identified with the Christian faith. Remarkable as it may seem, old records show that bulls were sacrificed on Eilean Ma-Ruibhe, and at Applecross also, so recently as 1678.

Eilean Ma-Ruibhe is a small island. Eilean Suthainn, the Eternal Isle, is so large that it appears from the shore to be part of the mainland. Here grow old Scots firs, and on the island is a small loch, believed to be deeper than Loch Maree itself. There is a small island on this insignificant loch, and on a tree growing on the island a pair of ospreys once nested. The nest is described in the late Osgood MacKenzie's *A Hundred Years in the Highlands*.

Loch Maree is a loch encircled by great hills. Most imposing

Slioch from Loch Maree.

of these hills is Slioch, standing a little apart from his fellows as a chief among his clansmen. Nearest to Slioch is Ben Lair, then come Meall Mheannidh and Beinn Airigh Charr. A peak close to the summit of Beinn Airigh Charr bears the name Spidean Moirich or Martha's Peak. A woman named Martha, perhaps herding the cattle which in former times were pastured on the high tops in summer, was seated here one fine summer's day and was winding thread on her spindle. The spindle fell from her hand down the steep rocks to the north-east. Martha endeavoured to recover it, but fell over the rock and was killed.

On the April morning when I climbed to Meall Mheannidh the

Slioch.

spring sun shone warmly. A night of wind and rain had cleared away most of the snow and each burn was bank-high with brown impetuous water, so that the violets and primroses were drenched in spray. Near the hill-top I passed beside a lochan which lay beneath thick ice and deep snow, and saw a pair of ptarmigan in their spring plumage sunning themselves on a rocky knoll where a hen snow bunting was flitting from stone to stone. The snow at this height was soft and dazzlingly white. Below each snowfield the hill was drenched with the water which flowed from the melting snow. Even on the hill-top the air was warm. Far below me a fitful breeze played upon the waters of Loch Maree. On the western horizon rose the north coast of Skye. Between the hill where I stood and the sea was a country of lochs, peat bogs, and small tarns. Beneath me, on the opposite side of the hill to Loch Maree, lay the beautiful Fionn Loch, encircled by snowy hills. From the shoulder of Beinn a' Chàisgein Mhór a great waterfall leaped to the dark waters of Loch Dubh. An old raven flew overhead, and later dropped down to her nest in a long swift glide. The south wind fell light. I sat in pleasant

Loch Dubh, by the Fionn Loch.

sunshine and warm airs. But at evening the weather changed. Storm clouds, black as night, gathered to the south. Across the dark skirts of the Maiden wisps of grey mist formed and grew. Dusk came before her time, and brought a storm of rain, hail and bitter cold, whitening afresh the brow of Slioch and sending the raven to shelter as the last of the golden sunset shone warmly upon the advancing storm.

CHAPTER IX

THE SANCTUARY OF APPLECROSS

From Gairloch and Loch Maree southward to the Kyle of Loch Alsh, where is the terminus of the railway, the coast-line is rugged and mountainous. By sea the journey is easy for the yacht-owner, but there is no road along the coast for the motorist. From Kinlochewe a road crosses to Loch Torridon, and by following the south shore of Upper Loch Torridon it is possible to reach Shieldaig and cross the hill to Loch Carron and Strome Ferry. Here is a good motor ferry for cars, and the Kyle of Loch Alsh, the crossing-place to Skye, is only a few miles beyond it. But this itinerary leaves out Applecross, and Applecross historically is one of the most interesting places in the west because of its religious associations.

Maol Rubha, whose island on Loch Maree I have written of, is, next to Columba or Calum Cille, the most renowned saint in the Scoto-Irish Church. His day is April 21; he was born in the year 640, and became abbot of Bangor in Ulster. In 671 he crossed to Scotland and founded the church of Aporcrossan (Applecross) in A.D. 672 or 673, and here his burial-place is still to be seen. At Applecross Maol Rubha presided as abbot for fifty-one years. It is narrated that he was discharging his sacred calling on the Black Isle on the east coast of Scotland when he was seized suddenly with illness, and knowing that the end of his life on earth was at hand he gave directions that " four red men from Applecross " should carry his remains to his western sanctuary beside the Atlantic. The people of the Black Isle neglected to fulfil the saint's dying injunctions, for they wished his sacred remains to lie in their own churchyard.

But when the body was placed on rests and laid outside the chamber where the saint died, the united efforts of all the people assembled there to carry the remains to burial were unable to lift them. Realising that an unseen power was working against them, they sent over the hills westward for four Applecross men, who lifted and carried the coffin with such ease that they halted only twice from the Black Isle to distant Applecross. In the *Annals of the Four Masters* we are told that Maol Rubha died on April 21 in the year 721, having lived eighty years three months and nine days.

Even for the western Scottish mainland Applecross is remote. It can be reached from Kyle of Loch Alsh each afternoon in an hour by the Stornoway mail steamer, but from October to May the mail boat does not call at Applecross on her return journey from Stornoway in the early hours of the morning, and at that season of the year the luckless traveller who may wish to leave Applecross must board the good ship " Loch Ness " on her afternoon call, cross the stormy Minch to Stornoway, then cross once more to Kyle during the darkest hours of a winter night. His alternative is to cross the mountain road to Strathcarron by way of the Bealach nam Bó, the Pass of the Cattle. This road is one of the highest in Scotland, and is usually impassable because of snow-drifts until May.

It was on a misty afternoon of April that a friend and I left the warmth and comfort of the turbine mail steamer and leaped into the pitching ferry boat on the stormy bay of Applecross. A fresh westerly wind was raising a short steep sea. The shore was far off, and our craft was small. We sat precariously amongst mailbags, stores, and luggage, while rain and salt spray swept the ferry boat. For more than thirty years the two ferrymen of Applecross have met successive steamships in the bay, by day and night. They counted the day on which we were embarked a comparatively fine one, and their skilled oarsmanship landed us, a trifle moist perhaps, but intact, at the slip. Here we were met by the kind friends who were to

E

show us the country of the old Celtic saint, and during our
stay at Camusterach, surrounded by views which, even for the
west highlands, were beautiful above the ordinary, we learned
something of a district which the Gaelic-speaking natives still
speak of as A' Chomraich, the Sanctuary.

Where the waves break on the low shore of Applecross and
curlews call on the grass fields Saint Maol Ruibhe is buried. Two
rounded stones mark the saint's grave, which lies east and
west, and not north and south like the more recent graves near
it. There is a tradition that a more imposing stone of red granite
was sent from Norway as a tribute to the memory of Maol
Ruibhe from the king of Norway's daughter, but the stone in
some way was broken when the manse was being built.[1] Fragments of what may be that old stone have been lately discovered.
There was a belief that the earth from the grave of Maol Ruibhe
had miraculous powers. He who left the Sanctuary on a
journey fraught with peril was accustomed to carry a little of
the earth with him. This ensured a prosperous journey and a
safe return to Applecross. No one could be slain in battle
with the holy earth shielding and protecting him.

Other famous men of olden times are buried here. At the
entrance to the churchyard is an ancient upright slab bearing
the figure of a collared cross. This great stone is more than
nine feet high, and is to the memory of Ruadhri Mór Mac
Caoigean who was slain by the Norsemen. He is believed to
have been a chief of great strength and valour. The renowned
Red Priest of Applecross is also buried here.

The Sanctuary of Applecross has a " girth " or circumference
of six miles. It was formerly marked by stone crosses. The
last of these crosses stood on the *dùn* at Camusterach. The
stone was over eight feet in height and showed traces of a cross
on the western face. This priceless relic was destroyed by the
religious zeal of a Stornoway mason. He believed the cross to

[1] When the broken gravestone of the Saint was being carted away the
master-mason fell from some scaffolding and fractured his skull upon it.

be a relic of popery, and after he had seen a priest on several occasions visit the stone, he broke it in pieces with his big hammer —he was repairing the Free Church at the time, and so had this weapon handy.

The Sanctuary is now but a name, yet in the rude days of twelve hundred years ago it must have been known and revered far and wide. The fugitive, hard-pressed and exhausted, with enemies close on his track, must have seen with joy the emerald slopes of Eilean nan Naomh, the Holy Isle, beside the Applecross shore, and the austere monastery of Aporcrossan below him at the margin of the sea. Upon banks of primroses and wild hyacinths he perhaps threw himself to the earth, and as he prayed with gratitude looked out westward to where the sun cast a silver pathway over the ocean to Skye, the home of mystery and of the great Cuillin range.

Once, and once only, was the Sanctuary of Applecross violated. Norsemen landed from their galleys and paid no heed to the circle of stone crosses. We do not know what excesses they committed here, but shortly after they had rowed out again seaward a swift fate overtook them, for their craft sank although the ocean remained calm and the wind light. Now, in more peaceful days, the memory of the past still lingers in the Applecross country. There is a healing power in the solitudes of the Sanctuary. In spring the daffodils are golden in the gardens of Camusterach and the young leaves of the sweet-smelling poplar scent the sea air. It is one of the charms of that country that although it is on the sea the sea winds do not reach it. Stately trees grow to the tide and in the old woods roe deer feed, careless of passers-by. At sunrise the mavis sings his song, and out to sea eider drakes call softly. In the natural harbour at Camusterach fishing boats lie at anchor, or put to sea to set their nets for cod and hake which they carry south to the market at Kyle or Mallaig. The Holy Isle is green while yet the hill grass is brown as at mid-winter, for there is warmth beside the ocean at the time of spring.

Very early one morning my friend and I bade farewell to Applecross and took the hill road leading to Strathcarron and the railway. It is a long walk, but even had we been minded to go by car we could not have done so, for the road at the watershed (as we found later) was still snow-bound. This road is unique in Scotland. It rises from the sea to a height of almost 2,100 feet, then drops to sea level again on the far side of the pass of Bealach nam Bó. As we climbed towards the clouds that raced eastward we looked back across the sea, and watched rain-storms blot out the Cuillin hills. A bitter wind blew in on us, and twilight descended on the hill. We saw no bird on our walk to the watershed except an old raven hurrying with food to his nesting rock where his brood doubtless awaited his coming with impatience. But when we reached the cold hill pass we came upon a pair of ptarmigan dosing close to the side of the road. They were remarkably tame, even for ptarmigan. The cock bird had already grown his summer plumage, but his wife was still speckled with the white feathers of winter, and when disturbed she raised her wings high above her head with a charming gesture. The male ptarmigan was reluctant to fly, and fed on the heather shoots almost at our feet, but when his more timid mate took wing he dutifully followed her, croaking as he flew. Almost on the watershed a great drift of snow lay upon the road. It was perhaps six feet deep, and was frozen so hard that it bore a man's weight with ease. Some tinkers had succeeded in crossing with their carts, but they had been forced to go a considerable distance off the road, over ground so rough that the ponies had apparently been taken from the shafts and the carts dragged by man power. Our view was restricted. Through gathering clouds and flurries of wet snow Loch Torridon gleamed wanly far away to the north. Beinn Bhàn was in gloom; about its slopes dark clouds were gathering and the hill-top was invisible.

The way from Applecross to the watershed is easily graded, but as we reached the pass we saw our road disappear over what at a distance appeared to be a sheer precipice. Through a rift in the mist curtain we looked down upon Loch Kishorn 2,000 feet below, and saw that the road led into a deep corrie with grim precipices on either side, the general appearance recalling the austerities of Glen Coe. We wished for a little sun. The bitter wind with the dampness of wet snow on its breath sought out the most sheltered places and moaned amongst the black rocks and spires that ended in the clouds. Into this gloomy corrie the road wound in a series of curves so sharp that the average car could scarcely negotiate them without reversing. The wind was at our back. Chilly and damp, we hurried downward, past waterfalls and mossy rocks, and now Loch Kishorn was at hand and the songs of curlew rose from beside the tide. We looked back. The hill road over which we had come was already hidden in the clouds that crept ever lower, and soon hill, glen and corrie were shrouded in a grey pall of cold rain which continued as we rounded Loch Kishorn, crossed the hill to Lochcarron and from Jeantown travelled west along the shore of the loch to the old Castle of Strome and the ferry beside it.

CHAPTER X

APPLECROSS TO SHIELDAIG

THE country of Applecross is, as I have written in the last chapter, at the back of the world. Its remoteness may be realised to the full by a walk northward to Shieldaig along the coast—a distance of some twenty-five miles.

The coast track is not broader than a stalking path, so that no horse and cart can use it and no motor-car venture along it. The narrow path is well kept, and is the more appreciated because in Scotland to-day there are few paths left to the pedestrian for his undisputed use, and he has been driven from the main roads because of their hardness and the speed of motor traffic upon them.

This Right of Way of Wester Ross-shire deserves to be better known, for it leads through a fine wild country where the hills and the sea are the walker's companions, and red deer stand beside the track to watch him pass. My first visit to Applecross had been in the spring of the year. It was October when I again visited the district. The weather was wild when I boarded the steamer at Kyle. A northerly gale was bringing showers of snow to the hills and stinging hail squalls to the seaboard. It was uncertain whether the Applecross ferry boat could put to sea in such weather (I afterwards heard that the only other passenger for Applecross had remained behind at Kyle to avoid the risk of being carried over the stormy sea to Stornoway), but the friendly captain of the mail boat was optimistic, for the wireless had given him the cheerful news of an intense anticyclone over Iceland, and the weather of western Scotland is influenced largely by the conditions prevailing over

Iceland. His optimism was justified, and after a fast and comfortable passage of less than an hour we were abreast of Applecross and I was relieved to see the ferry boat already afloat on the green waters of the bay to meet us. The short afternoon was drawing to a close as I was landed, on the crest of a wave, at the Applecross slip. A walk of eleven miles along the coast northward lay between me and my destination for the night, and drifting snow already covered the hills. The path first skirts the Bay of Applecross, and here was shelter from the wind. A great number of red-breasted mergansers were sheltering on the calm waters near the shore, and from the hillside above me the roaring of a stag came down the wind. But I had soon passed beyond the sheltered zone, and for the next three hours the northerly gale was my companion. Mile after mile the track led northward, sometimes close to the sea, sometimes high above it. I looked westward, across Raasay, to Skye, and saw the Cuillin wrapped close in hurrying snow clouds. That stern hill range was this day the gathering-place of storms, and when the clouds for a moment lifted the hills were seen grey with the first snows of autumn against a wintry sunset. Dusk was near when I saw a line of waves white on the shore ahead of me. The coast so far had been rocky, but here, unexpectedly, I came on a small sandy bay on which the northerly swell was breaking. The sands were red, and burned as though they held the last of the sunset that had now faded from the sky. The small sand dunes were red also, and in one place a trail of sand lay upon the green grass where it had been drifted on a westerly gale. Here was a scene to delight the eye of an artist, and yet I have never seen a painting of this lonely shore. The foreground was green *machair*, on which an old ruined dwelling stood : this led to dull red sand dunes and smooth moist sands on which breaking waves caught the ebbing light. Beyond was the heaving sea stretching away to Eilean a' Cheò, where the Cuillin rose austere to the driven clouds. Beyond the line of waves advancing on the shore a gannet was fishing for his supper. Backward and forward he flew, a mysterious white figure faintly seen. Once, twice, thrice, a fourth time, he plunged beneath the grey waters, and when I last saw him his appetite for his evening meal was still unsatisfied. And now the track crossed a burn where stunted rowans carried a meagre crop of berries and the *sphagnum* moss on the banks was coloured an unusual and beautiful deep red-brown, seeming to glow with hidden warmth. Northward I hurried in gathering twilight, and saw the lighthouse on South Rona burn brightly seaward and the last of the fires fade from the western sky. After darkness had fallen I realised that the road was even more lonely than I had imagined. The track passes the two small townships of Lòn Bàn and Kalnakill, and it might be imagined that it would lead through them, but as the path deviates neither to the right nor to the left it leaves both these townships considerably below it, and this must be a matter of considerable inconvenience to them. In the darkness Lòn Bàn showed no single light from its windows, but the swell was heavy here, and the great waves, leaping in upon a rocky shore, gleamed white and ghostly beyond the dark line of the heather. Occasionally I was aware that I was approaching an invisible house or township because of the smell of peat, carried far on that eager north wind. Once I saw a small light moving uncertainly over the ground : someone was seeking his house by the light of an electric torch.

Through a dark and unknown country I walked. From time to time the young moon showed dimly through racing storm clouds and her light was welcome. Gradually, as the miles drew out, the beacon on South Rona shone more warmly, and beyond it I could see faintly the light of Troddday, off northern Skye. At last, about eight o'clock, I reached a small township which I subsequently learnt was Cùaig. At the first house where I knocked there was no reply, but at the second I was more successful. This house was full of men and boys, and I interrupted a *céilidh*, or evening gathering, of the old-fashioned sort. I mentioned to the man of the house that I was walking to Ri-Aulaidh. He told me that it would be impossible for a stranger to find the place in the darkness, but kindly offered to guide me with a lantern. For perhaps a mile we continued along the path, then struck across the moor. There was no track of any sort, and walking was by no means easy, even with the aid of that friendly lamp. We now approached the invisible sea and heard the roar of the waves, then saw a dark shape loom up suddenly through the gloom. Here were my quarters for the night. My guide knocked on the door, and a kindly welcome was given the wanderer. Although my hosts believed that the ferry boat could not have put out to the steamer that afternoon they had nevertheless prepared for me a true highland welcome, and one which I shall not easily forget. A warm fire of peat and coals lighted the room and supper was soon prepared. I sat down to lythe, caught the previous day off the rocks, hot tea, scones, and oatcakes baked by skilled hands, fresh butter in unlimited quantities—everything indeed that could cheer the heart of the weary walker. Late that night I looked from my bedroom window over an invisible ocean to the faint light on Trodday isle, and yet I had no indication of what the view was like by day. Next morning, therefore, when I awoke I at once scanned land and sea with eagerness. I have rarely seen a more beautiful view than that which greeted me from the small window of the lonely house on the edge of the mainland of Scotland. Almost beneath me was a sandy bay margined with smooth boulders of red Torridon sandstone. Across the sound lay Rona, with the long northerly swell breaking white upon its outlying reef. Beyond Rona was Beinn Storr of Skye rising white against a horizon of serene blue. Upon the distant north coast of Skye huge seas were hurling themselves. They glistened in the morning sun. Beyond Skye the hills of Lewis and Harris rose from the rim of an ocean which still heaved restlessly from the gale which had subsided with the dawn. On the shore of the little bay beside the house lay the wreck of the " Shiela," the Stornoway mail boat which must have been familiar to many travellers to the

Isles. On her passage from Stornoway to Kyle one New Year's eve she had steamed at full speed in the blackness of a stormy moonless night on to the rocks at high water. Here she had come to rest, almost on the heather, but the sea is dragging her back, so that her stern, even at low water, is now partially submerged. On the further shore of this bay is a cave, accessible only at low tide, where a whisky still was hidden in former days, but the smugglers have long gone, and now the rock pigeons which roost in the cave have the place to themselves.

Northward was the Sacred Cave (An Uaimh Shianta), which perhaps received its name because of some forgotten association with Saint Maol Ruibhe. Between the house and the shore was the croft. Here wandered sheep, hens and stirks, all remarkably tame. The sun shone upon the russet bracken fronds which formed a close thatch for the byre. It shone upon the chrysanthemums in the tidy garden. An air of quietness and peace was here.

After breakfast I left the house, and in sunshine crossed the moor, past a small loch which lay without a ripple beneath the cloudless sky, to join the path which led to Shieldaig, far up Loch Torridon. As I reached the higher ground I saw the snowy slopes of Tom na Gruagaich rise, cloud-wreathed, beyond Loch Torridon. Perhaps the sprite which gave the hill its name was to-day revelling in the first snows of autumn, and was leaping about the precipices of Sgùrr Mór, which raised its shapely peak to the idly drifting clouds. At the township of Fearnmore I reached Loch Torridon, a fine sea loch some fifteen miles in length, and looked across to the peaks of the Shieldaig Forest and the Torridon Forest, where snow showers moved slowly past on the decreasing north wind. As I walked east along the loch I gradually left behind me the influence of the open sea. The swell on the rocks became less. Trees and briars now appeared beside the shore, and I was soon walking through a wood of hazel and birch, with bracken up to my shoulders. The path now climbed 600 feet, now dropped again to sea level, and these ascents and descents made the way to Shieldaig seem long.

At intervals I passed small townships beneath which a
sturdy motor boat (sometimes two of them) lay at anchor.
The people of all this wide district are dependent for their
stores on a small steamer which is sent to them each fortnight
by a paternal Government.[1] To-day this vessel followed me up
the loch, calling out the boats from successive clachans by long
and strident blasts on her siren. As I approached Shieldaig
the sinking sun was shining on the hills and was lighting up the
shores of Loch Torridon. Shieldaig must have been famous for
its herrings when the Norse ruled this western country, for the
name of the place is Norse, and is in reality Síld-Vík or Herring
Bay. I found that the woods here were partly of Scots pine,
and titmice flitted through the thick branches, while an old
blackcock flew strongly over my head. Green and gold were the
bracken fronds; the birches too were of the same colours. The
air was so clear that Harris rose up far westward, beyond the
intervening hills and the sea.

During the whole of my two days' walk I had seen no horse,
nor do I think that there is one in all that district. The tilling
of the land must therefore be done by hand, but the hay-fields
and the oat-fields are small, and the chief harvest is gathered
from the sea. I was interested to notice that no hay-stacks
and no oat-stacks were to be seen, for the hay and the corn are
kept in barns, which are thatched with bracken, and not with
rushes and yellow iris as in most parts of the west. It is a pity
that the industry of spinning and weaving has gone from this
country. In one of the townships is a weaver, but she is a Harris
woman, and has brought her art with her across the Minch. But
perhaps the *gruagach* who lives amid the snows of Beinn Ailiginn
has retained the knowledge of the old things—she who dwells
beside the Loch of the Night which lies near the Hollow of the
Water Monster—and will impart that knowledge to unborn generations when the highlands of Scotland come to their own again.

[1] This small cargo steamer no longer runs, and the people of the
district have difficulty in getting their stores.

Skye from Kyle.

CHAPTER XI

THE COUNTRY OF LOCH ALSH AND THE GATEWAY OF SKYE

Loch Alsh in Wester Ross-shire stands at the sea gates of the Isle of Skye. It looks west to the hills of that great island, and before sunrise on a still winter morning of hard frost the Cuillin and the lesser hills around them are a country of almost fairy-like beauty. In the frosty sky the twinkling stars and orange planets pale. Dawn rides across the heavens from the east. The Cuillin, white and phantom-like, catch the first cold light of dawn. *Gradually they warm to the glow of the eastern sky. The sun's rays reach their snowy slopes and they are suffused with rosy light. Above the hills the cold blue of the zenith is tinged with orange. The sea lochs are as yet in deep shade. They might be the fjords of northern Norway beyond the Arctic Circle, and the Cuillin might be the snowy spires of the distant Lofoden Islands. A summer sunset over Skye has been seen and admired by many. A winter sunrise is a thing of immeasurably greater beauty, but few have watched the sun god bring back life to the frozen Cuillin at the coming of a windless and cloudless winter's day.

The country of Loch Alsh has much old history. It saw King Haco's fleet sail south through the narrows which bear the king's name to-day, and come to anchor, awaiting the ebb tide, at Sgeir na Cailliche, the Carlin's Stone, that is mentioned in the historic Haco Saga. Twice daily the tides contend at the entrance to Kyle Rhea. Before the time of steam, vessels were obliged to anchor at the entrance to this narrow sound and await the pleasure of the tide. Kyle Rhea, according to an old legend, is named after one of the Fianna or Fingalian giants.

The legend is that Fionn, Oscar, Caoilte, Diarmid and the rest of the Fianna were hunting the red deer in Skye while their wives were living together in a house on the mainland shore of the strait. While the women slept some enemy fired the house. The warriors saw the thick smoke rising from the thatch. They hurried across the hills of Skye to the shore of the sound and each hero, lifting himself upon his spear, leaped across that channel of the fast-flowing tide. But one of the Fianna met with disaster. As Reidh was hoisting himself up on the shaft of his spear the shaft broke and Reidh, falling into the sea, was swept away and drowned. Since that day his name is immortalised in the name of the sound, for it is Caol Reidh, the Narrows or Strait of Reidh.

The western terminus of the old Highland Railway (now the London Midland and Scottish Railway) is at Kyle of Loch Alsh, and from the railway pier the mail steamers to Skye, Stornoway and the Outer Hebrides sail. Here also is the ferry across to Skye, over which motor-cars and passengers are carried on a short sea passage of less than ten minutes.

Two main roads from the country to the east converge near the village of Kyle of Loch Alsh. One is from Inverness, by way of Achnasheen and Strome Ferry; the other is from Inverness and Fort William and the country to the south. This road reaches Kyle of Loch Alsh by way of Cluanie, Loch

Duich, and Dornie Ferry, which crosses the upper arm of Loch Duich, known as Loch Long.

The village of Kyle of Loch Alsh is thus of considerable importance, and there are several hotels where the traveller can stay before he continues his journey to Skye or the Outer Hebrides.

On the pleasant shore of Loch Alsh at Balmacara Bay is Uaimh a' Phrionnsa, the Prince's Cave. The tradition of the place is that Prince Charles Edward hid here, perhaps after his journey across Skye from Mugstot to Kingsburgh and Portree. The cave is well hidden. It is high up on a precipitous bank, where small oaks find a root-hold in the niches of the rock, and its whereabouts is to-day known to few persons. East of Balmacara, where the winter sun shines warmly even on the short frost-laden days of December, is the site of an old clan fight. Blàr nan Saighdearan, the Battle of the Archers, was the name of that fight of long ago, when the men of Loch Alsh contended with the MacCrimmons of Glen Elg and drove them back across Loch Alsh to their own country. On the high ground above Kyle Rhea, close to the present boundary between the counties of Ross and Inverness, the MacCrimmons, believing themselves safe from pursuit, lay down and fell asleep. As they slept the Mathesons from Loch Alsh fell upon them and killed them to a man. A cairn of stones marks the place and is named Carn Cloinn Mhic Cruimein, the Cairn of the Clan MacCrimmon. It is said that sweet music, the music of the Sidhe, has been heard near this old cairn. Below the cairn is a small tongue of heathery hillside, lying between two burns. It is known as Teanga na Comhstri, the Tongue of Contention, since this strip of land for long was debatable ground, and was claimed in turn by Inverness-shire and Ross-shire.

At one time the country of Loch Alsh carried a large population, and the cattle were sent up to the shealings for the summer months. This indeed was the custom throughout the highlands, but surely few had to journey so far to their shealings as the

Eilean Donnan Castle, Loch Duich.

people of Loch Alsh, who drove their cattle each summer to the distant upland country east of Loch Monar. In those days it was said that Coille-mór of Loch Alsh, now deserted, was the home of 67 families, and that Matheson of Loch Alsh could raise 700 men in Gleann Udalain where the buzzard now sits on a sunny rock and surveys a lonely glen. In the churchyard at Kirkton are crowded graves, one with an old recumbent flagstone showing a warrior with hands folded over the hilt of his claymore. This stone is said to have been prepared by Ciar MacMathan and carried on his back from the slopes of Sgùrr Mór, some distance away.

Beneath a cloudless sky I climbed the slope of Gleann Udalain, past Cnoc a' Chrochaidh, the Hanging Knoll, to the highest point of the hill road that leads eastward to Strome. Here, 700 feet above the sea, I looked down on the old castle of Eilean Donnan standing in bright sunshine at the entrance to Loch Duich, a loch named after Saint Dubhthach of Tain. For days a frost of unusual intensity had prevailed on the western sea-board and Loch Duich resembled an Arctic fjord, for it was frozen across, and the sun was reflected from the ice that held its salt waters. Here the tribe of the shag or green cormorant could no longer fish until the south wind slackened the bonds of ice on this dark sea loch. That old castle of Saint Donnan's Island could tell of years of strife. It was built at least 700 years ago and occupies the site of a Caledonian vitrified fort. The old "Statistical Account" states that Colin Fitzgerald, son of the Earl of Desmond (from whom is descended the great family of Seaforth), was made constable of Eilean Donnan Castle because of the valour he showed at the Battle of Largs in 1263. In the year 1539 Donald Gorm of Sleat made a determined raid upon the castle, which was defended with great bravery by its small garrison. Donald Gorm was pierced in the thigh by an arrow. The wound in itself was not serious, but the Chief of Sleat, angrily wrenching the barbed arrow from his leg, severed an artery and bled to death. In the "Statistical Account" it is also told how the castle was once taken from the King's troops by stratagem. A neighbouring tenant applied to the governor of the castle for assistance in the reaping of his corn, for he said that he understood, from the face of the skies and the croaking of the ravens, that a heavy storm was impending. The governor unsuspectingly ordered the garrison to assist in harvesting the field, and when the soldiers returned to the castle they found the gate barred against them and the men of Kintail in possession. The account continues : " The oldest inhabitant of the parish remembers to have seen the Kintail men under arms, dancing on the leaden roof of the castle, just as they were setting out for the Battle of Sheriffmuir, where this resolute band was cut to pieces."

In May 1719 His Majesty's ship " Worcester " bombarded and destroyed the castle of Eilean Donnan, garrisoned at the time by a Spanish regiment under William, fifth Earl of Seaforth. For almost 200 years the castle remained a ruin. In 1913 its restoration was begun by Colonel MacRae Gilstrap, whose grandfather seven times removed (the Reverend Farquhar MacRae, whose time was 1580–1662) was appointed by Colin, Earl of Seaforth, as Constable of Eilean Donnan. The castle is now restored and for a time each year Colonel MacRae Gilstrap makes his home in the castle of his ancestors.

Loch Duich is MacRae country. The River Shiel, flowing from the south-east, and hurrying down Glen Shiel, a dark glen with the lofty Sisters of Kintail rising from sea level to a height of 3,500 feet, enters the loch. Near the head of Glen Shiel was fought, in 1719, the Battle of Glen Shiel. Two Spanish frigates arrived at Loch Duich, having on board the Earls Marischal and Seaforth, the Marquis of Tullibardine, some field officers, and three hundred Spaniards, along with arms for two thousand men. This small force was joined by Seaforth's men, but the other Jacobite clans, with the lesson of 1715 still fresh in their minds, stood aside until a stronger force of foreign aid was forthcoming. The highlanders and their Spanish allies had

F

taken up a position at the pass of Glen Shiel, but on the arrival of the Government forces from Inverness under General Wightman they retired to the pass at Strachell. Here General Wightman attacked them and drove them from one position to another until night. The highland and Spanish force then dispersed. Seaforth, Tullibardine, and other officers, retired to the western isles, and the Spaniards surrendered themselves prisoners of war.

In December the sun sets early, and dark shadows crept across the icy surface of Loch Duich while yet the snows on the Sisters of Kintail were afire. Full-orbed, large and golden, the moon rose out of the East, and as she climbed high in the star-lit heavens, dimming the light of the Pole Star and the Plough, a long line, as of silver clouds, was seen on the far western horizon. That silver ghostly line was the Cuillin range, where virgin snows reflected the cold light of the moon through the long frosty hours of a winter night.

Castle Maol, Skye.

CHAPTER XII

THE ISLE OF SKYE : THE KYLEAKIN COUNTRY

SKYE is the greatest of the Hebrides. It is a long narrow island ; from Duntuilm in the north to the Point of Sleat in the south by road is almost 80 miles, and considerably further than the distance from Edinburgh to the English border. The area of Skye, with its islands of Raasay, Scalpay and the lesser isles, is 690 square miles and the population at the 1931 Census was 10,407 persons, including 354 on Raasay.

One of the first historical mentions of Skye is in Adamnan, about the year 800, where it is recorded that Columba met and baptised an old man named Artbranan :

" When the blessed man was staying for some days in the Scian Isle (Skye), striking with his staff a small piece of ground of a certain place near the sea, he thus speaks to his companions : ' Wonderful to say, O my children, this day on this spot of ground a certain aged heathen, who has kept his natural goodness throughout all his life, will be baptised, and will die, and will be buried.' And behold, after the interval of about one hour, a vessel arrived at the same port, in the bows of which a certain decrepid old man was borne, the chief of the Cohort of Geona, and two youths, lifting him out of the ship, set him down before the eyes of the blessed man. And he, having received the word of God from the Saint

67

through an interpreter, forthwith believing, was baptised by him, and after the ministrations of baptism were completed, as the Saint had prophesied, he thereupon died in the same place, and there his comrades bury him, a cairn being raised over him.   And this is to be seen to-day on the seashore, and the river of the same place in which he had received baptism is to this very day called by the inhabitants by his name, Dobur Artbranani."

Professor Watson in his work, *Celtic Place-names of Scotland*, writes : " The only place-name in Skye that involves *dobur*, so far as is known to me, is Tot-arder in Bracadale, where ' arder ' is for ' ard-dobhar,' which means, as it stands, ' high water.' The place is on the seacoast, and so far agrees with Adamnan's description, but the data are insufficient for identification. This is the only known instance of *dobur* known to me in the islands ; on the mainland it is common."

The Norsemen colonised Skye, and a memorial to their three centuries of occupation is found to-day in the place-names of the island, which are mostly Norse.   Hunish, Trodday, Fladday, Vaternish, Husabost—these are strong viking names, quite distinctive from the soft Celtic place-names like Loch Caluim-cille.   The two most important old families of Skye are the MacDonalds and the MacLeods, and the latter family trace their descent back to the Norsemen.

The visitor who crosses the narrows from Kyle of Loch Alsh on the mainland to Kyleakin in Skye at once enters a land of Norse associations.   Kyleakin is Haco's Sound—named after King Haco of Norway who led the last great Norse expedition to the isles of Scotland which ended at the Battle of Largs in 1263.

As he approaches the Skye coast the visitor sees the old ruin of Caisteal Maol, where a Norwegian princess levied toll of all ships passing through the narrows. A chain was stretched across the sound to hold up shipping, and the mark of the chain on a small pillar-like rock is still to be seen on the shore of Skye immediately opposite the lighthouse.

Could one cast one's vision back to an August day of the year 1263 a great fleet might be seen to approach Kyleakin from the

north. King Haco, summoned from Norway in his old age
to the help of the people of Skye because of their ill-treatment
at the hands of the Scottish king, was sailing south to give
battle with their enemy. The proud fleet, their sails golden
in the sunlight, steered east through the narrows and arriving
at the broad waters of Loch Alsh came to anchor at Sgeir na
Cailliche, the Carlin Stone, at the entrance to Kyle Rhea.

In this western country the Norsemen doubtless felt at home.
They were in a land of fjords and of great hills which cast their
shadows far across the sea; the Cuillin perhaps reminded them
of the narrow peaks of their own land. Not a few of the isles
folk who greeted the fleet when it came to anchor were themselves
Norse; others had married Norwegian wives, tall and fair, and
comely to look upon. We do not know how long the fleet remained
at anchor beside the Carlin Stone. Against the flood tide they
could scarcely have sailed through Kyle Rhea, for the tide here
flows so swiftly that a steamer cannot pass without a struggle,
and a small coaster may sometimes be forced to let go her
anchor where King Haco's fleet lay, there to await the ocean's
pleasure. Looking up from their sheltered anchorage near
Sgeir na Cailliche, the Norsemen saw three hills of Skye towering above them, blue and smiling in the August sunshine.
Beinn na Cailliche (this must not be confused with the hill of
the same name above Broadford), Beinn Bhuidhe, and Sgùrr na
Cóinnich are the names of these three hills, and Sgùrr na Cóinnich, the highest of the three, exceeds his neighbour Beinn na
Cailliche by five feet, and stands just 2,400 feet above the waters
of the sound beneath.

These hills rise in a lonely part of Skye. They may be climbed
from Kyleakin, or may be reached by a hill road which leaves
the main road between Kyleakin and Broadford. This road,
which crosses a pass 900 feet high and leads to the small township of Kyle Rhea, reaches the watershed close to Sgùrr na
Cóinnich. The hill slopes above the road are dry, and in August
the heather is purple upon them. As one climbs one looks down

on the great tidal river of Kyle Rhea. The day on which I climbed the hill a small coasting steamer was attempting to force her way through the Kyle to the north, but the strong ebb sweeping down upon her was too powerful for her engine, and she finally gave up the contest and anchored in the still waters of a bay. With each upward step that I made the view increased in beauty. On the south horizon rose the hills of Mull and as I reached the hill-top, where the heather gives place to grass and a few ptarmigan have their home, I saw a glorious view over land and sea. Most peaks are delightful because of the distant view which they give. Sgùrr na Cóinnich indeed shows the climber wide views of Mull and Ardnamurchan, Coll and Moidart, but it is the near prospect which is the most inspiring.

Around the base of the hill winds a great fjord that stretches from Trotternish of northern Skye to the wooded slopes of Sleat in the south of the island. I looked north and saw the white waves break upon green Pabbay and the long swell from the north hurl itself in foam upon the low reefs of South Rona. Beneath me was Caisteal Maol; beyond it rose Beinn na Cailliche of Broadford, showing on its rounded summit a great cairn of stones. A Skye tradition narrates that a Norse princess was buried here—perhaps the same lady who levied toll on the ships which passed beneath her castle beside the tides of Kyleakin.

Eastward, through Loch Alsh, I saw the historic castle of Eilean Donnan and pictured that day of four centuries ago when the great Donald Gorm harried the castle with a fleet of 50 galleys and met his own death there. In my chapter on the Loch Alsh Country I have described how the Chief of Sleat was pierced in the thigh by an arrow shot at him by Duncan MacRae, the Constable of the castle.

The site of another old castle—that of Glen Elg—was visible across the narrows of Kyle Rhea. This castle was at one time a stronghold of the MacLeods of Dunvegan, who were the Lords of Glen Elg as far back as the thirteenth century. There is a curious tradition regarding the old castle of Glen Elg, namely, that the MacLeods left it because a young child fell out of one of the windows and was killed. Exactly the same story is told of the ruined castle of Duntuilm in northern Skye to account for the MacDonalds leaving that old building.

When I climbed Sgùrr na Cóinnich each near and distant hill was in clear sunshine, but towards evening a chill breeze from the north brought an increasing army of grey clouds to the Cuillin range. These clouds swirled around Sgùrr Alasdair and hid from view the great pinnacle on Sgùrr Dearg. From the cone of Blaven they trailed out into space like a great cloud of smoke.

Far below me a golden eagle appeared for a moment, then was lost behind a shoulder of the hill. Soon the great bird, accompanied by its mate, appeared once more and the pair soared magnificently close above my head, searching the ground carefully for hares, which are numerous on the hill.

At sunset Beinn Sgriol, across the sound, was aflame while the shades of night were falling on Kyle Rhea, where the young flood tide had overcome the last of the ebb. Beyond Sleat, where the sands of Morar were grey in the dim light, the young moon appeared and prolonged the hour of sunset light—that mysterious hour when past and future join hands across the present and old things are made new.

Blaven, Skye.

CHAPTER XIII

SLEAT OF SKYE

SLEAT has been called the Garden of Skye. Whether the traveller reaches it by sea from Mallaig, or by road from Kyleakin or Broadford, he has the same impression of a kindly, fertile district. The traveller approaching Sleat by land from the north passes near the old ruins of Knock and Caisteal Camus and then sees on his right hand Armadale Castle, the residence of the old family of MacDonald of Sleat, who still own a large part of Skye. Beyond Armadale is the village of Ardvasar, and the traveller may continue along the shore by the track which leads to the Point of Sleat, where are small sandy bays of great charm.

Sleat (a Norse place-name meaning the Level Land) is a broad promontory leading out into the Atlantic, but it is the Level Land only in comparison with the Cuillin giants which rise to the north of it, or with rocky Blaven that towers so magnificently

72

across Loch Eiseord, or with rounded Beinn na Cailliche where the summer sun shines warmly upon a princess's lonely grave.

Sleat is one of the few districts in Skye where are to be found large numbers of well-grown trees. Beside Armadale Castle are splendid silver firs and stately lime trees and ashes.[1]

Johnson and Boswell were the guests of Sir Alexander Mac-Donald at Armadale. In the *Journey* Johnson writes as follows:

"As we sat at Sir Alexander's table, we were entertained, according to the ancient usage of the North, with the melody of the bagpipe. Every thing in those countries has its history. As the bagpiper was playing, an elderly Gentleman informed us, that in some remote time, the Macdonalds

Cill Chriosd, Skye.

of Glengary having been injured, or offended by the inhabitants of Culloden, and resolving to have justice or vengeance, came to Culloden on a Sunday, where finding their enemies at worship, they shut them up in the church, which they set on fire; and this, said he, is the tune the piper played while they were burning."

It is interesting to know that this tune, known as Cill Chriosd, is played to-day in competitions at the great highland gatherings by the foremost pipers of the day, and is considered by some who are skilled in such matters to be the finest composition of its type in existence. The usual history of the tune is that the massacre took place in the church of Urray, not far from Strathpeffer, and that the families massacred were MacKenzies.

[1] Dr. Samuel Johnson expresses admiration of the ash trees in 1773.

On September 5, 1773, Boswell walked to the parish church of Sleat, and mentions that there were then no church bells in Skye, but that there had been bells in the past. The bell-less state of most of the Skye churches continues.

In the sheltered glens of the promontory are birches and hazels, and old oaks scarred by Atlantic tempests. But on the high backbone of Sleat no tree stands. The land here is a maze of rocks and peat hags; of unstable bogs where the *cannach* or bog cotton waves white feathery heads and the cross-leaved heath opens pink waxy flowers in summer sun; of lonely lochs and lochans where the trout leap unseen; where the red grouse at dawn throws his challenge to the quiet air unheard by human ears; where the golden eagle, seeking new territory from its home in Rhum across the sea, sails on broad wings into the sunset; where the red deer, wandering at evening, graze the crofters' oats at Tarskavaig and Tokavaig.

When the sun shines and the air is cleared of haze by the vital north wind it is good to climb to the highlands of Sleat. The way from Armadale leads first across green fields where swallows flit low above the dew-drenched grass. When one has reached the high ground above Ostaig and pauses awhile beside the smiling waters of Loch nan Uamh, one sees a vision through a gap in the hills of the blue Atlantic and the Outer Hebrides rising clear on the distant horizon. One continues to climb, and at last reaches the highest ground, where rocks and peat hags form a difficult country for the walker. Here and there are dry banks purple with bell heather and ling—the bog cotton flowers with the bog asphodel in damper sites.

From the highest ground of Sleat the view is wide and varied. Across the sea to the south are the white sands lying between Morar and Arisaig. It was on the Smooth Mile, not far from these sands, that Mac Gille Chaluim, MacLeod of Raasay, battled with Colann gun Cheann, a headless spectre of ill-repute. This sprite used to waylay and kill passers-by on a piece of moor named as the Smooth Mile which began where Morar railway

Tormore, Sleat, Skye.

station stands in these prosaic days. All who attempted to remove the spectre came to a violent death. MacLeod of Raasay, a man of great courage and remarkable strength, was asked to rid the country of this demon. He met Colann gun Cheann in the blackness of midnight and a long and desperate struggle took place. Iain Garbh (as MacLeod of Raasay was named in the west) towards the dawn began to overcome the spectre. It is at dawn that ghosts feel their strength ebbing, for by earliest cockcrow they must be gone. Colann gun Cheann became weary and was now no match for MacLeod of Raasay, who picked him up and took him under his arm, for he

Sound of Sleat, Skye.

wished to carry him to the nearest light to see what appearance his adversary had. The spectre implored MacLeod of Raasay to release him and his captor answered, " I will not let you go until you swear by the Book and by the Candles that you will leave this district for ever." Colann gun Cheann swore the oath, then flew away, singing sadly to himself as he disappeared. Since that dawn he has made his home on Beinn Eadarra in the north of Skye, and the song that he sang on his banishment is sung to-day in the Trotternish district of Skye by young and old.

Beyond the white sands of Morar, beyond Ardnamurchan and its hills, rise the peaks of Mull—Beinn Mhór and the twin tops of Dùn dà Ghaoith. Near at hand, on the Sound of Sleat, can be seen the herring fleet. A long line of drifters, from Inverness, Buckie, Banff and Kirkcaldy in Scotland and from Yarmouth and Lowestoft in England, steer out west from Mallaig to the Coll Banks or Barra Head, or perhaps to the fishing grounds in the Minch off Lochmaddy. From this height they seem toy vessels with their brown smoke forming a cloud above and around them. They steer towards mountainous Rhum, and Canna rising blue from the sea, and disappear on the horizon towards the hills of South Uist—Hecla and Beinn Mhór, Corodale and Stulaval—that climb mistily from the far Atlantic.

Across Loch Eiseord tower the Cuillin. From Garsven, tapering grandly at the south, to Sgùrr nan Gillean with its sharp and airy summit to the north, all the peaks of this majestic range rise clear, blue, and very dark. They are full of mystery, stern yet attractive. They speak of old times—of the days of Norse raids, of clan fights, of a wandering Prince with a price upon his head. Near the Cuillin, but distinct from them, Blaven rises magnificently to the clouds.

From the high ground of Sleat is no great distance to the western shore of the promontory. In all Skye, most beautiful of islands, there is no more beautiful country than this western shore. At Ord one stands beside the tidal waters of Loch Eiseord, and sees a great palm dwarf the other trees of that old garden. This palm is at least twenty feet in height. The people of the place tell me that it is a fresher green in mid-winter than in summer, for its leaves are untouched by the mild frosts that prevail here. There is a ruin of a very old chapel beside Ord. It is named on the maps Teampuill Chaon, and commemorates St. Comgan, patron saint of Lochalsh. To-day, hay is made above the old nameless graves which are beside St. Comgan's chapel at Ord—graves which were old at the time of the '45, and whose history is now quite unknown. Rather less than a mile east of this old ruin is a small wood named Coille a' Ghasgain which marks the entrance to the old Sanctuary which the chapel gave. Once he entered St. Comgan's Sanctuary a man, whatever his crime might have been, was safe from pursuit. This Sanctuary of Sleat is now less widely known than the Sanctuary of St. Maol Rubha at Applecross on the mainland not far distant from it, which I have described in an earlier chapter.

Beside the waters of Loch Eiseord, where sea-trout leap of a summer evening and solans fly backwards and forwards at their fishing, oak, ash and birch, hazel, bracken and bramble, clothe the ground to the tide. In summer the hay and the oat harvest occupy the crofters' time. The workers look up for a moment

Rhum from Skye.

to watch a passing yacht as she steers across a golden path on the ocean, then bend once more to their work. The sinking sun gilds Dunscaith farther along the coast, and shines upon the great boulder where Cuchulainn tied his deer hounds, Luath and Bran, when at night he returned from the chase. But on the Cuillin the sun does not shine. Here the sky darkens. Mist rolls in upon Sgùrr Dearg, on Bruach na Frìthe, on the rugged ridges of Sgùrr a' Mhadaidh. The clouds rise steam-like and each hill in turn is overwhelmed by the mist army, but sentinel Blaven stands free of cloud as the last of the sunset burns crimson in the far west.

Concerning the old fortress of Dunscaith there is much Celtic lore. It was the *dùn* or fort of Scàthach, a great and warlike queen, and to Dunscaith came Cuchulainn to learn from the renowned queen the arts of war. Scàthach is mentioned as the instructress of Cuchulainn in a very old tract entitled *Verba Scàthaige,* the Words of Scàthach. It is assigned by the scholar Thurneysen as it stands to the first half of the eighth century, but Thurneysen adds that the date of actual composition may be earlier. The tract is a metrical prophecy in a very difficult language concerning the future of Cuchulainn. There is a short prose introduction to the poem as follows :

" Here begin the words of Scàthach to Cuchulainn on the occasion of their parting from each other in the eastern quarters of the world after Cuchulainn had completed full learning of warfare with Scàthach. There-after Scàthach prophesied to him what should befall him, and she told him of it to the end through knowledge that enlightens."

Tir Scàith, the Land of Scàthach, is mentioned in a manuscript of the early twelfth century. The manuscript is entitled " Leabhar na h Udhri," and it contains a tract called " Siabur-charpat Con Chulainn "—the Phantom Chariot of Cuchulainn.

In this old account Cuchulainn is made to appear in his chariot to Laegaire, King of Ireland, when Patrick came on his mission in the year 432. Cuchulainn here recounts certain of his most famous deeds. Professor W. J. Watson has kindly given me the following translation of one interesting passage :

" Another expedition I made when I went to the Land of Scàth. Therein was Dún Scàith with locks of iron; I laid hand thereon. Seven ramparts there were around that fortress; unlovely was its hue. A palisade of iron there was on every rampart, whereon were nine heads. Each court had doors of iron, against which one might not prevail. I chanced against it with a kick, so that it fell in faggots. In the fort there was a pit. Ten snakes guarded it across its edge; it was an evil. Then I attacked them, though the throng was huge, so that I made small gobbets of them between my two fists. A swarm of toads was let loose about us, creatures bitter and beaked. They clung about my snout. Ugly dragon-like monsters fell upon us. . . . Then I attacked them, when . . . I ground them into fragments between my two palms. There was a cauldron in the fort. Calf of the three cows, thirty cattle in its maw were not a full charge for it. They would frequent the cauldron—delightful was the bond. They would not depart from it any whither until they had left it full. Much gold and silver was therein; wondrous was the treasure. I bore away that cauldron, besides the daughter of the king. The three kine we bore away; they swam the sea. Two men's burden of gold each bore on its back. When we had put out to ocean, folk would deem it vast, the crew of my curach were drowned by the relentless storm. Then I oared my course, though it was a sharp peril. Nine men were on each of my hands, and thirty on my head. Eight men on my two thighs clung to my body. It was thus I swam the ocean until I was in port."

After the time of the Norsemen Dunscaith was a fortified castle of the MacDonalds of Sleat. In the sixteenth century it was besieged and taken by Alasdair Crotach of Dunvegan, the MacLeod chief who is buried in the cathedral church of Rodil. Dunscaith to-day is a picturesque ruin, open to the storms that rush in upon it from the Atlantic and shriek about its ancient walls. Distant indeed is the day when Cuchulainn first saw the place, guarded by a bridge that none might pass over. Yet Cuchulainn with his hero's leap crossed the bridge, and with the point of the sword at Scàthach's breast, made her swear that she would instruct him in all the arts of war. The Cuillin have not changed since that day. Their blue jagged peaks hold the summer sun or call down the passing clouds that are borne on the south wind from Cuchulainn's country of Ireland. The woods of Tokavaig were perhaps musical with the song of birds in Cuchulainn's time as to-day.

Standing amid surroundings so romantic and picturesque it is little wonder that there are many traditions concerning the origin of Dunscaith. It is said that it was built by the fairies in a single night. Through the centuries MacLeod and MacDonald contended for its possession. From the castle the great war pipe must often have summoned the neighbouring clansmen. Within the strong walls the *clàrsair* or harper must have sung and the *seanachaidh* must have narrated the deeds of daring done by the illustrious ancestors of his patron. The war galleys must often have sailed into Loch Eiseord, bringing to those in the castle grim tales of victory or defeat across the sea.

But now the harper has gone and the strains of the pipe are

heard no more on the *dùn* of Scàthach—except, it may be, when a wandering piper seeks to recall by *ceòl mór*, the classical pipe music, the spirit of the past, and plays an old tune with sadness and longing in it, and the call of the sea. And as he plays he looks south towards Erin beneath the horizon and his thoughts go back to that day when Cuchulainn, his *curach* overwhelmed, swam the ocean with nine men upon each hand, eight men on each thigh, and thirty upon his head, while the beaked toads barked savagely upon the surf-beaten shore to see the hero escape.

G

Roag, Skye.

CHAPTER XIV

LOCH CORUISK AND THE CUILLIN

DUNSCAITH looks across Loch Eiseord to Kilmaree, where was an old chapel dedicated to St. Maol Rubha. There is also a remarkable cave, named the Spar Cave, on the shore of the loch not far from the site of the old chapel. The road to Kilmaree and Strathaird leaves the main road at Broadford, and skirts the shoulder of Blaven. The end of the road is at Elgol, a small village where it is possible to hire a motor boat to the shores of Loch Scàvaig, whence it is only ¼ mile to Loch Coruisk.

Near Broadford, at the foot of Beinn na Cailliche, are the ruins of Coire Chatachan. After leaving Armadale Johnson and Boswell were most hospitably entertained at Coire Chatachan by the MacKinnons. They revisited the house on their return journey through Skye, and its highland hospitality was again remarked upon by the travellers. In his account of the first night of their second visit to Coire Chatachan Boswell writes :

" Dr. Johnson went to bed soon. When one bowl of punch was finished, I rose, and was near the door, in my way upstairs to bed ; but Corrichatachin said, it was the first time Col (MacLean of Coll) had been in his house and he should have his bowl—and would I not join in drinking it ? The heartiness of my honest landlord and the desire of doing social honour to our very obliging conductor induced me to sit down again. Col's bowl was finished ; and by this time we were well warmed. A third bowl was soon made, and that too was finished. We were cordial, and merry to a high degree ; but

Sligachan, Skye.

of what passed I have no recollection, with any accuracy. I remember calling Corrichatachin by the familiar appellation of Corri, which his friends do. A fourth bowl was made, by which time Col, and young M'Kinnon, Corrichatachin's son, slipped away to bed. I continued a little with Corri and Knockow; but at last I left them. It was near five in the morning when I got to bed. I awaked at noon, with a severe head-ache. I was much vexed that I should have been guilty of such a riot, and afraid of a reproof from Dr. Johnson. About one he came into my room, and accosted me, ' What, drunk yet ? ' His tone of voice was not that of severe upbraiding; so I was relieved a little. ' Sir,' said I, ' they kept me up.' He answered, ' No, you kept them up, you drunken dog.' This he said with good-humoured English pleasantry."

North of Coire Chatachan the road winds round the head of a long sea loch, by name Loch Ainort, after passing close to the hilly island of Scalpay. At the head of Loch Ainort is a magnificent view of the surrounding hills, and a great waterfall pours out a milky flood on the hill-side here after rain. The old road climbed a steep hill named Druim nan Cleochd, but the new highway skirts the shore, passing Sconser, where there was an inn at the time of Johnson's visit, and turns inland at Sligachan. At the Sligachan river is to be seen perhaps the most grand hill scenery in all Scotland. Across the glen rise the Cuillin giants, the majestic cone of Sgùrr nan Gillean dominating the scene.

There is a fine walk through Glen Sligachan to Loch Coruisk, held by some to be the most beautiful loch in Scotland. Sir Walter Scott writes thus of Loch Coruisk :

" We were now under the western termination of the high ridge of mountains called Cuillen or Quillin or Coolin, whose weather-beaten and serrated peaks we had admired at a distance from Dunvegan. They appeared to consist of precipitous sheets of naked rock, down which the torrents were leaping in a hundred lines of foam. The tops of the ridge, apparently inaccessible to human foot, were rent and split into the most tremendous pinnacles. . . . From the bottom of the bay (Loch Scavaig) advanced a headland of high rocks, which divided its depth into two recesses, from each of which a brook issued. Here it had been intimated to us that we would find some romantic scenery, but we were uncertain up which inlet we should proceed in search of it. We choose, against our better judgement, the southerly dip of the bay, where we saw a house which might afford us information. We found, upon inquiry, that there is a lake adjoining to each branch of the bay, and walked a couple of miles to see that near the farm-house, merely because the honest highlander seemed jealous of the honour of his own loch, though we were speedily convinced that it was not that which we were recommended to examine. . . .

Marsco, Skye.

" We returned and re-embarked in our boat, for our guide shook his head at our proposal to climb over the peninsula, or rocky headland which divided the two lakes. Arrived at the depth of the bay we found that the discharge from this second lake forms a sort of waterfall, or rather a rapid stream, which rushes down to the sea with great fury. . . .

" Advancing up this huddling and riotous brook, we found ourselves in a most extraordinary scene; we lost sight of the sea almost immediately after we had climbed over a low ridge of crags, and were surrounded by mountains of naked rock, of the boldest and most precipitous character. The ground on which we walked was the margin of a lake, which seemed to have sustained the constant ravage of torrents from these rude neighbours. We

Loch Scavaig, Skye.

proceeded a mile and a half up this deep dark and solitary lake. The mountain vapours which enveloped the mountain ridges obliged us by assuming a thousand varied shapes, changing their drapery into all sorts of forms, and sometimes clearing off altogether. It is true, the mist made us pay the penalty by some heavy and downright showers, from the frequency of which a Highland boy, whom we brought from the farm, told us the lake was popularly called the water-kettle. The proper name is Loch Corrisken, from the deep corrie or hollow, in the mountains of Cuilin, which affords the basin for this wonderful sheet of water."

Scott did not approach Loch Coruisk by Glen Sligachan, but by sea. It would appear from his narrative that he first landed at

Camusiunary and was taken by his guide to Loch nan Creathaich, a solitary loch beneath the steep rocks of Blaven. The "highland boy" was later in the employment of the father of Mr. James Cameron, Tallisker. Mr. Cameron tells me that the man used to speak of the day when he acted as guide to Sir Walter Scott, whom he described as "a tall, lame man, with shepherd's tartan trousers."

I do not think Dr. Johnson would have appreciated the Cuillin. Boswell remarks in his *Journal* that when he and Johnson passed through Glen Shiel the learned doctor was not greatly impressed with the "prodigious" mountains in that place:

"Dr. Johnson owned he was now in a state of as wild nature as he could see; but he corrected me in my inaccurate observations. 'There' (said I) 'is a mountain like a cone.' Johnson, 'No, sir. It would be called so in a book; and when a man comes to look at it, he sees it is not so. It is indeed pointed at the top; but one side of it is larger than the other.' Another mountain I called immense. Johnson: 'No; it is no more than a considerable protuberance.'"

Writing of the Cuillin Boswell observes :

". . . the Cuillin, a prodigious range of mountains, capped with rocky pinnacles in a strange variety of shapes. They resemble the mountains near Corté in Corsica. They make part of a great range for deer, which, though entirely devoid of trees, is in these countries called a forest."

Men's minds have changed towards the hills since the days of Johnson and Boswell, and of all the ranges in Great Britain none attracts so strongly as the Cuillin of Skye. When seen from a distance—from the snowy summit of Ben Nevis or the small cairn that marks the top of Hecla in the Outer Hebridean island of South Uist—the Cuillin rise on the far horizon, graceful and beautiful as dream mountains. From the country nearer to them—from delightful Morar, from Kyle at the sea-gate of Skye, from Skye herself—the Cuillin are so majestic that the eye is drawn to them again and again. They dwarf the lesser hills; they rise blue to the summer sky; they are inspiring on a day of storm when the grey wrack streams through their corries where the eagle soars and the raven drifts like a miniature eagle above the highest summit.

The Cuillin from Portree Bay, Skye.

It is curious that the peaks of the Cuillin should so nearly approach one another in height. Sgùrr Alasdair, their chief (named after a Skye man who was poet and mountain lover, Sheriff Alexander Nicolson), is 3,251 feet above sea level. Sgùrr nan Gillean is 3,167 feet, Bruach na Frìthe 3,143 feet, Sgùrr Dearg 3,206 feet and Sgùrr na Banachdich 1,367 feet.

The peaks actually rise close to one another, but many of them are guarded from the average walker by precipices and treacherous screes. Yet some of the finest Cuillin peaks can be climbed without difficulty. To reach the summit of Bruach na Frìthe by way of the Fionn Choire is a pleasant walk which a child might undertake. Sgùrr na Banachdich presents no difficulties to the walker of average ability. Sgùrr Alasdair is not really difficult, by what is termed the Great Stone Shoot. But the so-called Tourist Route up Sgùrr nan Gillean is certainly NOT easy; indeed Sgùrr nan Gillean is one of the hardest of the range to scale without a rope.

On a fine summer day there is no more delightful experience than to wander through the dark corries of the Cuillin or to climb to their airy summits. The hill flowers, even in late summer, are brightly-coloured and varied—lowly blossoms that creep over the ground to hide from the fierce mountain winds. The tormentil on the highest and most wind-beaten ridges opens its yellow flowers to the August sun and the wild thyme is purple on steep slopes. The highest spring in the Cuillin is near the head of the Fionn Choire of Bruach na Frìthe, and is encircled by a delightful rock garden, where the white flowers of the starry saxifrage and the mauve blossoms of the northern rock-cress cover the ground and the emerald moss. The waters of this well are crystal-clear and are ice-cool even on the hottest summer day. This little oasis is surrounded by screes and stern rocks, and is the more beautiful on that account. On the bare rocks three thousand feet and more above the sea the tiny alpine willow grows. Its home is in crevices, where its small leaves are green and vigorous despite the storms from the Atlantic that rush over them.

Were it not for the hill plants the Cuillin would be a desolate country for the nature lover, for bird life here is scarce. On the higher Cuillin slopes one is above the home of the red grouse, and ptarmigan are rare. The golden eagle has become, I think, less numerous here, and the raven does not nest on the Cuillin, but flies up to their high corries after the young are strong on the wing. It is possible to walk on the hills through the day and see no bird of any kind, and the silence of those lonely hill-tops is immense. Animals, too, are scarce on the Cuillin. A blue hare or two haunt certain of the summits, such as Bruach na Frìthe and Sgùrr na Banachdich, and on the more southerly of the range deer are seen, but to-day the lower slopes of the Cuillin are sheep ground rather than deer forest. Yet so long as he has the view and the hill flowers as his companions the climber is never lonely. The views are unrivalled and it is one of the charms of climbing the range by the north slopes that the view is seen early in the climb. Before he is half-way on his journey the climber has risen above the intervening hills and already looks over the Minch to the Outer Hebrides. Before he has climbed to a height of 3,000 feet he sees, if the day be very clear, two hazy isles rise from the Atlantic at a vast distance from him. These islands are St. Kilda and the rocky isle of Borreray which rises some five miles to the north of it. It may be a guide to climbers if I mention that, when seen from the summit of Bruach na Frìthe, Borreray rises immediately behind Eaval, a hill near the south end of the island of North Uist. During the climb up the northern slopes of the range the view north and west is extensive, but to the south nothing is seen by reason of the steepness of the slope which towers above the climber. Then, in a second of time, when the ridge near the summit is reached, all that hidden view is revealed. I have sometimes told a climber to close his eyes during those last few yards in order that when he opened them the wonder of the view might be the more complete. Beneath him lies the dark jewel of Loch Coruisk; across the sea the sands of Morar appear like snow, and behind them are many hills, among which is the highest hill in Britain—Ben Nevis. On the south horizon are the hills of Mull, and nearer rise the hills of Rhum and the Scùir of Eigg. On the far horizon towards the north-east, hill upon hill of Wester Ross and distant Sutherland are seen.

There are days when the climber on the Cuillin is hidden in white, eddying mist and there are days, rare indeed, but memorable because of their beauty, when he climbs above the clouds and is greeted by the sun shining from a cloudless sky of deep blue. Above the mist-sea rise the jagged forms of the neighbouring peaks. The ocean is invisible. A cloud hides the abyss of more than one precipice. Here, on his pinnacle above the swaying sea of cloud, the climber is far removed from the troubles of the world. Sometimes after a day of happiness spent amid the hill silence the wanderer on the Cuillin may see towards evening a dark cloud gathering, and the rumbling of thunder may reach him. The thunder cloud approaches ; the mutter of the thunder becomes louder, while lightning flickers across its edge. A thunderstorm in the heart of the Cuillin is a sublime experience.[1] The thunder echoes and re-echoes between the hills. Lightning plays about the tops, and the hill summits appear to be pounded by some invisible hammer of the gods as through the increasing gloom sparks fly from the shattered rocks. Torrential rain, illumined by the lightning, drenches the hills. Nature is aroused, immense forces are abroad, and man stands puny and helpless before them. But the storm gradually drifts away on the wind. The sky brightens and the thunder is less loud and menacing. Soon the blue arch of the heavens appears, the setting sun shines in glory, and the Cuillin are serene and beautiful as before the coming of the storm. Before the onset of thunder and rain silence had prevailed on the range, but now is heard the rushing noise of innumerable waterfalls. These hurry to the glens, and thence to the mother ocean who smilingly awaits them.

[1] Thunder is rare on the Cuillin in summer, but is not infrequent during westerly storms in winter.

Outer Hebrides from Loch Bracadale, Skye.

CHAPTER XV

BRACADALE AND DUNVEGAN

NORTH of the Cuillin, on the west of Skye, is Tallisker, the old home of the MacLeods of Tallisker and now the residence of a highland gentleman well-versed in highland history, and with a profound love for Tallisker, of which the learned Dr. Johnson wrote :

" Tallisker is the place beyond all that I have seen from which the gay and the jovial seem utterly excluded, and where the hermit might expect to grow old in meditation, without the possibility of disturbance or interruption. It is situated very near the sea, but upon a coast where no vessel lands but when it is driven by a tempest on the rocks. Towards the land are lofty hills streaming with waterfalls. The garden is sheltered by firs or pines, which grow there so prosperously that some, which the present inhabitant planted, are very high and thick."

Boswell, in his account of Tallisker, was dissatisfied with the court before the house, which was " most injudiciously paved with the round bluish-grey pebbles which are found upon the seashore; so that you walk as if upon cannon-balls driven into the ground." He also mentions that in a quarter of an hour he looked at no less than fifteen different waterfalls near the house and drank of Cuchulainn's well, finding the water of it admirable.

The house of Tallisker to-day is remote and solitary as in Johnson's time, and old trees still stand in the grounds and

shelter the garden, which is not without flowers from late
January, when the snowdrops blossom white as snow beneath
the old trees, until December, when the hydrangeas hold their
blue flower-heads to the short winter day and the last of the
roses slowly open their petals.

North of Tallisker are the broad waters of Loch Bracadale,
where King Haco, after the battle of Largs, on his passage north
to Norway (which he was destined never to reach), anchored
awhile to repair his ships. On the south shore of Loch Bracadale
is the settlement of Harris crofters known as Port nan Long.
The people here make the home-spun and hand-woven tweed
which is so distinctive of the Outer Hebrides, and when the
Duke and Duchess of York were the guests of MacLeod at
Dunvegan Castle in the summer of 1933 they paid a special
visit to this settlement to see for themselves the various processes
in the making of the tweed. On one of the islands of Loch
Bracadale, Ouay or Wiay by name, flax was formerly grown,
and Donald MacLeod of Ose has an old tablecloth spun of flax
grown on Ouay.

At the north entrance to Loch Bracadale are three curious
pillars of rock called MacLeod's Maidens. The Mother, as the
largest of the three stacks is called, has now only two daughters,
but there is a tradition of MacLeod's Country that a fourth
column formerly existed, and that it was broken cleanly across
near the base during a great storm. The flat base of the fourth
column may be seen to-day. Near the Maidens are a number
of unusual sea caves.

North of Loch Bracadale is MacLeod's castle of Dunvegan—
one of the oldest inhabited castles in the British Isles. The
castle is built upon a rock beside the tidal waters of Loch Dunvegan and is now (1934) the home of Sir Reginald, twenty-
seventh chief of the clan. The MacLeods of Dunvegan go back
as a family to the mists of antiquity, and are believed to be
descended from Niall of the Black Knee, King of Ulster in the
tenth century. One of the most renowned of the MacLeod

lairds was Sir Roderick, commonly called Rorie Mór, that is, Great Rory. This name was given him not because of his stature but because of his greatheartedness. His own room in the castle was in ear-shot of a small waterfall which lulled him to sleep, and since his day, three centuries ago, the fall has gone by the name of Rorie Mór's Waterfall. Above his bed was this inscription : " Sir Rorie M'Leod of Dunvegan, Knight. God send good rest." Rorie Mór's drinking-horn is still at Dunvegan. It is a bull's horn, the mouth ornamented with silver, and holding rather more than a bottle and a half. Each chief of MacLeod was expected, as a proof of his manhood before he was permitted to bear arms, to drink it off full of claret without laying it down.

Johnson and Boswell visited Dunvegan, and Sir Walter Scott stayed one night at the castle in 1814. He then, at MacLeod's suggestion, visited Loch Coruisk, which he has immortalised in " The Lord of the Isles," and when on shore at Strathaird explored the Spar Cave, that

> " mermaid's alabaster grot
> Who bathes her limbs in sunless well
> Deep in Strathaird's enchanted cell."

A letter from the Wizard of the North is preserved at the castle of Dunvegan. It reads as follows :

" DEAR MADAM,
" I have been postponing from day to day requesting your kind acceptance of my best thanks for the beautiful purse of your good workmanship with which I was some time since honoured. The hospitality of Dunvegan will long live in my recollection, and I am not a little flattered by a token which infers that my visit was not forgotten by the Lady of the Castle. I venture to send (which has long delayed this letter) a copy of a poem which owes its best passages to MacLeod's kindness and taste in directing me to visit the extraordinary scenery between his country and Strathard, which rivals in grandeur and desolate sublimity anything the Highlands can produce. The volume should have reached you in a quarto shape, but while I sought an opportunity of sending it behold the quartos disappeared and I was obliged to wait for the second impression, of which I now send a copy. I shall be proud and happy if it serves to amuse a leisure hour at Dunvegan. It has had one good consequence to the author, that it has served to replenish the purse with which the Lady MacLeod presented

him. Yet he has so much the spirit of the old Bard, that he values the purse more than the contents. Should MacLeod and you ever come to Edinburgh I will scarce forgive you unless you let such a hermit as I am know of your being in the neighbourhood of his recess and I would have particular pleasure in showing you anything that might interest you. I do not despair of (what would give me the most sincere pleasure) again being a guest at Dunvegan. My eldest girl sings Cathail Gu La—excuse Saxon spelling—and I hope to send you in a few weeks a very curious treatise on the Second Sight (not for sale) from a manuscript in 1691 which fell into my hands. Hector MacDonald has promised me the means to send it. I beg my respectful compliments to Miss MacLeod, my kindest remembrances to the chieftain and my best wishes to the little tartan chief and nursery.

"Believe me with much respect,

"Dear Madam (for I will not say Mrs. MacLeod, and Lady M— is now out of fashion),

     "Your honoured and obliged and truly grateful,

                      (Signed) WALTER SCOTT

Edinr. 3 *March*, 1815."

Rather more than thirty years before that time Johnson and Boswell were MacLeod's guests at Dunvegan. Johnson's description of the place is interesting. He writes :

"Dunvegan is a rocky prominence, that juts out into a bay, on the west side of Sky. The house, which is the principal seat of Macleod, is partly old and partly modern; it is built upon the rock, and looks upon the water. It forms two sides of a small square : on the third side is the skeleton of a castle of unknown antiquity, supposed to have been a Norwegian fortress, when the Danes were masters of the Islands. It is so nearly entire, that it might have easily been made habitable, were there not an ominous tradition in the family, that the owner shall not long outlive the reparation. The grandfather of the present Laird, in defiance of prediction, began the work, but desisted in a little time, and applied his money to worse uses.

"As the inhabitants of the Hebrides lived, for many ages, in continual expectation of hostilities, the chief of every clan resided in a fortress. This house was accessible only from the water, till the last possessor opened an entrance by stairs upon the land.

"They had formerly reason to be afraid, not only of declared wars and authorized invaders, or of roving pirates, which, in the northern seas, must have been very common; but of inroads and insults from rival clans, who, in the plenitude of feudal independence, asked no leave of their Sovereign to make war on one another. . . . When this house was intended to sustain a siege, a well was made in the court, by boring the rock downwards, till water was found, which though so near the sea, I have not heard mentioned as brackish, though it has some hardness, or other qualities, which make it less fit for use; and the family is now better supplied from a stream, which runs by the rock, from two pleasing waterfalls."

It was at Dunvegan that Johnson was distressed by a cold, and Miss MacLeod made him a large red flannel nightcap.

It is interesting to know that the MacLeods were thinking of leaving Dunvegan Castle as inconvenient at that time. MacLeod's lady wished to build a house about five miles from the castle and to make gardens and other ornaments there, but Boswell said to her :

> " ' No, no; keep to the rock : it is the very jewel of the estate. It looks as if it had been let down from heaven by the four corners, to be the residence of a Chief. Have all the comforts and conveniences of life upon it, but never leave Rorie More's cascade.' ' But (said she) is it not enough if we keep it ? Must we never have more convenience than Rorie More had ? He had his beef brought to dinner in one basket, and his bread in another. Why not as well be Rorie More all over, as live upon his rock ? It is all very well for you, who have a fine place, and every thing easy, to talk thus, and think of chaining honest folks to a rock. You would not live upon it yourself.' ' Yes, madam (said I), I would live upon it were I Laird of M'Leod, and should be unhappy if I were not upon it.' Johnson (with a strong voice, and most determined manner), ' Madam, rather than quit this old rock, Boswell would live in the pit; he would make his bed in the dungeon.' "

No less renowned than the MacLeods were the MacCrimmons, who were for centuries their hereditary pipers. The MacCrimmons held their lands rent-free, and their college of piping was at Borreraig on the opposite shore of the loch. To this college came pipers from every part of the highlands of Scotland, and even from Ireland, to be instructed. Johnson " had his dinner exhilarated " while at Dunvegan by the piping of a MacCrimmon and mentions that " there has been in Sky beyond all time of memory, a college of pipers, under the direction of Macrimmon, which is not quite extinct."

With MacCrimmon to play him into the fight, and the Fairy Flag to give him victory, MacLeod's state was a fortunate one. The magic property of the Fairy Flag (which hangs on the wall of Dunvegan Castle to-day) was that, when unfurled, it magnified the MacLeods sevenfold in the eyes of their enemies. But its enchantments were limited, and could be used on three occasions only.

Tradition states that it was twice unfurled—at the battle of Glendale in or about the year 1490 and at the battle of Trumpan at Vaternish in 1580. The third and last occasion on which the Fairy Flag was unfurled was in fulfilment of a most remarkable prophecy by Coinneach Odhar, the seer. The prophecy was as follows :

" When Norman (son) of the Third Norman, the son of the slender, bony, English lady, should die by accidental death; when MacLeod's Maidens should become the property of a Campbell; when a fox should have her young in one of the turrets of the castle; and when the Fairy Flag should be taken out of its box for the third and last time and unfurled, then the glory of the MacLeods should depart, a great part of their land would be sold, and a curach or coracle would be large enough to carry all the tacksmen of the name MacLeod across the sea loch. But in later times a MacLeod named Iain Breac would arise who would redeem the estates and would raise the power and honour of the house of MacLeod to a high degree."

The fulfilment of the prophecy (all unfortunately except the last part of it) came about as follows. In the summer of 1799 an English smith who was staying at Dunvegan, and one named Buchanan, business manager to MacLeod, secretly broke open the iron chest in which the Fairy Flag was kept. They found inside the chest several boxes of scented wood, each fitting perfectly within the other, and in the last box was the Fairy Flag. By exposing the flag for the third time they destroyed for ever the miraculous power which it possessed, but worse results were to come of their action. Almost at once came the news that Norman, son of the third Norman, had been blown up in H.M.S. " Queen Charlotte " while serving as a Lieutenant in the Navy. A short time afterwards the property of Orbost, on which were the rocks known as MacLeod's Maidens, was sold to Angus Campbell of Ensay. Then, remarkable to relate, a tame fox belonging to Norman, son of the Third Norman, had a litter of cubs in the west turret of the castle. When the prophecy was made there were more than forty tacksmen of the name of MacLeod on the estate. Not one remains to-day. Before the Great War there were hopes that the youthful Iain Breac, son

H

of the late Canon Rory MacLeod of MacLeod, would fulfil the concluding part of the prophecy, but he was killed in the war, and there is now no male heir in direct descent.

There are several traditions to account for the coming of the Fairy Flag to Dunvegan. One of them describes the crusading of an early chief. He was opposed at a certain ford in the Holy Land by a fairy, with whom he fought. On his overcoming his adversary she gave him the Fairy Flag. A second tradition narrates that one day of long ago a fairy entered the room where the infant chief was lying and taking the child on her knee wrapped about him the mystic fairy flag, singing a strange croon to him as she did so. The air and the words were so unusual that the nurse remembered them, and in time it came to be thought that any member of the chief's family to whom the fairy song was sung in infancy would be protected from harm through life. When the present chief was born in 1847 his nurse sang the Fairy Lullaby to him.

There is in the castle of Dunvegan a very old Communion Cup, thought to have belonged to Niall Glún-dubh, Niall of the Black-knee, who, as I have mentioned earlier in this chapter, was King of Ulster in the latter part of the tenth century. This cup is ten inches high, and is made of wood with fine silver work on it. Each side of the cup has its own pattern. On all four sides appear triangles, emblems of the Trinity, and circles, emblems of Eternity. The circles and the triangles are arranged with the greatest skill. The sacred use of the cup, which stands on four short silver legs, is shown by the letters I H S four times repeated inside the rim.

Dunvegan Castle is a place of associations of the past. The old dungeon with its rusted chains and weighted manacles, the Fairy Room, the Banqueting Hall where the MacCrimmons played, the Sea Gate through which the chiefs descended to their waiting galleys, the old portraits hung in the dining hall, the Prince Charlie relics—all these things are precious in an age of hurry and unrest.

North of Dunvegan is the peninsula of Vaternish, where stands the ruined church of Trumpan. How it came to be a ruin is one of the grim tragedies of the west. Between the MacLeods and the MacDonalds of ClanRanald a bitter feud existed. Perhaps the MacDonalds remembered that black day when many of their clan in Eigg were massacred by the Mac-Leods. Be that as it may, the men of ClanRanald planned a deadly revenge. One Sunday they sailed across the Minch in their galleys from their island territory of South Uist, and surprised the MacLeods at worship in the little church.

MacLeod's Tables, Skye.

" Picture the dismay of the worshippers when there is a loud shout at the church door, and they turn to see the door guarded by armed men, triumphant and without pity. Escape is impossible. Resistance is useless, for the men are unarmed in the church. As the congregation stand there—the women and children terrified, the men defiant yet powerless against the claymores that guard the narrow door—wisps of pungent smoke enter the church and soon the crackle of flames is heard. ClanRanald's men have fired the church !

" Shrieks and wailings echo through the doomed building, while outside the chief of ClanRanald's piper plays wild and scornful music to drown the cries of the dying. Unperceived in the dense smoke, the solitary survivor of the massacre squeezes herself, inflicting mortal injuries on her person as she does so, through the narrow slit at the corner of the church which serves as a window. . . ."

But before the men of ClanRanald could escape, the MacLeods came up from Dunvegan, and a desperate fight was fought on the green shore beside Ardmore. Uncertain for some time was the issue of the fight :

"Of a sudden the MacLeods are miraculously increased in numbers in the eyes of their enemies. Where they stood in scores they now stand in hundreds. The Fairy Flag has been unfurled! The tide of battle now goes against the raiders. ClanRanald and his men make for the shore in disorder. To their dismay they find their galleys left high and dry by the ebbing tide, and it is impossible to launch them across the great boulders and slippery stones while the MacLeods do not pause in their harrying. Disheartened, and with their means of escape cut off, the MacDonalds sell their lives dearly. The battle becomes a slaughter, but the defence is sufficiently strong to permit of a single galley being launched. In her a few of ClanRanald's men make their escape and return to South Uist with their bad tidings."

CHAPTER XVI

TROTTERNISH OF SKYE

ON June 29, 1746, a small boat might have been seen to approach the peninsula of Vaternish at Ardmore. The boat contained Prince Charles Edward and his guide, Flora MacDonald, who hoped to land on Skye after a perilous crossing from South Uist. They found, however, that the MacLeod militia held the shore of Vaternish (the MacLeods were against the Prince in the rising of '45), and as they were fired on by the militia they rowed out of range as fast as they were able to. Some three miles north of Ardmore they rowed into a narrow creek near a waterfall, and remained there for a short space to rest the men and eat some food. It was fortunate for them that there was no wind at the time, and thus the sailing vessels along the coast were unable to pursue them. After their short rest they rowed across the broad mouth of Loch Snisort and landed at a small shingly beach at Kilbride near Mugstot House, at that time a residence of the MacDonalds of Sleat. MacDonald had not supported the Prince, but his wife, Lady Margaret, a lady greatly beloved by the people of Skye, was well-disposed towards him, and through her diplomacy and skill the Prince escaped the cordon of troops in the district and reached Kingsburgh, where he stayed that night with MacDonald of Kingsburgh, continuing his journey next day to Portree.

On landing in this northern district of Skye, which is named Trotternish, the Prince found a treeless though fertile country, which in olden days went by the name of the Granary of Skye. Its most northerly point is Hunish, and near that promontory are the ruins of Duntuilm Castle, once a Norse fortress and at a later time the strong home of MacDonald of Sleat. The castle has now been a ruin for two hundred years, and there are two traditions to account for its state. According to one tradition a young child of the family was being held up to the window by its nurse, perhaps to see the galleys approach across the Minch, when with a sudden struggle it got free of the nurse's grasp and fell from the window to the rocks below. This tragedy so upset the family that they could no longer reside in the castle. The

Duntuilm, Skye.

second tradition tells that the restless spirit of Donald Gorm, a great warrior of the family, was in the habit of haunting the place and making it so unpleasant for the inmates that they left it. Duntuilm is in perhaps the most beautiful part of Skye. The view from the castle to the rocky island of Tuilm in the bay, and the hills of Harris rising above the sea twenty miles across the Minch, is of an exceptional character, whether seen in summer or at the close of a short winter day, when the rosy sunset bathes the shore in the early afternoon.

Duntuilm is full of reminders of the past. On the shore

beneath the castle is the hollow hewn out of the rock where the MacDonald galleys were kept. Leading from the hollow to the sea is to be seen on the surface of the rock (from half tide to low water) the narrow groove along which the galleys were drawn when they were being launched. Now small fishing boats are kept where the galleys rested, but the groove in the rock is still used when a boat has to be launched. To the south of the castle is a small green knoll where MacDonald sat in judgment on his people, having the power of life and death in his hands. Beside the present high-road is a low knoll named the Hanging Knoll. The dungeon of the castle is choked with earth. Could it but speak it might tell of dark deeds. Here perished Uisdean or Hugh, a kinsman of Donald Gorm Mór of Sleat. Close to the ruined castle is the old garden, made from ground brought from seven kingdoms—England, Ireland, Norway, France, Spain, Germany and Denmark. Hay is made to-day in the old garden, and so rich is the soil that the crop is heavy, although no top-dressing is applied to the ground.

Early on a December morning, when the storm wrack is hurrying past on the arms of a south-westerly gale, the full moon, shining behind the castle, lights up its dark walls and shines golden on the storm-harried waters of the Minch. Equally beautiful is a December moonrise on a winter afternoon in calm frosty weather. One afternoon when fishing on the Minch I watched the sky slowly brighten behind the castle so that the old ruin gradually stood out dark and noble against the increasing light. The moon was long in appearing, but at last it climbed into the sky, golden, immense, benign. Shafts of aurora flickered on the northern horizon; in the south-west the planet Venus was so bright that she threw a golden pathway on the sleeping waters. In winter in Skye there are days and nights more beautiful than any July or August can give.

Between Duntuilm and Flodigarry (the place of Flora Mac-Donald's early married life) is a grim and dark peak marked on the map as Sron Vourlinn, but called by the people of the district

Sron Bhiornal. The tradition of the country is that during the Norse occupation of Skye a princess lived in Dùn Dabhaid (as Duntuilm was then called). Her name was Biornal, and before she died she asked that she might be buried high on the hills so that her tomb might look across the sea to Norway. There is nothing to-day to mark her grave—no great cairn as on Beinn na Cailliche—but tradition tells that she was buried on a grassy ledge about seventy feet below the hill-top. Here the hill falls in a sheer precipice, so that her body must have been lowered by ropes to the ledge, if this be indeed her burial-place.

Sron Bhiornal is a picturesque height of some fifteen hundred feet. Almost always it is dark and gloomy, but when the winds of autumn and winter sweep over the land this gloom is intensified and, as often as not, the hill is hidden by swirling clouds that are bred in Atlantic solitudes. But sooner or later comes a day when the wind falls, the clouds rise from the hills, and the low sun shines upon the rain-sodden bogs and streams that flow bank-high. The small crofting township of Kilmaluag is a good base for the climb to Sron Bhiornal. Kilmaluag commemorates Mo-Luoc of Lismore, a much-loved contemporary of St. Columba.

From Kilmaluag the climb is at first gradual, and snipe rise with harsh cries from the sodden ground, but soon the dry slopes of the hill are reached—the territory of the buzzard and the raven. The hill-top where Biornal lies is narrow and wind-swept. Her resting-place is the first soil of Skye to feel the breath of the north wind from Norway and the view north and east is remarkable. Like a golden seal crouching in the dark Minch the island of Trodday lies almost at the climber's feet. At a greater distance are the Shiant Islands and beyond them the low sun shines upon the sea cliffs of Lewis. The peninsula of Tiumpan and the entrance to Stornoway harbour are clear.

On the day when I stood on the hill-top the south wind increased, and flurries of air wandered over the Minch where two trawlers were fishing. Above the Sound of Rona drifted grey

clouds.   Upon the peaks of the Scottish mainland snow lay deep.
One of the hills beside Loch Maree was covered by a cloud so
light that, even at this great distance, the sun was seen shining
on the snow through the cloud.   When, perhaps a minute later,
I again looked at this hill the mist had vanished and the snowy
slope was clear.   Grey mists, white, ice-cold peaks, the long
northerly swell breaking on the rocks of Rudha Réidh—such was
the view to the east.

North End, Skye.

I continued south along the ridge to the high ground above
the Quirang—that remarkable labyrinth of rocky castles, towers
and bastions in the midst of which cattle were hidden in former
times during a raid—and here reached the snow.   From the
snowy slope rose a scabious flower.   It was curious to see its
dark blue colour in a country on which winter had already laid
her hand.   Hitherto the view southward had been hidden, but
when I reached the hill-top above the Quirang I could see far in
that direction.   In deep shadow Beinn Storr rose, the snow

which covered it a pale blue-grey in the ebbing light. Beyond this hill of pinnacles rose the Cuillin, their upper slopes in mist, and billowy sun-bathed clouds in their corries also. Far to the south rose the snow-powdered heights of Rhum, an island whose name, written in the form *Ruimm*,[1] appears in the *Annals of Ulster* as long ago as the year 676. The two flat-topped hills in MacLeod's Country, known as MacLeod's Tables, were hidden

The Quirang, Skye.

in drifting rain showers, through which slanting shafts of sun-light shone. Across the hill-top where I stood a flock of snow buntings flew. From a rocky perch three grey crows rose with harsh unmusical cries, and a few minutes later five ravens flew over my head. The peaty pools were bound by ice an inch thick; a chill wind swept the hill and brought with it a flurry of snow. West, the sky was dark and lowering, and

[1] It is here written in the genitive case.

across the Minch showers drifted. They hid rocky Iasgair, and shadowed Fladday where the long swell broke heavily. Far to the west rose the islands of the Sound of Harris—Pabbay, Berneray, and others. St. Kilda was already hidden in misty rain which an Icelandic depression was bringing to the Outer Hebrides. On the shore of Skye beside the Minch at Camus Mór rose the church that is now abandoned, and which was built more than a hundred years ago by Lord MacDonald. A still older church was unroofed by a gale so violent that it swept the sheaves of oats into the sea. That church was a thatched building, and on the day following the storm one of the congregation, meeting the minister, said to him, " I am thinking it is a sad thing to see our church with the thatch blown from its roof." To which remark the minister replied, " And I am thinking of a sadder thing, and that is the many sheaves of corn that were swept out to sea in yesterday's storm."

I left the snowy hilltop, and as the light failed, reached the low ground, and heard the clamour of wild geese. I passed close to Martin's home—he who was governor to MacLeod of MacLeod's children and also to MacDonald of Sleat, and who wrote that classic book on the Western Isles at the close of the seventeenth century—and saw, dark against the flashing lighthouse on Scalpay of Harris, the ruins of Duntuilm.

CHAPTER XVII

THE BACKBONE OF SKYE

SOUTH of Sron Bhiornal and the Quirang rise a long line of hills. Between these hills are old paths crossing from the east to the west of Skye through hill passes that often are hidden in the clouds.

Before roads were made in the island these hill paths were well-trodden, but now they are seldom used, except by a shepherd with powerful voice giving orders to his collie from afar, or a sportsman after blue hares on the high tops.

One of the highest of the hills that rise from the northern wing of Skye is Beinn Eadarra (2,003 feet), and a few hundred yards south of this hill-top is a *bealach* with an interesting history. The name of this gloomy and awe-inspiring defile is Bealach a' Mhorghain, the Shingle Pass, and on dark winter nights when the west wind moans among the black precipices and the gloom is rendered still more intense by the Atlantic mist, a headless spectre is said to haunt the pass and to sing a sad song. I have in another chapter [1] narrated how he—the Colann gun Cheann—was long ago expelled from Morar, where he fought a fierce fight with Iain Garbh of Raasay, and was banished to Skye.

North of Beinn Eadarra are two hill passes—Bealach Uig and Bealach nan Coisichean. Beneath Bealach Uig to the east a dark lochan lies in deep twilight overhung by a precipice. One day a shepherd and his wife were on the hill, and to amuse themselves were rolling great stones from the high ridge into the loch, where they fell with vast splashes. Of a sudden a more violent turmoil was visible in the middle of the loch and the man and his wife saw a fierce black horse swim to the shore,

[1] *Vide* p. 74.

climb from the peaty water, and look in fury around him. The onlookers now realised that they had disturbed the dreaded *each uisge* or water horse itself—that fearsome steed with the power to change at will into human form—and in terror crouched behind the rock they had been about to roll into the loch. With wet gleaming flanks the water horse stood there awhile, then sprang again into the lochan and dived beneath the waters.

The country of Beinn Eadarra is wild, even for the Isle of Skye. For miles north and south is a precipice almost uninterrupted except where it is broken by the hill passes, many of them marked by old moss-grown cairns. On the narrow ledges of this precipice rowan trees grow (the cliff faces east and thus is sheltered from the prevailing winds) and ravens make their home. The golden eagle formerly nested on the precipice, and the survivor of a pair of these noble birds haunted the rocks for a number of years after she had lost her mate. One September day when I was walking along the moor at the top of the precipice I became aware of a remarkable thing. Bumble bees were flying east above my head at great speed, but on reaching the edge of the cliff were at the mercy of the wind. The uprushing current lifted them high into the blue sky, and blew them back to the more sheltered zone. The bees fell exhausted into the heather and grass but they did not accept defeat. After a rest of a few seconds on the ground they again rose into the air, and flying very low sought to evade that uprising stream of air. Time after time they essayed a passage, but I do not think one was successful in flying beyond the rock. I imagined that the bees had set out from their homes in the quiet of the morning to search for honey, and now on their return found a wind barrier in their way. They were perhaps obliged to pass the night on the hill-top.

The view from Beinn Eadarra is one of the finest in Skye. On a clear winter day, when the winds of ocean for a brief space are at rest and the sun shines, one can look over a vast seascape. One day I recall of outstanding beauty. Deep snow covered all

Storr Rock, Skye.

the hills of the mainland. From Loch Carron, from Loch
Torridon, from Loch Broom, they rose. Each was enfolded in a
mantle of spotless white, and grey clouds floated about the lower
slopes. Northward the view was bounded by the long flat-
topped hills of the Reay Country. The distant island of Handa
was low on the horizon. The lighthouse on Rudha Storr caught
the winter sun, and beneath the lighthouse came from time to
time the sudden gleam of a great wave that broke upon rocks
sixty miles distant from Beinn Eadarra. West, across the Minch,
were the Outer Hebrides, and far west of the Outer Hebrides
St. Kilda,[1] like an island of dreams, rose on the distant horizon,
the low sun framing its great precipice of 1,300 feet—a cliff so
lofty that from its top the roar of the Atlantic surf is scarcely
audible. The Celtic name for St. Kilda is Hirt, a name which
in English may be translated Death. The name may have
arisen because of the use of the island as a prison. A man
convicted of sheep-stealing was banished to Hirt : a man who
had offended his chief found himself an unwilling passenger in a
sailing boat breasting the great Atlantic swell that surges
eastward, as he was borne towards an island whence there was
little chance of escape. But in time a thriving community
came to live upon the island that has lately been deserted, and
as I looked upon Village Bay and saw the pale sun on the slopes
of Connachair I thought of those people who have now made
new homes on the Scottish mainland. The men of St. Kilda
had curious notions of the wearing of the kilt. When the
people of that island landed at Oban from the vessel which
had brought them to the mainland, a well-known highlander
of the district who had come to welcome them was thus
addressed : " Are you not ashamed, you who have the Gaelic,
to go about in so indecent a manner, with your knees exposed ! "

So clear was the air that I could that day identify various
houses on Berneray in the Sound of Harris, perhaps thirty

---

[1] When seen from Beinn Eadarra, St. Kilda rises slightly to the left
of the Sound of Harris.

miles from where I stood, and could see a lobster fisherman's boat with tall brown sail feeling its way among the outlying reefs of the island. The sun shone on the small sands of Shillay and on the wide sands of Pabbay where is the site of an ancient MacLeod stronghold. Across the island of North Uist lay the low group of the Monach Isles, their lighthouse rising against the western sky.

One summer day from Beinn Eadarra I saw through the glass two sailing vessels steering south past the Monach Isles. They closely resembled (and I have little doubt were) the Breton smacks which were fishing lobsters that summer round the outermost skerries of the Outer Isles and, under sail, with no motor to aid them, made more than one voyage from the Outer Hebrides to Brittany with their catch. They were fishing illegally and the following year were driven back to France by a French fishery cruiser.

The isles of the Minch are seen clearly from Beinn Eadarra. Fladday Chuain—Fladday of the Strait—is always picturesque. This island was to have been one of the hiding-places of Prince Charlie after Culloden, but for some reason the Prince did not go there. It was so confidently believed in Skye that he was in hiding on Fladday that Donald Roy MacDonald was sent to the island by Lady Margaret MacDonald with food, money, and clothes for the royal fugitive. Fladday Chuain is now un-inhabited, and the last man to live on the island was a native of the Isle of Mull. He was known as the Muileach Mór, the Big Man from Mull, because of his stature and strength. When he left Fladday he settled in Skye at Kilmuir, and on the first Sunday of his residence in Skye was seen by scandalised neighbours to be ploughing his ground. They came and remonstrated with him. "This is the Lord's Day, Donald," said they, "and surely it is not seemly for you to plough your land on a Sunday." But the Muileach Mór, not in the least disconcerted, made answer, "Indeed, my friends, on Fladday I lost count of Sundays long years ago, and it is wishing to be back on Fladday I am now, for no one would interfere with me yonder."

On Fladday Chuain is a very old burial-ground, and just below the surface of the ground rested, until recently (it has now unfortunately been broken), a skull said to belong to the monk O'Gorgon, a man of great stature who had his cell on the island and was a contemporary of Columba.

The Cuillin seen from Beinn Eadarra against the cloudless glory of a winter sky, primrose-tinted and serene, are always

Portree, Skye.

memorable, and the snow which rests lightly on them gives them an added majesty. West of the Cuillin tops is Rhum, and south-west of Rhum, beyond Canna and the lighthouse upon Hyskeir, can be seen a hill of distant Tiree.

In glowing splendour the winter sun set behind MacLeod's Tables and the young moon climbed above Beinn Eadarra. A woodcock sprang from the hill near me and flew owl-like above the heather. In cold grandeur the high peaks beside

Loch Torridon rose into the evening sky as the lighthouse on Scalpay of Harris was lit and flashed its friendly message to the ships that sail the Minch, and to the hill country of Beinn Eadarra also.

The traveller who reaches the north promontory of Skye has two alternatives before him. He can either return by the road he came—through Kilmuir, Uig and along the shore of Loch Snisort to Portree—or he can make his way along the east shore of the island—past Flodigarry, Staffin and the Beinn Storr

The Cuillin Hills from near Storr Rock, Skye.

country to Portree. At Staffin again he has two alternatives. He may continue along the coast, or may cross the backbone of the hills by a mountain road to Uig. If he should decide to travel by the east side he passes near a loch with an unusual history because of a miraculous well that is beside it.

Martin Martin writing of the well in the year 1700 says :

"The most celebrated well in Skye is Loch Siant well. It is much frequented by strangers, as well as by the inhabitants of the isle, who generally believe it to be a specifick for several diseases, such as stitches, headaches, stone, consumption, megrim. Several of the common people oblige themselves by a vow to come to this well, and make the ordinary touer about it, call'd Dessil, which is performed thus : they move thrice round the well, proceeding sunwise from east to west, and so on. This is done after drinking of the water, and when one goes away from the well it's a never-failing custom to leave some small offering on the stone which covers the well. There are nine springs issuing out of the hill above the well, and all of them pay the tribute of their water to a rivulet which falls from the well. There is a little fresh-water lake within ten yards of the said well. It abounds with trouts, but neither the natives nor strangers will ever presume to destroy any of them, such is the esteem they have for the water. There is a small coppice near to the well, and there is none of the natives dare venture to cut the least branch of it, for fear of some signal judgment to follow upon it."

Loch Sianta, as the loch is named, is distinguished from the neighbouring lochs by the clearness of its water. Its grey-green depths are mysterious, and in them can be seen to swim the descendants of the " Sevin fair trouts " [1] which the great MacDonald introduced into the loch centuries ago.

There are few people who go to-day to the Holy Well of Loch Sianta ; there are few indeed who know where the loch lies, for, although it is close to the road, it is hidden from it by a sharp heathery ridge. The people to-day no longer invoke the miraculous power of the well. But the trout of the loch, and the mavis that sings in the sacred coppice, perhaps recall the old days when people from far and near, by sea and by land, came ill and infirm to the spring and left it restored by faith to health.

South of the Sacred Well and its loch is Staffin, where a broad bay of grey sand replaces the rocky shore. Near Staffin is the celebrated Kilt Rock, named because of its fancied resemblance to a kilt ; this rock is part of the cliff, and is of columnar formation, resembling the pillars of Staffa. It stands on the shore, not far from the main road.

If the traveller should decide to cross the hill road from Staffin to Uig he will be repaid by a very fine view from the highest part of the road, and when he descends to Uig beyond the watershed he will find himself in a sheltered bay, where the

[1] Macfarlane's *Geog. Coll.*, Vol. 2, p. 151.

rivers Conon and Rha enter the sea each through a well-wooded gorge. From Uig to Portree the road first keeps near the upper reaches of Loch Snisort and passes not far from Kingsburgh house, where, as I have described in another chapter,[1] Prince Charlie was sheltered for a night when he landed a fugitive in Skye in 1746. Less than thirty years later Johnson and Boswell were the guests of MacDonald of Kingsburgh. Boswell writes of his visit:

> " Mr. MacDonald of Kingsburgh was completely the figure of a gallant highlander. He had his Tartan plaid thrown about him, a large blue bonnet with a knot of black ribband like a cockade, a brown short coat of a kind of duffil, a Tartan waistcoat with gold buttons and gold button-holes, a bluish philibeg, and Tartan hose. There was a comfortable parlour with a good fire, and a dram went round. By and by supper was served at which there appeared the lady of the house, the celebrated Miss Flora MacDonald. [Flora MacDonald was at this time the wife of Mac-Donald of Kingsburgh.] She is a little woman, of a genteel appearance, and uncommonly mild and well-bred. To see Dr. Samuel Johnson, the great champion of the English Tories, salute Miss Flora MacDonald in the isle of Sky was a striking sight."

During their visit Johnson slept in the bed used by Prince Charles Edward, and on the following day heard from Flora MacDonald herself of her successful efforts to bring the Prince safely to Skye from the Outer Hebrides, although Government vessels patrolled the Minch, MacLeod militia patrolled the coast, and there was besides a reward of £30,000 on the royal fugitive's head.

From Kingsburgh is a matter of ten miles to Portree, the capital of Skye and named, it is usually believed, to commemorate the visit of James V in 1540. Each year two events of considerable importance are held at Portree. One is the Gaelic Mod or Musical Festival, the other is the Skye Gathering. The Gathering is held on the flat grassy crown of a small hill above the bay, and is perhaps the most truly highland of all the meetings held in Scotland.

In summer there are many cars on the roads which converge upon Portree. Each year a greater number of visitors arrive

---

[1] Page 101.

in Skye. They arrive by car, by bus, and by boat. Some have their caravans behind their cars, some sleep in tents, some in hotels, some in more humble lodgings. The great island of Skye casts her spell upon them, and they return to the mainland with minds and bodies refreshed, and with the resolve that they will revisit the scenes of beauty which have so greatly impressed them.

CHAPTER XVIII

RAASAY

SOME two miles east of Skye stands Raasay, a long hilly island 14 miles long and 4 miles broad, of high wind-vexed moorlands, green pastures, and (in a few places) fine woods extending to the shore.

For more than five centuries Raasay was the home of the MacLeods of Raasay, but the old family have now gone from the island, although I spoke to a MacLeod who told me that his grand-uncle was gillie on Loch na Mna when the last MacLeod of Raasay fished it. The island of Raasay is now owned by the Department of Agriculture for Scotland.

Raasay is an example of how the face of the land can be altered and improved by the judicious planting of trees. The west side of the island is covered with plantations and old trees which give shelter from the wind. The east face is bare and treeless, except for a few natural woods of birch and hazel. On the eastern shore of Raasay, near the north end of the island, are the ruins of Brochel Castle, the early home of the MacLeods of Raasay. Dean Munro in the sixteenth century writes of two castles, " Brolokit " and " Kilmorocht," " with twa fair orchards at the said twa castles ; the island perteining to Mac-ghyllichallan of Raarsay be the sword, and to the bishope of the isles be heritage." The Dean also writes of the island as " having maney deires, pairt of profitable landes inhabit and manurit." The " deires " still remain, and there is good deerstalking on Raasay to-day.

There is a tradition on Raasay that Brochel Castle was built by the MacSwans, who held the island before the MacLeods of

Raasay. Brochel Castle stands on a naturally fortified rock and is a picturesque ruin, looking across the sea to Applecross and the high hills of Ross-shire.

No greater contrast could be imagined to the wild country of Brochel than Raasay House, on the opposite side of the island. Here is a situation full open to the sun, sheltered by fine old trees, and with a glorious view across the sea to the dark Cuillin of Skye.

The first MacLeod of Raasay, whose Gaelic patronymic was Gille Chaluim, was a MacLeod of Lewis, and after him the successive heads of the family were known as Mac Gille Chaluim. It will be remembered that in the time of the '45 MacLeod of Dunvegan made cause with the Hanoverian troops, but MacLeod of Raasay followed the Prince to the mainland, and before setting out on that desperate enterprise he reviewed and spoke words of encouragement to his men who had assembled, to the number of one hundred and more, on the green in front of Raasay House. According to the island tradition of the " rising," twenty-six pipers went from the island, and sixteen of them returned. MacLeod of Raasay himself was wounded, but made his way back to the island and was for some time in hiding in a cave near the house. Before taking arms for the Prince, he had wisely made the estate over to his son, who remained on the island, and the story goes that the son when he afterwards claimed the property swore in a Court of Law that his father was below the ground, and that he had walked over him. This evidence was indeed strictly true, and was accepted as a proof of old Raasay's death. It is likely that the old highlander remained " below the ground " until the evil passions of the years following the " forty-five " had died away.

Raasay house was fired by the King's orders, after Culloden, but shortly afterwards a new house was built on the old site, and that house stands to-day, although it has been greatly added to since then, the centre part remaining as the old Raasay House. Here can be seen the room in which Johnson slept during his visit to the island, and it is believed that the bed is the same as that which stood in the room on a September day of the year 1773 when Johnson and Boswell, after a rough voyage, landed on Raasay and were most hospitably received. We have it on Boswell's authority that the wind made the sea very rough and that Dr. Johnson was heard to remark, "This is now the Atlantic. If I should tell at a tea-table in London that I have crossed the Atlantic in an open boat, how they'd shudder, and what a fool they'd think me to expose myself to such danger." But all the inconvenience suffered by the learned doctor on that occasion was the loss of his spurs, which were swept overboard. Thirty people sat down to supper that night in Raasay House, and there was highland dancing to the music of a fiddler. Doubtless there were good pipers on Raasay in those days, but the time of the most renowned piper of the island was later. This man was John MacKay, commonly known in the lore of the island as Iain mac Ruaidhri of Eyre. He was an orphan, and was brought up by Malcolm MacLeod of the Raasay family. John MacKay was a herd boy, and used to practise pipe tunes on a chanter made of the stalk of the yellow iris when he was herding the cattle on the hill. Malcolm MacLeod at the time was teaching the pipes to another young lad, and Iain mac Ruaidhri sometimes overheard the two pipers, and unknown to them, eagerly learnt the lesson intended for another. Then one day Malcolm MacLeod chanced to hear young MacKay play, and was so impressed with his music that he had him sent to the MacCrimmon college at Borreraig, and also to the great MacKays of Gairloch. It is interesting to realise that from John MacKay, through his son Angus, the traditional playing of *piobaireachd* or classical pipe music has been handed down to pipers of the present day.

In a recess leading out of one of the rooms of the old part of Raasay House are stains in the stone floor. They are believed to be bloodstains, and cannot be washed out. A picturesque tradition accounts for the presence of these stains. A brother of MacLeod of Raasay—a doctor—had climbed to the top of Dun Caan, the highest hill on the island, with his sister. She, unknown to him, had been interesting herself in magic, and on seeing a boat on the sea fifteen hundred feet beneath them, said to her brother, " If I wished to sink that boat I could do it." Jestingly her brother replied, " Put her down, then, if you are able." By incantations she conjured up a storm. Angry waves pressed in upon the boat, and when her brother in alarm told her to quieten the wind, she sadly replied that she was powerless to do so. The boat soon afterwards sank, and its inmates were drowned. Brother and sister returned to Raasay House, and her doctor-brother then told her that she looked ill. She denied feeling ill, but he said it would be necessary to " bleed " her (bleeding was the cure for most ailments in the old days). After he had drained a certain amount of blood from her he asked her what colour the candle's flame appeared to her. " I see it yellow," she replied. Again he drained her blood, and again asked her the colour of the candle's flame. " I see it red," she replied. A third time he opened the vein and again asked her the same question. " I see it blue," she replied, " and now I understand your purpose, which is to take my life." When she had said this she fainted away, and died from loss of blood. Her brother had deliberately killed his sister in order that the honour of the old family might remain untarnished.

When Johnson and Boswell visited Raasay they were shown, on one of the low rocks which fringe the shore below Raasay House, a cross below old Celtic scroll-work incised on the stone. Before this cross the Raasay family used to pray—perhaps on first reaching their island by sea. There were at one time the remains of eight crosses near here; they surrounded the chapel behind the house and marked the " girth " of the Sanctuary, on entering which a man was safe from his enemies. The chapel is now in ruins, and I saw no signs of any of the old crosses. The climate of Raasay is mild, and in the shelter of the woods semi-tropical trees, such as the eucalyptus, grow at a remarkable rate. Fuchsia hedges are a feature of the island, and are striking when the plants are in flower. The shelter and warmth attract many woodcock in autumn and winter, and the woodcock shooting on Raasay is perhaps the finest in the north-west of Scotland. Grouse are found in considerable numbers on the island, but blackcock, which were plentiful in Johnson's time, have almost disappeared, just as they have almost vanished from the Isle of Mull during late years.

On one of the lochs of Raasay—Loch Storab by name—there is a small island with a curious history. Long ago, when the Norsemen conquered the Hebrides, the son of the King of Norway came, unknown, as a fugitive from Lewis to Raasay, and hid on this small isle. His shelter in time was discovered, and the men of Raasay attempted to leap from the shore to the island to capture the man. Storab, a person of great height, had been able to jump with ease from the island to the shore, and had been in the habit of going by night to a farmer's wife for food, but when the men of Raasay found that they could not reach the island they began to drain the loch. When Storab realised this he sprang ashore, and hurrying to his benefactress asked her to hide him. This she did not dare do, and Storab, when leaping over a ravine, was fatally injured by an arrow fired at him. When his sister Biornal heard of his death at the hands of the people of Raasay she was filled with indignation and sorrow. She burnt the isles of Raasay and Rona and asked that when she died she might be buried on high ground, where she could look across to Raasay. Her tomb is still pointed out on a narrow ledge just below the summit of Sron Bhiornal in northern Skye.[1]

Dun Caan, the high hill of Raasay, was at one time believed to be as lofty as the Cuillin. It is a fine hill, of distinctive appearance, and can be seen from the Outer Hebrides.

On a September day of sunshine I climbed to its summit, and looked east across a blue and tranquil sea to Crowlin Island and

[1] *Vide* Chap. XVI.

Applecross. To the north were the lands of the MacKenzies of Gairloch, who were often at variance with the MacLeods of Raasay, and in a grassy corrie immediately beneath the top of Dun Caan I noticed a few old stones which are said to mark the graves of MacKenzies of Gairloch and MacKenzies of Applecross, killed by the men of Raasay in a clan fight here.

If Raasay and the Gairloch folk were often at enmity it was otherwise with the MacLeods of Raasay and the MacDonalds of Sleat. In his *Tour* Dr. Johnson mentions that there was an old friendship between the families of Raasay and Sleat, and that "whenever the head of either family dies his sword is given in the keeping of the head of the other." At the time of Johnson's visit Raasay had in his keeping the sword of the late Sir James MacDonald of Sleat. Can that sword have been the broken claymore belonging to Iain Garbh who was drowned (some say by the incantations of the Witch of Staffin) on passage from Lewis to Raasay in his galley, which was kept by the family as a treasured possession?

As I sat on Dun Caan on a September morning I could see the sunlight sparkle on Loch na Mna, the Loch of the Woman, where a fearsome *each uisge* or water horse lurked. The loch received its name because a certain blacksmith lost his wife here. She was abducted by the water horse, and the bereaved husband accordingly set a trap for the creature. An Gobha Mór, the Big Smith, built a stone hut on the shore of the loch with an opening in the wall nearest the water and then killed and roasted a wether-sheep in the hut. The wind blew the savoury smell towards the loch and the greedy water horse made its way into the enclosure by the entrance left for it. The smith had his irons ready in the fire, and rushing with them at the *each uisge,* killed it. The monster was examined, and after death was found to be a soft mass like a large jelly-fish !

Times have changed on Raasay. No longer do Mac Gille Chaluim and his eldest son, Rona, sail from the grim old pile of Brochel, with a piper at the prow of the war galley. No longer does Iain mac Ruaidhri send out on the sea wind the strains of some warlike *piobaireachd*. No longer does the *each uisge* emerge from the peaty depths of Loch na Mna in search of human prey. The small cave beside the shore where Morag,[1] the Prince, hid is now empty. But a September sunset bathes Raasay as it did in the time of Johnson's visit and from the high ground of the island the sun may be seen to sink in splendour behind MacLeod's Tables in Skye, bathing them in rosy light and caressing the house of Raasay, serene in an untroubled old age.

[1] Prince Charles Edward was known in the Hebrides as Morag by those who were in the secret of his hiding-places.

CHAPTER XIX

THE COUNTRY OF KNOYDART

NORTHWARD from Mallaig, and between that small seaport and Glen Elg, is a wild country of dark sea lochs and gloomy hills, often mist-shrouded. Loch Nevis and Loch Hourn lie here. If we credit popular tradition Loch Hourn means the loch of the Nether World, and there is perhaps no loch in all Scotland which can be so dark, and no loch so overshadowed by great hills which tower above its head to the very skies.

Between Loch Nevis and Loch Hourn is the broad peninsula of Knoydart—the Country of Knoydart as its own people call it. This land is old Glengarry territory (except when two generations of the Grants of Glen Morriston obtained a footing in it) and traditions of the MacDonells of Glengarry linger here to the present day. The Country of Knoydart and the lands of Loch Hourn will long remain unspoiled. Here are no speedways; the roads are narrow and primitive although they are broader than the roads of the Applecross country. In Knoydart, as in Applecross, the high-road is the sea, yet it is possible for a moderately good walker to cross from Mallaig to Inverie on Loch Nevis by motor boat, walk by way of Glen Dulochan over the *bealach* to Glen Barisdale and Loch Hourn, cross this loch and continue to Glen Elg and its hotel in the course of a single day.

Sailing from Mallaig to Inverie one passes the two small townships of Mallaig Bheag and Mallaig Mhór and then, landing on the further shore of Loch Nevis, enters Glen Dulochan, through which an ancient and little-used track climbs by way of Loch Dulochan to the *màm* or hill pass and continues to Glen Barisdale on the far side of it. Heavy rain was falling as I climbed this track one September morning. The raindrops hissed upon the loch in the glen, refreshing the waters which were shrunken from many weeks of drought, and in the mist-filled corries the white waterfalls were awakening the music of the hills, silent for so long. At a height of rather more than 1,000 feet above the Atlantic the path reaches the watershed. Here, this sombre morning, I stood and looked down to the depths in which Loch Hourn lay. It resembled a lake of the infernal regions. Above it rose vast hills, grim, ghostly, and nebulous through banks of fog and soft-stealing rain showers. Never in Scotland have I seen hills giving the impression of such vast size. Here the clan of the *uruisgean* or spectres must roam; here the *each uisge* and the *tarbh uisge* or water bull perhaps fight fierce battles. I do not think the *daoine sìth*, the hill fairies, are here. The country of Loch Hourn is too vast and forbidding for the " little people." It was in Glen Barisdale that I heard the legend of the Bull of Barisdale. This supernatural creature had but three feet, and its tracks were " a paw and a claw." Its roaring was so fearsome that the belling of the stags seemed feeble indeed when the Bull gave tongue. That thunderous cry would come now from one corrie, now from another at a considerable distance from it. On one memorable occasion the tracks of the Bull of Barisdale were followed through deep snow until they climbed a precipice. The trackers then wisely declined to go further, and returned home secretly glad at having avoided closer contact with the monster.

Glen Barisdale is a place of interest to the lover of trees because of the old natural-sown Scots pines which grow here. I had not previously seen veterans of the Old Caledonian Forest so far west, for the climate of the Atlantic seaboard is less favourable to these conifers than the drier Central Highlands where, in the Cairngorms, the Scots pine grows as high as the 2,000 feet level. Yet these firs of Glen Barisdale are healthy and well grown, and twist their gnarled roots about the naked rocks. In former days these firs must have been more numerous than now, for along the river which flows through the glen are remains of old dams which were used to float the timber down to Loch Hourn. There is a tradition that a great fire which began in the forest of Achnacarry swept westward on an easterly gale, until it had reached the Barisdale "march." Here the stumps, and even the tree trunks, of blackened firs are still to be seen in the peat. Perhaps that great fire was in the time of Coll of Barisdale, who was out in the '45, and led a life full of adventure even for those exciting days. The MacDonells of Barisdale were descended from Ranald IX of Glengarry, whose youngest son, Archibald, was the first of the Barisdale family. Archibald was "out" with Dundee at Killiecrankie, and afterwards fought under Glengarry's banner at Sheriffmuir. True highland hospitality was dispensed at the old house of Barisdale, a house containing " 18 fire rooms, besides as many more without chimney."

The most celebrated of the Barisdale family was Coll, commonly known as Colla Bàn, because of his fair appearance. He held the appointments of Captain of the Watch and Guardian of the March on the west side of Inverness-shire. Colla Bàn joined Prince Charles Edward at the head of the Knoydart men, who, it is said, made a very handsome appearance, and he so distinguished himself that he was made a Knight Banneret at the pursuit after Prestonpans. After Culloden Barisdale was captured, but was permitted to return home on the condition that he supplied information as to the whereabouts of the fugitive prince. The information which Coll gave to the Government (since he had no intention of betraying Prince Charlie) was that the Prince was with friendly Campbells in Perthshire, while his royal master was all the time in hiding in the Hebrides. When his information was proved false, Cumberland dispatched a party of Ross-shire militia to burn down Barisdale House. The ruins of the old house are still to be seen near the modern building. Coll then attempted to escape to France on board a French man-of-war, but the Prince, believing that Barisdale had indeed plotted against him, made him prisoner. From France he escaped, only to be once more imprisoned in Britain on his return. He died in captivity in Edinburgh, and was perhaps the victim of great injustice. His son, who at the age of twenty was also " out " in the '45 and greatly distinguished himself, was after Culloden sentenced to be hung, drawn and quartered, but this harsh sentence was remitted because of his youth.

Near Glen Barisdale the waters of Loch Hourn are more kindly than elsewhere. Here are white shores, and islands purple in late summer with heather bloom. One low isle is emerald green, and on it is a very old burying-ground, with no gravestones of modern days to deface it. The sea thrift grows over these old graves, and sea-gulls on white wings drift like angels of peace above them. Near this burying island is a low strand where a crone who " had the sight " was in the habit of searching for shellfish to feed herself in her black house. Barisdale and she in some way fell out, and in order to spite the old crone the laird gave orders that the shore should be ploughed up in order to disturb her shellfish. She thereupon (this is the story as told by an old *seanachaidh* or story-teller) put a curse upon him, saying that the time would soon come when Barisdale would lose his possessions, and when he and his family would themselves be compelled to subsist upon shellfish, but before these things should happen the sea would flow in upon his fertile lands. The sea loch did indeed encroach upon the rich land here, and not long afterwards Barisdale passed from the possession of the old family. On one of the islands of Loch Hourn the laird is said to have sat in judgment on his people. On another isle, Eilean a' Phìobaire or the Piper's Island, a piper of the old days was accustomed to practise on his *feadan* or chanter and his *pìob mhor*, and perhaps composed *ceòl mór* with the crooning sea music in his ears.

To sail down Loch Hourn is to pass through a waterway between great hills; the traveller might be deep in the recesses

of some Norwegian fjord. The huge corrie of Labhar Bheinn is
the home of red deer, foxes, and curling mists. On the opposite
side of the loch is Beinn Sgriol, 3,196 feet high, whose slender
summit may tower above the clouds that hide its steep heathery
slopes. Below this hill is Arnisdale, its white-harled " big
house " sympathetically blending in tone with the purple heather
that approaches it so closely. Near the house cluster the
village crofts. Here was once a prosperous herring fishing
industry, but now the herrings do not enter the loch in such
numbers as formerly.

From Arnisdale to Glen Elg a narrow road, with a good surface
for the walker, leads first through bracken, birches and oaks,
then across the open moor. One looks south to Ardnamurchan,
and sees its lighthouse rise needle-like on the far horizon, and
south-west to the Scùir of Eigg and the dark heights of Rhum.

The mouth of Glen Elg is beside Kyle Rhea, the narrow strait
separating the Isle of Skye from the mainland. The narrows
are named after Reidh, one of the Fianna or Fingalians. The
story of the origin of the name I have told in a previous chapter.[1]

Kyle Rhea was formerly the main crossing-place between
Skye and the mainland. The old slips are still to be seen, but
this ferry is seldom used nowadays, for the ferries at Kyle of
Loch Alsh and Armadale have taken its place.

From Glen Elg a road leads eastward to Loch Duich and
Cluanie. It crosses the formidable Mam Rattagan pass, but
from Glen Elg the gradient to the watershed is easier than
from the shore of Loch Duich on the east side of the pass.
It was in the woods of Glen Elg that MacLeod killed the fierce
wild bull from which the famed drinking horn of Rory Mòr,
which hangs on the walls of Dunvegan Castle, was made.

It is possible to travel by car from Glen Elg, by way of Loch
Duich, Glen Shiel and Tomdoun, thence westward along the shore
of Loch Quoich to the head-waters of Loch Hourn. At the head
of Loch Hourn one receives again the impression of descending

[1] Page 61.

K

to the nether world at Kinloch Hourn, which lies far below. Even on a summer day the hills are so high as to intercept the sun. In winter the twilight of early morning must linger here until dusk, hurrying from the east, throws her cloak over the loch three hours after midday.

CHAPTER XX

In the last chapter I have described the country of Knoydart, from Loch Nevis, across Loch Hourn, to Glen Elg. Let us now return from Kinloch Hourn by way of Loch Quoich and Loch Garry and, entering the Great Glen at Loch Oich, travel west along the shore of Loch Lochy to Achnacarry and Loch Arkaig. Here is Lochiel's Country, perhaps the most romantic district in all the Western Highlands.

Many of the great highland families have had to part with their lands, which are now in the possession of strangers. But Lochiel, Captain of Clan Cameron, and its twenty-fifth chief, still lives where his people have lived from time immemorial, and it will be a bad day for the western highlands when there is no longer a Lochiel at Achnacarry.

In Lochiel's Country the past and the present join hands. In the castle at Achnacarry are priceless relics of the '45, and of still earlier times. The most interesting of the '45 relics is perhaps a silver flask given to the Gentle Lochiel by Prince Charles Edward with the following inscription on it : " Snuff Box or Dram Cup, while skulking in ye Highlands, given by him to Lochiel A.D. 1747, at Paris." On the castle wall hangs the clan banner, which escaped the hands of the English after Culloden. MacLachlan of Coruanan, hereditary standard-bearer to the Lochiel of the day, wrapped the standard next his skin that evening of disaster, and carried it safe to Lochaber—and in the family of the Coruanan MacLachlans it remained until recent years, when it was given to Lochiel. On the castle wall near the standard are a claymore, or two-handed sword, used at the Battle of Harlaw, an old targe (pierced thrice by deadly thrusts which must have caused grievous wounds to him who carried it) on which is written in bold lettering, " Fear God, Honour the King," and the gun with which Sir Ewen of Lochiel, perhaps the most renowned of a long line of outstanding chiefs, killed the last wolf in the highlands.

At Achnacarry, beside the friendly Arkaig river, which sings a soft lullaby, or an eager song of triumph, according to the season and the weather, it is easy to visualise the days of the '45. The old castle was burned to the ground by Cumberland's troopers. Not a trace of it remains. But the beech avenue stands high and green and stately, and if one looks at it closely one notices that the trees are planted in a curious manner. At the beginning of the avenue they are carefully spaced; farther on they grow so closely together that the stems press one upon another. The explanation is that when Lochiel in 1745 crossed the hills to meet Prince Charlie he hoped to dissuade the Prince from his reckless enterprise, and thought soon to return to his planting of the beech avenue which he had planned. But dark days came to Lochiel. His lands were confiscated, Lochiel died in France, and the beeches were left to grow as they had been temporarily set into the ground. Near this avenue are older trees, and on them are still to be seen the hollows which supported the beams on which were hung the kettles of Cumberland's troopers. On the wooded hill-side above the castle stood the hut to which Lochiel retreated when in hiding. To-day the last traces of that hut have gone. The site of it was marked by willows, and when the woods were felled during the Great War, these guiding trees were cut down also. Not far from where the hut stood is a cave where the fugitive Prince is said to have rested.

When the dipper sings his autumn song beside the hurrying waters of the Arkaig he sings quietly. He and his clan have lived here for many generations, but the osprey, who for so long had her eyrie on Loch Arkaig, has gone, never, it is to be feared, to return. Despite watchers and barbed wire entanglements the osprey's nest was frequently robbed, and on their journeys to and from their winter quarters in the south the birds themselves, both young and old, fell victims to unscrupulous gunners.

For its size the Arkaig must be one of the shortest rivers in Scotland. It is little more than a mile in length, and flows from Loch Arkaig to Loch Lochy. Loch Arkaig, a long narrow loch more than twelve miles in length, is sheltered by high hills. On a still autumn evening, when the last of the sun-fire lingers on Fraoch Bheinn and the moon rises golden in the east, salmon leap and play in the still waters of Loch Arkaig and the clan of the bats flit delicately and uncertainly above the old oak woods and the dark pines of the Caledonian Forest.

On the north shore of the loch the road to Glen Dessary winds through the oak woods. The tree is still standing behind which Cameron of Clunes awaited his special enemy, an English officer of the army of occupation. The story may be told in a few words. During the troublous times that followed the '45 one of Cumberland's officers made himself so disliked by his brutal and overbearing behaviour that Cameron of Clunes determined to take his life. The officer was the owner of a handsome white horse, which made him easy to recognise. He heard of this plot against his life, and arranged that on the day in question a brother officer, Major Monroe of Culcharn, should ride his horse. This highland officer, who was serving in the Hanoverian army, unsuspectingly did so, and as he rode at nightfall along the side of Loch Arkaig he was shot dead by Clunes, who in the failing light recognised the horse but failed to recognise the rider.

On Loch Arkaig is a wooded isle which was, according to one tradition, the burying-place of the MacPhees. It was probably on this island that the renowned Sir Ewen of Lochiel confined three English colonels and Colonel Duncan Campbell. He had surprised and captured these officers near Inveraray, and took them " to Locharkike to ane isle there." Loch Arkaig never freezes. " Its water is admirably light and delicat, being well stored with salmond and other fishes," says an old account, which goes on to describe how Sir Ewen, who in time came to have a great regard for his prisoners, organised a deer drive for them. Some hundreds of his clansmen, skilled hunters all of them, made a long line across the hills, and enclosed a great number of deer. They drove these deer to an appointed place, and actually prevented them from breaking out while the prisoners killed them with their broadswords. The old pines of Glen Mallie beside Loch Arkaig must have been striplings on the day of that memorable deer drive.

When a part of this pine forest was felled some twenty years ago a number of the oldest trees were spared. They are believed to be almost 300 years old. Even the splendid pine forests of the Cairngorms have, I believe, no trees to compare with them in age. One of the old Glen Mallie firs is known as the Three Sisters because of its three stems. On a dark day, when mist covered the hills, I first saw this tree, and as I looked upon it the sun for a few minutes pierced the clouds, and shone full upon the Three Sisters, so that the tree stood out from the dark hillside in radiant beauty. That old tree during its long life must have seen many things. It must already have been well grown when Prince Charles Edward, a fugitive with shattered dreams, journeyed, disconsolate, westwards along Loch Arkaig. Cumberland's troops may have camped in its shade. During many years it must have seen the osprey sail across to its island nest, carrying in his talons fish for the hungry brood. It has watched the *each uisge*, or water horse, playing upon the surface of the loch, before it was banished by the thoughts of a materialistic age. Lord Malmesbury in his Memoirs writes (1857): " My stalker, John Stuart at Achnacarry, has seen it twice, and both times at sunrise in summer, when there was not a ripple on the water. The creature was basking on the surface; he saw only the head and hind-quarters, proving that its back was hollow, which is not the shape of any fish, or of a seal. Its head resembled that of a horse. The highlanders are very superstitious about this creature. They believe that there is never more than one in existence at the same time."

As one walks along the Mile Dorcha (the Dark Mile) at sunset the water horse, and other mysterious beings, seem more real than many a creature of the material world. Invisible stags roar hoarse and menacing challenges from the depths of the forest. A wild cat ambles across the track with long, easy strides that appear deceptively slow. A heron shrieks: overhead a flight of mallard pass. The last of the sunset burns pale upon the snows of Ben Nevis—so long as snow lies on the Ben all is well with Lochiel and his house—and night lays her hand lightly upon Lochiel's Country.

Between Lochiel's Country and the Glengarry lands of Knoydart great hills tower to the clouds. The eagle, the raven, the hill fox, and the red deer, have their home here, and traces of human handiwork are seen in General Wade's old track which leads from Glen Dessary, beside Loch Arkaig, westwards to the Atlantic tides of Loch Nevis. The hill pass at the head of Glen Dessary is named Mam na Cloiche Airde, the Pass of the High Rock, and the name is singularly apt. At the head of Loch Arkaig two glens lead away west. One is Glen Pean, in Gaelic Gleann Peathann, the other is Glen Dessary, in Gaelic Gleann Deiseirgh, the Glen with a Southern Exposure. Glen Pean crosses to Loch Morar. Prince Charlie traversed it at least once during his " skulking in ye Highlands," and Cameron of Glen Pean and MacDonald of Glen Alladale met the Prince subsequently at Ranachan in the Loch Ailort country, and discussed future plans with him there. Glen Pean is a narrow glen, and does not rise to any great height above the sea. Near its head-waters is Loch Leum an t-Sagairt, the Loch of the Priest's Leap. The story is that a priest was in hiding, and was surrounded by soldiers. On every side his escape was hindered. Only by jumping across the loch, which is several hundred yards wide, could the hunted man win free. But leap it the saintly man did, aided, some say, by supernatural powers, and made good his escape. Since that day the Loch of the Priest's Leap has been the name of this lonely tarn. Glen Dessary was the old home of the Camerons of Glen Dessary, a cadet branch of the Lochiel family. It was Miss Jenny Cameron of Glen Dessary who rode at the head of the men from Kinloch Arkaig to meet the Prince at Glen Finnan. She was mounted on a white horse and wore a green jacket. Scarcely a trace remains of the old house of Glen Dessary, and the barracks, where Cumberland's troops were quartered, are not easily recognised to-day, although the firmly built walls are still standing beside the road at the mouth of the glen. Perhaps two miles up Glen Dessary from the site of the old barracks, on the far side of the river near the only house that stands hereabouts, is a small knoll known as Cnoc Dhuic, the Duke's Knoll, where Cumberland's soldiers had their camp on one occasion.

It was a dark day in autumn when a friend and I made our way up Glen Dessary by General Wade's old track. Beside Loch Arkaig the leaves on the rowans were dark red, and were even more beautiful than the ample crop of scarlet berries, on which fieldfares from Norway were feeding eagerly. A pair of swans swam on the dark waters of the loch. On Guilven and Streap across the glen the mist rose and fell, and Sgùrr na h-Aide for a moment showed his graceful peak. The hill grasses in the glen were yellow and gold beneath the dark sky, through which a haloed sun for a short time shone palely. Near the foot of Glen Dessary General Wade's track unaccountably disappears for a short distance. One theory is that two parties of soldiers, one from Loch Nevis, the other from Loch Lochy, worked to meet one another, but made an indifferent joining. Perhaps an urgent summons was received by them to proceed elsewhere. This track—it cannot be called a road—of the General's is not one of his best, even making allowances for the hand of time, which is gradually hiding his work. In a number of places the path almost disappears, and it is rough, wet and stony throughout its course.

Ahead of us as we walked, Sgùrr na Cìche rose steeply, gloomy and mist-capped. From its precipitous sides many burns were falling in grey spray. At 1,000 feet above sea level we reached the watershed and Mam na Cloiche Airde. Here three cairns stand beside the track. They mark the bounds of three old territories—Lochiel, Lovat and Glengarry. Of the three Lochiel is the only property remaining in the hands of the old family. It is fitting, therefore, that Lochiel's cairn should be by far the largest and most strongly built of the three. On the pass rather more than a mile west of the watershed are two small lochs, on the shores of which scattered rowan trees grow. On the shore of the second loch a collection of mussel shells lay. It was curious to find them at this height and at this distance from salt water. Perhaps the shellfish were used as bait for trout, but it is more likely that they made a light meal for some wanderer travelling to the east, who had gathered them on the shore of Loch Nevis at low tide and had carried them up to the lochan. We were discussing the origin of the mussel shells, when we saw approaching us a party of travellers. Two pleasant-faced lads were driving before them a stirk and a young bull; a couple of sagacious and friendly collie dogs completed the party. They were crossing from Loch Nevis to Loch Arkaig on their way to Fort William for the sales, and were moving slowly, for the beasts were ill at ease in their unaccustomed surroundings. Few cattle now use the pass, but at one time many drovers must have crossed here. Ruined shealings are still visible beside the track and they were apparently built before General Wade made his path through the hills, for the bridle track deviates in order to pass near them. We conversed with the drovers and, cheered by their highland courtesy, watched them pass slowly out of sight. We had now entered a country of high rocks, gloomy gorges, and mist-covered peaks. The scene was stern and grand. Somewhere above us a stag roared. A pair of golden eagles circled overhead, and were mobbed by a pair of grey crows : the eagles, as is their custom, treated the furious attacks of the hoodies with contempt. We continued on our westward journey perhaps a couple of miles beyond the watershed, then (since the surrounding rocks and knolls still hid the view westward) we climbed a little way up Sgùrr na Cìche, and soon were in sight of the white-capped waves of Loch Nevis far below us. The tide was low, and a long line of golden sea wrack was visible along the shore. On the far western horizon Eigg showed faintly, and the dim outline of Rhum appeared like some distant cloud. A small yacht steered towards the mouth of Loch Nevis. Beside the shore scattered houses could be seen; through the narrows the tide flowed like a river in flood. We had intended to descend to Loch Nevis by the path, continue along the shore of Loch Nevis to Tarbet, and then cross the narrow neck of land to Loch Morar, but a heavy storm was approaching us, and we decided to return to Achnacarry. Far up the hill-side above us a stag with strong broad antlers was wandering restlessly in search of hinds. In a grassy sheltered hollow near us a hind and her calf were lying. Although winter was near, the milkwort, the louse-wort, and a *ranunculus* still held their flowers towards the dark sky and beside wee burns the yellow saxifrage's leaves were dark green and full of vitality.

The air grew heavy; still more sombre became the heavens. A rain-storm hid Eigg and approached the green slopes of Mallaig Bheag. We finished our " spying," turned east, and with the wind at our backs set out for Loch Arkaig, invisible beyond the hills. Soon the rain reached us. It fell upon us in sheets, as only a west highland rain can fall. The hills ran water. Sgùrr na Cìche was the birthplace of innumerable milky torrents. Majestically the rain-filled mists swept across the rocky slopes where the eagles, unperturbed, faced the squalls. Darkness came early to Glen Dessary. In the gathering dusk we splashed our way down the glen and reached Loch Arkaig in the blackness of a moonless night.

CHAPTER XXI

BEN NEVIS

BEN NEVIS, reaching a height of 4,400 feet above sea level, is the highest mountain in the British Isles, being rather more than 100 feet higher than Ben MacDhui, chief of the

Glen Nevis.

Cairngorm range. It stands at the head of Loch Linnhe, in Lochaber.

The derivation of the name Nevis is uncertain. The Gaelic name of the hill is Beinn Nimheis, and popular tradition describes it as the Hill of Heaven. The river Nevis probably named the hill, and Professor Watson is inclined to believe that the name is identical with the Old Irish " neim," and may mean the " venomous one." Glen Nevis and its river had a bad reputation in old days. A sixteenth-century bard writes of Glen Nevis :

> " Glen Nevis, a glen of stones,
> A glen where corn ripens late,
> A long, wild, waste glen,
> With thievish folk of evil habit."

It has also been written of as " a glen on which God has turned His back."

The old people were awed by the darkness and gloom of Glen Nevis, from which the Ben towers mightily to the clouds. The pastime of mountaineering was then unknown, and it must have been rare indeed for any man to have climbed the hill. Then came the time when an observatory was built on the summit of Ben Nevis and for the best part of half a century hourly observations, both by day and night, were made here. The observers had thrilling experiences. The winter hurricanes, sometimes blowing at a speed of over two miles a minute, threatened to sweep them, with the furiously driven snow, over the great precipice that dropped sheer from beside the observatory. The record of one of the observers (*Forty Years on Ben Nevis*, by W. M. Kilgour) is a book which all who love the Scottish hills should read, and it sometimes recalls the Everest expedition on a smaller scale. Northern Lights, St. Elmo's Fire, Glories, Fire-balls, wonderful rainbows spanning the heavens, the blackness of an approaching storm, all these things were watched with appreciation by the small band who lived together in their mountain fastness on the Roof of Scotland.

The observatory, alas, has been abandoned, but it was built so firmly that it should stand for many a day. Its reports in these days of flying would be of considerable value, for it stands in the path of the storms which approach us from the Atlantic.

One summer night that I spent on the summit of Ben Nevis remains as a clear memory. When I reached the plateau the sun had already set in the glens beneath me, but the hill-top was still bathed in its last rays, and the lingering snow-fields were faintly pink in its glow. The low sun passed just above the Cuillin summits in distant Skye, so that their jagged peaks stood out in sharp relief, and finally sank below the horizon beyond the hills of Knoydart. For fully three-quarters of an hour after the sun had set its rays still shot high into the northern sky, and throughout the short night the horizon west and north held the afterglow, while in the east a waning moon struggled to pierce the mist with her silvery rays.

By dawn the face of the landscape had changed. During the brief hours of dusk a pall of white mist, creeping stealthily west from the distant North Sea, had covered all the highlands. From this vast sea of mist the tops of the highest hills rose clearly. Never, either before or since, have I seen so unusual and wonderful a sight. Before the sun rose upon it the mist was grey and cold. Very gently the sun warmed that ocean of mist, so that a rose-coloured glow suffused it. On this glowing aerial sea the shadow of the Ben was thrown for many miles towards the south-west. On the hill-top scarcely a breath of wind stirred, but several thousand feet below me the cloud moved westward, and during its slow journey towards the Atlantic assumed in places the form of gigantic billows which rose above the average level of the mist sea as they flowed over some insignificant hill that barred their way. Even at ten o'clock the vast cloud canopy was still unbroken, and now reflected the rays of the sun with brilliance. High above the mist to the east the Cairngorm Hills were visible; Cairn Toul (4,241 feet) being especially prominent across fifty miles of the Scottish highlands. To the southward of it LochnaGar, on the King's Forest of Balmoral, climbed above the cloud. Of all the peaks rising from the mist sea, Schiehallion, " fairy Hill of the Caledonians," was the most striking, its tapering cone rising grandly to the blue of the sky. West, the two peaks of Cruachan just topped the cloud, but here the level of the mist was higher, and hid all but the summits of the highest hills. Sgùrr a' Mhaim, across Glen Nevis, raised its crater-shaped corrie to the bright sunshine, and through my glass I saw two stags reach its ridge, and look down into the white ocean of cloud beneath them.

There are few flowering plants on the plateau of Ben Nevis, for the season of growth here is a very short one, but a small colony of plants of the starry saxifrage (*saxifraga stellaris*) flower here at an elevation of 4,300 feet above the sea. This is, I believe, the highest point at which any flowering plants are found in Britain, for it is slightly higher than the summit of Ben MacDhui, where the cushion pink (*silene acaulis*) is found.

I have stood on the summit of Ben Nevis on fine clear days, yet I have still to look forward to seeing the hills of the northern coast of Ireland. The distance is so great that it is only very occasionally that these distant hills are visible. The observatory staff have placed it on record that they CAN be seen on days of extreme visibility.

The climb I have described was in the middle of July—at the height of summer. Another day on which I climbed the Ben was in May. Summer that year came early to Lochaber. The birches, swaying their young green leaves in the soft breeze, were happy in the warmth of the sun. Fields of wild hyacinths scented the air. Only on the brow of Ben Nevis did winter linger. Down in Glen Nevis the river flowed low and clear. Glen Nevis is on the eastern border of Fort William. The climber takes the road up the east side of the glen, and at a farmhouse finds the beginning of the path to the hill-top. The ascent is easy and daring spirits have even driven motor-cars and motor bicycles to the summit of the Ben, but this is not to be recommended. The ordinary mortal will be thankful if he reaches by his own unaided power the highest land in the British Isles.

As I climbed, this May day, Ben Nevis seemed to tower to the blue sky, and the strong sun gleamed on its great snow-fields. The bleating of lambs was heard. Beside the springs of clear water the green leafy rosettes of the starry saxifrage took the place of the pink flowers of the lousewort which had been seen at lower levels. On the path a ptarmigan's feather lay, but no voice of bird was heard that day upon the Ben which rose, grim and mighty, from a flower-strewn base.

From the half-way hut the view was already remarkable. Delicately pencilled on the north-west horizon rose Rhum. In the middle foreground was Loch Eil, its waters pale blue and calm. A herring drifter steamed out from the Caledonian Canal, and steered away for the open sea and the summer herring fishing in the Isles. I continued to climb, and at the 3,500 feet level entered the country of the snows. At first the snow lay in small fields, but before I had arrived at a height of 4,000 feet I was walking across an unbroken expanse of glistening white. Ben Nevis, like most hills, is deceptive. The summit appears close at hand and the climber is cheered. But now, as he thinks to stand on the summit, yet another snowy slope rises ahead of him, and this too must be surmounted, painfully and slowly, if the snow be soft. Many insects rested on the snow-cap. The warm wind had carried them up from the lower slopes and they had alighted on an inhospitable waste. Across the snow they crept. After sunset they would have neither the power to rise nor the knowledge where to fly to escape the frost, and few would survive the night. Across the abyss of Glen Nevis Sgùrr a' Mhaim rose. Its eastern crater-shaped corrie where I had seen the two stags on a midsummer day years before was now filled with unbroken snow. Bidean nam Beann, highest of Argyllshire hills, rose from dark Glen Coe, and near it was Beinn Bhéir.

Great clouds, inky-black and menacing, approached the plateau of Ben Nevis. They hid the sun: they curled and eddied, with primrose edges and awe-inspiring centres. A twilight fell on the Ben. From white, the snows changed to pale grey and themselves appeared intangible and cloud-like.

Across this Arctic waste rose a line of stone cairns that used to guide the observers to the summit in mist and snow, in the days when the observatory was occupied. At last I was close to the hill-top. Along the precipice a great cornice of snow extended into space. It was impossible to know whether I was standing above firm ground or was suspended by the frozen snow over an abyss of 2,000 feet. No Arctic tundra could have been more lonely. There must have been an average depth of twelve feet of snow on the hill-top. Yet in the glen beneath me the birches were in leaf, and violets and wild hyacinths were growing among the uncurling bracken fronds.

From the unbroken snowy surface the flat roof of the abandoned observatory and its chimney projected a few inches. The roof might have been a large flat rock. It was sun-warmed and pleasant to sit upon. Here I rested, looking over a wide country of hill, glen and sea, smiling and sun-lit.

West and north rose hill upon hill. Beyond Lismore, low and green, was the Isle of Mull. Its highest hill, Beinn Mhór, was the only peak, north, south, east and west, on which a cloud rested. Beyond the cliffs of Gribun in Mull I fancied I could make out Iona. Far beyond Ben Resipol of Ardnamurchan rose the isles of Coll and Tiree on the hazy Atlantic. A hundred miles distant from where I sat were the hills of South Uist in the Outer Hebrides. Hecla, Corodale, the long ridge of Beinn Mhór —all were distinct. Bearing north, the Cuillin hills formed the horizon. So clear was the air in this direction that each sharp top could be distinguished. Upon Sgùrr nan Gillean a snow-field shone. The glass showed the Inaccessible Pinnacle of Sgùrr Dearg rising black against the sky. Even the great cairn on the summit of Beinn na Cailliche was visible. A sea of primrose mist, drifting before a northerly wind, swirled about the slopes of Glamaig. To the south the view was not so clear. Schiehallion was seen, but was less imposing than she had been on that early morning when I had watched the sun shine upon the aerial sea. To the east the Cairngorms were in strong sunshine.

Cairn Toul I recognised, and Brae Riach with its snow-filled corrie, and, across the depths of Lairig Ghru, the shoulder and summit of Ben MacDhui. It is a far cry from Iona, Coll and the Outer Hebrides to Schiehallion and the Cairngorms— from Jura (seen on the horizon southward) to the Cuillin of Skye and the hills of Ross-shire.

The ascent of Ben Nevis had been arduous. The descent was swift and easy. Down 2,000 feet of the hill I was able to follow a snow-filled gulley. The gradient was so steep that it would have been scarcely possible to have descended here under ordinary conditions, and at times I seemed in danger of disappearing over a snowy precipice. The snow, however, was soft and gave excellent footing. I heard beneath my feet the rush of a hill torrent, flowing unseen through a snow tunnel. The snow was blinding in the intensity of its light. I glissaded quickly down this almost vertical snow slope, and as I moved had the curious illusion of being suspended in space. Near the half-way hut I came upon the path and here, looking back, I saw great thunder-clouds gathering above the Ben, but the lower slopes of the hill were in brilliant sunshine.

That night, from the birches of Loch Eil, I looked back on to Ben Nevis. Above the lesser hills it towered, massive and imposing. In the evening light the great cornice fringing its summit was lemon-tinted. The lower slopes, snowless and in shadow, were of a deep blue. A thunder-cloud lay beyond the summit of glowing snow. Thus Ben Nevis appeared at the coming of summer. In June the snows on its crown gradually lessen, and disappear in July, but there is one snow-field in the north-east corrie which has never been known to melt, and they say in Lochaber that if snow should disappear from the Ben, the hill would revert to the Crown.

L

Inverlochy Castle.

CHAPTER XXII

FORT WILLIAM WEST TO THE LAND OF MORAR

FROM Fort William west to Loch Ailort and Morar is as beautiful a country as can be found in all Scotland—a land of history and romance. Inverlochy, Fassiefern, Achdalieu and Glen Finnan—these are magic names that will continue to cast their spell. The waters of the Lochy, flowing grandly from dark Loch Lochy, enter Loch Linnhe beside Fort William. On the bank of the river near the estuary are the ruins of Inverlochy Castle. The history of this castle goes back to very remote times. In the eighth century a treaty was signed here between Achaius, who succeeded to the throne of Dalriada in 787, and Charlemagne, King of France. In the early part of the fifteenth century the first battle of Inverlochy was fought when young Donald Balloch of the Isles attacked a greatly superior force of King James I of Scotland under Huntly. The islesmen " wielded their broadswords and Lochaber axes with such ferocity that at least one thousand of the Royal army were slain, among whom were the Earl of Caithness, together with many knights and barons." But Inverlochy Castle is more renowned to-day for the second battle of Inverlochy, fought in

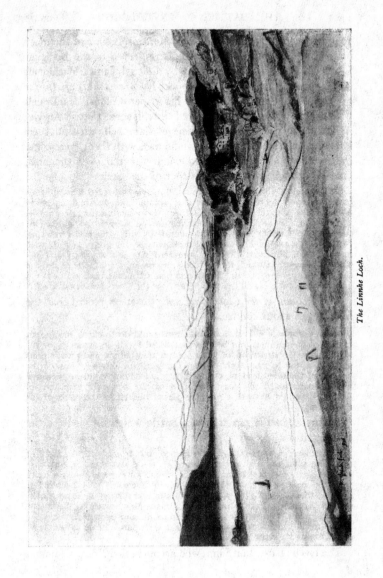

The Linnhe Loch.

1645 between Argyll and the Great Montrose. One of the most interesting accounts of this battle is preserved in the Bodleian Library. It is a paper written by Colonel James MacDonell and is quoted in a little-known work, *The MacDonells of Antrim* by the Rev. George Hill. In his paper Colonel MacDonell writes that when they received intelligence that " Argyle, Achenbracke and the whole name of Campbell, with all their forces and a great number of lowland men with them, were come to Inverloughy," they made a counter-march over the hills, arriving at night within musket-shot of the castle.

" That night," the account continues, " Argyle embarked himself in his barge, and there lay till the next morning, sending his orders of discipline to Achenbracke and the rest of the officers there commanding the battle, which on all sides being pitched, and their cannon planted, the fight began ; the enemy giving fire on us on both sides, both with cannon and muskets, to their little avail. For only two regiments of our army, playing with musket shot, advanced till they recovered Argyle's standard and the standard-bearer, at which their whole army broke. . . . Little or none of the whole army escaped us, the officers being the first that were cut off. There Achenbracke was killed with 16 or 17 of the chief lords of Campbell."

The *Account of the Clan MacLean* puts it on record that the fight began about sunrise.

" The Campbells did all that brave men could do to check the furious assault of the royalists, but being disheartened by the impetuosity of the attack and the desertion of their leader, they threw away their arms and attempted to gain their boats. Campbell of Skipness, one of the bravest of the rebel leaders, on being brought before Montrose, declared had he entertained the least suspicion of the cowardly character of Argyle, he would have that morning placed himself in the ranks of the royal army."

Montrose, in the report of the battle which he made to the King, writes :

" Our men did wonders, and came immediately to push of pike and dint of sword, after the first firing. The rebels could not stand it, but after some resistance at first began to run; whome we pursued for nine miles together, making a great slaughter, which I would have hindered if possible that I might save your Majesty's misled subjects. Some gentlemen of the Lowlands that had behaved themselves bravely in the battle, when they saw it all lost, fled into the old castle, and upon their surrender I have treated them honourably, and taken their parole never to bear arms against your Majesty."

The Gaelic bard, Iain Lom, who accompanied Montrose on his

campaign, composed stirring verses on the Battle of Inverlochy, and as a tribute to his services in heartening Montrose's army he received the appointment of Poet-Laureate to the King.

A short distance west of Inverlochy is Corpach. In the days when Iona was the Sacred Isle, the Great Glen from Inverness to the west saw many funeral processions of the mighty pass through it. At Corpach (the Place of Bodies) galleys were waiting to convey the illustrious dead westward down Loch Linnhe to the distant island of Columba. Few people know that in the word Corpach there is a memorial to those old kings

Loch Linnhe and Hills at Spean.

and chiefs whose names are now forgotten. From Corpach the road to the west winds beside the shore of Loch Eil, through woods of birch and oak. Many fine old birches grow here. In winter their branches are sometimes weighed down by snow: each tree is then delicately traced in white. But spring comes early here and the birches of Loch Eil are a mist of green while winter lingers in the high glens to the east. On the shore of Loch Eil is Achdalieu, memorable because of the historic encounter between Sir Ewen Cameron of Lochiel and an English officer. The story is as follows. In the year 1654 three hundred men from the Fort William garrison landed from their boats near Achdalieu and proceeded to cut

down Sir Ewen's trees.   It was only natural that Lochiel and
some of his clansmen (who had been watching these proceedings)
should have attacked the invaders of his territory.   The Fort
William garrison gave way slowly, and Sir Ewen and the officer
commanding the party engaged in mortal combat.   After a hard
struggle Lochiel disarmed his adversary, but the English officer
then leaped upon him, and as he was a much more powerfully
built man seemed likely to get the better of the highland chief.

" They tumbled up and down till they fixt in the channell of a brooke,
betwixt two straite banks, which then, by the drouth of summer, chanced
to be dry.   Here Lochiel was in a most dismall and desperate scituation,
for being undermost he was not only crushed under the weight of his
antagonist, who was an exceeding heavy man, but likewise sore hurt and
bruised by many sharp stones that were below him.   Their strength was
so far spent that neither of them could stirr a limb, but the English gentleman, by the advantage of being uppermost, at last recovered the use of his
right hand.   With it he seized a dagger that hung at his belt and made
several attempts to stab his adversary, who all the time held him fast.
He (the Englishman) made a most violent effort to disengage himself, and
in that action raising his head and stretching his neck, Lochiel, who by this
had his hands at liberty, with his left suddenly seized him by the right, and
with the other by the collar, and jumping at his extended throat, which he
used to say ' God putt in his mouth,' he bitt it quitt throw and keept such
a hold of his grip that he brought away his mouthfull !   This, he said, was
the sweetest bite ever he had in his lifetime."

The burn where this epic fight was fought is still pointed out
beside the shooting lodge at Achdalieu.   In an old Cameron
record it is said that the clansmen had been told that the English
garrison of Fort William were of simian form, and being simple folk
believed the tale.   After the fight, therefore, they turned over a
number of the slain, and were not a little disappointed to find that
they had no tails, but were of like appearance to themselves.

On the shore of Loch Eil is the old house of Fassiefern,
sheltered by surrounding trees.   At the time of the '45 Fassiefern (in Gaelic am Fasadh Fearna, the Alderwood Station) was
the home of Lochiel's brother John.   On his way to meet the
Prince at Borrodale Lochiel called at Fassiefern to see his
brother, and said he was resolved to tell the Prince that as
he had arrived in Scotland with neither money, nor troops, nor

Falls of Morar.

arms, it would be folly for him (Lochiel) to be concerned in the affair.　John approved his brother's sentiments, but advised him to go no farther on his way to Borrodale, suggesting that he should rather send a letter to the Prince.　For, he said, " Brother, I know you better than you know yourself, and if this Prince sets his eyes on you he will make you do whatever he pleases."　He was right.　Lochiel, after speaking with Prince Charles Edward, felt that as a loyal and honourable man he could not stand aside, and a few days later placed himself and his clan at the disposal of the Prince.　One would give much to know the thoughts of Lochiel's brother when Prince Charles Edward, four days after the raising of the standard at Glen Finnan, passed a night at his house and while there heard of the march of Sir John Cope from Stirling.　The bed on which the Prince slept at Fassiefern is now at Callart, where also I was shown his waistcoat, beautifully embroidered.

From the head of Loch Eil the road continues west to Loch Shiel and historic Glen Finnan.　When Prince Charles Edward, sailing up Loch Shiel from the west that August day of 1745, landed below Glen Finnan and found no welcoming clans to meet him his spirits fell.　But after a two hours' wait he was cheered by the distant music of the bagpipe, and saw approaching him Lochiel and his clan—a fine body of men to the number of between seven and eight hundred.　So delighted was the Prince at the appearance of Lochiel's men that he resolved to raise his standard without waiting for the other clans who were expected to join him.　There were present at this ceremony (besides the Camerons) the laird of Morar with one hundred and fifty men. The standard was unfurled by Tullibardine, who " took his station on a small knoll in the centre of the vale where, supported by two men, he displayed the banner and proclaimed the Chevalier de St. George as king.　The flag used was of silk, of a white, blue and red texture, but without any motto."

The birches were green and the heather was purple that August day when a great adventure was begun.　In the misty air of the loch is still the echo of pipes, and now a memorial stands to those who laid down their lives for a cause which they championed reluctantly, but with a high sense of highland chivalry, for one who had come among them to place his life and fortune in their hands. The standard was raised only a few hundred yards from the county march between Argyll and Inverness. West of Glen Finnan and Loch Shiel is Inverness-

Prince Charlie's Monument, Loch Shiel.

shire; south are the rugged lands of Argyll. The road to the west climbs beside the small Amhuinn Schlatach to a height of 400 feet above the sea, then drops to Loch Eilt (the Hinds' Loch) through a pleasant glen known as the Muidhe. Here the birches are early in leafing and in April primroses and violets cover the mossy ground beneath the trees. No breath of cold north wind reaches the Muidhe, and the warm spring sun shines full upon its sheltered slopes. Below the road lies the blackened trunk of a great oak tree beneath which Prince Charles Edward is said to have hidden or sheltered during his wanderings after Culloden. Loch Eilt is a fresh-water loch of great beauty, with islands where Scots firs grow, and shelving bays where sea-trout of great size are caught. I doubt whether there is any other loch on the mainland of Scotland where the sea-trout are so heavy. Beyond Loch Eilt the Atlantic is reached at Loch Ailort.

When the rain-laden wind from the south sweeps across the Rough Bounds [1] the country of Loch Eilt and Loch Ailort is one of sublime grandeur. Down each steep hill-side milky torrents rush. Madly they leap, and their spray mingles with the soft Atlantic rain. Loch Eilt, receiving to herself many burns, rises fast and sends her river roaring in flood to Loch Ailort, whence great sea-trout press up the swollen waters to the loch beyond. But at midsummer the hills are dry and Loch Eilt day after day reflects the burning rays of the sun. Yet, whether the sky be rain-filled or smiling blue, this western land retains its charm and tells of the romance and chivalry of past times, of

> " Old unhappy far-off things
> And battles long ago."

North-west of Loch Ailort are the broad waters of Loch nan Uamh, sometimes written Lochnanuagh. The loch is historical because it was on its shore that Prince Charles Edward first set foot on the Scottish mainland, and when all was lost after Culloden he succeeded, after hair's-breadth escapes, in boarding a French frigate on the same loch at which he had arrived with high hopes and courage the preceding year. There are many caves in the highlands where the Prince is said to have hidden, and one of them is on Loch nan Uamh (the Loch of the Caves) on the shore near where Arisaig House now stands. Beyond Loch nan Uamh is the beautiful country of Arisaig, where in the burial-ground are sculptured stones of great antiquity. From Arisaig the road skirts the coast, and passes the White

[1] The Rough Bounds is an old name given to the mountainous western fringe of the Scottish mainland lying between Morar and Loch Hourn.

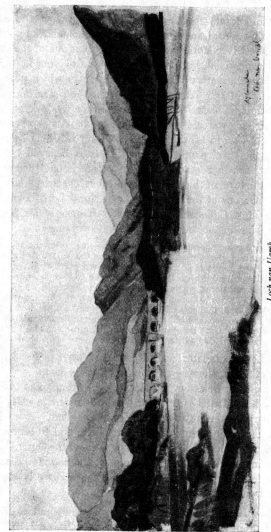

Loch nan Uamh.

Sands of Morar where weeping birches grow at the edge of sands that gleam snow-white in sun and shade. Across these sands the River Morar enters the sea. It is one of the shortest rivers in Scotland, but it flows swift and full from Loch Morar, and its waters are of that pale green tinge which pure water shows. Professor Watson in his work, the *Celtic Place-Names of Scotland*, explains that the name Morar was originally Mordhobhar, big-water, and he remarks that it is " probably the biggest *dobhar* in Scotland." Loch Morar is a long fresh-water loch, some twelve miles in length. It is believed to be the deepest loch in Scotland, and its bottom is one thousand feet below the level of the Atlantic, which lies less than a mile to the west. On one of the islands of Loch Morar Lord Lovat was in hiding after Culloden. In Browne's *History of the Highlands* is the following account of Lord Lovat's capture :

" After having the mortification of witnessing, from the summit of a high mountain, the conflagration of his seat of Castle Downie by the king's troops, Lord Lovat took refuge in the western parts of Inverness-shire, and finally concealed himself in the hollow of a tree which grew on a small island in Loch Morar, where he was apprehended early in June by a party from the ' Furnace ' sloop of war. When discovered he was wrapt up in a blanket ; and, though he had between five and six hundred guineas in his pocket, had been obliged to live twelve days in his miserable retreat on oatmeal and water. Being unable, from his great age and infirmity, to ride, he was carried in a litter to the royal camp at Fort Augustus." [1]

Lord Lovat was later beheaded at the Tower of London in his eightieth year, showing great bravery at the last.

Some three miles beyond Morar is the fishing port of Mallaig, where heavy catches of white fish are landed in early spring, and herrings during the remainder of the year. From Mallaig there is a daily steamer service to Skye, and to Stornoway in Lewis, and on certain days to other ports of the Outer Hebrides, while in summer a motor ferry crosses the Sound of Sleat twice daily from Mallaig to Armadale in Skye. There is also a car ferry from Mallaig to Armadale in summer.

[1] Another and perhaps more reliable account mentions that Lord Lovat escaped from the island to Meoble, where he subsequently surrendered to the King's forces.

CHAPTER XXIII

ROIS-BHEINN : A PEAK OF MOIDART

FROM the sheltered waters of Loch Ailort in the Rough Bounds rises a fine hill, Rois-bheinn by name. The height of this hill is approximately three thousand feet, and because of its situation it gives an unusual view.

It is one of the virtues of the mild western seaboard that there is often warm sunshine here when the rest of Scotland shivers beneath swirling snow showers and bitter winds, and when I reached the hospitable inn at Loch Ailort after a cold journey from the snow-swept uplands of Inverness-shire I found there brilliant April weather. After sunset the stars shone clear in the cloudless sky and at sunrise next morning the ground was frost bound, but the April sun has power, and an hour after sunrise the air was already warm. The hills were brilliant, and Loch Ailort sparkled like the enchanted loch which Bran of old visited on his voyage west to Tir nan Og. Primroses flowered upon south-facing mossy banks, and amongst them were violets of deep blue. The birches unrolled their first delicate green leaves ; the first green feathery needles of the larches swayed in the breeze : the Spirit of Spring showed her radiant form, breathing lightly and mystically upon the sun-lit west. To-day the waters of Loch Ailort were so still that it was impossible to tell where the loch ended and the land beyond it began : the birds swimming on the loch formed each a ripple which broadened and spread far across the placid surface.

As I climbed I saw the islands of the west one by one appear. First to show was the Scùir of Eigg, then Rhum, with clouds resting lightly on its hills was seen, but for long the high ground of South Morar hid the Cuillin of Skye. South Morar was in shadow, and because of this deep shade the first view of the Cuillin was startling in its beauty. It was heralded by a brightening of the distant horizon northward. When I had climbed a few steps after seeing this brightening of the edge of the sky there appeared, mysterious across land and sea, the snows on Sgùrr na Banachdich, forming a glowing zone on the horizon, where soft pale clouds rested. Sgùrr na Banachdich alone was in sunshine, but the whole range of the Cuillin were clear—a mighty band with splintered ridges that rose in a great amphitheatre from the blue floor of the Atlantic. He who has seen the Cuillin from afar has no doubt in his inmost heart of the existence of Tir nan Og, the Celtic Isle of the Blest.

Every moment the scene westward was changing. A light westerly breeze from the Atlantic drifted in through the mouth of Loch Ailort; from a great moorland fire on Rhum pale creamy smoke rose to merge with the mist that floated around the highest hill of that mountainous island. Upon the Atlantic were luminous pools, reflecting the clouds. Then came the Black Wind from the north. From the country of Loch Nevis a gloomy cloud drifted south. Beneath its shade the hill lochs of Ardnish changed colour. No longer were they of that glorious blue of the earlier hours : their depths now were amethystine and the lochs shone like jewels in a dark setting. From Rois-bheinn, too, the sun vanished. Ice held the pools and tarns; ice bound the cushions of sphagnum moss; the snowdrifts of winter were hard as a high-road to walk upon. Across the hill a pair of ptarmigan flew, the male bird as he alighted uttering his snorting croak. From the hill-top a golden eagle rose and soared idly in wide spirals. In the corrie below me unseen ravens were croaking. Beside Samalaman at the mouth of Loch Ailort the Atlantic swell from time to time gleamed as it broke upon that rocky coast. On the edge of ocean rose the far-off hills of Barra.

The north wind bore down upon the western country, sweeping

dark lines on the surface of the Atlantic. As yet it had not reached beyond the mouth of Loch Ailort, but on the distant Sound of Sleat were crested waves that gleamed momentarily like a sea-gull's plumage when the bird leans toward the sun. Across Sleat itself shadows of clouds borne on the north wind passed swiftly. Upon distant Loch Slapin, too, were white waves.

A few minutes before I reached the hill-top the north wind arrived at Rois-bheinn. At once the air became bitterly cold. Hurrying clouds on the frost-laden wind obscured the sun. There was scanty shelter behind the cairn. On the hill-top large cushions of moss campion and sea thrift were growing.

It was only when the summit of Rois-bheinn had been reached that the view south could be seen. On Beinn Mhór Mull passing clouds rested, and on the snowy corrie of the hill was the greyness which shadow gives to distant snow. Distinctly the great cliffs of Ardmeanach beyond Gribun showed. South-east of Mull was Scarba. Farther to the east rose Cruachan Beann, imposing in unbroken snow. Nearer at hand, winding sinuously inland, were the great lochs of Sunart and Shiel, the one a fjord of ocean, the other a deep fresh-water loch. Looking down upon Loch Moidart I could see Castle Tioram, the ancestral home of the ClanRanalds. Beyond Ben Shiant of Ardnamurchan were the fertile islands of Coll and Tiree, hazy on the plain of the Atlantic.

Dark showers were now forming. To the west of Eigg a spiral of snow hung suspended between sky and ocean. Beyond Soay and the lofty rocks of Tallisker the hills of North Uist were faint on the horizon. Far to the north-east the hills of Applecross showed.

The north wind had now reached all the Atlantic that was within my view, yet Loch Ailort remained calm. At one place a green cloud appeared to be mistily mirrored in the loch : a strip of white sand lying fathoms deep gave this curious illusion. The flood tide crept into the loch. It came in the form of an arrow-head, unhurried yet with mighty power, showing a white wake where it moved noiselessly through sleeping waters. Moidart and Arisaig, Mull, Rhum and Skye, the long thin blue line of the Outer Hebrides far to the west—all these formed a picture of extreme beauty. I left the wind-swept hill-top and within an hour was basking in warm sun beside the tide, where was the scent of the sun-warmed needles of the old pines, the fragrant leaves of the larch, and the opening flowers of the daffodils, and on my long walk up to the head of Loch Ailort at dusk I was guided by a luminous window, low in the quiet sky towards the north.

CHAPTER XXIV

THE LAND OF MOIDART

WHERE the Atlantic, sweeping in past Ardnamurchan, bathes the rugged western shores of Inverness-shire, is to be found a country of beauty that is strong in reminiscences of Prince Charles Edward. No modern soul-destroying roads have as yet been driven through this country: it is as unspoilt as on that day nearly two hundred years ago when the Prince sailed its waters, or wearily climbed its steep hill passes. In this western land, where hill, sea and fertile glen meet in splendour, Loch Moidart winds eastward between wooded hills. It is a narrow loch, unusually sheltered for an arm of the Atlantic, and on its shores stand Castle Tioram [1] and Kinlochmoidart House.

The MacDonalds of Kinlochmoidart were a brave and chivalrous race, and did not hesitate to aid the Prince at his summons. Prince Charles Edward crossed from Loch Ailort of Kinlochmoidart (it is uncertain whether he travelled by sea or crossed the *bealach* from Glen Uig), and when at Kinlochmoidart addressed a letter to one " Mr. Peter Smith," asking for his support. In this historic letter, which was dated from " Kinloch, August ye 14th, 1745," the Prince writes that he proposes to set up the King's Standard at Glen Finnan on August 18th. When he wrote that letter the Prince was the guest of Donald MacDonald of Kinlochmoidart, a man " exceedingly cool-headed, fit for either the Cabinet or the field." During the victorious southward march of the Prince's army a Captain MacDonald (who is claimed by the Kinlochmoidart family to have been their ancestor, but whom some authorities consider

[1] Described in Chapter XXV.

Moidart from Eigg.

was MacDonald of Tirnadrish), figures in a pleasing incident. *Blackwood's Magazine* in 1817 published an account of the occurrence, written by Lady Clerk of Penicuik, who as a baby was the heroine of the episode.

"This incident" (she writes) "occurred November 15, 1745. My father, Mr. Dacre, then an officer in His Majesty's Militia, was a prisoner in the Castle of Carlisle, at that time in the hands of Prince Charles. My mother (daughter of Sir George le Fleming, Bart., Bishop of Carlisle) was living at Rose Castle, six miles from Carlisle, where she was delivered of me. She had given orders that I should immediately be privately baptised by the Bishop's chaplain (his Lordship not being at home) by the name of Rosemary Dacre. At that moment a company of Highlanders appeared, headed by a Captain MacDonald, who, having heard there was much plate and valuables in the castle, came to plunder it. Upon the approach of the Highlanders an old grey-headed servant ran out and entreated Captain MacDonald not to proceed, as any noise of alarm might occasion the death of both lady and child. The Captain inquired when the lady had been confined. 'Within this hour,' the servant answered. Captain MacDonald stopped. The servant added, 'They are just going to christen the infant.' MacDonald, taking off his cockade said, 'Let her be christened with this cockade in her cap : it will be her protection now, and after if any of our stragglers should come this way : we will await the ceremony in silence.' Which they accordingly did, and then went into the coachyard, where they were regaled with beef, cheese, ale, etc. They then went off without the smallest disturbance. My white cockade was safely preserved, and shown to me from time to time, always reminding me to respect the Scotch, and the Highlanders in particular. I think I have obeyed the injunction by spending my life in Scotland, and also by hoping at last to die there. (Signed) ROSEMARY CLERK."

It is stated that the writer of this letter showed her Jacobite relic to George IV when he visited Scotland in 1822.

MacDonald of Kinlochmoidart was captured while on a secret mission. He was beheaded, and his head was impaled on one of the city gates of Carlisle, where it remained for years. After his death the estate was for forty-one years in Government hands, and was administered by Butter of Faskally. Kinlochmoidart's two sons were educated at the Scots College in Paris. Alexander, the elder, served afterwards in a Highland regiment and towards the end of his military career commanded the 71st Highlanders. The second son served in the French army. The Government, curiously enough, did not restore the estate to Alexander despite his distinguished career, and it was said that when he was old and frail, and suffering from his wounds, his spirit often wandered away to Kinlochmoidart. His three fondest wishes were :

> " A couch from the heather of Torloisg,
> A drink from the Sorrell well.
> And half an hour with Father Uisdean."

To-day a grass-grown wall shows where the old house of Kinloch stood. The present Kinlochmoidart House is built near it, and in the garden are four great yew trees beneath which Kinlochmoidart's bedridden mother was laid when the house was burned by Government troops after Culloden. It is believed that the troops camped beneath these trees, which are said to be more than a thousand years old.

From Loch Ailort, where the Prince's vessel " Le Doutellier " lay at anchor in the shelter of Eilean nan Gobhar, a rough hill track crosses the *bealach* from Irine to Kinlochmoidart. One climbs near old ruins of summer shealings where in September the yellow saxifrage has still golden flowers, and after crossing the watershed at Loch nam Paitean looks down on the waters of Loch Shiel and Loch Sunart, golden in sunshine, while on the far horizon Beinn Shianta and the hills of Mull call down the ocean clouds. Kinlochmoidart House is seen in a deep glen a thousand feet below the watershed. The old yews rise against the golden fields of ripening oats and beyond the house are seen the historic beeches known as the Seven Men of Moidart, planted to commemorate the seven leading followers of the Prince on his arrival in Scotland. One of the seven trees was uprooted by a winter gale, and its place in the line is now taken by a younger tree. The descent from the hill pass to the glen is steep, and soon after breathing the invigorating air of the heights one finds oneself on the Prince's Walk, almost at sea level, beneath spreading trees, and looking into the clear waters of the Prince's Well.

Kinloch, as its name implies, stands at the head of Loch Moidart. As one walks seaward beside the loch one passes a high rock, beneath which great boulders lie. This is the Plate Rock, and there is a tradition that MacDonald of Kinlochmoidart hid the family plate here before he left with the Prince on that desperate enterprise which still grips the imagination of the world. From this rock there is a fine view across Loch Moidart to Castle Tioram and the wooded slopes of Eilean Shona. On Shona Beag (as the eastern part of the isle is named) I have the memory of meeting a delightful personality—the last representative of the MacDonalds of Kinlochmoidart. I crossed to the isle at ebb tide, towards sunset. The air was still. The loch lay mirror-like. Across the narrow channel, dry but muddy, I walked slowly, at each step sinking into the glue-like mud where white cockles lay. In mid-channel I happened to look towards the west. There I beheld, through a narrow opening between the hills, the Scùir of Eigg, rising remote and nebulous. It appeared like some phantom precipice, ethereal and mystical, bathed in the golden light of the sinking sun. I walked a few paces forward. The vision had gone. I could no longer see beyond the smiling wooded slopes which surrounded me.

Shona Beag is an isle with an old-world atmosphere and an air of peace. In a sheltered house, with Raeburns and cherished relics of the Prince on its walls, I was shown the remains of a bagpipe of considerable interest. The chanter, the mouthpiece, and the top of one of the drones are preserved. They were given to Donald MacDonald of Kinlochmoidart (direct ancestor of him who showed them to me) by the last representatives of the MacIntyres, before they emigrated to America. The MacIntyres were the hereditary pipers to the MacDonalds of ClanRanald. One of the last pupils of which there is a record at the MacCrimmon college of piping at Borreraig on Loch Dunvegan in Skye was a MacIntyre. For some time before they left for America in 1790 the MacIntyres lived at Uldary, at the head of the River Moidart, and since they did not wish to take the old pipe with them, and looked upon Donald

MacDonald as their chief, they gave him their old *píob mhór*, or great pipe, and told him the lore that was bound up with it. They said that the MacDonalds had followed its inspiring strains into the Battle of Bannockburn, and from that day the pipe had ensured victory in any battle where it was played. The old *feadan* or chanter has one extra hole in it, below the last hole for the scale. This is the fairy hole and was made at the advice of a friendly elf, who said that with it the chanter would play music the like of which had never been heard before; it would inspire those who marched to it, and would strike fear into the hearts of the enemy. The scale holes of the chanter are well-worn. It doubtless has played, at the touch of master fingers, that fine old *piobaireachd* "My King has Landed in Moidart," and has awakened the echoes of Loch Moidart to the strains of "ClanRanald's Gathering." The mouthpiece is four-sided and not rounded as in the bagpipes of recent times: it is also remarkably light. The drone-top, and also the chanter and the blow-pipe, give the impression of great age.

It was with regret that I left the fairy-like island of Shona Beag. As dusk was falling I was rowed across the narrows, through which the flood tide was flowing in a swift broad stream where young saithe disported themselves. I had yet a long road before me, for I had to cross the hill to Glen Uig, and thence along the shore of Loch Ailort. I saw on my walk that evening many cairns built beside the path. Some were of great age; a few were almost new. They marked the resting-places of those who were carrying the mortal remains of their loved ones from the shore of Loch Ailort to the sacred Eilean Fhìonain on Loch Shiel. To mark where the coffin rested, each man of the party placed a stone to form a cairn, and these cairns now stand, strong and abiding, while the memory of those who rested here has long since gone. The path climbs heathery slopes, and looks down upon the clachan of Glen Uig and the waters of Loch Ailort.

Dusk had fallen as I passed through Glen Uig. Blue peat smoke rose slowly from the houses. From the west came the flashes from the small lighthouse on Eigg : the hills of Rhum were faint. Out on Loch Ailort rose Eilean nan Gobhar, the Isle of Goats. The story is told that one day when a French and a British frigate were hotly engaging one another, and while all the world was standing on the shores of the loch watching the stirring sight, an old man was seen to kneel beside the sea. With tears streaming down his furrowed cheeks, the ancient's lips moved in silent prayer. After a time someone asked him whether his prayers were for those on board the French vessel (an ally of Prince Charlie) or the crew of the Britisher. The old fellow, surprised at the ignorance of his interrogator, made answer thus : " My thoughts were not of either vessel. It was my goats on Eilean nan Gobhar I was thinking of, for I see that the island is now in the line of fire."

CHAPTER XXV

IN CLANRANALD COUNTRY : LOCH SHIEL AND CASTLE TIORAM

In the last chapter I made passing reference to Loch Shiel and Castle Tioram. The following is an account of a journey I made from Glen Finnan westward by water to the far end of Loch Shiel, and thence by road to Castle Tioram, which stands beside the Atlantic tides of Loch Moidart.

When, in the fourteenth century, John of Islay divorced his wife, the lady set about building Castle Tioram. This event, according to tradition, marked the beginning of the rule of the ClanRanalds in Moidart and far beyond its confines. The castle of this proud highland family is in a mountainous district of the west highlands—a land of mist-shrouded corrie and wind-tossed waterfall, known to old writers as a part of the Garbh Chriochan or Rough Bounds, which extend from Loch Sunart in Ardnamurchan to Loch Hourn. From the sea (and it must always be remembered that in early times the ocean was the highway in the western highlands) Castle Tioram is easily approached, but eastward it is beset with hills, and a land journey to it cannot have been easy. Doubtless the Captains of ClanRanald had a galley upon Loch Shiel, and sailed down Loch Shiel on their return from forays to the east.

Loch Shiel, a fresh-water loch, is some fourteen miles in length, and a small steamer each day sails up from Glen Finnan to Acharacle at the head of the loch, and leaves again the following morning. On the loch is an island named Eilean Fhionain, or St. Finan's Isle. It has been a place sacred alike to Protestants and Catholics for many generations, and was the burying-place of the ClanRanalds until the close of the sixteenth

century.   Saint Finan, who had his cell upon the isle in the
seventh century, was a contemporary of Columba, and is believed
to have been given charge of Swords by Columb of the Cell.[1]
He is styled *Labur*, the Infirm, and has his day on March 16,
one day before the day of the more widely known St. Patrick.
The saintly atmosphere of Finan the Infirm pervades the grassy
isle of his meditations to this day.   It is in the soft breeze that
sweeps down from Ben Resipol and sends the small waves to
break on the shores of the isle : it is in the scent of the many
wild-flowers that grow here.   Above forgotten graves the
broom sways golden branches.   Each summer night mild-
eyed hinds swim in silent procession across to the island, and
graze here until the flush of sunrise on the hill-tops warns them
that it is time to return to the high corries.   The numerous
graves on Eilean Fhìonain are of persons in every station of
life.   Here lie the remains of chief and crofter, some in the
shelter of the small ruined chapel, others on shores drenched
by winter spindrift.   On the southern shore lie the Protestants ;
on the northern shore the Catholics.   The centre of the isle
divides the two faiths.

   The chapel of Eilean Fhìonain is of great interest.   Little
is known of its early history, but it is perhaps built on the site
of the cell of St. Finan.   The builder is believed to have been
Alan MacRuairidh, one of the early ClanRanald chiefs.   In the
middle of the seventeenth century the chapel became a ruin.
The altar remains.   It is of rough stone, and on it is St. Finan's
bell.   This small bell, which tradition affirms was brought from
Ireland by St. Finan himself, has rested before the High
Altar for certainly two hundred and fifty years, and a curse will
fall on anyone venturing to steal it.   The voice of the bell
is gentle and musical ; it tells of old sacred things.   It has seen
the dead chiefs of ClanRanald borne with much ceremony in
their galley to the holy island.   It has seen those sent to the
island to do penance kneel before the stone crucifix which

---

[1] The name by which Columba was often known.

neither summer sun nor winter storm can harm. The face of the Christ on this small cross is arresting, for it is full of simple humility, and of an aloofness from this world and its desires. Few figures of Christ can be more striking.

Beside the altar are the graves of many illustrious dead. Conspicuous is the gravestone of John of Moidart who died at Castle Tioram in 1584. This stone is worked with beautiful Celtic design, and a claymore is engraved on it. Many clansmen doubtless assembled on the island when he, the first to be styled Captain or chief of ClanRanald, was laid to rest, and the strains of a pibroch echoed across Loch Shiel as the funeral galley drew alongside St. Finan's Isle. Beside the burying-place of John of Moidart are the grass-grown graves of some of the earlier leaders of the clan, scarcely visible now above the green mantle of the island. Near the chapel are rough crosses, unusual in shape. These are said to have been hewn by Donald Mór MacVarish rather more than one hundred years ago. The graves they mark are nameless.

It was on a warm still day of early autumn that I crossed to Eilean Fhionain and then, after visiting the island, returned to the north shore of the loch and walked towards the west, through woods of birch, where the bracken was already bronze. Along the old road I had the sense of the past living again in the present. The sun was low, and shone through the autumn haze. This old road, which might well be called the Way of Pilgrimage, or the Road of the Cairns, leads from St. Finan's island to Castle Tioram. Almost throughout the length of the road are cairns. They stand singly, in twos and threes, in scores. In one place I counted upwards of forty of them. It was interesting to see that most of the cairns were built beside burns. Here funeral parties rested with their burdens in the heat of the day, and drank from the clear waters that flowed to Loch Shiel. That night I reached the village of Acharacle, and next morning, in clear sunny weather, with Rhum mist-enfolded on the western horizon, I continued west to Castle

Tioram. So long ago as the year 700 Adamnan was impressed by the salmon of the Shiel, and as I crossed the river at the bridge I could see a very heavy fish lying quietly in the deep clear water, just where the river Shiel leaves the loch. From Shiel Bridge I walked through woods of oak, and thought of the ancestors of these trees which were felled to repair the monastery of Iona.

Swiftly the Shiel flows on its short course from its loch to the mother ocean. Beside the river dragon-flies darted on quivering wings. Ben Resipol was hidden in white mist : only its top showed above the cloud. When the hill-tops rise above the clouds it is a sign of a fine day to follow, so that I had hopes of a pleasant walk as I passed through wooded country until the estuary of the Shiel was reached, the trees abruptly ended, and the sea was visible. Along the shore the road twisted, and soon the walls of Castle Tioram were seen outlined against the wooded slopes of Eilean Shona, across the loch.

Castle Tioram takes its name from Eilean Tioram, the Dry Island. The island is well named, for it is an island only at high spring tides. At all other times it is joined to the mainland by an isthmus or *doirlinn*. The *doirlinn* of Castle Tioram is a spit of shingle where the sea thrift grows, and oyster catchers doze away the heat of the day. Mild-eyed cattle crossed the isthmus to graze on the green grass of Eilean Tioram. The sun was warm. No breeze drifted in from the Atlantic, where, on the blue horizon, the Isle of Muck [1] showed clearly. As I sat beside the castle a fishing boat stood out from Loch Moidart towards the surf fringe beyond Eilean Shona and I thought of the times when ClanRanald's galley, on its voyage from Castle Tioram to the chief's lands in South Uist, had steered a similar course.

Castle Tioram to-day is a ruin, but it is a well-preserved ruin, and in this respect differs from another MacDonald stronghold—Duntuilm Castle in Skye. In the year 1715 Castle

[1] Eilean nam Muc, Isle of Pigs.

Tioram in a few hours became a blackened shell. Allan Mór of Moidart, on setting out to join the Old Pretender on the Braes of Mar in 1715, had a presentiment, like Donald Bàn MacCrimmon before the '45, that he would not return. He therefore, so the story goes, gave orders to one Roderick Mac-Donald to set fire to the place after he had left it. By a remarkable coincidence Ormicleit Castle in South Uist (his castle in the Isles) was burned on the same day, the fire there originating at the roasting of a stag. In the massive walls of Castle Tioram the marks of the beams are still to be seen, and these marks show that the ceilings of the castle must have been low. I was shown a piece of one of the old beams; it was of resinous pine. With this inflammable material it must have been easy to fire Castle Tioram.

In the ruined castle the remains of the kitchen can be seen. On one side of this room is the beehive-shaped oven; on the other is the well. Thus the cook at Castle Tioram had not far to go for water, but one at least of ClanRanald's cooks had difficulties here of another sort. That old crone was cook to Donald the Cruel, and her one failing was that she was fond of snuff. At times she was not above taking a pinch from the chief's snuff-box, and finally she became so bold that she stole the snuff-box itself. Her crime was discovered and she was sentenced to be hanged on the Hanging Hill that overlooks the castle. On being led out to her death she took a last pinch from her master's box (how she had retained it we are not told), then with a defiant gesture threw it far over the waters of the loch.

Donald the Cruel had so many crimes to his account that at length Satanic powers approached him. He was disturbed by a huge toad, which attached itself to him with sinister persistence. Repeated efforts were made to outwit the toad. On one occasion it was enticed into the castle dungeon, and was locked in just before the chief sailed away in his galley to the Isles. " At last," said Donald the Cruel as the sail was hoisted, and he felt the heave of the ocean swell, " at last I am free of my unwelcome guest." Scarcely had he spoken these words when the breeze freshened from the south and the sea quickly rose. The sails were reefed. Waves leaped angrily upon the galley. When the storm was at the height of its fury the toad was seen breasting the seas. The creature soon overhauled the galley and swam in its wake, eyeing the chief with malignant stare. At first the Captain of ClanRanald refused to take the creature on board, but the waves became so threatening that at last he was compelled to do so. Immediately the gale subsided and the sea calmed.

The only occasion on which Castle Tioram fell was in the sixteenth century, and that was not in fair fight. A strong force under Argyll had unsuccessfully besieged it for five weeks, and at the end of that time, apparently baffled, sailed away in their galleys. The MacDonalds then left their stronghold, and many of them set out for their homes to obtain news of their relatives. That night the Campbells stealthily returned, steering in by the narrow north channel where they were invisible behind Eilean Shona, and surprised and overpowered the small guard that had been left in Castle Tioram. But next day the tide of battle turned swiftly. The MacDonalds, hurrying up from all sides, drove the enemy to their galleys and put to the sword those who did not escape.

From Castle Tioram a road leads by way of Shiel Bridge to Salen on Loch Sunart, winds along that narrow sea loch to Strontian, and thence, by way of Glen Tarbert, to Loch Linnhe and Ardgour. From Ardgour it is possible either to cross the ferry to the farther side of the loch at Ballachulish, or to continue along the shore of Loch Linnhe and the shore of Loch Eil, and join the Fort William road at Drumsallie, on the county march between Argyll and Inverness, as I have described in Chapter XXXII.

CHAPTER XXVI

EIGG : THE NOTCHED ISLE

OF Hebridean islands Eigg is one of the most distinctive. It is recognised from afar by its Scùir—a precipitous hill which rises gracefully from the southern end of the island, and attracts

Eigg.

to itself the soft ocean clouds which so often drift in from the Atlantic. Looking across from Arisaig or the sands of Morar on a summer evening one sees the Scùir of Eigg rising ethereal on the horizon. From Sleat of Skye, too, Eigg is often inspiring because of its deep spiritual blueness, and from the northern coast of Mull it is one of the most distinctive of the isles. Eilean

Eige is the Gaelic name of the island, and it means the Isle of the Notch. In Adamnan's *Life of Columba* (A.D. 700) it is written of as Egea Insula.

The patron saint of Eigg is Donnan, whose genealogy is obscure. He is commemorated in Kildonan, in Eigg, and probably also in Eilean Donnan in Kintail. Saint Donnan was massacred on Eigg, whither he had gone to preach the religion of his master, Columba. With Donnan were slain his fifty-two followers. It has been suggested that the murderers were Norsemen, but the Eigg massacre took place before the earliest Norse invasion, and old records merely call the assailants "piraiti" or pirates. There were roving bands of pirates in the Isles long before the Vikings appeared. A curious tradition accounts for this massacre. It is said that Saint Donnan in some way aroused the anger of a proud queen, who hired unscrupulous men to exterminate him and his band.

Their bones were found by Martin many centuries after. Martin, writing about the year 1700, says, "There is a church here in the east side of the isle, dedicated to Saint Donnan, whose anniversary they observe. About thirty yards from the church there is a sepulchral Urn under the ground. It is a big stone hewn to the bottom, about four feet deep and the diameter of it is about the same breadth. I caused them to dig the ground above it, and we found a flat thin stone covering the Urn. It was almost full of human bones, but no head among them, and they were fair and dry. I inquired of the natives what was become of the heads, and they could not tell, but one of them said, perhaps their heads had been cut off with a two-handed sword and taken away by the enemy." This Urn of headless bones confirmed the old tradition of the massacre of Donnan and his followers, but it seems as though the natives of the island at that time did not know of the tradition, although elsewhere in his book Martin writes of "St. Donnan, the celebrated Tutelar of this Isle."

The murder of Donnan and his devoted followers belongs to

the remote past : another, and more recent, massacre, is still spoken of in the Isle of Eigg. The MacLeods of Harris and the MacDonalds of ClanRanald had long been at enmity. The pretext for the crime known as the Massacre of the Cave of Eigg was the maltreatment by the men of Eigg of certain messengers who had been sent to them by the MacLeods. It was also said that one of the MacLeod chiefs had made himself unpopular on the island because of his amorous escapades, and

Scuir of Eigg.

had been tied to a boat and set adrift on the Minch. In revenge for these indignities a strong force of the MacLeods sailed from Skye to Eigg in their war galleys. It was the season of early spring—the most bitter time in the whole year in the Hebrides. A north wind blew mercilessly upon the green waters of the Minch beneath a hard blue sky. The Cuillin were deep in snow. Even Eigg was snowbound to the shore. From Rudha Thalasgeir on Eigg the approach of the galleys was observed and the alarm was given. There was fear in the hearts of the people when the news was brought to them, for most of the men were absent from the island at the time. On the eastern shore of Eigg is a great cave. The entrance is partially hidden by a burn which flows in a small white waterfall from the moor above, and drops immediately over the cave's entrance. To this cave all except two of the island families hurried, the men assisting the small children and carrying the infants across the high ground. The two families who did not accompany the rest hid in another cave, farther along the coast. The MacLeod galleys landed, the men with difficulty leaping ashore in the strong wind that sent the cold spray against the frozen rocks. A film of drifting snow lay above the island that bitter March day, for the north wind was blowing the powdery snow before it in clouds, and was piling up great drifts in the sheltered hollows. Almost as soon as they were made, the footprints of the fugitives to the cave were covered in by the drifting snow, and when the MacLeods searched the houses and found them empty, and saw no footmarks in the ground, they doubtless imagined that the population of Eigg had escaped them. They searched the island, satisfied themselves that no person remained on it, then embarked and set sail towards Skye. The wind now became less violent and one of the men of Eigg left the cave and climbed to the high ground to see whether the coast was clear. His action brought disaster on the island. He saw the galleys departing, but they also saw him, and at once put about. The friendly wind no longer drifted the snow, and when the enemy landed, they were able to follow the watcher's footmarks back to the cave. Here the whimpering of children and the barking of dogs told them all they wished to know. In the latter part of the sixteenth century there was little mercy shown to an enemy in the highlands. The entrance to the cave was narrow. To escape, and even to fight, was impossible, for a MacLeod claymore would have put a swift end to any person crawling laboriously from the cave's mouth. The leading men of the MacLeods then conferred among themselves. A ruthless plan

N

was decided on. The nearest houses were stripped of their thatch for kindlings, and when the course of the burn had been altered so that it no longer flowed over the cave's mouth a great fire was lighted at the entrance, and wet fuel was piled upon the flames. Within the cave arose cries and lamentations. Children were wailing; their terror-stricken mothers had no heart to comfort them. Thick clouds of smoke rolled into the sky and into the cave. At the far end of this underground passage there is little air at any time, and gradually the people within were overcome by the smoke. The cries, the moanings, and the shouts lessened. At long intervals came a gasping sob and when these too ceased the men of Skye embarked beneath the stars, leaving a smouldering fire at the entrance to what was now a cave of the dead.

Through the centuries that followed the whitening bones of the victims remained in the cave. It is not so long since they were gathered and reverently interred. They were found in family groups—father, mother and children mingling their dust in that dark recess. The two families (in some accounts only one family is mentioned) who were in hiding in another cave escaped the massacre. Thus in a few hours was the population of Eigg virtually wiped out. At the present day there are living on Eigg only one family who are original natives of the island; all the rest are settlers from neighbouring islands or the mainland.

In Skene's *Celtic Scotland* (Vol. III. p. 428) is an interesting account of the massacre. This report is believed to have been prepared for the use of James VI and must have been written before 1595, as James Stewart of Appin, who died in that year, is mentioned as being alive. The account, after mentioning that Eigg " will raise 60 men to the weiris," goes on to say, " there is mony coves under the earth in this isle, which the country folks uses as strengthis,' hiding them and their gear therein." We read that in March 1577 the people with " ane callit Angus John Mudzartsonne their capitane " fled to one of these " coves " and that the MacLeods " smorit the haill people thairin to the number of 395 persones, men, wyfe and bairnis." It has never been settled beyond doubt whether this massacre was in revenge for a crime of equal turpitude, the massacre of the MacLeods in the church at Trumpan in Skye by the MacDonalds of Clan-Ranald (ClanRanald owned both Eigg and the Outer Hebridean island of South Uist). The MacLeods assert that the massacre of Trumpan preceded that of Eigg. The MacDonalds aver that their raid on Trumpan was in revenge for the Eigg massacre. The evidence is rather in favour of the MacDonald version of the event, as some authorities give the date of the Trumpan crime as three years after the massacre of Eigg.

Let us recall briefly the course of the massacre at Trumpan (which I have described in chapter XV) and the Battle of the Spoiled Dyke which was fought the same day. One Sunday morning in summer ClanRanald's galleys reached Trumpan on Vaternish of Skye and, surrounding the small church during the service, set fire to it and burned to death those within. MacLeod's clansmen cut off the raiders before they could reach their galleys, and the Battle of the Spoiled Dyke was fought. The MacLeods were being hard-pressed when the miraculous Fairy Flag was unfurled. One galley only escaped. The rest of the incendiaries were slain and the stones of a dyke were heaped above their bodies.

The days of summary and ruthless vengeance have long since gone and Eigg is now peaceful. Its most illustrious son of the present day is the Reverend Kenneth MacLeod, who has perhaps done more than any man to rescue the old music of the Gael, in danger of being lost in this age of unrest. Eigg is full of music. Even the sands of the seashore sing when one walks upon them. These Singing Sands lie, white and gleaming, on the western side of the island. Here is the broad Bay of Laig, where gannets fish among the breakers and at dusk the clan of the shearwaters fly inland from the darkening sea. Beside these white singing sands of Laig there is green *machair*, where many sweet-scented flowers blossom, and the crimson orchis

blends with the yellow of the iris and trefoil. Eigg is an isle
of flowers. The scented dog rose blossoms on the shore and
on the hills, while the sea cliffs at midsummer are white with
dryas octopetala, crimson with the cushion pink, and golden
with roseroot. High on the slopes the bell heather flames, and
the wild honeysuckle twines among the rocks. By day buzzard
and raven sail above the cliffs of Eigg. At dusk the shearwaters speed in from the sea to their nesting burrows on the
cliffs, and throughout the nights of spring and summer make
wild music there. But as the glow of the lighthouse on
Ardnamurchan pales and the outline of Rhum across the Sound
becomes clear the shearwaters sink into slumber and the robin
and mavis, taking their places as musicians, salute the approaching day.

CHAPTER XXVII

THE OUTER HEBRIDES

WEST of Skye and Mull a long chain of islands rise from the stormy Atlantic. These are usually named the Outer Hebrides, and sometimes the Long Island, because when seen from a vessel approaching from the west they appear to be joined together. The Outer Hebrides are just short of 120 miles in length; they lie from north to south, and Lewis, the most northerly member of the group, is in Ross-shire while the other isles are in the county of Inverness. They can be reached from Oban, Mallaig, or Kyle of Loch Alsh, and there are also steamers from Glasgow. The word Hebrides is what is termed a ghost-name. It originated from the misreading of Ptolemy's name " Ebudae." Ptolemy wrote : " Above Ivernia (the north of Ireland) are the islands called Eboudai." Marcian, according to Stephanus of Byzantium, wrote Aiboudai, and Pliny Hebudes. The Outer Hebrides (naming only the more important) are Barra, South Uist and Benbecula, North Uist, Berneray, Harris and Lewis. Each island is distinctive, with its own peculiar atmosphere, but each island has this in common—it is the home of kindly, hospitable people. Even to-day many of the Outer Hebrideans have never seen a train, and my wife recently travelled with a woman who was making her first journey on a steamer and her first journey by train, yet she had often seen seaplanes passing her home! The people of the Outer Hebrides are Gaelic-speaking, and some of the older generation are unable to speak any English. Formerly all the Hebridean houses were thatched, and chimneys were unknown. The peat fire (peat is the fuel burnt universally in the Outer Hebrides) was placed in the centre of the room, and was kept alight night and day. The smoke found its way out of the house through the open door, and through a hole in the roof. When Prince Charles Edward landed on Eriskay in the Sound of Barra in 1745 he spent the night in a house belonging to one of the people of that island and he found the peat smoke so trying to his eyes that he was obliged to go often to the door to get air. "What a plague is the matter with that fellow," said his host indignantly, "that he can neither sit nor stand still, and neither keep within nor without doors?" Sometimes it is impossible, on entering a room of an old-fashioned Hebridean house, to distinguish the people within it. The peat smoke is liable to make the eyes smart and the breath falter of one unaccustomed to it, but these old "black houses" are healthy and well ventilated, and I believe they are more healthy to live in than the modern buildings with chimneys and slated roofs which are now being built in their place.

The Island of Barra is said to take its name from Saint Barre of Cork, and at Cill Bharr, the Church of St. Barr, on that island there was an image of the saint in Martin's time and his anniversary was observed on September 27. Barra was old MacNeil country. MacNeil of Barra lived in his castle on the small isle of Kismul, which rises about a quarter of a mile from the shore at Castlebay. Martin desired to see the castle of Kismul about the year 1700, but found it no easy undertaking. When he arrived at the shore he heard that MacNeil and his lady were absent from the place. "I saw the officer called the Cockman, and on old Cock he is. When I bid him ferry me over the water to the island he told me that he was but an inferior officer, his business being to attend to the tower, but if (says he) the Constable, who then stood on the wall, will give you access, I'll ferry you over. I desired him to procure me the Constable's permission, and I would reward him, but having waited some hours for the Constable's answer, and not receiving any, I was obliged to return without my seeing this famous fort. I was told some weeks after that the Constable was very apprehensive of some design I might have in viewing the fort and thereby to expose

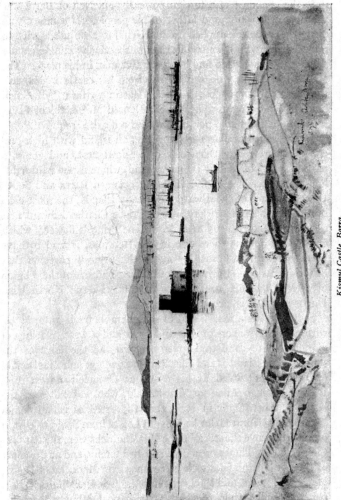

Kismul Castle, Barra.

it to the conquest of a foreign power." MacNeil of Barra was the uncrowned king and father of his people. If a man's wife died, the widower applied to MacNeil for a suitable wife to replace her, and if a woman lost her husband, she in like manner petitioned the chief to find her a suitable man in his place. The MacNeil of Barra who was absent from his castle in Martin's time was the thirty-fourth chief. Martin writes: "Mackneil holds his lands in vassallage of Sir Donald McDonald of Slate, to whom he pays 40 l. per annum, and a hawk if required."

To the south of Barra is Mingulay, an island with high precipices where many thousands of sea-fowl nest, and across a narrow sound beyond it is Barra Head, where a powerful lighthouse stands. The Sound of Barra, between Barra and South Uist, is a place of shoal water and many islands, the most celebrated of which is Eriskay, where Prince Charles Edward first set foot on Scottish soil in 1745. "The Prince's flower," which grows here and nowhere else in the Hebrides, is said to have been brought from France by one of the Prince's party on that historic occasion. Barra and South Uist, because of the religion of their old chiefs, are mainly Catholic to-day; North Uist, Harris and Lewis, are Protestant.

South Uist is a long island of innumerable fresh-water lochs, with an eastern shore of hills and rocks and a western fringe of glorious white sand and green *machair*, at the edge of the shore. This island is old ClanRanald country, and MacDonald of ClanRanald lived at his castle at Ormicleit, now a ruin. It was through Allan of ClanRanald, who was killed at the battle of Sheriffmuir in 1715, that the breed of island ponies became so celebrated, for he brought horses from Spain to Uist in order to improve the stock. The MacMhuirichs were the bards of ClanRanald. They were a distinguished family, and at the court of the Lord of the Isles took precedence over MacLean of Duart, MacNeil of Barra, and MacLeod himself. The MacMhuirich poets were descended from the famous Irish poet Mhuireadhach Ua Dalaidh, who was obliged to flee to Scotland about the year 1213 because he had split open the head of O'Donnell's steward with an axe when the steward had the presumption to demand rent from him. I have referred to the destruction of Ormicleit Castle in Chapter XXV.

No longer do the MacMhuirichs recite their verses by the shores of Uist, but the island to-day is the home of more pipers than any other district of Scotland. Each winter Pipe Major John Mac-Donald [1] holds a school of piping in South Uist, and each summer games are held on the *machair* beside the Atlantic. On the great dunes of white sand the summer sun shines with brilliance. There is a carpet of wild flowers on the *machair*. Yellow

Barra from S. Uist.

bedstraw, milkwort, silver-weed and clover perfume the air. South across the sea are the hills of Barra; west, as far as the eye can reach, are the blue waters of the Atlantic. Under these inspiring conditions the pipers of South Uist play old battle-pieces, salutes and laments, some of them composed by the MacIntyres, hereditary pipers to the MacDonalds of ClanRanald.

It is pleasant to wander in Uist when the strong summer sun shines down upon the island and the rains and storms of winter are forgotten. It is pleasant to cross the Minch from the mainland when the sea is blue and smiling and the fulmar petrels and solans which glide gracefully around the vessel are snow-white above green waters. There are, perhaps, fog banks on the Minch,

[1] Pipe Major John MacDonald, M.B.E., of Inverness is universally conceded to be the finest player of *piobaireachd* at the present day.

and the tops of Outer Hebridean hills are veiled by wandering ocean mists. Curious mirages are seen on days of heat and sea fog. The island hills suddenly change shape. Phantom precipices appear and confuse the eye; the base of a hill shrinks and the shape of the peak becomes like some giant mushroom, so that he who sees this illusion feels that he has been placed beneath a spell, and that the Druid cloak of Manannan, god of the sea, has been waved before his eyes. There is delight in watching the herring fleet from Mallaig steer out to Hebridean waters, the white foam of many bow waves glinting in the sun, the brown coal smoke from many funnels trailing out to leeward; there is pleasure in steaming slowly up Loch Boisdale and seeing South Uist, fair to look upon, in the golden sunshine of a summer evening.

Here in Uist one stands on the rim of the material earth and looks away west towards that Land of the Spirit which the Celtic seers long ago named Tir nan Og. To him who stands at sunset on the *machair* of Uist, Tir nan Og is not hard to visualise. Lower and lower sinks the sun and at last, glowing, quivering and full of splendour, he dips below the grey bank of fog which rests above the far horizon as though to hide the secrets of Tir nan Og from mortal gaze. The sea is first opal, then changes to turquoise beneath the evening sky. The last air of the breeze has died away; the flowers of the *machair* close their petals. The heavy trout of the *machair* lochs now cruise round the sun-heated shallows, rising occasionally to the flies which float lightly on the surface. Twilight comes, and the orange rays of the Monach light pierce the dusk. A number of grey geese rise from the *machair* where they have been feeding, and fly inland with loud cries. Terns on graceful pointed wings haunt the shores of the lochs, a red-necked phalarope swims lightly by, picking small insects off the water with quick dainty movements, and as the dusk deepens a short-eared owl flies silently across the *machair*. For a few hours the low summer moon floods land and sea, then at sunrise the ocean mist spreads over the island, and from a dim dew-drenched world are heard the wailing cries of wandering curlew. Gradually the climbing sun disperses the mist, and at midday no single cloud is to be seen from the zenith to the far horizon. Above the *machair* the air quivers. There is no wind. Out on the western horizon is the cobalt line of the Atlantic. Along the edge of the *machair* are low stone walls where the tangle weed of the sea is burnt for its ash. The sun has shone upon these low walls until they are hot to the touch; one might think a fire had been kindled here. The cattle stand contentedly on the smooth wet sands at the edge of the ebbing tide. A light breeze rises, rippling the ocean around a low skerry where the crew of a lobster boat are lifting their creels. This done they hoist the brown sail and steer south towards Barra, which rises blue on the horizon. Small waves break on the white shore with soft sighings. Hecla, one of the three great hills of South Uist, towers to the blue sky; the west slopes of Beinn Mhór [1] are soft and green. Far eastward rise the Cuillin of Skye and the Cuillin of Rhum. The *machair* land is green with oats and barley, golden with corn marigolds, red with poppies, purple and white with the flowers of the potato. At the margin of the sands the sea aster opens its mauve flowers; in boggy hollows the damp earth is covered with a close carpet of the pink blossoms of the bog pimpernel. On an island of one of the *machair* lochs a ragwort colony flames golden beneath the sun. At the margin of the green *machair* is a long line of white sand, stretching away north and south as far as the eye can reach into the haze of distance.

South Uist is separated from North Uist by the island of Benbecula. Between South Uist and Benbecula is a tidal channel known as the South Ford which at low spring tides is dry. Between Benbecula and North Uist is a much wider channel, known as the North Ford. There are a number of islands rising from the North Ford, which is more difficult to cross than the South Ford, and although a trap can drive over it at low tide,

---

[1] Beinn Mhór means the Great Hill. There is a Beinn Mhór in Mull and a Beinn Mhór in South Uist.

the ford is never entirely dry. If the tide is in, it is possible to cross the North Ford by boat, and sail through pale green waters above white sands where the sea swallows play above the tidal streams. A mirage may lift the Monach lighthouse, fifteen miles to the west, into the summer air; may lift the Atlantic waves that advance upon lonely Baleshare so that they appear to break mysteriously in the sky; may lift up St. Kilda fifty miles westward into the heavens.

One lands upon North Uist, and finds it no less pleasant than South Uist, but entirely different. North Uist also has a *machair* on its western seaboard. From this flower-covered and scented *machair* one looks across to the remote island of Hasker and sees its fine natural arches.

Travelling north along the west side of North Uist, long an island possession of the MacDonalds of Sleat, one passes in turn Balranald and Tighearry, the Hosta *machair* (perhaps the most beautiful *machair* land in all the Hebrides), Griminish with its dark rocks, remote Vallay, and green Lingay. At Newton Ferry one reaches the north shore of the island of North Uist, and here one can cross the Sound of Harris to Rodil, or else can break one's journey on Berneray, an island of white sands, green *machair*, and clean thatched houses with small crofts. At either end of this island two small hills rise to a height of a few hundred feet. Elsewhere the ground is level, and there is little shelter from Atlantic storms. West, on the far horizon, rise the dream islands of St. Kilda; east, across the Minch, are the hills of Skye, often in deep shade when the sun shines brilliantly on the Outer Hebrides. The visitor to Berneray may notice that there are many small fields on the island, but no fences nor stone walls enclose these small fields of oats, barley and bere. How, then are the growing crops protected from the live-stock of the island? Each animal on Berneray—cow or calf, stirk, horse and sheep—is tethered. Sheep are usually tethered in pairs, the other animals singly. It is not unusual to see even a domestic fowl tethered at the end of a string ! A vigorous cow may at times pull up her

N. and S. Uist from Harris.

tether pin and enjoy a furtive meal of succulent oats or barley
before she is discovered and is driven back to her rightful
quarters, but the people of the island take these little episodes
with calmness. Another interesting thing about Berneray is
that there is no hay on the island, as it will not grow on the pure
fine sand, and the winter feed of the cattle is oats and barley.

Berneray, like other islands of the Outer Hebrides, burns peat
as its fuel, but there is no peat moss on the island and the peat
has to be cut, dried and stacked on an island several miles
distant. In July and August, when the peats are dry, they are
loaded into sailing boats, and it is a pretty sight of a summer's
afternoon when the flood tide is rising to watch a procession of
boats approaching Berneray, their tall brown sails set to the
breeze. As they near the island the boats separate and each one
makes for its own landing creek. Immediately the boat arrives
eager helpers hurry down to the shore and leap on board,
carrying creels with them. These creels are speedily filled with
peats, and the shore workers hurry, burden on back, a little way
above the tide and throw down the peats on the grass.

Most of the Berneray men have served on yachts, and lobster
fishing is carried on during a part of the year. Some of them
weave Harris tweed—though it is more difficult to sell this tweed
than formerly because of unfair foreign competition—and when
the tweed has been woven there is the *luadhadh* or shrinking of the
web. At this ceremony there is much merriment and the singing
of Gaelic songs with a rhythm specially adapted to the pounding
of the tweed. At the *luadhadh* or waulking half a dozen women
or more sit at a long table. The web of cloth is soaked, and as it
is passed round the table each woman slaps and kneads it with
both hands, the workers keeping time by singing one of the
waulking songs. The peat fire glows on the earthen floor,
sprinkled with white sea sand, and the little gathering is full of
good cheer. Without lies the *machair* scented with clover and
blue with fields of harebells, and the low-toned music of the
Atlantic surf is the accompaniment to the cheerful singing.

The traveller who crosses the Sound of Harris from North Uist to Harris may land at Leverburgh, of which the older name is Obe (now a dreary collection of abandoned houses) or at peaceful Rodil. At Rodil is the old cathedral of St. Clement's, an ancient and picturesque church. In Dean Munro's time (the middle of the sixteenth century) the tradition was that St. Clement's was founded and built by MacLeod of Harris in the thirteenth century. St. Clement of Rome, who was banished from Rome to the Crimea, and was there murdered by being thrown into the sea with an

St. Clement's, Rodil, Harris.

anchor round his neck, was the patron saint of the MacLeods. Within the church is a very beautiful old tomb to " Alexander Macclod, domino de Dunvegan, 1528." Alexander was the chief known usually as Alasdair Crotach, who gave the great MacCrimmon pipers their lands of Borreraig in Skye. In the churchyard are many old graves. On one of them is the following inscription :

" To the memory of Donald Macleod of Berneray, son of John, tutor of MacLeod, who in vigour of body and mind resembled the man of former times. His grandfather and grand-uncle were knighted by King Charles II for their loyalty and distinguished valour in the Battle of Worcester, where the standard of the House of Stuart, to which he was attached, was displayed. A.D. 1745, though past the prime of life, he took arms, had a share in the actions of that period, and in the Battle of Falkirk vanquished a dragoon hand to hand. From that time he lived at his house of Berneray, universally beloved and respected. In his 75th year he married his third wife, by whom he had nine children, and died in his 90th year, the 16th of Dec. 1783."

Harris and Lewis are one island. At Tarbert the Atlantic almost flows into the Minch, but there is a narrow neck of land here which divides the two seas, and thus it is possible to walk, or travel by motor-car all the way from the Sound of Harris to the most northerly part of Lewis. On the west of Harris are the beautiful sands of Borve, and from them are seen the islands of Taransay, Scarpa and Gasgeir.

At Tarbert is the port of the mail steamer and a good hotel. North of Tarbert the road winds through the hill country of Harris and skirts the base of Clisham,[1] the highest of Outer Hebridean hills. At Loch Seaforth, the boundary of Lewis and Harris, a long and narrow loch resembling a Norwegian fjord runs far inland through the hills, and from the Lewis boundary to Stornoway, the capital of Lewis, the road is through wild and lonely scenery. Lewis is interesting because it is the only district of the highlands and islands where the summer shealing still lives. In early summer the people of the townships, having sowed their oats and planted their potatoes, set out to the moors with their cattle. In the small thatched shealings they remain until the end of summer, and by bringing their cattle with them they allow the grass of the townships' grazing to have a period of rest and to grow a crop sufficient for the winter feed. At one time the people of the highlands everywhere went to the summer shealings; the shealing procession has been poetically described by Alexander Carmichael in his great work *Carmina Gadelica*.

On the west of Lewis is the very remarkable stone circle of Callernish. MacCulloch, in his *Western Islands*, thus describes it:

" The form is that of a cross, containing at the intersection a circle with a central stone, an additional line being superadded on one side of the

---

[1] Usually known to Hebrideans as " The " Clisham.

longest arms and nearly parallel to it.   Were this line absent, its form and proportion would be nearly that of the Roman cross or common crucifix. The longest line of this cross, which may be considered as the general bearing of the work, lies in a direction 24 degrees west of the meridian.   The total length of this line is at present 588 feet, but there are stones to be found in the same direction for upwards of 90 feet further, which have apparently been a continuation of it, but which having fallen, like others, through different parts of the building, have sometimes been overwhelmed with vegetation, leaving blanks that impair its present continuity.   The whole length may therefore with little hesitation be taken at 700 feet.   The cross line, intersecting that now described at right angles, measures 204 feet, but as it is longer on one side than the other its true measure is probably greater also, although I was not able to discover any fallen stones at the extremities; the progress of cultivation having here interfered with the integrity of the work.   The diameter of the circle which occupies the centre of the cross is 63 feet, the lines ceasing where they meet the circumference.   The stone which marks the centre is 12 feet in height.   The heights of the other stones which are used in the construction are various, but they rarely reach beyond four feet : a few of seven or eight feet are to be found, and one reaching to thirteen is seen near the extremity of the long line.   The additional line already mentioned extends northwards from the outer part of the circle, on the eastern side.   It is, however, very defective, a great number of the stones being absent towards its northern extremity; although there is apparent evidence of their former continuity, in one which remains erect and in others which have fallen from their places.   I could not discover any traces of a line parallel to this on the western side; but as some inclosures have been made in the immediate vicinity, it is possible that such might have originally existed; notwithstanding the superstitious reverence with which the Scots in general regard these remains, and the care with which, in their agricultural operations, they commonly avoid committing any injury to them.   The intervals between the stones vary from two to ten feet or more, but it is probable that the larger spaces have resulted from the falling of the less firmly rooted pillars which occupied those places.   The number of stones in the circle is thirteen, independently of the central one, and the number in the whole building, either erect or recently fallen, is forty-seven. The aspect of this work is very striking, as it occupies the highest situation on a gentle swelling eminence of moorland; there being no object, not even a rock or stone, to divert the attention and diminish the impression which it makes.   The circles found in the vicinity are less perfect, and present no linear appendages; their average diameter varies from forty to fifty feet, and one of them contains four uprights placed in a quadrangular form within its area.   I may add to this general account that solitary stones, apparently of a monumental nature, are found in this neighbourhood, as well as in the island of Bernera and in other parts of Lewis.

" The cruciform shape of the structure described above is a remarkable, and I believe a solitary, circumstance.   It has not at least been noticed among the numerous descriptions of these erections which antiquaries have given to the public.   It is true that in some of the cromlechs or smaller monuments, a disposition of the stones resembling that of a cross has sometimes been remarked, but it seems in all these cases to have been the result

O

Carloway, Lewis.

either of accident or necessity. No monuments in which that form is
obviously intended have been traced higher than the period of the introduction of Christianity ; nor was it indeed till a later age, that of Constantine,
that the cross became a general object of veneration. From that time its
use is common ; and it is frequently found applied, under a great variety of
structures and forms, to numerous objects, civil and military, as well as
ecclesiastical. Those cases in which the figure of the cross has been found
marked or carved on stones of higher antiquity, which had served either for
the purposes of sepulchral memorials or Druidical worship, appear to have
resulted from the attempts of the early Catholics to convert the supposed
monuments of ancient superstition to their ends ; either from economical
motives or from feelings of a religious nature. But such attempts cannot
be supposed to have given rise to the peculiar figure of the structure here

Callernish.

described. The whole is too consistent and too much of one age to admit
of such a supposition ; while, at the same time, it could not under any circumstances have been applicable to a Christian worship. Its essential part,
the circular area, and the number of similar structures found in the
vicinity, equally bespeak its ancient origin. It must therefore be concluded
that the cruciform shape was given by the original contrivers of the fabrics,
and it will afford an object of speculation to antiquaries, who, if they are
sometimes accused of heaping additional obscurity on the records of antiquity, must also be allowed the frequent merit of eliciting light from darkness. To them I willingly consign all further speculation concerning it."

From the standing stones of Callernish, a remarkable unknown memorial of an unknown age, one travels north mile after
mile through a country of moors and bogs and lochs, but as one
reaches the Butt of Lewis, the most northerly part of the island,

the land suddenly changes to white sands and green *machair*. From the lighthouse on the Butt of Lewis there is to be seen as sublime a view as any in the Hebrides. Forty miles northward over the Atlantic is the island of North Rona, an island that is now uninhabited and is the home of sea-birds and seals. Far to the east is the high land of Cape Wrath. To stand at the brink of the sea precipice beside the lighthouse at the Butt of Lewis and look over the Atlantic northward to Greenland and Iceland, and west towards the coast of Labrador, is a memorable experience.

In the Minch east of Lewis are to be seen a group of bold rocky islands—the Shiant Isles. These, like North Rona, are now uninhabited; they were one of the last haunts of the sea or white-tailed eagle before that fine bird of prey was exterminated in Scotland. The daily mail steamer between Mallaig, Kyle of Loch Alsh and Stornoway passes near the Shiant Islands. Stornoway is the capital of the Outer Hebrides. A large fishing fleet is based here during a considerable part of the year, and heavy catches of herrings are landed. The old castle of Stornoway was besieged and captured by Huntly in 1506, but in 1554 it successfully withstood the attack of the Earl of Argyll. This old castle of the MacLeods of Lewis remained as a ruin until the year 1882, when its stones were removed to permit of town improvements.

CHAPTER XXVIII

GLEN COE

CLAN warfare in the highlands was bloody and cruel. The MacDonalds of ClanRanald surrounded and set fire to the church at Trumpan* while the MacLeods were worshipping within, and the MacDonells of Glen Garry took a similar venge-

In Glen Coe.

ance on the MacKenzies at the church of Urray in Mid Ross. The MacLeods of Dunvegan wiped out the population of Eigg by suffocating them in a cave where they had hidden. Why, then, does the massacre of Glen Coe stand out in unenviable prominence among all the dark deeds of clan warfare? It is, I think, because at Glen Coe the sacred code of highland hospitality was deliberately and callously violated.

Glen Coe is in northern Argyll, in sight of the county of

Inverness across the tidal waters of Loch Leven. It is a wild and gloomy glen, a fit place for the tragedy that was enacted here on a bitter February dawn in the year 1692. Great hills rise almost sheer from the glen. Chief of them is Bidean nam Beann (3,766 feet high), the most lofty peak in Argyllshire. Near it stand other peaks almost as high. Beinn Fhada (the Long Hill) is 3,500 feet above sea level, Stob Coire an Lochain reaches a height of 3,657 feet, while at the head of the glen the Great Herdsman of Etive rises in gloomy austerity to an altitude of 3,345 feet above the Atlantic. Through a dark gorge the river Cona or Coe enters the glen and flows swiftly seawards. In Glen Coe the Fingalians hunted the red deer and on the rocky flank of Aonach Dubh is Ossian's Cave, while near the foot of the glen, to the east of the river, is a fine peak named Sgùrr na Féinne, the Fingalians' Hill. Below this hill is Loch Leven, and the islands of this loch have associations with early days. The largest of the isles is Eilean Mhunna, generally spoken of as St. Munn's Island. The ownership of this island was claimed by the Camerons of Callart and the MacDonalds of Glen Coe. Each in turn took a crop of hay off it. Finally, it was agreed that the MacDonalds of Glen Coe should have undivided ownership of the island. Near Eilean Mhunna is a smaller island, Eilean a' Chomhraidh or the Isle of Discussion. This was the meeting-place of those persons who had disputes with their neighbours on the land question, and perhaps on other matters besides. When their disputes had been settled satisfactorily the erstwhile disputants sailed up the loch to Eilean na Bainne. This is the Isle of Covenant or Ratification ; here the agreements were drawn up and sealed.[1]

From Glen Coe several side glens wind into the hill country and are soon lost to view. The chief of these glens is Gleann Leac na Muidhe, a grassy glen thickly populated at the time of the massacre. Few people now live in Glen Coe, but in 1692 a large population inhabited the glen. Every yard of suitable ground

[1] This information I received from the late Canon MacInnes, of Glen Coe.

was at that time under cultivation. In places the slopes rose so steeply that low walls of turf and stone had to be built to keep the soil from being washed away by the winter floods. Upwards of one thousand cows were pastured in the glen, besides horses, sheep and goats.

Although the massacre of Glen Coe took place more than two hundred and forty years ago, the old people of the glen speak of it to-day as though it were a recent event and, even now, no Campbell is happy in Glen Coe. Most of the older people are Episcopalians, and I believe St. Mary's of Glen Coe is the only Episcopal church of Scotland at the present time where a Gaelic service is held each Sunday. A broad road, straight as a railway line, has now been driven through Glen Coe. No longer does the traveller follow the old picturesque track along which cattle and sheep from the western seaboard and the Isles were driven to the Falkirk market. The late Canon MacInnes, one of the oldest sons of the glen and a man of much lore and old history, told me that he remembered, as a boy, the herds being driven southward through the glen. He often used to ride bareback on the unbroken island ponies as they passed, and when he was tossed he would go home and say nothing about it. The drovers of seventy years ago, he told me, sometimes wore the kilt, but even when they were not in highland dress they had broad bonnets, occasionally so much the worse for wear that their owners' hair could be seen sticking out through the holes!

The old road, with all its associations, has gone, but the new speedway has not spoiled the appearance of the glen as much as I had feared. The worst feature is, I think, an unsightly bridge near Kingshouse, at the head of the glen. An advantage of the new road is that its broad and even surface permits the driver of a car to look about him and admire the scenery as he could never have done on the old road. He can see, for example, how aptly named is the rocky knoll marked on the maps as the Study. But he should first know the history of the word. "Study" is broad Scots for "Anvil," and the Gaelic name for the rocky spur is Inneoin, meaning an Anvil. Thus the map-name "Study" is wholly misleading, but the Gaelic name is a remarkably apt one, for that part of the hill-side has a close resemblance to a smith's anvil.

As I climbed Glen Coe on a night of full moon at the season of the roaring of the stags, I seemed to hear an echo of that grim tragedy of long ago. The events which led up to the massacre are somewhat as follows. The chiefs of the highland clans were required to swear allegiance to King William's government before the first day of January 1692. MacDonald of Glen Coe put off the distasteful task until the last possible minute. Mac-Iain (to give him his Gaelic title) was a man " of stately and venerable presence," and it is likely that at his time of life he was reluctant to travel far from home at the dead of winter. When he could no longer put off the matter he rode his pony to Fort William, and called upon Colonel Hill in order to take the oath of allegiance. Hill told the old chieftain that he was not qualified to swear him, and that it would be necessary for him to ride to distant Inveraray, to swear before Sir Colin Campbell of Ardkin-glas, the sheriff. The weather, we are told in a contemporary letter, was " extreme " and MacIain made his way with difficulty along roads almost impassable with snow-drifts, arriving at Inveraray one day late. So great was his haste that he did not call and tell his family his plans, although he passed within six miles of his house. That one day was to have disastrous consequences for MacIain and his clan, for when he reached Inveraray he found the sheriff was from home, and so had to wait impatiently three days for his return. When Sir Colin arrived he at first declined to swear MacIain, since the time allowed by the proclamation for taking the oath had expired, but when it was represented to him that the snow-bound state of the roads had added greatly to the length of the old chieftain's journey he yielded, and administered the oath to MacDonald and his attendants on January 6.

MacIain, his anxious mind reassured, returned to his glen, and was living there quietly when, one day at the end of January,

a party from the Earl of Argyll's Regiment, to the number of
120 men under the command of Captain Campbell of Glen Lyon,
were seen approaching. Glenlyon and MacIain were none too
friendly, for the MacDonalds of Glen Coe when returning from
the battle of Killiecrankie had raided the cattle of Glen Lyon,
and had cleared the glen of the herds. Accordingly, when the
Campbell regiment was seen the people of the glen had their

Glen Coe.

suspicions instantly aroused. MacIain's elder son, at the head
of twenty men, went forward and demanded from Glenlyon his
reason for coming into a peaceful country with a military force.
Glenlyon asserted that they had come as friends, and he and
his officers " gave Parole of Honour that they would do neither
MacIain nor his Concerns any Harm." They requested that
they might find quarters with the people of Glen Coe, giving as
their reason the " thronged " state of the garrison at Inverlochy.
Alexander, the younger son of MacIain, was married to Glen-

lyon's niece, and so it was only natural that the chieftain and his people should have accepted the word of honour given by the commanding officer of the party. As the days passed mistrust gradually gave place to goodwill, for the soldiers were friendly and many were doubtless Gaelic-speaking men like the families with whom they lived. For a fortnight the military party remained in Glen Coe. The men themselves may have been unaware at first of the sinister nature of their errand, but the higher command had sent them there for a definite purpose, and on February 12 the following letter was received by the officer stationed at Ballachulish, who in turn communicated it to Captain Campbell of Glen Lyon :

" SIR,
         Persuand to the commander in chief's and my Collonel's orders to me for putting in execution the service commanded against the rebells in Glencoe, wherein yow, with the party of the Earl of Argile's regiment under your command, are to be concerned, yow are therefore forthwith to order your affairs, so that the several posts already assigned by yow be, by yow and your several detatchments, fallen in action with precisely, by five o'clock to-morrow morning, being Saturday : at which time I will endeavour the same with those appointed from this regiment for the other places. It will be most necessary that yow secure the avenues to the south, that the old fox, nor none of his cubs, may gett away. The orders are, that none be spared from 70 of the sword, nor the Government troubled with prisoners. This is all untill I see you, from
                                        " Your humble servant
                                              (Signed) JAMES HAMILTON.

" P.S.   Please order a guard to secure the Ferry and the boats there, and the boats must be all on this syde the Ferry after your men are over."

Let us picture the scene at the time this letter, almost incredible in its baseness, was written. We know that deep snow covered the glen and that the cold was intense. The Earl of Argyll's Regiment was quartered up and down Glen Coe. The late Canon MacInnes told me that, according to the tradition of the glen, MacIain himself was not (as has been usually inferred in the accounts written of the massacre) at his house at Invercoe, but was living at his sheep farm in Gleann Leac na Muidhe, farther up the glen. The old chieftain, " of great integrity, honour, good nature and courage," was unsuspecting of treachery to the last. Perhaps his nature refused to believe that Scotsmen and highlanders could, at a moment's notice, turn against those from whom they had, from day to day, accepted many kindnesses. At all events, as a letter written on April 20 of the year of the massacre puts on record, " the very last day of his life he played at cards with Captain Campbell of Glen Lyon till six or seven o'clock at night." The parting between the two men was most friendly, and Glenlyon actually accepted an invitation to dinner on the following day.

By its very villainy, the plot for the massacre partially miscarried. Some of the better natures among the soldiers rebelled against the part they were called upon to play, and it was because of this that MacIain's two sons escaped. Alexander, the elder son, apparently was the only member of his family who mistrusted Glenlyon, and on the night before the massacre his suspicions made him leave the house. Seeing a party of soldiers in the snow he approached them unseen under cover of darkness, and overheard one of the men say to the other that there were some things which even a private soldier could not be expected to do, and that he was willing to fight the men of the glen, but he held that it was base to murder them. His companion replied that duty was duty, however unpleasant it might be. Alexander, his suspicions confirmed, returned to his father's house, and warned MacIain of his peril. But even then the old man refused to leave. He thought his son's suspicions were exaggerated, but he agreed that Alexander should continue his watch, and should keep him informed of any further developments. These events took place in Gleann Leac na Muidhe.

About the same time, lower down the main glen, a soldier quartered on two brothers named Eanruig asked his hosts to take an evening walk with him. Addressing a large stone in the field, the soldier spoke thus to it : " Grey stone, if I were you, I would be shifting from here, for great things will happen to-night." The brothers reacted differently to this obvious warning. One of them did not return to the house, and thus escaped the massacre. The other, believing that the soldier was indulging in a form of pleasantry, went to his bed that night as usual, and paid for his rashness with his life.

At five o'clock the following morning, before the pale fingers of dawn had fired the eastern sky, the silence of the snow-bound glen was broken by the report of a gun or small cannon. This was the signal for the massacre to begin, in three different places simultaneously. The soldiers, disposed five or three in a house according to the number of people they were to murder, at once set about the horrid business. MacIain (his sons had endeavoured to warn him a second time but had found the house closely surrounded by troops) as he lay sleepless on his bed heard stern shouts and a beating upon his door. " Hurriedly drawing on his breeches," we read, " he hastened to the door, to receive a mortal wound from a gun fired at point-blank range. He fell back into the arms of his lady, who uttered a dreadful shriek. She was stripped naked, ruffians pulled the rings from her fingers with their teeth, and she received such treatment that she died the following day." Meanwhile deeds of violence were being done in other houses. Men and boys were killed without mercy. One young lad, whose parents had been massacred before his eyes, ran wildly from the house, and offered, in return for his life, to be the officer's servant for the rest of his days. A knife thrust into his heart was the answer given him. A woman with her baby struggled through the snow to the bed of a burn on a precipitous hillside, where she hid. An officer noticed her footprints in the snow, and sent a soldier after the pair. The man unwillingly obeyed, but on going beyond the officer's sight killed a dog and, returning, showed the blood on his sword as a proof that he had carried out the order. The officer believed him, and so the woman and her child escaped.

Thirty-eight of MacDonald's people were murdered in cold blood. Double that number perished in the mad flight across the hill passes, " wrestling with a storm, in mountains and heaps of snow." Colonel Hamilton, stationed at Kingshouse with

400 men, was ordered to march down the glen before daybreak, and cut off those who sought to escape towards the south. Whether, according to one tradition, he thoroughly disliked the work and made the severe weather an excuse for arriving late on the scene, or whether the snow did indeed delay him, he certainly arrived tardily, and his delay undoubtedly saved many lives, for the people had taken to the hills before he reached the glen. He contented himself with firing the houses and driving the cattle, horses and sheep down Glen Coe and across Loch Leven to be divided among the garrison at Inverlochy. He is also credited with having killed an old man of over eighty, the sole remaining member of the clan of the MacDonalds whom he found in the glen. In a contemporary letter it is mentioned that 900 cows, 200 horses, besides a great many sheep and goats, were driven from the glen. These figures alone show that Glen Coe must have supported a considerable population at the time.

MacIain's clansmen, taken by surprise, were seldom able to defend themselves in the blackness of that hour before a winter dawn, but it is known that at least three men of Argyll's regiment were killed. The grave of one is still pointed out. It is beneath a very old hawthorn bush which, in the tradition of the glen, was of a considerable age even at the time of the massacre. The tree is carefully protected by Lord Strathcona, who now owns that part of the glen where it grows. Two other soldiers were buried at a place called Cladh nan Guibhneach, near the old road. The word *Guibhneach* is dialectic for *Duibhneach*, a man of the Campbell clan, from *Duibhne*, the eponymous ancestor of the House.[1] Cladh nan Duibhneach is the Burial-place of the Campbells.

Most of the MacDonalds who survived the massacre made their way across a high hill pass that leads out of Gleann Leac na Muidhe to Loch Etive. The women were scantily clad, some in their night attire, carrying babies and young children. Great snow wreaths obliterated the track. The frost was intense.

[1] For this information I am indebted to Professor W. J. Watson.

Weary, perished with cold, struggling up the pass with icy fear at their hearts, there is little wonder that many fell down and died in an inhospitable country. And those who succeeded in crossing the pass and reaching dark Glen Etive—what welcome awaited them there? We can infer something of that welcome from a letter addressed by Secretary Dalrymple to Colonel Hill, the Governor of Fort William. Dalrymple writes: " The earls of Argyle and Breadalbane were promised that they (the Mac-Donalds of Glen Coe) shall have no retreat in their bounds; the passes to Rannoch would be secured." A party of troops were also to be stationed on Island Stalker on Loch Linnhe, to cut off the fugitives if their line of retreat should pass near the coast.

Deplorable as the massacre of Glen Coe was, it fell far short of the original bloody plan. The Master of Stair, in a letter to Sir Thomas Livingston on January 7—five weeks before the massacre—writes: " You know that these troops posted at Inverness and Inverlochie will be ordered to take in the house of Innergarie and to destroy entirely the country of Lochaber, Lochiel's lands, Keppoch's, Glengarie's and Glenco," and he adds: " I hope the soldiers will not trouble the government with prisoners." His plan miscarried because Lochiel, Glengarry and Keppoch all took the oath of allegiance in good time. But his special hatred was directed against the MacDonalds of Glen Coe, for in another letter to Livingston, written on January 30, he says: " I am glad Glenco did not come in within the time prefixed."

The effect of the massacre upon the highlands, and indeed upon Britain as a whole, was profound. Lochiel, Glengarry and other chiefs at once rid themselves of those troops quartered on them, and made common cause, and for a time it seemed as if a great rising were probable. And what of the feelings of the murderers? " Glenco," says a contemporary letter, " hangs about Glenlyon night and day, and you may see him in his face." Glenlyon and his descendants fully believed that the curse of Glen Coe was upon them, and that in this curse lay the root of their subsequent misfortunes.

On a day of north wind, when the hill-tops were white with freshly fallen snow, I crossed Glen Coe and climbed the side glen where MacIain met his death. There is now but one house in that glen, and yet it can be seen from the old ruins that here was once a numerous population. The site of MacIain's house is barely visible, for a hill torrent has brought down much debris through the centuries, and has buried part of the ruins. The present occupant of the land, while lifting potatoes some years ago, came upon an old pipe chanter here. The chanter may have belonged to MacIain's piper. It was given away, and its present whereabouts is unfortunately unknown. At the same spot old plates and dishes were also dug up, and it is not long since MacIain's hearthstone was still visible. From this narrow glen the hills rise steeply. The pass winds unseen among the clouds and is so formidable that even the deer seldom cross it in winter. But on that tragic February day men, women, and even small children, toiled up this bleak pass, and through the drifting snow looked down upon red flames rising eagerly from what, only the evening before, had been a happy township.

CHAPTER XXIX

FORT WILLIAM AND THE APPIN COUNTRY

FORT WILLIAM, now an important town of the west coast, is built in the shadow of Ben Nevis, and at one time was the terminus of the West Highland Railway. The importance of the town has largely increased during recent years because of the great works carried out by the Grampian Electricity Company, works which are not yet (1934) completed. A tunnel has been driven through Ben Nevis, bringing to the town a great volume of water from Loch Treig in the hills, and further water power has been obtained from distant Loch Laggan.

Fort William received its name from an old fort which was built at the north end of the town. The fort was built of earth by General Monk in 1655, and in the time of William III was rebuilt of stone. The function of the fort was to keep order in what the Crown considered to be a lawless highland district.

There are two noteworthy things to be seen in Fort William to-day. The first is the West Highland Museum, a museum which is full of interesting old highland relics and owes much to the enthusiasm of the late Mr. Victor Hodgson of Onich; the second is a remarkably fine statue of Lochiel, twenty-fifth Chief of the Clan and father of the present chief, who was for long Member of Parliament for Inverness-shire and was a man greatly beloved throughout the highlands. Each year the well-known highland games of the Lochaber Gathering are held in Fort William, and periodically the Gaelic National Festival of Music and Literature is also held here.

From Fort William[1] (the Garrison, it is still called by Gaelic-

[1] At least one of the old rooms of the Fort is still in use at the present time.

speaking people) to Oban by the coast is a distance of just under
fifty miles.   The district is better seen on foot than in a car, for
a motor-car passes all too quickly through a country that is full
of variety and beauty.   For the first few miles the road skirts
the margin of " An Linne Dhubh," as the upper part of Loch
Linnhe is named.   Across the loch are the trees and lofty hills
of Conaglen, where, rather more than one hundred years ago,
MacDonell of Glengarry, perhaps the last great highland chief
who lived royally in the old tradition, lost his life after the ship-
wreck of the vessel in which he was sailing to Glasgow.   Off the
low cape of Corran, where a lighthouse stands, the sea loch
narrows, and then broadens greatly a little distance to the south-
west, where the lower part of Loch Linnhe begins.   It should be
noted that Loch Linnhe, like the word Hebrides, is a " ghost "
name, and the correct name of this celebrated sea loch is really
" An Linne Sheileach," the second part of the name (according to
some authorities) meaning salt water which is largely mixed with
fresh.   It is certainly true that in wet weather the rivers and
innumerable burns which empty themselves into the loch
pour into it a vast volume of fresh water.   Beyond the village
of Onich is the Ballachulish ferry, and here are two alternatives
open to the traveller by car.   He may either ferry his car across
the mouth of Loch Leven, and in this manner enter the county of
Argyll, or may drive past Callart (full of old associations) to Kinlochleven at the head of Loch Leven, and return down the farther
shore of the loch, passing the mouth of Glen Coe, to south Ballachulish.   Kinlochleven is a thriving town, and some of my readers may
remember the fierce verbal battle which was fought a few years ago
between the counties of Inverness and Argyll when the county of
Argyll endeavoured unsuccessfully to claim the whole of the town,
which stands partly in Argyllshire and partly in Inverness-shire.

At South Ballachulish, within a stone's throw of the ferry, is a
small wooded knoll.   Here, in the year 1752, took place an event
which stirred the highlands from end to end—the hanging of
James of the Glen for the murder of him who has sometimes been

P

known as the Red Fox, Colin Campbell of Glenure.   It is now almost two hundred years since Campbell of Glenure fell dead from two shots fired from what has been immortalised as the Black Gun of the Misfortune, as he was travelling southward along the old road on the hillside between Ballachulish and Kentallen while on his way to evict certain Jacobite tenants from the estate of Ardsheal.   An old cairn stands at the place where Glenure died, but few persons have seen it, for the present road does not pass within sight of the spot.   After the two shots had been fired a man with a gun was seen running away up the hill, but he was too far off to be recognised by Glenure's attendants and to this day there is doubt as to who he really was.   James Stewart of the Glen, who then lived at the farm-house of Acharn in Duror, brought suspicion upon himself and was arrested because of injudicious remarks he had been overheard some time previously to pass on Campbell of Glenure.   He was subsequently tried in the old court house of Inveraray and paid the penalty, as some people think unjustly, with his life.   Protesting his innocence to the last, and forgiving those who had brought him to his death, he was hung from a gibbet erected on this knoll.   It was on a day of fearful tempest, the month being November, and after the unfortunate man had been hung his body remained, chained to the gallows, for several years.   It was closely guarded by soldiers, and when at length the bones of the skeleton were shaken to the ground by the wind they were carefully replaced and were fastened by wire.   More than two years after the hanging, the skeleton fell to the earth during a storm on January 30, 1755, but was again hung up on February 17 of the same year.   It was firmly believed that the holes in the ground where the gibbet formerly stood could not be filled in. I recently spoke with an old man who told me that as a boy he had himself, in a spirit of light-heartedness, filled in the holes, but when he visited the place shortly afterwards he found that they had opened again.   At length the skeleton of James of the Glen was taken away secretly, but none dare touch the gibbet until a man " not altogether right in his mind " threw it into the loch. Here the tides took charge of the sinister emblem, and cast it ashore at Port na Croise in Appin. The people of the district cast the hated object once more into the sea and it was borne by the currents to the shore of Morvern. Here again it was washed ashore at Port na Croise, the Port of the Cross—an event not without significance in the minds of the country people. The people of Morvern feared to touch the gibbet, but at length a farmer had it removed and made into a bridge.

In Appin, James Stewart of the Glen was universally believed to be innocent of the crime for which he was hung. There were certain families of the district who knew who the murderer of Glenure was, but their oath of secrecy was so binding that the mystery remains unsolved to the present day. Allan Breac, soldier of fortune, was by some believed to be the man seen running up the hill after the shots were fired, and tradition narrates that he was accompanied by Cameron of Mamore, but the identity of the real murderer has never been disclosed by the few families who have handed down the secret from one generation to another.

Let us visualise that day of 1752 when Campbell of Glenure and the sheriff officer and his servant, were travelling along the narrow road at Lettermore. Campbell of Glenure on his mother's side was a Cameron of Lochiel, and was by all accounts a decent easy-going fellow who acted as factor on the confiscated Ardsheal estates for the modest sum of ten guineas a year. At one time he and James of the Glen were on friendly terms and the letting of the farms of the forfeited estate was largely left to James. But after a time the factor was cautioned by the higher authorities to be more stern in his dealings, and his former popularity was replaced by mistrust and dislike. Then came the day when Glenure was on his way to evict Jacobite families, the journey in single file along a narrow road, two shots fired in quick succession, and a dying man unselfishly calling upon his companions to save themselves and leave him to his fate.

The hanging of James Stewart of the Glen has left an impression on the district almost as profound as the massacre of Glen Coe. The wind that drifts up the narrows of the sea loch and the mists that crowd in upon Beinn Bhéir still whisper the secret. On a late September day I stood on the little knoll where that tragedy was enacted. It was one of those beautiful autumn days when the spirit of peace enfolds hill, glen and sea. The air was scented; about Beinn Bhéir the mist was wreathing darkly. The place was full of the spirit of old times and the flood tide surged into Loch Leven through the narrows as it has done twice daily since the Appin murder. Across Loch Linnhe gleamed the waterfall of Ardgour that is named MacLean's Towel. The MacLeans of Ardgour have been for centuries on the land from which they derive their title. They escaped the troubles of the neighbouring clans during the eighteenth century, and have continued in uninterrupted succession ever since that day, in the early fifteenth century, when the first MacLean of Ardgour with the good-will of the Lord of the Isles drove MacMaster from his Ardgour lands at the point of the sword.

A few miles to the south-west of the present house of Ardgour is a cave on the shore of Loch Linnhe where Stewart of Appin was in hiding during the troublous times of the '45.

It is perhaps in spring that Ardgour is most beautiful. The house is surrounded by rhododendrons of many kinds, and when the swallows arrive in April they flit above an aerial carpet of crimson, pink, mauve and white, while the grassy banks are scented by innumerable daffodils, primroses and wild hyacinths. In summer the sun shines down upon Ardgour with almost tropical heat. I remember one June day when the sun rode high in the heavens, the air was calm, and scarcely a cloud rested against the deep blue of the sky. But with awe-inspiring swiftness a thunder-cloud, born above Ben Nevis, grew and spread over the face of the land. For a time the sun still shone, intensifying the black canopy of cloud that grew menacingly above the hills. Twilight descended on Ardgour—a twilight that was broken by a blinding flash of lightning. And now came flash after flash, while peal upon peal of thunder broke the stillness and suspense of nature. The rain fell in torrents, shaking the leaves of the old trees as though a summer gale were agitating them. Thunder reverberated among the hills; from Glen Coe to Ardgour the air was full of deep roarings and echoings. MacLean's Towel increased in size and leaped exultingly from the high hills to the sea loch. But, amid that scene of tumult, the swallows flitted happily around the old house, heedless of the lightning and the crash of the thunder, and intent only in capturing insects for their hungry broods in their nests.

South of Appin the road winds past Duror and Ardsheal through a sheltered and wooded country. Here in the fourteenth century ruled Iain Dubh nan Lann, Black John of the Sword-blades, a mighty fighter. A picturesque old castle is seen on a small island of Loch Linnhe, near the mainland. It is known as Castle Stalker, described in MacFarlane's *Geographical Collections* as " A pretty tour in the Appin built on a rock in the sea, verie near the land, callit Iland Stalker." This castle, which is a simple square tower, is believed to have been built by Duncan Stewart of Appin for King James IV during his hunting excursions in the district. Duncan Stewart himself was appointed keeper of the castle. The island on which the castle stands and from which it receives its name is Eilean an Stalcaire, the Island of the Stalker or Deer Hunter.

The road to the south leads past Achnacon and Fasnacloiche, Druim na Mhuic and Barcaldine. On the shore of Loch Nell the traveller reaches, at the village of Ledaig, what perhaps may have been the historical Beregonium—the seat of the ancient Pictish monarchy. The original name of the place according to the late Alexander Carmichael was Barr na Gobhann, the Ridge of the Armourers, and he believed it to have been Latinised by George Buchanan into Beregonium. It was also known as Dùn mhic Uisneachan, the Fort of the Sons of Uisneach. This old fortified site is a small green hill by the shore of the loch. The

Atlantic swell breaks with deep sighings on the long beach of pebbles at the foot of Beregonium, and beyond the line of waves are the green deeps of the sea. The main pass which leads to the top of the small green hill is known by the old people as Bealach Banruinn Fhionnghail, the Pass of Fingal's Queen. Few traces remain to-day of the royal fortified castle where Pictish kings had their home. On the autumn day when I stood on the *dùn* the

Dunstaffnage.

air was hazy, and it was scarcely possible to see the hills of Mull, faint across the sea. Whins and brambles grew on the slopes of the little hill, and over the top flitted a tortoise-shell butterfly— a fragile emblem of to-day passing lightly and carelessly above the more enduring works of a past age. Beregonium was a vitrified fort, and it is believed that there were no fewer than seven forts on the same hill and the ridge which leads from it. On the opposite side of the public road stood Dùn Bhalaire, the name perhaps commemorating Balor of the Evil Eye, the mighty Fer

Bolg whose glance was death to him on whom that eye might rest.

The whole district of Beregonium is rich in tradition. South, across the swift stream of Lora, is the old castle of Dunstaffnage where the Lia Fail (the Stone of Destiny, on which the early Irish kings were crowned) rested for a time. This stone is said to have been brought across the sea from Ireland by Fergus Mór, the first king of Dalriada. The Lia Fail remained at Dunstaffnage until it was removed by Kenneth MacAlpine to Scone. There it was encased in a chair of wood, and in 1296 Edward I carried off the stone with its chair to England. It was placed below the throne in Westminster Abbey, and has remained there until the present day. North-west, across the blue waters of the sea, rises the Island of Lismore, where, according to local tradition, the Pictish Royal Family were buried. On a lesser isle of Lismore, Berneray by name, grew a yew tree so large that a thousand persons might find shelter beneath it. Tradition narrates that Columba preached below the mighty branches of this venerable yew and prophesied that a curse should rest on him who should at any time injure the tree. The life of that man, said the saint, would be short, and his inheritance would not be lasting. The tree is said to have been cut down by one of the Lochnell Campbells and a stairway made from it for his new castle. The malediction was fulfilled : the life of the builder was short and the castle was twice burnt to the ground.

When the sun sinks behind the Mull hills and Beregonium is bathed in a glowing aura the spirit of the past descends upon the place. One can visualise the royal galleys approaching up the loch and kings and great men alighting on the dark rocks beneath the royal fortress, for there is an echo of the past in the soft sighings of lonely waves breaking on a quiet shore.

CHAPTER XXX

GLEN ETIVE : THE LAND OF DEIRDRE

> Glen Etive !
> There I built my first house;
> Lovely its woods after rising.

ONE summer evening when the world was young, Fergus of royal Irish lineage sailed up Loch Etive in his war galley the " Iubhrach." From the bay at the head of the loch, Fergus, emissary of King Conchobar, gave a great shout that was caught up by the Herdsman standing sentinel at the head of the glen. The shout re-echoed through the corries of Ben Starav; the ptarmigan upon the stony face of Bidean nam Beann heard it; the stags of the Royal Forest of Dalness lifted their heads from the fresh green grass.

Deirdre, fairest of women, and her lover Naoise, most comely of men, were sitting in their hunting booth playing at draughts. Deirdre, with the second sight upon her, knew that shout of Fergus. She knew also that it foretold disaster to her beloved. She therefore endeavoured to persuade Naoise that he had heard the voice of no stranger but a native of the glen. Thrice was the great shout repeated. Naoise could no longer be restrained. He leaped to his feet, knowing that this indeed was Fergus, Knight of the Red Branch, and sent his brother down the glen to welcome him. How Deirdre and Naoise crossed the sea with Fergus to Ireland in the " Iubhrach " and how tragic disaster overtook them is told unforgettably as one of the " Three Sorrows of Story Telling," and as the galley sailed westward down Loch Etive Deirdre sang her lament of simple beauty that has come down to us through the long years.

The old traditions concerning Deirdre and the Sons of Uisneach are fast dying in Glen Etive, but the site of Deirdre's home is still known. It is on a grassy slope across the river from the lodge at Dalness. A hundred years ago the old people of Glen Etive could point to the three apple trees of Naoise and his brothers Ainnle and Ardan, but the whereabouts of that old garden is now unknown. Even the names of the three Knights of the Red Branch have been forgotten, and the name of Deirdre alone remains as a faint memory in the glen.

On a stormy day of autumn I saw Glen Etive from the source of the river at Lochan Màthair Eite (the Mother-loch of Etive) to the sea. The rowans that day were dark rose-red. Objects of beauty, they sheltered in the gorges (clinging to the naked rocks with sturdy roots) from the storms that were brewed by the nymph of Etive on the loch far beneath. The golden leaves of the birches were set adrift on the gusts that bent and harried the old trees. Winter was near. At the head of the glen rose the snowy cone of the Buachaille Mór [1] over which the speeding mists from time to time drew a thin grey veil. Glen Etive drops quickly to the waters of the sea. Beside the clear impetuous river fieldfares and redwings, Norse invaders to the Celtic west, clustered upon the berry-laden rowan trees, eagerly devouring the ripe fruit.

Where the river Etive turns abruptly from west to south-west was Deirdre's home, on the grassy slope that rises from the south bank of the river. Here was her *grianan* or sunny bower, and the small peak of Stob Grianan perhaps commemorates the place. The hill-sides are dark and frowning and hard to climb. Across the river from the *grianan* a waterfall of great height leaps from the mists. Here Deirdre roamed the hills with Naoise. Together they hunted the red deer. They were supremely happy in one another's company and had no thought for the dark tragedy that was soon to come to them. Surely an echo of their sadness remains in Glen Etive to-day. But there is none living who saw them, save perhaps Eiteag, the

[1] The Great Herdsman, a well-known hill at the head of Loch Etive.

goddess of the glen and the loch. Eiteag is not often abroad, these years, but in earlier times she was feared because of the sudden storms she raised on Loch Etive, sending the ships driving wildly before the squalls as the spindrift from the loch sought the lowering clouds.

But Deirdre as she sat within her *grianan* was beyond the reach of the loch and its petulant goddess. She saw the eagles sail high overhead and cross the brow of the Great Herdsman. The salmon that crowded the linn pool at Dalness were her companions. She could watch the hinds as they crossed from Glen Etive to Glen Coe through Lairig Eilte, the Hinds' Pass, and see the stags as they climbed at sunrise of a summer morning from the shadowed glen to the splendour of the high tops. At night the distant murmur of the great waterfall lulled her to sleep; she awoke to see the sun golden upon Buachaille Etive Mór.

Old traditions with difficulty withstand the present age of unrest, but at Dalness is to be seen a relic of one of the most famous trials in the history of the highlands—the gun by which Campbell of Glenure, the Red Fox, met his death. In Chapter XXIX I have written of this, called usually the Appin Murder. James Stewart of the Glen, before a Campbell jury, was convicted of the murder of Glenure at the court house at Inveraray. He was, as most people believed and still believe, convicted unjustly. The secret of who killed the Red Fox has been handed down to the people of the Glen Coe district from one generation to another and is still guarded closely in their hearts. Could this old rusty gun but speak it might settle a controversy that is likely to continue far into the future.

Many steep hills rise from Glen Etive. One of them is Beinn Fhada, the Long Hill, which reaches a height of 3,500 feet. After a night of storm came a morning of clear sunrise and light airs, and from the head of Glen Etive Beinn Dobhrain and its surroundings hills were seen to rise clear of mist to the quiet sky. From Dalness, the home of the hereditary keepers of the Royal Forest, a friend and I climbed to

Beinn Fhada by way of the Lairig Eilte, a very old right of way
leading across to Glen Coe. A few hundred yards up the Lairig
a number of great boulders lay near the track. They are
known as the Clachan Reamhair. On the path, a little way
beyond them, is a flat stone which is known as Clach an t-Suidhe,
the Stone of the Seat. There is a tradition that Campbell of
Inverawe signed the title-deeds of Dalness on this stone, Mac-
Donald of Dalness keeping him at the place while he (Inverawe)
sent his servant home for the deeds. The inference is that
Campbell obtained the title-deeds by some trickery. The Mac-
Donalds of Dalness were a sept of the MacDonalds of Glen Coe.
They were generally known as Clann Reubhair or Clann Reum-
hair. Reubhar or Reumhar is a personal name. It is, Professor
Watson assures me, a very rare Gaelic personal name, and he
knows of no other instance of the name in Celtic literature.

At the watershed between Etive and Coe we left the Lairig
and climbed a steep grassy face to the ridge of Beinn Fhada.
From the glen and the corries came the roaring of stags. Big
stags could be seen to roam restlessly in search of hinds, and
others, more fortunate than they, were busy rounding up their
ladies and anxiously watching the movements of rivals. A pair
of grey crows crossed high above the hill-top, then dropped in
wild corkscrew dives into the deep corrie. On the ridge at
3,000 feet puffs of icy wind rose from the sunless depths of the
corrie beneath us. Away to the south were the bens of Jura,
faint in gathering haze. Far below us Loch Etive led away west
into the grey distance. Down in Glen Etive the sun shone upon
Stob Grianan, the Sunny Peak where was Deirdre's bower that
was " thatched with the royal fern, and lined with pine and
with the down feathers of birds." It is said that deer of the
hill could be shot from the window and salmon could be caught
from the door of the *grianan*. Loch Etive, almost eighteen
miles long, is one of the few Scottish lochs to-day which have
no road near them, and therefore to reach the head of the loch
from the west it is necessary to travel by sea, passing on the way

the great granite quarry at Bonawe. The loch is one of the few sea lochs in the west where sea-trout rise to the fly in salt water.

Clouds rested on Cruachan Beann, but Stob Ghabhar and the other peaks of the Black Mount Forest were clear. Far to the east was the graceful cone of Schiehallion. A pair of ptarmigan rose from the hill-side near us. Snow covered the hill-top; the sun for a few brief moments shone, and the snow at once became so dazzling that the eye was almost blinded. Then the sun was hidden; with incredible swiftness a dark cloud spread from the west across the whole of the sky. Through deepening gloom the hills of Mull were seen and the long green island of Lismore. Beyond Lismore the Lady's Rock was dark. To the east Ben Nevis was in mist, but the snowy slopes of Ben Alder caught the last of the sunshine. Flurries of wind played upon Loch Etive : the water sprite was awakening. Waves were lapping against the small island that was named after the Sons of Uisneach long ago.

Nearly three thousand feet below us was Coire Gabhail, where the cattle of Glen Coe were driven during a raid. The sides of this corrie are so steep that it was possible by placing a tree across the only entrance to hide the cattle from view and to keep them from wandering back to the main glen. Less than a mile from us rose the snowy top of Bidean nam Beann, highest of Argyllshire peaks. The Ordnance map names this hill Bidean nam Bian, but according to the late Canon MacInnes of Glen Coe, a scholar and native Gaelic speaker, the correct name for the hill is Bidean nam Beann, which may be translated, the Chief of all the Hills. The Canon pointed out to me how aptly the old people named this hill, as accurate surveying has determined that it is indeed the highest mountain in the county of Argyll.

The day wore on. Somewhere a raven croaked; stag answered stag. The clouds thickened and mist advanced on the rising and backing wind : a storm seemed imminent. The autumn day faded and at dusk increasing showers of rain hid hill and glen and the stormy waters of Loch Etive.

CHAPTER XXXI

THE COUNTRY OF LORNE

In the early years of the sixth century three princes of Ireland, Loarn, Fergus and Angus, sailed north to Alba and there founded three distinct settlements. Angus occupied Islay, Jura, and

Lorne.

Iona. Fergus took Cantyre, Cowall and the southern districts of Argyll. Loarn laid claim to the territory which still (more than fourteen hundred years later) bears his name. Fergus, the youngest of the princes, survived his brothers and united the three settlements : he formed the kingdom of Dalriada and was proclaimed its king. The new kingdom soon absorbed Mull and Morvern, Ardgour, Lochaber and Ardnamurchan, and finally stretched from Ardnamurchan Point to the Firth of Clyde.

It is believed that Loarn, and subsequently Fergus, lived partly in the old castle of Dunstaffnage which stands near the entrance to Loch Etive, a few miles north-east of Oban. At a

Cruachan from Firth of Lorne.

later date Dunstaffnage was traditionally occupied by the Scottish kings down to the time of Kenneth II, but was abandoned as a royal residence in the ninth century. From that

Seil.

time until the year 1300 there is no mention of Dunstaffnage in the annals of Scotland, the reason being doubtless that the district of Lorne was held by the Norsemen during most of that period.

The traveller to Dunstaffnage and Oban may take the road

Entrance to Oban Bay.

from Ballachulish through the country of Appin, or may make his way from the east, across the windy moor of Rannoch, where, at Druimliart beside Inveroran, are the ruins of the home of that immortal bard of the Gael, Duncan Ban MacIntyre, he who is known as Donachadh Bàn nan Oran, Fair-haired Duncan of the Songs. From Loch Baa with its pleasant islands the traveller, crossing the Blackmount Forest, may descend friendly Glen Orchy (Gleann Urchaidh), of which Deirdre sings in her lament on leaving Alba—" Glen Urchain ! that was the straight, fair-ridged glen." At the foot of Glen Orchy is the old ruined smithy at Barachastalain, the home of the MacNabs, hereditary smiths and armourers to the Campbells of Breadalbane since 1440. On nearing the head-waters of Loch Awe and the mouth of the Orchy the traveller sees the ruined castle of Kilchurn. Tradition makes this castle a former strong fortress of the MacGregors, who were long ago driven from Glen Orchy by the Campbells. It is said that the Knight of Lochow gave the glen and the castle to his son Colin, the founder of the house of Breadalbane, and that the MacNabs in the year 1440 were employed to do all the iron work in the building (or rebuilding) of the castle of Kilchurn. In Pennant's time the MacNabs were still in their old house. Pennant writes : " On an eminence on the south side of this vale dwells M'Nab, a smith, whose family have lived in that humble station since the year 1440, being always of the same possession. The first of the line was employed by the Lady of Sir Duncan Campbell, who built the castle of Kilchurn when her husband was absent. Some of their tombs are in the churchyard of Glen Urqhie; the oldest has a hammer and other implements of his trade cut on it." Pennant also mentions that the great tower of Kilchurn Castle was repaired by the Lord Breadalbane of the 1745, and was garrisoned by him " for the service of the Government in order to prevent the rebels from making use of that great pass across the kingdom, but is now a ruin, having been lately struck by lightning."

The traveller to the west leaves Kilchurn Castle on his left and skirts the north shore of Loch Awe to the impressive Pass of Brander, where a great fight was fought between Robert the Bruce and the Lord of Lorne. The river Awe flows strongly through the pass in a series of deep pools and swift rushes which retain much of their strength even during a prolonged summer drought, and as a salmon river it has a great name. I believe the average size of the Awe salmon to be unequalled in British rivers, and the same angler caught (in different years) two salmon of approximately 56 lbs. weight here. The river reaches the sea at Loch Etive, on the farther shore of which is Ardchattan Priory, named after Saint Catan. The priory was founded in 1230 by Duncan MacCoul, ancestor of the MacDougalls of MacDougall. It is on record that in the year 1500 Somerled MacDougall was abbot of the priory and that in 1617 the establishment was annexed to the Bishopric of Argyll.

West of Ardchattan is Connel, and here the traveller sees the flood tide surge in mightily to form the cataract known as the Falls of Lora. From the shore of Connel the hills of Mull appear, and there is no more beautiful sight on a summer day than these fine hills rising blue on the west horizon across the floor of the ocean. Near Connel is the historic castle of Dunstaffnage (which I have already mentioned), where old Coll MacDonald of Islay, treacherously taken near his castle of Dùn Naomhaig,[1] was hung by his Campbell enemies from the mast of his own war galley, laid across a gully near the castle for that sinister purpose. The *Account of the Clan MacLean*, describing the murder of MacDonald, known usually as Coll Ciotach, places it on record that " the final and more melancholy part of the ceremony was performed in the cleft of a rock in the immediate neighbourhood of Dunstaffnage Castle. Across this cleft the murderers placed the mast of MacDonald's own galley, and, leading him forward with the halter round his neck, he was suspended to the mast, and perished amid their fiendish yells."

Sir James Turner, writing of the events which led to the seizing

------

[1] See Chapter XLVIII.

Q

and hanging of Coll Ciotach, mentions that "before we were masters of Dunnevig the old man Coll, comeing foolishlie out of the house where he was governour, on some parole or other, to speak with his old friend, the captaine of Dunstaffage castle, was surprised and made prisoner, not without some staine to the Lieutenant Generall's honor." This "old friend," the captain of Dunstaffnage, was a Campbell, and Dunstaffnage has been held by the Campbells (in earlier times it was a MacDougall possession) ever since the day when that district of Lorne came into their

Ganavon, Oban.

possession through the marriage of Colin Campbell, first Earl of Argyle, with Isabella Stewart, daughter of the last Lord of Lorne. In the year 1541 Dunstaffnage Castle was appointed by James V as the principal messuage of the lordship of Lorne (see *Orig. Paroch. Scot.*, Vol. II. p. 117).

It is perhaps evening when the traveller reaches Oban, and sees the bay still and peaceful and the sails of the white yachts that float bird-like upon it mirrored in its water. Oban is the town with the finest view, not only in Scotland but, I should say, in the British Isles. It has some-

times been called the Charing Cross of the highlands, for
steamers sail from it to the Outer Hebrides, Iona, Mull and
Skye, Fort William and Inverness, and indeed to every seaport
in the west. It is crowded with hotels, yet accommodation in
summer is not easy to secure, for the number of tourists is very

Dunollie, Oban.

great. At the entrance to Oban Bay stands the historic castle
of Dunollie, the residence from time immemorial of MacDougall
of MacDougall, chief of his clan. Dunollie is five times mentioned in the *Annals of Ulster*, first in the year 686, and subsequently in 698, 701, 714, 734. Professor Watson, in his *Celtic
Place-Names of Scotland*, writes thus of Dunollie : " The ancient
tale of Táin Bó Fráich, the ' Driving of the Cattle of Fráech,'

tells how Fráech, son of Fidach, a hero of Connacht, who was contemporary with Cuchulainn, had his cattle stolen. Some of them were taken to Cruthentuath in the north of Alba. Fráech followed, recovered his cattle, and he and Conall Cernach came from the east past Dún Ollaich maic Briuin, the 'fort of Ollach son of Brión,' across the sea from the east to Aird hua nEchtach in Ulster. Hogan places this fort in Ulster, but it is certainly, in my opinion, Dunollie in Scotland."

The MacDougalls trace back their direct descent from Loarn, brother of Fergus who founded the kingdom of Dalriada. The old castle of Dunollie is now a ruin, but MacDougall of Mac-

Lynne of Lorne.

Dougall, the present chief, lives beside it in the house which his great-grandfather about the year 1746 built of stones taken from the old castle. The family tradition is that the roof of the castle began to leak and the chief of the day decided to abandon it. The castle of Dunollie sheltered the family for many centuries; it has perhaps seen King Haco of Norway's fleet join the galleys of the Lord and chiefs of the Isles in the lee of the green island of Kerrera across the Sound. But at the time the castle was abandoned there was less interest in preserving old things than there is to-day, and now the restoration of the castle would be a costly undertaking.

Sir Walter Scott had pleasant memories of Dunollie. He writes: "Nothing can be more wildly beautiful than the

situation of Dunollie. The ruins are situated upon a bold and
precipitous promontory, overhanging Loch Etive and distant
about a mile from the village and port of Oban. The principal
part which remains is the donjon or keep, but fragments of
other buildings overgrown with ivy attest that it had been once
a place of importance, as large apparently as Ardtornish or
Dunstaffnage. These fragments include a courtyard of which
the keep probably formed one side; the entrance being by a
steep ascent from the neck of the isthmus, formerly cut across
by a moat, and defended doubtless by outworks and a drawbridge. Beneath the castle stands the present mansion of the
family, having on the one hand Loch Etive with its islands and
mountains, on the other two romantic eminences tufted with
copsewood. There are other accompaniments suited to the
scene : in particular a huge upright pillar or detached fragment
of the sort of rock called plum-pudding stone upon the shore,
about a quarter of a mile from the castle. It is called Clach a'
Choin or the Dog's Pillar, because Fingal is said to have used it
as a stake to which he bound his celebrated dog Bran. Others
say that when the Lord of the Isles came upon a visit to the
Lord of Lorne, the dogs brought for his sport were kept beside
this pillar. Upon the whole a more delightful spot can scarce
be conceived and it receives a moral interest from the considera-
tions attached to a residence of a family once powerful enough
to confront and defeat Robert Bruce and now sunk into the
shade of private life. It is at present possessed by Patrick
M'Dougall, Esq.; the lineal and undisputed representative of
the ancient Lords of Lorn. The heir of Dunolly fell lately in
Spain, fighting under the Duke of Wellington—a death well
becoming his ancestry."

When the poet Wordsworth visited Dunollie in 1831 a captive
eagle kindled his sympathy, as the following lines testify :

> " Dishonoured rock and ruin that, by law
> Tyrannic, keep the Bird of Jove embarred
> Like a lone criminal whose life is spared.
> Vexed is he, and screams aloud."

Two years later Wordsworth again visited Dunollie. This time he writes that

> " The captive bird was gone.
>
> .   .   .   .
> .   .   .   .
> But, climbing a tall tower,
> There saw, impaved with rude fidelity
> Of art mosaic, in a roofless floor,
> An eagle with stretched wings, but beamless eye."

The mosaic of the captive eagle remains to this day. It is a rude representation in rounded pebbles, larger than life, of what was probably a white-tailed or sea eagle, a bird now extinct in Scotland.

Standing one autumn evening after sunset on the earthen floor which holds the mosaic of the eagle I looked out to Mull and saw the orange beacon on Lismore flash its message. Nearer at hand was Kerrera, a large grassy island having at its seaward end the ruined castle of Gylen, a former strong tower of the MacDougalls. It was on Kerrera that Alexander II of Scotland died in 1249 of a fever when endeavouring to assert his rights in a district which at that time regarded Norway, and not Scotland as its mother-country.

In a peaceful house, sheltered by the ivy-covered *dùn* and many old trees where jackdaws call and swallows flit gracefully during long summer days of sunshine, the chief of MacDougall and his family live quietly. Here are to be seen varied and priceless relics such as few highland families possess to-day. Most valued of them all is the Brooch of Lorne. This brooch was worn by Robert the Bruce at the battle of Dalrigh, between Crianlarich and Tyndrum, fought in the early years of the fourteenth century between the Bruce and MacDougall of Lorne. One of MacDougall's followers laid hands on the king and was killed for his rashness by a strong blow from the royal claymore, but with his dying grasp he tore off the king's cloak and with it the shoulder brooch. In the year 1647 a detachment of General Leslie's army besieged and took Gylen Castle, and the Brooch

Sound of Kerrera.

of Lorne, which was in the castle at the time for safe-keeping, was found and carried off. It became the spoil of Campbell of Inverawe, then serving under Colonel Montgomery, the captor of Gylen Castle. By the descendants of Inverawe the brooch was carefully preserved down to 1826, when it was purchased by General Duncan Campbell of Lochnell. This distinguished officer then most generously presented the brooch without reservation to the MacDougall family, who have held it since. The large crystal set in that old brooch is unusual. Under whatever conditions of light it may be viewed, a warm glow, as from a peat fire, burns within its depths. Surrounding the large central crystal are a number of pearls, set in a circle. The centre of the brooch unscrews, and within is a small box which formerly contained a small piece of bone (perhaps a saintly relic) and a piece of very old MacDougall tartan, hand-spun and much faded. When Queen Victoria sailed up Loch Tay the royal barge was steered by the chief of the MacDougalls, who wore the Brooch of Lorne in his plaid. The Queen so greatly admired the brooch that she asked MacDougall whether she might wear it during her historic row down the loch.

In addition to the Brooch of Lorne there are preserved at Dunollie to-day two crystals which have been in the family since time immemorial. They were believed to bring success to the clan and were carried into battle. These crystal balls are said to have been brought from the Holy Land by an early Lord of Lorne at the close of a crusade. They were believed to possess great healing powers. On one occasion (some say before the battle of Scamadale) the larger crystal was accidentally dropped into a burn during the march and was cracked on a stone. Thereupon one half of the fighting men of the clan turned back with dark thoughts of mistrust at the ill-luck this disaster must bring to them.

At Dunollie are preserved two fine old targes and also a small horse of bronze on which is seated a man with a withered leg. This bronze was discovered beneath the ruins of the old castle

Gylen Castle, Kerrera.

and is believed to represent Iain Bacach, Lame John, Lord of Lorne, a man of courage and renown (despite his infirmity) who ruled the district of Lorne in the thirteenth century.

In 1715 Iain Ciar, Dusky John, the MacDougall chief of the day, rose under the Earl of Mar for the Jacobite cause, and was presented by the Chevalier with a special medal for bravery in the field. On the failure of the rising, the MacDougall estates were forfeited, and for twelve years the chief was in hiding, sometimes in his own district and sometimes in Ireland. It is said that his hiding-place near Oban was a cave named Uaimh Chrom, the Curved Cave, at Lerags on the north shore of Loch Feochan. He was pardoned in 1727 and died in 1737. His lady, who held the Castle of Dunollie for him when he was fighting under Mar at Sheriffmuir, was a granddaughter of Sir Donald MacDonald of Sleat. The clan MacDougall had already suffered severely in the wars of Montrose, for they were assisting the MacDonalds in their castle at Dunaverty when it was surrendered to Leslie. I have in another chapter mentioned the disgraceful massacre which followed the surrender.[1] The MacDougalls were " extirpated verie neere," but Sir James Turner, adjutant in Leslie's army, rescued " one young man MacCoul, whose life I begged." With the exception of this youth Turner bluntly states that " every mother's son was put to the sword."

The MacDougalls, broken by the rising of 1715, took no part in the '45. There is a family tradition that the wife of the chief at the time of the '45 poured a kettle of boiling water over his foot in order to prevent his taking arms for Prince Charles Edward. After the close of the campaign of 1745 the Mac-Dougall estate was restored and now in its old age the Castle of Dunollie is serene. Beneath it the tides ebb and flow, and when the sun sets in glory behind the hills of Mull and the western sky is fired with rosy light the bay of Oban reflects the pageant of beauty, as it did in those early days when the galleys of the

[1] See Chapter XLIV.

vikings sailed majestically into the bay and anchored beneath the old ivy-covered walls through which the winter wind sings a sorrowful song.

I append an old document in the possession of the present chief of the MacDougalls, and which he has kindly allowed me to make use of :

TENOR of a SIGNATURE for a CHARTER under the Great Seal in favour of ALLAN McDOUGALL of DUNOLLY of the Lands of DOWACHA, SOROBA, etc., 20th September, 1686.

KING JAMES VII as King, Prince and Steward of Scotland, considering that the whole Lands and Offices pertaining to Archibald late Earl of Argyll fell in the hands of the late King Charles II by the forfeiture pronounced upon the said Earl on . . . December 1681, and that the said late King by Great Seal Charter dated 17th March 1682 ordained the superiorities of the said lands and estate of Argyll to be consolidated and annexed to the Crown; " As also out of the regaird his Majesties said deceast royall brother hade to the great service and sufferings of the deceast Duncan McDougall of Dunollich and his predecessors in the tyme of the lait troubles and rebellion under the Usurper his lait Majesty wes lykewise pleased by the said signatur to grant unto him his airs maill and successors as much land nixt and adjacent to the Castle of Dunollich as would amount to ane hundred punds sterling money yearlie, to be designed be the commissioners therin named," the said late King by a Signature dated at Windsor Castle 19th June 1684 granted and disponed the lands and others after mentioned to the said Duncan Mc-Dougall, erecting the same in a barony. But as the said Signature " hes become useles to the said Duncan McDougall and his representatives " through the death of the King and of the said Duncan himself, before the same could pass the seals, and as the present King is desirous to renew the same in favour of Allan McDougall now of Dunollich, brother german of said Duncan : THEREFORE his Majesty with consent of his

Officers of state ordains a Charter to be made and passed under the Great Seal granting and disponing to the said Allan McDougall and his heirs male and assigns whomsoever heritably and irredeemably the following lands :—The 29 merk land of the Isle of Carvora, 3 merk land of Dunollichbeg, 8 merk land of Glensheallache, 4 merk land of Colgin, 8 merk land of Ardnaway, 8 merk land of Dowacha, 6 merk land of Sorrabay, and 10 merk land of Molleig (excepting the two merk land of Sondachin); as also the 3 merk land of Dunollichmoir, 2 merk land of Clythchoymie, and 4 merk land of Penniefou all in the Lordship of Lorn and Sheriffdom of Argyll, together with the office of bailiary within the bounds of the said lands : all which lands pertained heritably to the said deceased Duncan McDougall and his predecessors, holding of the late Earl, and now held of the Crown in the manner foresaid. ALSO the two " tounes and lands of Leraggs with pertinents, 1½ merk land of Achichlachuth, 4 merk land of Torrintuirk and Aichyleich, 4 merk land of Culcullaren, 1½ merk land of Binchallich, 3 merk land of Belliemenoch, 2 merk land of Camishvachan, and 4 merk land of Blairnagour, with all the pertinents," which lands pertained heritably to the late Earl, fell to the Crown by his forfeiture, and were in terms of the late King's Charter and the decree of the Commissioners therein named dated 15th April 1684 assigned to the said Duncan McDougall (therein designed of Lorne) in satisfaction of the sum of £100 sterling yearly, the trustees for Argyll's creditors being thereby bound to denude in favour of said Duncan as from Martinmas 1683. MOREOVER his Majesty " for the good true and faithful services done and performed to his Majesty and most royall progenitors of ever blessed memorie be the said deceast Duncan McDougall and the said Allan McDougall now of Dunollich and their predecessors and haveing speciall regaird to their great services and sufferings in the tyme of the late Usurper when their whole lands and estait wer laid waste, their houses burnt, and their father and grandfather with the most of their kinsmen all murdered in cold blood for their loyaltie and constant adherence to his Majesties service And more especially his Majesty haveing good and sufficient prooff of the said Allan McDougall now of Dunollich his constant faithfull and loyall service done to him In his being present at and assisting with his men followers and freinds in suppressing and defeating the lait bold and dangerous rebellione attempted contryved and carried on against us our authority and government by the lait Earle of Argyle in the year 1685, And his Majesty being now sensible of the mean conditione of that ancient and loyall familie and of their said services and sufferings upon ane loyall account and being desyreous in some measure to recompense the same," therefore of new grants dispones and confirms to the said Allan McDougall and his heirs male and assignees whomsoever heritably and irredeemably All and sundry the lands and others above mentioned, disjoining them from all other baronies or earldoms and erecting them into a free barony to be called the Barony of Dunolich, whereof the manor place of Dunolich is to be the principal messuage. Dated at Windsor 20th September 1686.

CHAPTER XXXII

MORVERN

The country of Morvern, sometimes spelled incorrectly on the map as Morven, is a mountainous district of north Argyll extending north-east from the Sound of Mull to Loch Sunart. So deeply does Loch Sunart bite into the land that it forms a

Old Ardtornish, Morvern.

peninsula, with the neck at Glen Tarbert, a glen of some eight miles in length, joining the head of Loch Sunart with Loch Linnhe. The Gaelic name for Morvern is A' Mhorbhairn, from *muir*, the sea, and *bearn*, a gap, so that the meaning of the name is the Sea-gap.[1]

[1] "Celtic Place Names of Scotland," by Professor W. J. Watson.

The traveller who sails up the Sound of Mull past the Morvern coast sees a ruined castle standing on a promontory beside the narrow entrance to a sea loch. The castle is Ardtornish, and the sea loch is Loch Aline, in Gaelic Loch Àlainn, the Lovely Loch.

Ardtornish was one of the castles of the Lord of the Isles. Here in the year 1380 died John of the Isles, on whom the Church bestowed the appelation of " the good John of Islay "

Kingairloch, Cruachan in the distance.

because of his liberality. For centuries now the castle of Ardtornish has been a ruin, and could a Lord of the Isles return to earth to-day he would be astonished to find a community from St. Kilda, the most remote island of his kingdom, living in happiness on the farther shore of Loch Aline, opposite his castle. The evacuation of St. Kilda a few years ago brought to a close a long history of an island community whose life was always a hard one. It was believed that the people of St. Kilda would never find happiness away from their beloved island. It is true that the older generation was reluctant to leave, but the younger people have settled to their new way of life. Some of them have been given employment by the Forestry Commission on the shore of Loch Aline, and when I visited them in the summer of 1933 I found a contented community, which I scarcely recognised as the same people I had seen on St. Kilda a few years before.

From Loch Aline a coast road leads along the shore of the Sound of Mull to Drimnin, formerly MacLean country, but for the last hundred years the home of the Gordons of Drimnin. One is here at the entrance to Loch Sunart, where is the deeply indented Island of Oronsay. It was believed that German submarines might use this island as a hiding-place in the early days of the Great War, when the Grand Fleet were anchored in Loch nan Ceall on the west coast of Mull, but no evidences were ever found of hostile craft frequenting the place.

The shore of Morvern was the home of a family of renowned Gaelic ministers, whose preaching became celebrated throughout the world wherever those of Gaelic extraction had settled. Dr. Norman MacLeod, a man of great stature and breadth of mind, devoted his life to the cause of his fellow-countrymen, and his name is still remembered with honour throughout the highlands.

On the shore of Morvern is an historic cave known as Somerled's Cave. Here the great Somerled, King of the Isles, was at one time in hiding. I have found none who can tell me where this old cave is situated, for I think that there have been more changes in the families of Morvern than in other parts of the west.

It is possible to ship one's car from Oban to Tobermory and, having visited Mull, to re-ship the car at Tobermory or Salen and (care being taken that the tides suit) drive it off the mail boat at Loch Aline pier. From Loch Aline there is a road through the hills to Ardgour and thence to the head of Loch Eil, where the Fort William–Mallaig road is joined. It is a very narrow road, with turns and twists to terrify the motorist who is used to the speedways of the mainland. During the drive I trusted that I should not meet the car belonging to a

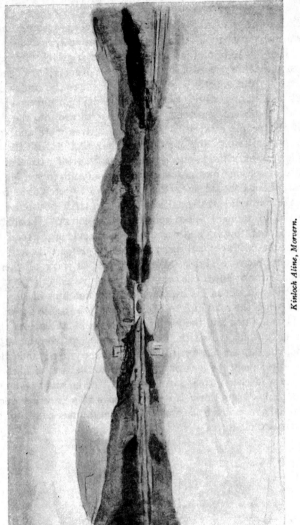

Kinloch Aline, Morvern.

R

well-known peer of the district, who has the reputation of frequently urging his driver to make greater speed.

" Here," one is told, as one passes over a stretch of road so narrow that there is just room for a car, " Here is Threadneedle Street." And a little way on, " This is where the bridge gave way on a stormy winter morning before daylight during a great flood. No harm was done. The car overturned into the river, but the people escaped." And as one drives more and more slowly, and rounds one blind corner after another with the hair rising on one's head, one is told by a cheerful native of the place of various narrow escapes. My only adventure on this road, which I should say is the most difficult stretch of highway in the western highlands, was when a small post-office car hurtled at topmost speed round a blind corner. Fortunately my car was stopped, and was drawn to the side of the road, and the miniature racer had just room to squeeze past me and continue its meteoric career. For the driver on this road there is no opportunity to see the country, but the passenger, if he is not travelling in fear of his life, sees first the high hills of Morvern, then, when the road dips to Loch Linnhe, the sheltered beauties of Loch a' Choir and the verdure of Lismore. At Ardgour there is a ferry which crosses the loch to the main road on the farther side, but cars are not ferried, so it is necessary to continue along the west side of the loch past Conaglen to the head of Loch Eil, where wild cherry trees surround many of the small crofts and in late April and early May are laden with a crown of snowy blossom above which the first swallows of summer pause on their northward flight.

CHAPTER XXXIII

ARDNAMURCHAN

ARDNAMURCHAN, sometimes known poetically as Rìoghachd na Sorcha (the Kingdom of Sorcha), is the most westerly promontory of the Scottish mainland. The place-name Ardnamurchan is a hard nut for scholars to crack, but those of us who are romantically minded perhaps favour the derivation Aird nam Murdhuchan, the Height of the Sea-nymphs. Ardnamurchan was the northern boundary of the kingdom of Dalriada, founded by Fergus Mór, and later was the division between the north isles and south isles of the Hebrides. Its wild rocky promontory juts far out into the Atlantic; Ben Resipol guards it to the south and the hills of Rhum and Skye stand sentinel northward.

It was by way of Ben Resipol that I entered what an old account speaks of as the " firme land " of Ardnamurchan, and from the cairn on that lofty hill looked on to a country of lochs and lochans and white bays of ocean sand to distant fairy isles that rose from the blue Atlantic. On the far-distant horizon the lighthouses of Skerryvore and Dubh-hirteach stood out from a sea of burnished gold, and the houses of the low island of Tiree were dark against an ocean background, while on the rim of the Atlantic I could see the hills of Barra and Uist. That evening I watched the sun gild the young foliage of birch and oak beside Loch Sunart and light up the ancient fortress of Dun Gallan, where courting eider drakes swam on the blue waters of the sea loch.

Ardnamurchan was formerly the territory of the noble highland family of MacIain, but there is a strong tradition that an equally illustrious clan, the Hendersons, were the rulers of the promontory before them. It is interesting that the old name for the Sound of Mull was Cuan mhic Eanruig, which may be translated Henderson's Narrow Sea. There is also a tradition that the Lochiel family at one time held part of Ardnamurchan.

The first MacIain of Ardnamurchan was Iain Sprangach, a son of Angus Mór MacDonald of Islay, and from Iain Sprangach were descended the MacIains, who held Ardnamurchan until they were driven out by the Campbells. Mingary Castle, the castle of the MacIains, has well withstood the ravages of time. In 1495 James IV visited the castle, and despite its rough usage by more than one besieging force it is still an imposing pile, venerable and massive, with a sea gate that leads down to the rocks where the flowers of the sea thrift, crimson and pink, made a natural rock garden of surpassing beauty on the April day when I saw the castle. From the sea gate of Mingary I looked across Port nan Spainndeach, the Bay of the Spaniards, where Lachlan MacLean of Duart unsuccessfully laid siege to Mingary Castle with one hundred Spanish soldiers who had been lent him from one of the ships of the Spanish Armada, which had taken refuge in Tobermory harbour. Across the arm of the ocean the hills of Mull rose blue in the track of the north wind. Where I now stood MacIain perhaps bade farewell to his lady before stepping into his galley which awaited him below the castle. That galley was painted white on one side and black on the other, from the thwarts to the water line, for MacIain often harried the lands of Lochaber, and by this ruse his galley was not recognised when it returned west down Loch Linnhe after one of his bold raids. Then, as to-day, Beinn Mhór Mull lifted her head nobly to the sky and Beinn Talaidh caught the last rays of the setting sun, but no echoing voices of men are heard to-day within the thick walls of Mingary, and the stout galleys which rowed out from the castle have long since crumbled to dust. Mingary Castle stands near Kilchoan, and it was to St. Comghan's church (after which Kilchoan is named) that the robust Episcopalian minister, Maighstear

Alasdair, was accustomed to walk each Sunday from his home at Dalilea. After preaching he returned across the hills. That great walk of between fifty and sixty miles is still spoken of in the district, although the conditions of life have changed much since that day.

The northern shore of Ardnamurchan is singularly beautiful. Here are bays of white sand and small green fields that lead down to them from the rough moorlands. The country is wilder than Moidart, which adjoins it. At a very remote part of the coast a small cave is hidden away amongst rocks and heather. Its name is Uaimh Chloinn Iain (the Cave of the MacIains), and its whereabouts is now known to very few. When in the year 1624 the Campbells devastated Ardnamurchan and reduced the castle of Mingary a number of the MacIains took refuge in this cave, thinking that here they would be safe. The ground was snow-covered at the time and when one of the fugitives ventured out, his footprints (despite the precaution he took of walking backwards on his return journey to the cave) were seen and tracked by one of the enemy who carried the news to Mingary. A strong Campbell force hurried to the mouth of the cave and a great fire was kindled at its entrance so that the MacIains within were suffocated by the smoke and fumes.[1] The cave is close to the sea and is on a raised shelf, and at the entrance is a great rock which divides the mouth of the cave into two small openings leading into black depths which the light of a match fails to illuminate. Below the cave the moss grows green and untrodden. Much driftwood lies upon the rocky shore here, and on the morning when I visited the cave a flock of eider ducks, buoyant on the north-east swell, were courting a little way out to sea. North were the Cuillin of Skye, blue and mystic; on the far west horizon Barra rose. On Skye two heather fires were lighted, and as I watched, the white smoke from them increased, and rose slowly into the air. As I stood beside the cave four wild geese

---

[1] In the chapter on Eigg I have recorded a similar tragedy from that island.

passed above it, gliding easily into the breeze. The Cuillin became less clear; grey showers of snow descended upon them, veiling their slender tops, but on Moidart and the land of Ardnamurchan the sun shone. Near the cave I was surprised to find a sprig of bell heather (*erica cinerea*) in blossom. It had evidently survived the winter and its small bell-shaped flowers, held to the April sunshine, were so unexpected that the finding of them will remain in my memory as a memorial to the Clann Iain, mercilessly killed within the cave on a snowy day three hundred years ago.

An old track, little used nowadays, follows the coast of north Ardnamurchan from Kilmory to the estuary of Kentra Bay, beside Acharacle on Loch Shiel. North of Kilmory the coast is rugged and the white sands which were pleasant companions are not seen again until Gortanfern is reached. On the sands here a battle was fought between a personage known as the Red Rover from Dublin and the men of the district, and old brooches and coins are found in the sand from time to time. I crossed that old battle-field, but found no relics of the fight, and saw only some flints and a ringed plover's nest with its four pear-shaped eggs laid on the bare sand. Here I met a highlander of the fine old type rarely seen to-day. Over six feet in height, with distinguished features, piercing blue eyes, white beard, and courtly manners, this man with his cultured and fluent Gaelic might well be the representative of a great highland family. His story as he told it to me was a romantic one. His ancestor was of the Lochiel family, and was sent by Lochiel of the day to the north coast of Ardnamurchan some four hundred years ago to protect the district from the attacks of a notorious Irish free-booter named Duin who had become a terror to the inhabitants. His mission successfully completed, Lochiel's emissary settled in the district, and his descendant with whom I spoke was the last of a long line who had lived in direct succession on the same piece of land. It brought the past vividly before me to hear the story of the narrator's great-great-grandfather who on the battle-field of Culloden saw his sister's son hard pressed and in protecting him broke his claymore and met his own death. I was told of the days when the kilt was worn universally in Moidart and Ardnamurchan, when a weaver lived in almost every house, when the fishing was good (now English trawlers scour the bays in defiance of the law) and when the men were content to live simple lives on the land, before the great cities had cast their unhealthy spell upon them.

With these old tales in my head I crossed the small burn where Domhnall Conallach MacIain, on his way to Lochaber to marry Lochiel's daughter, was killed by an arrow fired at him by Angus Mór of Strontian. The tide was high and so I did not continue my walk round the head of the bay but turned off to the north and, making my way through natural woods and scrub to the mouth of the loch, was ferried across the narrow channel to Ardtoe. Thence I walked through the wide peat moss of Kentra, above which lapwings flew in courting flight, to the small village of Acharacle, where the grass was already long and green and bees sucked the honey from the fragrant flower-clusters of the sycamore trees.

In bright sunshine next morning I sailed down Loch Shiel. Eilean Fhìonain, the Sacred Isle, was radiant in spring sunshine; the woods of Dalilea were green, and the sun shone full upon historic Glen Alladale that led up to the great hills. One of the crew of the small mail steamer played a *piobaireachd* on his bag-pipes as we approached Glen Finnan, and my thoughts went back to that summer day of 1745 when Prince Charles Edward sailed on the same course up the loch with hope high in his heart to write a chapter in highland history that will be remembered with honour so long as courage and fidelity be reckoned as virtues.

CHAPTER XXXIV

TIREE AND COLL

WEST of the Isle of Mull, and between it and the Outer Hebrides, are two low islands—Tiree and Coll. In an old nameless description, written about the year 1595, Tiree is thus referred to :

" Tierhie is ane Ile of aucht mile in of lenth, and in sum pairtis but thrie mile braid, and at the braidest is six mile braid. But it is commodious and fertile of corns and store of gudes. It is 140 merk land, and will raise to the weiris 300 men. It pertenis to great McClane of Doward (MacLean of Duart), gevin to him be McConneill (MacDonald). It was callit in all tymes McConnells girnell; for it is all teillit land, and na girs but ley land, quhilk is maist nurischand girs of ony other, quhairthrow the ky of this Ile abundis sa of milk that thai are milkit four times in the day. The yeirlie dewtie thairof is sa great of victuall, buttir, cheis, mairtis, wedderis, and other customes, that it is uncertain to the inhabitants thairof quhat thai should pay, but obeyis and payis quhatevir is cravet be thair maister for thair haill deuties, only to tak sa mony firlotts as micht stand side be side round about the haill Ile full of victuall, half meill, half beir, and it wes refuseit."

Tiree is still a most fertile island, and to-day is noted for its cattle-raising. The whole of the island is under crofts. The people of Tiree are vigorous and intelligent, and become sea captains, ministers, and school teachers. The beautiful white sands are a feature of the island.

It is believed that in Columba's time the monks of Iona grew a part of their corn on Tiree. Adamnan mentions two Columban monasteries on the island. One is at Campus Lunge, situated near the shore " over against Iona." This has been identified with Soroby, near the south-east end of the island. This monastery was under the charge of Baithene, Columba's foster-son, afterwards the successor of Columba in the abbacy of Iona.

Muir, who examined the old monastery of Soroby in 1865, writes of it as follows :

" The burying-ground . . contains nine or ten ancient slabs embellished with the usual devices, and the shaft of a cross, decorated on one of its faces with foliage, and on the other with the figure of St. Michael, Archangel, bearing a sword and shield, and trampling a dragon.   Under the figure is HAEC EST CRUX MICHAELIS ARCHANGUELI DEI ANNA ABBATISSA DE Y.   Under this is an ogee-headed niche, containing the figure of Death holding a spade in one hand, and leading off Anna with the other.   Besides these there is a ponderous cruciform pillar of granite, rising 3 feet 8 inches from a heavy plinth called Maclean's Cross.   This form is curious and quite unique, each face presenting the appearance of two distinct crosses, one of them laid against the face of the other.   On both faces there are slight traces of serpent-like animals and scroll-work."

The second Columban monastery on Tiree was at Artchain, the Fair Cape, but its whereabouts is at present unknown.

Tiree is perhaps the most wind-swept of the Hebrides, but it is an island with a charm of its own, both in winter and summer. In winter it is the home of innumerable birds.   On its lochs herds of Bewick's swans swim in a graceful, white-plumaged assembly, and before frost utter their musical call notes repeatedly. When the frost is binding the shallow water of the lochs the swans swim backwards and forwards without rest, night and day, keeping open a lane of water.   In the very early spring the swans leave Tiree.   They nest on the tundras of Siberia, and since in February (when they leave their island home) and long after that date the Siberian steppes are hidden beneath deep snow, the wild swans must have some half-way resting-place, where they pass the months of March and April, but where that resting-place may be is unknown.

On the broad green *machair* of Tiree hundreds of white-fronted geese make their winter home.   The island at that season abounds in snipe, and the snipe shooting in Tiree is as good as any in Britain.   The tide of birds on their northward migration passes along the shores of Tiree.   Here are seen on early May days many whimbrel and white wagtails.   Golden plover, with more handsome plumage than their British relatives, pause here awhile on their long flight to the Arctic nesting-places.   Late in May come the clan of the sea swallows to Tiree—the Arctic and the lesser tern. These nest along the sandy beaches, scraping out a small hollow in the dry hot sand and laying two, sometimes three, eggs. At this time the dunlin make their nests in a small tussock of grass in the *machair* land, and lapwings in their hundreds nest on the young grass slowly growing after its struggles against the icy north wind. On the sea cliffs at the south-west end of the island the fierce peregrine falcon nests, and often raids the crofters' chickens. The trout of the Tiree lochs are, I should say, the finest in all the Hebrides.

On a calm day of early summer there is no more delightful island than Tiree, but in winter the lack of shelter is a drawback and there is a saying that one can recognise a man of Tiree by reason of his peculiar walk—a walk that has developed from his almost daily struggle with winter storms. Tiree is tree-less. Formerly there was one tree, and it grew in the manse garden. A new minister came to the island, saw the small struggling tree—and promptly cut it down for firewood ! The island is part of the wide territory of the Duke of Argyll ; the island of Coll, lying to the north of Tiree and separated from it by a narrow strait, belonged formerly to the MacLeans of Coll. Johnson and Boswell were entertained by Coll during their tour of the Hebrides, their visit to the island being unpremeditated, and the result of a storm which prevented them reaching the shelter of Mull after what was at first a fair voyage from Skye. Coll is a long narrow island. When seen from the ocean, it is rocky and barren, but hidden away among the rocks is rich earth, and there is at least one farm of considerable size on the island, on which the celebrated Coll cheeses are made.

Both Tiree and Coll are in want of a good harbour. Some years ago an excellent pier was built at Gott Bay on Tiree, but in westerly storms a heavy swell runs into this bay, and a steamer cannot make the pier. I remember on one occasion arriving off Tiree after a hard struggle with a westerly gale. We closely approached the pier, but the force of the wind was such that nobody could venture to walk along the exposed pier to throw us a rope, and we were forced to put about and run for Coll. On that occasion we had taken on board some women passengers at Tobermory for Kilchoan (about four miles across the entrance to the Sound of Mull). It was too stormy for the Kilchoan ferry boat to come out to meet us, and the unfortunate passengers were carried on to Tiree, and (when we could not make that port) to Coll. At Coll they were borne half-fainting from the steamer to the ferry boat, and I remember the hardy captain saying to me, " Well, Mr. Gordon, they have, I think, had their ninepence worth." It should be explained that ninepence was the steerage fare from Tobermory to Kilchoan.

For several centuries Coll had a Norwegian history. It was the chief seat (according to Skene) of the Jarls who ruled the Isles under the King of Norway prior to the establishment of the Norwegian kingdom of the Isles.

In an old account of the island we read :

" Collow is ane Ile of 12 mile of lenth, 4 or 6 mile of breid in sum pairtis thairof. It is 30 merk land, and pertenis to the Laird of Collow, quhairin he has ane castell callit Brekauche (Breachachadh of to-day), quhilk defendis the half thairof, and hes three walls about the rest of the castell and thairof biggit with lyme and stane, with sundrie gude devises for defending of the tower. Ane uther wall about that, within the quhilk schippis and boittis are drawin and salvit. And the third and the uttermost wall of tymber and earth, within the quhilk the haill gudes of the countrie are keipit in tyme of troublis or weiris. It is very fertile alsweill of corns as of all kind of catell. Thair is sum little birkin woodis within the said Ile. Ilk merk land payis yeirlie as is declarit of the Ile of Mule, and will raise seven score men."

The Isle of Coll has seen many changes since the days of the Norsemen. Its woods have gone ; the old castle of Breachachadh, where harper and piper played to MacLean of Coll, is now a ruin. Strangers have come to the island to make cheeses and farm the land. When first I knew the isle an old piper lived here—one who had his teaching from an uncle who had it from the last of the great MacCrimmons—and I can still see that old piper of more than fourscore years playing on his *feadan* or chanter the immortal tunes formerly played in the great MacCrimmon college at Borreraig in Skye. But there was none in the island who cared to hear him play the pieces of *ceòl mór*, and now he has gone, and with him has gone from the island all knowledge of ancient pipe music.

Kilmore, Mull.

CHAPTER XXXV

THE ISLE OF MULL

More than three hundred years have passed since Dean Munro described the Isle of Mull as an island " 24 myles of length and as much in breadth, unpleasant indeed, but not unfruitfull of cornes. There are many woodes in it, many heardes of Deere, and a good haven for shippes."

A man's outlook has changed since the days of the Dean. In his time little or no regard was paid to the beauty of scenery ; men's thoughts were set rather on forays and the chase, and to a stranger the trackless isles (as they then were) of Mull and Skye must have seemed, as Dean Munro remarks, " unpleasant indeed."

But now our sense of beauty has been developed and strengthened. Each year our love for beautiful things and for beautiful scenery is growing, and most of us who know the West to-day hold Mull and Skye as the two most delightful islands of the Hebrides. Very few people, for example, would now agree with

Sir James Turner, who, about the middle of the seventeenth century, describes Jura as a " horrid isle, and a habitation fit for deere and wild beasts." We hear much to-day of the decadence of our race, but none can deny that our perception of grandeur in nature has been strengthened.

Mull and Skye are both great islands, and both are fertile. The hills of Mull are more grassy than the hills of Skye. In summer the delicate peak of Beinn Mhór Mull is green almost to the summit with the fresh greenness of a lawn in spring. From the hills of Gleann Mór a hay crop might well be reaped in August. The hills of Mull are kinder and less austere than their Skye brothers. In Mull there is no great mountain range like the Cuillin of Skye to dominate the island with its knife-like ridges and dark summits. The vegetation in Mull is more luxuriant than in Skye and the island gives the impression of being less wind-swept. Bracken has obtained so firm a hold of the lower slopes of the Mull hills that it has destroyed hundreds, even thousands, of acres of the best grazing land, for bracken thrives on rich ground. During a recent visit to the island I noticed that one industrious farmer had cut much of the bracken-infested hill slopes with the scythe—a heart-breaking task against long odds. In one respect Skye lags far behind Mull. In Mull the poorest crofter has a garden, small perhaps but tended with care, beside his house, and in June old-fashioned roses scent the air. In the outlying districts of Skye a garden is a rare thing.

Each district of Mull has its own atmosphere. The pleasant hazel-clad shore of Loch Scridain, the mist-covered heights of the Wilderness (now taken over by the National Trust as a sanctuary for wild life), the stern primitive country of Loch nan Ceall, the tall woods of Torosay, the birches and natural oak of Glen Lussa—all are distinctive and delightful in their own way. The traveller to Mull may land at Craignure beside Torosay, near the old Castle of Duart and, crossing Gleann Mór with its red deer and its green hills, may see the waters of Loch

Scridain gleam beneath him like a silver bar in the sunshine. The hills slope steeply towards Loch Scridain, and after rain each corrie is the home of waterfalls that shine like snow in the sun.

Aros Castle, Mull.

Near the head of Loch Scridain, at Pennyghael, an old cross stands between the road and the loch. On the cross are the letters (now scarcely decipherable) " G.M.B. 1582. D.M.B." incised on the east face of the shaft. The cross is to the memory of the Beatons, men skilled in the art of healing and hereditary doctors and *seanachaidhean* to the MacLeans of Duart. The old cross is on the lands of Penycross, which were given to one of the Beatons by MacLean of Duart who had been healed of a terrible wound by the skill of his physician, but these lands have long passed into other hands. In Campbell's *West Highland Tales* it is mentioned that there were three Beaton brothers famed for their skill in medicine. One of the brothers, John, went to Mull and was afterwards known as the Ollamh Muileach (the Mull Doctor). His tomb is on Iona. Another brother, Fergus, ministered to the people of Islay. The third brother, Gilleadha, was the herbalist, and was the most famed of them all. He was summoned to attend one of the kings of Scotland, but the doctors of the court, being jealous of his healing powers, poisoned him, and he died far from the western islands. The initials "G.M.B." on the old cross may be the initials of Gilleadha Beaton.

There is a Mull tradition that when one of the great Beatons (perhaps this same Gilleadha), was summoned to attend a king of Scotland he left a wise prescription for the people of the island during his absence. It was " Be cheerful, be temperate, rise early." Martin, writing of the disaster to the Spanish man-of-war " Florida " in Tobermory Bay, mentions that " the famous physician of Mull " was sitting on the deck of the vessel when she was blown up " by one Smallet of Dunbarton " and had a miraculous escape. Doctor Beaton was hurled a good distance by the force of the explosion, yet was uninjured and lived several years after his adventure.

If the traveller journeys through Gleann Mór (the Great Glen) to Loch Scridain and thence along the Ross of Mull to Iona he passes, near the head of the Great Glen, a chain of hill lochs. On one of these lochs is a small island, and on the island are the remains of a very old lake dwelling. This is reputed to have been the castle of Eoghan a' Chinn Bhig (Ewen of the Little Head), a warrior MacLaine of Lochbuie whose phantom was heard to ride furiously on a ghostly steed around the old castle of Moy on the shore of Loch Buie before a death in the Lochbuie family. Above the loch of Ewen's old castle, and quite near the road, is a great boulder named Clach Sguaban. In Mull tradition Sguaban was one of the Fingalian heroes, and one day he and another giant named Nicol were amusing themselves by hurling boulders at one another. Nicol was standing in Gleann Mór, while Sguaban was on the shore of Loch Spelve. These two places are hidden from one another by the hills, but presumably the Fingalian giants were of so vast a stature that they could see one another above the intervening ground. Tradition does not say what was the end of the homeric duel, but Sguaban threw his stone to where it now stands and Nicol hurled his boulder from Gleann Mór to the shore of Loch Spelve, where it may be seen to-day.

The Ross of Mull begins at Kinloch, at the head of Loch Scridain, and leads west as a long promontory to the Sound of Iona. Carsaig, Uisgean, and Erraid, Bunessan, Ardfenaig, and Fionphort—these names recall many a pilgrimage to Iona and a country, whether in storm or sunshine, of great charm.

Carsaig is remote, even for Mull. To reach it one must cross the hill road from Pennyghael, and as one arrives at the head of the pass one sees the track ahead apparently disappearing over a sheer precipice. Very steeply indeed does the road drop to the shore and Mr. Gordon of Carsaig, the hospitable laird, tells me that Carsaig is a difficult place to leave by road on a cold winter's morning, for the car begins its steepest climb from the door of the lodge. Carsaig is as it were a backwater, but a back-water of great beauty. On a summer morning following a night of rain the steep grassy slopes which lead to the sea are a fresh green. Each waterfall (and the Carsaig waterfalls exceed in their size and number even those of Tallisker in Skye, commented on by Boswell and Johnson during their visit) is a white tumultuous torrent swaying like a living thing in the sea breeze. On the rocks beneath the waterfalls the Atlantic surf breaks

S

white. Upon Colonsay, far across the sea, the Atlantic combers hurl themselves high into the sunlit air. On the shore near Carsaig is the Nuns' Cave, in Gaelic Uamh nan Cailleachan. Tradition narrates that persecuted nuns took refuge here when they were driven from Iona at the Reformation. Old carvings adorn the walls of this cave, which is large and roomy and capable, according to an old account, of concealing three hundred men. Most of these carvings are of crosses, one of them highly ornamented, but there is also a flower (perhaps a lotus flower) delicately incised on the rock. It is believed that the stone used in the building of the Abbey Church on Iona was taken from the Nuns' Cave.

In her *Guide to Scotland* the Honourable Mrs. Murray, writing about the year 1800, describes her visit to this cave. When she arrived at its entrance she found nearly one hundred head of cattle screening themselves from the hot rays of the sun in its cool recess and was deterred from entering by the filth which covered the floor. To-day no cattle wander near the cave, but wild goats spring from ledge to ledge of the great rocks that tower above it. As I stood at the mouth of the cave I could see the Atlantic surf advance with the rumble of thunder upon the smooth-worn rocks only a few yards away. At one time the sea must have flowed into the cave, but it does not reach it now and the wild strawberry ripens its small red fruit near the cave's entrance, where many wild-flowers grow.

To the west of the Nuns' Cave the rocks rise to a great precipice, so high that the ocean clouds often rest on the summit. Here is Gorrie's Leap, and the name commemorates a tragedy of olden days. MacLaine of Lochbuie organised a great deer drive, and told one of his men, Gorrie by name, to guard a certain defile, warning him that his life would be forfeit if he allowed the deer to pass him. The man did his best, but notwithstanding his efforts the deer escaped and the great drive was a failure. Gorrie did not lose his life, but he was rendered impotent in the presence of the assembled clan. He took his revenge swiftly.

Not far from him was the infant son of Lochbuie, held in the arms of his nurse. Gorrie snatched up the baby and fled with it to the highest part of the rock. He then leaped down to a ledge some yards below the summit where none dared follow him and delivered his ultimatum. Lochbuie, he said, should have his son back on condition that he should submit to the same indignity which he (Gorrie) had suffered. After a discussion the father, frantic with anxiety, agreed to the terms, but Gorrie, whether he did not believe that the operation had been performed or whether he wished his revenge to be more complete, leaped with a wild cry out over the abyss, holding the infant MacLaine aloft in one hand. Man and child were dashed to instantaneous death on the rocks far beneath, and at nightfall, when the sea mist enfolds the cliffs, is sometimes heard the echo of that terrible shout which numbed the hearts of all who heard it on a day of long ago.

There is no road along the south coast of the Ross of Mull. Few houses are here, and the coast is rough and difficult to traverse throughout its length. Towards the western end of the Ross the coast is lower and there are pleasant sands near Uisgean. Still farther west is the island of Earraid, known to all who have read Robert Louis Stevenson's *Kidnapped*. Some miles out to sea from Earraid, which is so near the coast that it is an island only at high tide, are the low Torran Rocks. Certain of these rocks are below the surface of the sea, and ships give them a wide berth. Earraid, which stands at the entrance to the sound of Iona, is the lighthouse shore station for Skerryvore and Dubh Hirteach. The coast of the Ross of Mull now recedes northward to Fionphort (the Fair Harbour) where the ferry boat crosses to Iona.

The visitor who is travelling to Fionphort and Iona by way of the Ross of Mull follows the road along the northern shore of the Ross. From the shore of Loch Scridain he looks across the loch to the heights of Ardmeanach. He then passes through the village of Bunessan, where the Glasgow steamer " Dunara

Castle " makes periodic calls, and after leaving the birch woods of Ardfenaig behind him has his first sight of the holy isle of Iona near Loch Poit na h-I, where the monks of Iona are believed to have done most of their fresh-water fishing. A few minutes later he reaches Fionphort beside the pale green waters of the Sound of Iona. If he is not minded to cross to Iona at once he can travel a short distance further along the coast of the Ross to the primitive village of Kintra. There was formerly a good deal of fishing done from this small village, and about the year 1800 the Duke of Argyll brought to Kintra from the Orkney Islands two families of fishermen to teach the people of Kintra how to fish with the long lines. This instruction was most successful, and John MacInnes of Iona tells me that as a boy he remembers seeing the room of a Kintra house full to the roof with huge dried ling, which were sold at a penny the pound.

From Fionphort or Kintra the traveller may return eastward along the shore of Loch Scridain and near the head of the loch cross to Loch nan Ceall (or Loch na Keal as it is incorrectly named on most maps) by way of Gleann Seilisdeir. He leaves Loch Scridain near Tiroran and after a gradual climb up a straight moorland road reaches the watershed, and has all at once a glorious view of Loch nan Ceall (the Loch of the Churches) with its hallowed island of Inchkenneth, and, farther out on the blue Atlantic, the Isles of Treshnish and Staffa. On Carnburg, most northerly of the Treshnish Isles,[1] MacLean of Treshnish is said to have hidden his friend Campbell of Skipness after the utter defeat of the Campbell forces at Inverlochy.

Inchkenneth, guarding the sea gates of Loch nan Ceall, has been from earliest times a sacred island. Cainnech, the friend and helper of Columba, gave it the name which it has retained through the succeeding thirteen and a half centuries. John of Fordun, who lived about 1385, mentions the island, calling it " insula sancti Kennethy." There is a ruined chapel on Inchkenneth, and in the burial-ground are some very old recum-

[1] See Chapter XXXVII.

Gribun and Loch nan Ceall, Mull.

bent stones. Perhaps the most interesting of the sculptured slabs is one showing the figure of a great warrior, powerfully built and caparisoned in a short tunic. In his right hand he holds a ball and in his left a claymore; his breast is covered by a targe. At his feet a dog is lying. There is nothing on this slab to show who the warrior may be, although an old MacLean stone is near it. Not far from the ruined chapel stands a Celtic cross, tall and delicately fashioned. When Johnson visited Inchkenneth in 1773 he mentions that he saw on one side of the altar of the chapel a bas-relief of the blessed Virgin and a small bell resting beside it. This bell, "though cracked and without a clapper, has remained there for ages, guarded only by the venerableness of the place." At the time of Johnson's visit Sir Allan MacLean was laird of the isle, and the distinguished visitor was delighted with his reception on an island where he found no "gross herdsmen or amphibious fishermen, but a gentleman and two ladies of high birth, polished manners, and elegant conversation." The evening of his second day on the island Johnson looked on with approval as one of Sir Allan MacLean's daughters played highland music on her harpsichord, while MacLean of Coll and Boswell danced a reel with the other young lady. It was not long afterwards that young MacLean of Coll was lost on a passage between Ulva and Inchkenneth. From Inchkenneth Sir Allan escorted Johnson and Boswell first to Iona and then to Loch Buie. One would have given much to have seen Dr. Johnson's face when MacLaine of Lochbuie haughtily asked him, "Are you, sir, of the Johnstons of Ardnamurchan or of Glen Coe?"

On the Mull coast south of Inchkenneth rise the rocks of Gribun. Here the coast resembles the wildest parts of the seaboard of Skye. The road from Iona and the Ross of Mull winds along the shore beneath great cliffs, sheer and in places overhanging. Even to-day the passage of this road is not without an element of risk. Great rocks from time to time leap from the precipices and rush down to the road and over it to the sea beyond.

A friend of mine tells me that one winter day when driving in his car along this part of the road he felt the ground tremble, and looking back saw that he had escaped a large falling rock by a few yards only. On another occasion the mail car found its way blocked by a landslide. The driver was searching for a turning-place when a second landslide occurred, this time behind him. He was able to go neither backwards nor forwards until the road was cleared. In February 1934 the Gribun road was blocked by a landslide and the mails had to be carried through Gleann Mór.

The Gribun rocks are soon passed, and the journey thence to the head of Loch nan Ceall is through one of the most delightful districts of Mull. Here terns hover on delicate white wings, curlews sing and oyster catchers make shrill music. When the woods of Gruline at the head of the loch are reached, mavis and blackbird, willow warbler and chiff chaff, chaffinch and tree pipit, add their softer songs to the curlew's far-carrying whistle.

Killundine, Sound of Mull.

CHAPTER XXXVI

THE ISLE OF MULL (*continued*)

Northward of Loch nan Ceall is Loch Tuath, the North Loch, where is the country of Torloisk. The lands of Torloisk were conferred as his patrimony upon Lachlan Og, son of Sir Hector Mór MacLean of Duart who was killed at the battle of Traigh Gruinard in Islay. From Lachlan Og the family of the MacLeans of Torloisk are descended.

Lachlan MacLean of Torloisk was one of those summoned in the year 1616 to attend before the Scottish Privy Council to produce sureties for his law-abiding behaviour.

It is perhaps at the entrance to Loch Tuath that the wildest country of Mull is to be found. Here stand the bold rocky promontory of Treshnish and the primitive *clachan* of Haunn, where small gardens surround the thatched cottages of the lobster fishermen. When I visited the place [1] I found old Malcolm MacDougall, a fine highlander over ninety years of age, still full of energy and hard at work outside his house. Old Malcolm was fishing lobsters out at the Treshnish Isles more than seventy years ago, and had the reputation of being one of the best men at the helm on that dangerous coast.

[1] In the summer of 1933.

A short distance north of Treshnish Point the rocky character of the coast changes suddenly and at Calgary a shore of white sand reflects the summer sun with dazzling brilliance. In this place is to be found the contrast of green trees which shelter the modern castle of Calgary and, only a few hundred yards away, the wild Atlantic treeless coast where the waves break in their might on the low sandy shore.

North of Calgary the coast is once more rocky, and at the north end of the island is a broad bay known as the Bloody Bay, where about the year 1480 a great sea fight was fought between John, Lord of the Isles, and his turbulent son Angus, who thoroughly defeated his old father in this engagement. Hector MacLean of Duart commanded the fleet of the Lord of the Isles and was taken prisoner. The eldest son of MacLeod of Lewis, who was also fighting for John of the Isles, was mortally wounded and MacNeil of Barra narrowly escaped falling into the hands of the fleet of Angus. Allan MacRuaraidh, chief or captain of ClanRanald, was one of the main supporters of Angus of the Isles in his challenge to his father, and had it not been for his powerful support the issue of that sea fight would probably have been very different.

After the battle the victorious galleys with their prisoners on board probably sailed into the bay of Tobermory, one of the safest and most sheltered anchorages in the Island of Mull.

From Tobermory (Tobar Mhoire or St. Mary's Well), which may be said to be the capital of Mull, to Craignure the Sound of Mull forms the east boundary of the island. The Sound is perhaps three miles across, and on the further shore is the land of Morvern, also the ancestral home of the MacLeans.

On the coast, some nine miles from Tobermory, is the ruined castle of Aros. In the year 1608 a great court was held within this old castle by Lord Ochiltree, Royal Lieutenant of James VI. Many highland chiefs attended the court. Gregory in his *History of the Western Highlands and Islands* tells us that " there were present Angus MacDonald of Dunyveg, Hector MacLean of

Dowart, Lauchlan his brother, Donald Gorme MacDonald of Sleat; Ruari MacLeod of Harris; Allaster his brother; and Neill MacIlduy and Neill MacRuari, two gentlemen in Mull, followers of MacLean of Dowart." After the court Ochiltree invited the chiefs to hear a sermon preached by the Bishop of the Isles on board the King's ship, and then prevailed upon them to dine on board with him. When dinner was ended Lord Ochiltree informed the astonished highlanders that they were his prisoners by the King's orders, and weighing anchor, promptly sailed for Ayr. The chiefs were brought before the Privy Council, by whose orders they were placed in the castles of Dunbarton, Blackness, and Stirling. Aros was apparently a MacLean castle at the time, for it was subsequently restored to MacLean of Duart, upon the promise of that chief to surrender it when required.

A few miles south of Aros Castle are the old chapel and burial-ground of Pennygowan. There are many old gravestones here, and the most interesting of them is perhaps one standing erect inside the ruined chapel. The tracery on this stone is of unusual beauty. On one side are graceful flowers, entwined. Beneath these patterns, at the foot of the stone, is a galley under full sail. On the opposite side of the stone is the figure of the Virgin Mary with Child, and here also is a very beautiful and delicate Celtic pattern. This old stone is interesting because it is upright and not, like most of the early stone slabs, recumbent. There is no writing on the stone, so the person whom it commemorates is unknown, but perhaps to those skilled in such things the type of galley might give some indication of the clan, though not of the actual person.

It is likely that the stone commemorates one of the MacLeans, for Mull is the old MacLean country, although new families, and new times, have come to the island. In Skye the old families remain. MacLeod, twenty-seventh chief, lives in his castle at Dunvegan, while MacDonald of Sleat still holds the lands of his ancestors around Armadale and Portree, and his deer forest in

the Red Cuillin.   But in Mull the lands of MacLean of Duart and
MacLaine of Lochbuie have passed into other hands and until
recently the Castle of Duart was a picturesque ruin.   It was
therefore a proud day for the clan when the veteran chief, Sir
Fitzroy MacLean of Duart, invited members of Clan Gillean [1] from
far and near to be his guests at the ancestral stronghold of the
clan, which he had with infinite care and labour restored.   On
that summer's day MacLean of Ardgour knocked with ceremony
upon the castle door.   The door swung open, revealing the chief
standing at the doorway, and when he stepped forward and called
out to the clansmen " Ceud Mìle Fàilte," " (a Hundred Thousand
Welcomes)," there was happiness in the hearts of all because of
the great day which a dispersed clan had lived to see.

The Chief of Duart still lives in his castle.   He is now (1934)
in his hundredth year, yet his memory is unimpaired and the
resonance of his speech is such as a younger man might envy.

Duart Castle stands at the southern entrance to the Sound of
Mull, where the tides of Loch Linnhe contend with mighty
Atlantic currents.   On the summer day of 1933 when I last
visited the chief in his castle, dark storm clouds hid Ben Nevis
and drew a curtain across the high hills of Ardgour.   Above the
summit of Beinn Bhèir, guarding the entrance to Glen Coe, was a
mystic halo of rainbow colours.   On the rocks of Duart white
waves were leaping, urged forward by the north-east wind which
had its birthplace in the black thunder-clouds that towered into
the sky at the head of Loch Linnhe.   On the south-east horizon
rose Cruachan Beann, her brow dark above a girdle of soft clouds.
I looked out from the castle to the white surf that now and again
engulfed the Lady's Rock and thought of the narrowly-averted
tragedy of that lonely rock.   The story is somewhat as follows.
Lachlan Cattanach MacLean of Duart had married Elizabeth,
daughter of the second Earl of Argyll.   For some reason (it is
generally believed because she failed to present him with an heir)
the chief of Duart determined to make away with her, and the

[1] The Clan MacLean.

unfortunate lady was taken out at low tide to the rock and left there to her fate. Her death appeared certain, for the Lady's Rock at high tide is deeply submerged, but, according to the *Account of the Clan MacLean,* some of the chief's own people rescued his lady and landed her on the shore of Lorne, whence she proceeded to Inveraray. Argyll did not revenge this callous treatment of his sister, but a few years later the chief of Duart was slain in Edinburgh in his bed by Lady Elizabeth's brother, Campbell of Achallader.

Duart Castle, Mull.

This chief of Duart, Lachlan Cattanach, had apparently so bad a character even at an early age that a Mod or meeting of the leading members of the clan was held in Mull, and at this meeting it was suggested that he should be excluded from the chiefship. It was perhaps unfortunate that this proposal was not agreed to, for when he succeeded his father in the year 1513 he showed a baseness of behaviour unique in a long line of MacLean chiefs who were renowned for their chivalry and honourable dealings.

Even in Martin's time—and that is almost two hundred and fifty years ago—Duart Castle had passed from the MacLeans. Martin wrote, " Duart was the Seat of Sir John Mack Lean, Head of the Ancient Family of the Mack Leans, and is now, together with the estate, which was the major part of the Island, become the Duke of Argyle's property by the Forfeiture of Sir John."

From Duart along the coast of Mull to Loch Buie as the eagle flies is no great distance. The MacLaines (for so they now spell their name) of Lochbuie, descended from the same ancestor as the MacLeans of Duart, were more fortunate than the Duart chiefs. During the seventeenth and eighteenth centuries they contrived to preserve their estate, although compelled (writes

Loch Buie, Mull.

Gregory in his *History of the Western Highlands and Islands*) " by the power and policy of Argyle to renounce their holdings from the Crown, and to become vassals of that powerful nobleman and his successors."

The ancestral castle of the MacLaines of Lochbuie is Moy, at the head of Loch Buie, and in the year 1616 it was decreed by the Privy Council that MacLaine of Lochbuie must reside in his castle of Moy, and that he and certain other highland chiefs and chieftains must appear before the council annually on the tenth day of July. It was further stipulated that Lochbuie should not use in his castle more than one " tun of wine " and that he should issue strict orders that none of his vassals should drink or purchase wine. It was also decreed that he, and other highland gentlemen, should send all their children above nine years of age to school in the Lowlands, to be instructed in the reading, writing and speaking of the English language.

Moy Castle is now a ruin, and the estate of Lochbuie is in other hands. The castle to-day is in an untouched state, and is in surprisingly good preservation although the upper walls—much overgrown with ivy—are in danger of falling. The old iron door of the castle has been removed for safety and better preservation, but the old wooden bolt is still in position. Beside the castle entrance is an alcove where the doorkeeper had his quarters. In the entrance hall is the well.

In the banqueting hall of Moy Castle is a curious raised portion built of irregular stones and mortar, and forming a kind of platform at the end of the room. At the bottom of the dungeon (which leads off the dining hall) was a rounded stone just emerging above the water, which was some nine feet in depth. The unfortunate prisoner in the dungeon had to stand or sit upon this stone, from which a false step in the darkness would have meant a speedy end to his troubles. The window openings in the castle are very small, and when I looked, on a June day of rain and wind, through the narrow window slit of the banqueting hall I saw through the gloom and haze of a summer's gale white waves racing in upon the low shore of the sea loch from the heaving Atlantic beyond it.

MacLean of Duart and MacLaine of Lochbuie were often at variance and were often on friendly terms. Mr. Robert MacMorran of Treshnish in the north end of the island gave me an interesting story (which he believes has never appeared in print) told him by an old *seanachaidh* or story-teller of Loch Buie fifty years ago. According to this old story it was customary for the two families of Duart and Lochbuie to send messages to one another by their best men during their periods of friendship. On one occasion Lochbuie sent Duart a message by his best man. The messenger never returned. This act of treachery terminated for the time being the friendly relations between the two families. Lochbuie bided his time. After a few years the friendship between the two families revived and Lochbuie's lady paid a visit to the Castle of Duart. When the day arrived for her to return home she asked that she might have Duart's best man to escort her. Her request was naturally granted. After crossing a burn near the head of Loch Spelve the lady's shoe thongs became unfastened and she requested her attendant to fasten her shoe. As he was stooping down to do so she stabbed him in the back and killed him. The stone where she rested her foot was shown to my friend who gave me the story, but he has now left that part of Mull and told me he was doubtful whether anyone in the district could point out the place to-day.

It must be remembered that in those days there were no roads in Mull and the Honourable Mrs. Murray in her *Guide to Scotland* (written at the beginning of the nineteenth century) mentions that when she visited the island there was only one road " such as can have any pretensions to that appellation, namely from Achnacraig to Tobermoire. A carriage might be run this road, and did so once for a wager; it was the first and only one that ever touched the land of Mull, and it was reshipped as soon as the wager was won."

To-day Mull has excellent stretches of roads, but one old pony track which has not been converted into a highway winds from Loch Buie along the coast to Carsaig. The distance is some five miles, and the track keeps close to the shore throughout its length. Here one walks to the sound of the Atlantic waves, and looks over the sea to Colonsay and, nearer at hand, to the Garvelloch Isles. A mile or rather more before Carsaig is reached an isolated rock, resembling a fortified castle, is passed near to the track. This is the Smithy Rock, and in a hollow of the rock the pack-horses were shoed, and until recent years the ring to which the horses were tied while being shod was still in its place.

Mull of the sweet singers and of the green woods, there is no island of the west that can compare with you in calm restful beauty, for the influence of Columba's spirit is still felt along your western shores and sea lochs which look out over the Atlantic to the white sands of Iona that gleam in summer sun and are not dimmed by winter storm.

CHAPTER XXXVII

STAFFA

STAFFA, a small island lying north of Iona and west of Mull, is for its size perhaps the most renowned of the Hebrides. It is famous because of Fingal's Cave, a wonderful cave or grotto on the south side of the island. Each day during summer the Iona

Staffa.

steamer calls (weather permitting) at Staffa and lands a large number of visitors to see this cave which Sir Joseph Banks, President of the Royal Society, first brought to the notice of the world in the year 1772. Early travellers wrote enthusiastic descriptions of Fingal's Cave. The French traveller Faujas St. Fond and the British explorers Pennant and the Honourable

Mrs. Murray have put on record their impressions of Staffa, or rather it is more accurate to say that Pennant (being unable himself to land on Staffa) has put on record the observations of Sir Joseph Banks.

I believe it will be of interest if I quote fully Pennant's *Account of Staffa, by Joseph Banks, Esq.* :

" In the Sound of Mull we came to anchor, on the Morvern side, opposite to a gentleman's house called Drummen : the owner of it, Mr. Macleane, having found out who we were, very cordially asked us ashore. We accepted his invitation, and arrived at his house; where we met an English gentleman, Mr. Leach, who no sooner saw us than he told us, that about nine leagues from us was an island where he believed no one even in the highlands had been, on which were pillars like those of the Giant's Causeway : this was a great object to me who had wished to have seen the causeway itself, would time have allowed. I therefore resolved to proceed directly, especially as it was just in the way to the Columb-kill. Accordingly, having put up two days' provisions, and my little tent, we put off in the boat about one o'clock for our intended voyage, having ordered the ship to wait for us in Tobirmore, a very fine harbour on the Mull side.

" At nine o'clock, after a tedious passage, having had not a breath of wind, we arrived, under the direction of Mr. McLeane's son, and Mr. Leach. It was too dark to see anything, so we carried our tent and baggage near the only house upon the island, and began to cook our suppers, in order to be prepared for the earliest dawn, to enjoy that which from the conversation of the gentlemen we had now raised the highest expectations of.

" The impatience which everybody felt to see the wonders we had heard so largely described, prevented our morning's rest; everyone was up and in motion before the break of day, and with the first light arrived at the S.W. part of the island, the seat of the most remarkable pillars; where we no sooner arrived than we were struck with a scene of magnificence which exceeded our expectations, though formed, as we thought, upon the most sanguine foundations : the whole of that end of the island supported by ranges of natural pillars, mostly above 50 feet high, standing in natural colonnades, according as the bays or points of land formed themselves; upon a firm basis of solid unformed rock, above these, the stratum, which reaches to the soil or surface of the island, varied in thickness, as the island itself formed into hills or vallies; each hill, which hung over the columns below, forming an ample pediment; some of these above 60 feet in thickness, from the base to the point, formed by the sloping of the hill on each side, almost into the shape of those used in architecture.

" Compared to this what are the cathedrals or the palaces built by men ! mere models or playthings, imitations as diminutive as his works will always be when compared to those of nature. Where is now the boast of the architect ! regularity, the only part in which he fancied himself to exceed his mistress, Nature, is here found in her possession, and here it has been for ages undescribed.

" Staffa is taken notice of by Buchanan, but in the slightest manner;

and among the thousands who have navigated these seas, none have paid the least attention to its grand and striking characteristic, till this present year.

" The island is the property of Mr. Lauchlan MacQuaire of Ulva, and is now to be disposed of.

". . . . With our minds full of such reflections we proceeded along the shore, treading upon another Giant's Causeway, every stone being regularly formed into a certain number of sides and angles, till in a short time we arrived at the mouth of a cave, the most magnificent, I suppose, that has ever been described by travellers. The mind can hardly form an idea more magnificent than such a space, supported on each side by ranges of columns and roofed by the bottoms of those, which have been broke off in order to form it; between the angles of which a yellow stalagmitic matter has exuded, which serves to define the angles precisely; and at the same time vary the colour with a great deal of elegance, and to render it still more agreeable, the whole is lighted from without; so that the farthest extremity is very plainly seen from without, and the air within being agitated by the flux and reflux of the tides, is perfectly dry and wholesome, free entirely from the damp vapours with which natural caverns in general abound.

" We asked the name of it. Said our guide, the cave of Fhinn. What is Fhinne ? said we. Fhinn MacCoul, whom the translator of Ossian's works has called Fingal. How fortunate that in this cave we should meet with the remembrance of that chief, whose existence, as well as that of the whole Epic poem, is almost doubted in England."

Twelve years after Sir Joseph Banks' visit to Staffa, Faujas St. Fond rowed out to the island from Mull. Concerning the name of the cave St. Fond has the following interesting note :

" Sir Joseph Banks is the first who gave the cave of Staffa the name of Fingal's Cave. I made the most minute enquiries of several persons well skilled in the Erse, Gaelic, or Celtic languages, and especially of Mr. MacLean of Torloisk and Mr. MacDonald of Skye, to know what relation this cave could have to the father of Ossian. And these gentlemen, as well as others, assured me, that the mistake was owing to the name being equivocal. The following is their explanation : The true name of the cave is An Ua Vine. An, the, Ua, Grotto, Cave, Cavern, Vine, Melodious. The name of Fingal in the same language is spelled and pronounced Fion in the nominative. But the Erse nouns are declinable, and the genetive of Fingal is Fine; so that if one wished to mention the cave of Fingal in the Erse language, he would write An Ua Fine. Thus between the Erse Vine (binn), Melodious, and the genetive of Fingal, Fine, there is no other difference than the change of the letter V into F, and some person not very well versed in the Erse language might have translated to Sir Joseph Banks the words An Ua Vine (in modern Gaelic An Uaimh Bhinn) by the Cave of Fingal, whilst the true and literal interpretation is, the Melodious Cave. In this case, the observation of Mr. Troil, on the agreeable sound which he heard issuing from the bottom of the cave when the water rushed in, is valuable, and comes in support of the true interpretation."

St. Fond's account of Staffa as he found it in 1784 is so interesting that I quote it verbatim.   The traveller rode from Salen to
Torloisk, where he was the guest of the MacLeans of Torloisk,
and visited Staffa from there.   On arriving at Torloisk St.
Fond was told that some visitors had that morning left Torloisk
for Staffa.

" They had embarked with a friend of the family and their own servants,
in two small boats.   But they had scarcely gone four or five leagues before
the weather suddenly changed, and the sea became stormy.   Mr. MacLean
thought it so rough that he was afraid they would not have been able to
land on the isle of Staffa, surrounded as it is with rocks, and that they
had been obliged to take refuge in the isle of Iona or Icolmkill, which is
fifteen miles from Staffa, and has a small creek.   We expected that the sea
would be a little calmer by the next day.   We repaired therefore, at an
early hour, along with Mr. MacLean and his family, to the water-side,
which was about three furlongs from the castle, to see whether the boatmen
would venture to come for provisions, but the sea was still more dreadful,
and totally impassable.   We now began to be very uneasy on their account.
They were eight in number, including the domestics, and they had only one
day's provision with them.   The evening arrived without any appearance
of them ; our anxiety was redoubled, and we passed a very unhappy night.
On the next day, which was Sunday, and the third day from their departure,
I rose at four in the morning to inspect the weather.   I discovered with
pleasure that the wind was beginning to fall, and that the sea was not so
high.   We went, before noon, to take a walk on the shore ; and at length,
with the aid of a good glass, we descried them at a distance.   They arrived
at one o'clock, to their own and our great satisfaction.   They were so
emaciated with fatigue, vexation and misery, were so much in want of food
and rest, and so uneasy, that they entreated us not to disturb them until
they were a little refreshed, and particularly relieved from a multitude of
lice that tormented them most cruelly.   ' Fly, fly from us,' said they,
' we have brought some good specimens of mineralogy, but our collection
of insects is numerous and horrible.'   We could not keep from laughing at
this address, their gait, and the restless motion of every part of their body.
They were instantly conducted to their apartments, where their first care
was to clean themselves, to eat a little, and to take a few hours' repose.

" In the evening they returned to the parlour, where they were received
with the greatest demonstrations of joy.   Their appearance was now
fresh and elegant ; but that did not hinder us from asking, whether we
might without risk come near to them.   ' We have cast off everything,'
replied they, ' and of all our evils there remains only the itch, respecting
which we can say nothing, as it is not yet developed.'   They then recounted
the circumstances of their unfortunate passage.   Notwithstanding the fine
appearance of the weather on the day of their departure, scarcely had they
gone six miles when a high wind worked the sea into a terrible commotion.
They would have willingly put back had not the rocks which skirt the coast
of Torloisk made it equally dangerous of approach at that moment ; more-

over the currents and the tide were also unfavourable. They were therefore obliged to keep the offing, and to brave the impetuosity of the billows, driven sometimes in one, sometimes in another direction, and every instant in danger of being swallowed up, but for the address and experience of the boatmen, accustomed from their infancy to this terrible sea.

" Having, at length, after many struggles and dangers, reached the isle of Staffa, they found it still more difficult to effect a landing. By the assistance, however, of the people of the isle, who, on seeing their distress, threw out some ropes to them, and by watching a favourable wave, they reached the shore without any other accident than that of wetting themselves to the skin. The coast, however, was too steep to admit of hauling up the two boats, which were obliged to put off again, and to take shelter in the isle of Iona or Icolmkill, about fifteen miles from Staffa.

" Our friends, continuing their recital, informed us, that the only two families living on this small island received them with the most affecting hospitality, and that the one which thought itself in the most easy circumstances invited them to enter their hut, where they were ushered into the midst of six children, a woman, a cow, a pig, a dog, and some fowls.

" There was laid out for them a remnant of oaten straw which had been used to litter the cow for several days before. This served as their seat, table and bed. A fire of bad peat, or rather ill-dried sod, lighted in the middle of the cabin, smoked them, at the same time that it dried their clothes and served to cook, in an indifferent manner, some potatoes, which, with a little milk, were the only articles of food the place afforded, and those in very small quantities. The provisions which they had brought with them were consumed at a single meal.

" The sea broke upon the island with such impetuosity and rushed with so much turmoil into the caves with which it is pierced, that the hut shook, and our adventurers could not shut an eye.

" Next day it rained incessantly until noon. The sea, far from calming down, raged with still greater fury, so that the boatmen could not venture to carry any supply of provisions from the isle of Iona.

" In the afternoon, the rain having ceased, the captives surveyed the island and visited Fingal's Cave. William Thornton took some views of it with much care; and they made a collection of the most curious stones, among which were some fine zeolites.

" In the evening they had the same reception, the same supper, and the same bed. A new incident, however, occurred. The master of the cottage, his wife and children, lived in such a horrid state of filth that the place was as full of vermin as of wretchedness. Detachments of lice approached from all sides to pay their respects to the new lodgers, who were soon infected with them. This was the most cruel of their torments, and formed the object of an occupation which did not allow them a moment's respite.

" On the third day the sea was somewhat calmer. Their distress was at its height. They walked repeatedly round the island, and ascended the highest part of it to look for the approach of the boats, which at length made their appearance, and came to deliver our poor friends from their afflicting captivity. After recompensing their hosts for their kind offices and hospitable attention, they took leave of them to return to Torloisk, where we had the happiness of welcoming them with all the ardour of friendship, congratulating them that they had got off so cheaply as to escape with only a few days of absistence.

"Finding them all safe, it was not without laughter that we heard them relate their misfortunes, and particularly the diverting episode of the lice. Their account brought to my remembrance, at the moment, a similar adventure which happened in the same isle, and probably in the same house, to Sir Joseph Banks, who set out from London in the year 1772 on a voyage to Iceland, in company with Solander, James Lind, Gore, Walden and Troil; and, in passing, paid a visit to the fine cave of Fingal, which he was the first to make known.

"On their arrival at Staffa they erected a tent, to pass the night under it; but the only inhabitant then on the island pressed Sir Joseph so strongly to come and sleep in his hut, that he out of complaisance consented, and left his companions under the tent. On leaving the hut next morning he discovered that he was completely covered with lice. He mentioned the circumstance to his host in terms of mild reproach. But the latter, who was touched to the quick, perked himself up, and assuming a tone of consequence, retorted haughtily and harshly that it was Sir Joseph himself who had imported the lice into his island, and adding that he had better have left them behind him in England."

Despite the experiences of the party, and the attempts of Mr. MacLean to dissuade him, St. Fond decided to visit Staffa himself, for, as he remarks, "curiosity overcame fear and prudence."

"The next morning at four o'clock, one of our boatmen came to inform us that the weather appeared to be promising, and that it was probable we should have a fine day. Having made the requisite arrangements the previous evening, we were soon ready, and reached the beach before sunrise.

"Our rowers were four young and bold Hebrideans, who appeared to undertake this short voyage with pleasure; the boat was very small and incapable of carrying a sail. Our four seamen seated themselves on their benches; Mr. MacDonald took the helm, William Thornton and myself sat down on a bundle of seaweed, and we put off under the auspices of the genius that presides over the natural sciences, to whom we made a short invocation. It took us hardly an hour and a half to double the point of the isle of Ulva, opposite to that of Mull, near Torloisk, whence we had sailed. We then entered the open sea, and soon found, that in these parts the ancient and majestic ocean has no need of being agitated by the northern blasts to rock up and down and to toss itself into big waves.

"Continuing our course, we had a view of the volcanic isles of Bac Beag and the Dutchman's Cap, with those of Lunga, Skye, Gometra, Iona, etc.

"We could not have wished for a more agreeable passage at so advanced a season. Our seamen, making Mr. MacDonald their interpreter, assured us that it was one of those extraordinarily fine days in this country which seldom come twice in the year. So to show their pleasure they began to chaunt in chorus the songs of Ossian. There is nobody in these islands, from the oldest to the youngest, who does not know by heart long passages or hymns of that ancient and celebrated bard.

" The songs began and continued a long time. They consisted of monotonous recitatives, ending in choruses equally monotonous. A sort of dignity, mingled with plaintive and melancholy tones, was the chief characteristic of these songs. The oars, which always kept time with the singing, tended to make the monotony more complete. I became drowsy, and soon fell sound asleep.

" I do not know how long this lasted, but I was awakened by the movement and noise of the seamen, and was told that we were near now close upon the isle of Staffa, and near some reefs which required some new manœuvres. Here I had an opportunity of witnessing, not without dread, the address and intrepidity of our sailors, who knew how to seize the favourable moments to avoid being dashed to pieces, and to choose the propitious waves which afford a safe passage over the reefs that make this landing so dangerous.

" Two of the inhabitants of the island soon ran towards us, and from the top of their rock threw down some ropes to us; with this assistance and the aid of a large wave selected on purpose, we disembarked amidst a cloud of foam.

" These two men led us, and our small crew, to a level spot on the top of the isle, where stood two houses or rather huts, constructed of large blocks of lava and broken prisms of basalt, and covered over with green sods, getting no light except from the door, which was only three feet high, and from the chimney, which consisted of a pyramidal opening in the middle of the hut.

" The women and children of the two families did not fail to come to us, and invited us to their habitations, but being already informed of their excessive dirt, we were inflexible; and preferred on good ground to receive their civilities and their compliments in the open air.

" Finding that it was impossible to prevail with us with the most friendly gestures, they resolved to do us the honours on the small esplanade in front of their dwellings.

" The men, women and children, with much gravity, first formed themselves in a large circle in which they placed us and our seamen. Then one of the women, disgustingly ugly and dirty, brought out a large wooden bowl filled with milk, with which she placed herself in the centre of the circle. She viewed us all round with attention, and immediately came up to me, and pronouncing some words, presented the bowl with a sort of courtesy. I held out my hands to receive it; but she drank some of it before she gave it to me. I followed her example, and passed the vessel to my neighbour, William Thornton. He gave it to Mr. MacDonald; and so on from hand to hand, or, more properly, from mouth to mouth, till every person had tasted of it. Having made our acknowledgments for this kindness, they immediately appointed two guides to accompany us to Fingal's Cave and all the remarkable places of this small isle. We ate a morcel of bread, to take the edge off our appetite during the walk; as it was agreed upon, that in order to lose as little as possible of so favourable a day, we should postpone taking our repast till we were seated in the boat on our way back. This allowed us sufficient time to see with ease all the objects of curiosity in the island, and particularly to direct our attention to that remarkable cave which we had come so far to see, and which we congratulated ourselves on being able to study on one of the finest days of the year. We went to work, therefore, without losing a moment of time. I soon arrived at the entrance of this marvellous monument, which, according to an ancient but fabulous tradition, was the ancient palace of the father of Ossian. I was obliged to put off my shoes in order not to slip in the depth of the cave, into which the sea rushes with great noise, and where one cannot advance but by walking with the utmost precaution along a sort of cornice on the right side, about fifteen feet above the surface of the water, and formed of a multitude of vertical basaltic columns, on the broken tops of which one must dexterously place one's feet, at the risk of falling into the sea, which runs in to the furthest recess.

"Attention is so much the more necessary here, as the cliff along the top of which one has to tread is entirely perpendicular, and the ledge is in some places at most two feet wide, formed of unequal prisms, very slippery, and constantly wet with the foam of the waves and the dripping moisture from above. The light, which comes only from the grand entrance and diminishes gradually as one advances inwards, serves to make the path still more difficult."

When the Honourable Mrs. Murray visited Staffa the island had been sold by MacQuarrie of Ulva and the laird of the island was "Ranald MacDonald, Esq., of the house of Boisdale." By this time both the families spoken of by St. Fond had left the island, for Mrs. Murray mentions that she saw only a few sheep and three red deer when she visited Staffa in the year 1800. When she paid a second visit to the island in 1802 she heard that in 1801 one of the deer had become so wild that it had almost killed a man, and on that account had been shot, and that the other two, which had formed the habit of following all boats leaving the island, had apparently "extended their convoy to too great a distance" so that they had been drowned. Goats had replaced the deer on Staffa in the year 1802.

The goats have gone from Staffa, and now only sheep remain. On the grassy top of the island are the small ruins, which have been tenantless for almost a century and a half. Gone are the days when a visit to Staffa was fraught with hardship and even peril. Each morning, during the summer months, a powerful motor boat crosses from Iona to Staffa and there awaits the arrival of the steamer, ferrying the passengers (sometimes to the number of several hundred) ashore. The visitors land, walk round the shore to Fingal's Cave, and then are shepherded back to the ferry boat while the two-funnelled steamer rolls idly at anchor perhaps a hundred yards off shore.

Could the two primitive families of the time of St. Fond revisit the island their astonishment would indeed be great. Civilisation has come to Staffa, but in winter the isle assumes once more its primitive aspect and the wild geese and the clan of the grey seals have the place to themselves.

CHAPTER XXXVIII

THE ISLES OF TRESHNISH

WEST of the Isle of Mull a group of attractive islands rise from the blue Atlantic. These are the Treshnish Isles, rich in historical associations and in bird life, and affording excellent grazing for cattle and sheep. Historically the most interesting of the group are Carnburg Mór and Carnburg Beag—two small rocky islands with grassy crowns, and separated by a narrow tidal channel, a place of fierce tides in stormy weather. Both of these islands were strongly fortified, and their name occurs often in highland history.

In the fifteenth century, when the Lord of the Isles still ruled the Hebrides from his castle of Finlaggan in Islay, Carnburg was in the keeping of that powerful highland chief, MacLean of Duart, but at a still earlier date it was held by MacDougall, Lord of Lorne. In an indenture between the Lord of the Isles and the Lord of Lorne in the year 1354 MacDougall surrenders to the Lord of the Isles the district of Mull and its lesser islands, but he makes the stipulation that the castle of Carnburg is not to be given to any of the race of Clan Finnon.[1] In 1493, when the Lordship of the Isles was forfeited, Hector MacLean of Duart was hereditary keeper of the castle of Carnburg and also of the castle " of Dunconnell on Scarba." This Dunconnell apparently refers to the old fortress of Dùn Chonaill, the most northerly of the group of the Garvelloch Isles.[2] It was the same Hector of Duart who was in command of the galleys of John, Lord of the Isles, at the battle of the Bay of Blood, when Angus of the Isles challenged his father's supremacy and defeated him on the north shore of Mull.[3]

In 1504 King James determined to reduce the castle of

[1] The MacKinnons. [2] See Chapter XXXIX. [3] See Chapter XXXV.

Carnburg, and sent a fleet north from Dunbarton with warlike
stores of every kind. Among these stores were " gun-stanes "
or stone bullets. The expedition apparently succeeded in its
object, but the royal garrison cannot have held the castle for
many years, for in 1514 Lachlan MacLean of Duart seized the
" royal castle of Carnburg " and afterwards, with the help of
MacLeod of Dunvegan, made himself master also of the castle of
Dunscaith in Skye.

In Martin's day (1700) " a small garrison of the standing
forces " held the castle of Carnburg, which was so highly fortified
as to be almost impregnable, and could be held safely by a small
force. Martin does not mention a persistent Iona tradition,
that the priceless library of the Iona monks was taken to Carnburg and buried there for greater security at the time of the
Reformation. It may be that the library awaits discovery
below the grassy slopes of the island.

One of the MacLaines of Lochbuie was at variance with
MacLean of Duart, his chief, who captured him and kept him
a prisoner on Carnburg because he did not wish him to have an
heir. He was looked after by an elderly woman, but when the
prisoner was visited a few months after he had been left on that
island the woman was found to be with child. She was at once
taken back to Mull, and a careful watch was kept over her.
When the time came for the child to be born, strict orders were
given that the infant was to be killed at once if it were a boy.
Immediately after the birth, the midwife ran out of the house to
say that the child was a girl, and thus the infant's life was spared.
But an hour or more after she had gone the woman gave birth
to a male child also. This baby was carried with the utmost
secrecy to a cave in the side of Beinn Fhada, where it was
guarded by a man and his five sons. It came in time to be
known that there was a male child concealed somewhere about
this hill and men were sent to the *airidh* or shealing where the
man and his five sons lived to demand that they should reveal
the whereabouts of the baby. They found the old man alone

in the shealing, and when they roughly questioned him he quietly refused to betray his trust. During the course of the day his five sons one by one returned to the shealing. Each as he entered the bothy was asked to reveal where the child was hidden. Each refused, and was slain in full view of the father. When the last of his sons had been killed the old man said that he now saw that his sons were faithful, and that he could die happy. He was then killed, and from that day the shealing was named Airidh na Sliseig, the Shealing of the Slicing, because the head was sliced or cut off each of the victims.[1] The child remained safe. He was taken by another protector and was reared in secret. When he had arrived at manhood his mother told him who his father was, and warned him that he must flee from Mull. He left the island and arrived in the north of Ireland, where he remained for a year and a day. He then returned to Loch Buie with twelve companions and made himself master of the castle by a ruse.

It was on a glorious day of summer that I sailed out from Iona, and as I steered through the pale green Sound that lay between shores of snow-white sand, saw the Isles of Treshnish rise from an ocean of deepest blue. East was Ulva, ancestral home of the MacQuarries, an island where the MacArthurs held their college of piping; west was the long low outline of Tiree and Coll. In the tidal streams of ocean many sea-birds fished. From Staffa we set our course for Carnburg, and at low water reached its tangle-covered rocky shore and landed on its dark rocks. Many birds were on the island. One saw eider ducks on their nests, curious-minded puffins standing at the entrance to their burrows, and shags which grunted and shrieked defiantly from unclean nests. The old ruins and fortifications of Carnburg stand on the flat grassy top of the island. Although the place has been a ruin for centuries it can be seen at a glance how strongly fortified the island was. A natural buttress of encircling

[1] The name remains to-day: the place is on the river Lussa, about three miles from its mouth.

rocks has been made more secure by a thick wall in which at intervals loop-holes are set. From these loop-holes arrows and guns were doubtless fired with deadly effect upon the enemies who were attempting to storm the island. The ruins of the castle and the chapel are on the highest part of Carnburg, a strongly built gateway giving access to them from the lower slopes. At this gate in old times stood the sentinel of MacLean of Duart, his keen eyes searching the sea for the approach of hostile craft. It is long since the last human watchman stood here, and that day his place was taken by a handsome puffin which stood proudly in the strong sunshine, a look of self-importance on its features. On the north-facing wall of the old chapel, where its dry root-hold was sheltered from the sun, was a glorious cluster of sea thrift. Its crimson blossoms gave a softening touch to this austere old chapel; it had perhaps blossomed there for many years. In the east wall were seen the remains of the font and the stone altar.

On this small island the Rankins, hereditary pipers to the chiefs of Duart, perhaps played a welcoming *piobaireachd* when the galley of the chief was seen to approach; the MacCrimmons themselves may have played here, when MacLeod visited the castle, and within the old walls harpers perhaps discoursed softer music. The human musicians have gone; the music of the wind and the waves remains, and the rush of the winter gale and the boom of the Atlantic surf thundering at the sea gate sing a solemn song for days that will not return. Carnburg Beag is also fortified, but from the information I have received it would seem that this island was occupied during a time of emergency only, and that its defenders crossed to it from the larger island where they lived.

It was late in the afternoon when we left Carnburg and sailed west into the Atlantic, passing Fladday where lobster fishermen live in summer, and rocky Sgeir a' Chaisteil, and landed on Lunga, a long island of distinctive appearance where humble families formerly had their homes. The remains of these old houses are visible; even the small heaps of stones which the people cleared off the land they cultivated with much toil, are unmistakable, although they are now grass-grown. The small fields retain their features. They were but a few yards long and less than that distance across—the wants of the people were simple and easily satisfied and they lived rather by the harvest of the sea than the harvest of the land. Even the tracks made by their cattle remain, yet Lunga is deserted to-day—except for its birds. No island with the bird population of Lunga could ever be lonely. Puffins in their hundreds lined the top of the rocks and showed no fear of man. Guillemots and razorbills flew backwards and forwards on important business; kittiwakes wheeled like drifting snowflakes over their nests on the dark rocks. All these bird people have from time imme-morial had their homes on Lunga and their ancestors lived here when the island sheltered a small population of human beings also. But there is one bird nesting to-day on Lunga which is a very recent arrival—the graceful fulmar petrel. These beautiful fliers lay one glossy white egg which they brood on some grassy ledge. Should the human wanderer approach too near for their peace of mind they spit out at him a thin jet of amber-coloured oily matter. Fortunately the fulmar's aim is none too accurate, for the oil is, to human nostrils at all events, somewhat unpleasant in smell.

On the north side of Lunga is a curiously shaped stack which is separated from the parent island by a deep chasm through which the waves thunder when the ocean ebbs and flows. This stack is Dùn Cruit, the Harp Rock, named of old because of its striking resemblance to a harp. The ledges of Dùn Cruit are the haunt of great numbers of sea-birds which provide music more harsh than the gentle chords of the harp.

Late that evening a course was set for the most outlying of the Treshnish Isles—Bac Mór, or (to give it a more modern name) the Dutchman's Cap. Presumably that name was given to the island by seamen because of its resemblance to a low-crowned hat. The Dutchman's Cap is a symmetrical island, with comparatively low ground at either end and a small hill near the middle. This island has no harbour of any kind, and is so exposed to the mighty waves of the Atlantic that even in summer a landing is impossible for days and even weeks at a time. But on this cloudless summer evening the ocean slept, and no rushing overfalls nor high-flung spray disturbed the rocky coast of the Dutchman. Green and long, the island grass swayed to the evening air. Fields of bird's-foot trefoil scented the breeze, and the last of the primroses lingered, half hidden, in sheltered nooks. The milkwort held its small flowers to the evening light and on the rocks beside the nesting sea-gulls the sea thrift blossomed pink and crimson. Even on the Dutchman's Cap, remote and storm-swept as it is, one sees the remains of human dwellings. Can it be that the people of Lunga used Bac Mór at one time for their summer shealings? There is a tradition in the north of Mull that the last man to live on the Dutchman's Cap was an outlaw. He had committed a crime so grave that he was banished by his own people to that lonely island where he lived alone for the rest of his life.

Fulmar petrels flew around our boat as we left the Dutchman's Cap. High overhead, on a steady course, a greater black-backed gull steered out towards Tiree, rising faint on the far horizon. On the coast and hills of Mull was soft sunlight, a delicate haze clothing them with beauty. The north wind fell asleep, and pools of glowing light lay here and there upon the ocean. Ten o'clock came—a quarter past—and at last the sun sank reluctantly below the Atlantic as our boat approached the Sound of Iona where the ebb tide flowed swift and strong past white sands.

CHAPTER XXXIX

IONA

" Seven years before doom
The sea will come over Ireland in one day
And over green grassy Islay,
But Columb the Priest's island shall swim."
Old Celtic Saying.

EVER since that far-off day in the early summer of the year 563 when Columba with twelve followers arrived in their *curach* from Ireland the small island of Iona has been illustrious, not only in Britain and Europe but throughout the world. Columba, of Royal Irish race, crossed the ocean to Alba of the East to preach the Christian faith. The old cave on Loch Caolisport on the coast of the Argyllshire mainland which bears his name seems to point to the fact that he journeyed slowly north along the coast of Argyll before crossing to the island with which he will always be associated, and which was presented to him as a gift by Conall, king of Dalriada. It was on the 12th day of May that Columba reached Iona, landing at a small bay on the south side of the island. To this day the bay is known as Port a' Churaich, the Harbour of the Coracle. Here is seen a mound which tradition affirms to be the place where the *curach* was buried, lest Columba should be tempted to return to the land of his birth, and around the mound are heaps of stones of various sizes supposed to have been raised by the monks as penances.

Before he reached Iona, Columba landed on Oronsay, an island joined to Colonsay at ebb tide, but when he climbed the small hill of Oronsay and could still see Ireland he decided to continue his voyage northward. Oronsay is still holy ground, and Mrs. Rogers of Ellary (by birth a MacNeil of Colonsay),

informs me that when she was a girl there were people living who
recalled that the men of the neighbouring island of Colonsay
used to bring their seed corn across the ford to Oronsay and
there build it into very small stacks along the roadside near the
ruins of the Priory, in order that their grain might be blessed by
resting through the winter on that sacred soil.

Columba had good reason to cast off all ties with the land of
his birth for the following reason. Finnian had brought from
Italy the first Vulgate Gospels ever seen in Ireland. He lent
the Gospels to Columba, who transcribed the manuscript for
his own use.

Trouble came of this, and believing himself wronged, Columba
with bitter words left the country of his birth. Before the saint
decided to make Iona his home he climbed on the clearest of
days to the top of the small hill which rises near the bay, and
scanned the southern horizon for the misty outlines of the hills
of Ireland. Then, since no trace of land was seen on that distant
horizon, he decided to found his monastery on Iona. On the
hill-top from which he had watched he built a cairn, which
remains to this day and is called Carn Cul ri Eirinn, the Cairn
with my Back towards Ireland. In a very old Irish poem
attributed to Columba the passage occurs

> " . . . that my mystical name be
>   Cul ri Eirinn."

There is no more beautiful name than Iona in the world to-day,
and none more renowned. It is interesting, therefore, that the
name should have arisen from the misreading of the letter u
for n in Adamnan's " Ioua." In the Gaelic of the present day
the isle is spoken of as I Chaluim Chille, the Island of St. Columba's
Church, after Calum or Colum Cille, Columba's Celtic name.
Iona is a small island, but there can be none so steeped in things
of the distant past. Because of Columba's fame, and the
miracles which he wrought, Iona became sacred and a burial-
place of kings, not only of Scotland, but of Ireland and Norway
U

also. Forty-eight kings of Scotland, from Fergus II to MacBeth, are buried in Reilig Odhran (Oran's Burial-ground). Here lie also the mortal remains of four Irish kings and eight Norwegian kings or princes, besides one king of France, whose gravestone, according to Pennant, was a red, unpolished stone placed about 70 feet south of Oran's Chapel.[1] One of the earliest accounts of Iona is from the pen of Dean Munro. When he visited the island about the year 1549 the Dean found three stone tombs, built in the form of little chapels. On one were the words "Tumulus Regum Scotiæ"; on the second were the words "Tumulus Regum Hyberniæ," and upon the third tomb was written "Tumulus Regum Norwegiæ." In the sixteenth century, therefore, the burial-place of the illustrious dead was unmistakable, but during the intervening years all trace has been lost of the original tumuli, and no man to-day knows exactly the position of those royal graves.

Many great highland chiefs were buried in Reilig Odhran. Here lies Angus Og, Lord of the Isles, a strong friend of Robert the Bruce and his ally at the battle of Bannockburn. Here lie the chiefs of Clan Fingon,[2] the MacLeans of Coll, the MacLeods of Harris, the MacIains of Ardnamurchan, the MacLaines of Lochbuie, the MacQuarries of Ulva, and other great highlanders.

Martin mentions that an Archbishop of Canterbury is buried on Iona. There is a curious and remarkable story concerning the building of Oran's Chapel, beside which are these historic graves. Columba desired to build a chapel, but the powers of darkness who had their home on Iona before he finally expelled them obstructed the work. Each night the wall which had been built with care during the day fell to the ground, and no progress could be made. It was then revealed to Columba in a vision that the chapel could not be built unless a human sacrifice were offered. In the Irish *Lives* it is written that Columba, addressing

---

[1] Simeon of Durham says that Ecgfrid, King of Northumbria, killed at Dunnichen in 685, was buried at Iona (Skene Celt. Scot. 1.266).
[2] The MacKinnons.

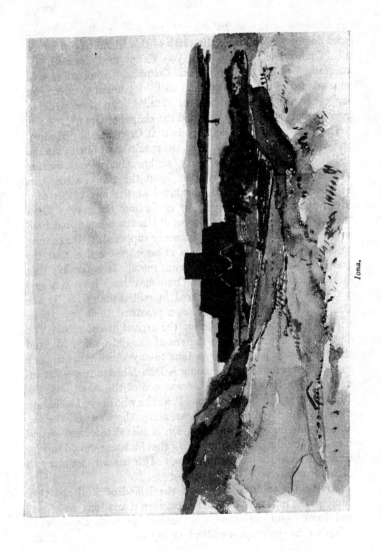

Iona.

the brethren, spoke as follows : " It is permitted to you that some one of you go under the earth of this island to consecrate it." Oran arose quickly. " If you accept me," he said, " I am ready for that." " Oran," said Columba, " you shall receive your reward of this. No request shall be granted to anyone at my tomb unless he first ask of thee." Oran then went to heaven, and Columb Cille founded the chapel of Oran.

The Iona version of the story is that Oran was buried alive, and when, the following morning, the monks went out to see the wall it stood firmly. The powers of darkness had been conquered by the sacrifice of a saintly man. But three days after Oran had been buried, Columba, sorrowful at the loss of his dear friend and kinsman, removed the earth from the grave. Oran thereupon spoke to him as follows : " Heaven is not as has been written ; neither is hell as is commonly supposed." On hearing so dangerous a doctrine Columba at once gave orders that the grave should be hastily filled in once more. It is possible that in this account the sacrifice of Oran may have been confused with the human sacrifices offered in still earlier days by the Druids, who are believed to have practised their mysterious rites on Iona for centuries before the arrival of Columba. The days of the Druids were in the era of the old Celtic gods, and there remains a place-name on Iona to-day which takes us back to that distant time. The name is Dùn Mhanannain—Manannan's fort. Manannan mac Lir was god of the ocean, and the Isle of Man is named after him. It was he who drove his chariot, drawn by his steed Splendid Mane, across the waves of the sea, and who hid himself at will in the Druid mist that formed around him at his bidding. It is interesting that his name should survive on an island which has been the home of Christianity for upwards of 1400 years.

The visitor to Iona may cross the Island of Mull and then traverse the mile of sea which lies between it and Iona, or he may sail from Oban, an interesting passage of some three hours. Whether he journeys overland or by sea he lands near the

Martyrs' Bay, and on his way to the abbey he walks near (and in some places actually on) Sraid nam Marbh—the Street of the Dead. This old track is now partly lost; it formerly led from the shore to Reilig Odhran. It was perhaps at Port nam Mairtir (the Bay of Martyrs) that the Norse invaders murdered sixty-eight men during the first recorded slaughter of Iona monks by the vikings in the year 806. The white sands and the pale green waters of the sea above them were on that day of terror stained deeply with human blood; and so it was fitting that the bodies of the illustrious dead should subsequently have been landed here by their clansmen to the sound of sorrowful piping and weeping. The coffin was landed from the galley, and was first laid on a small sacred grassy knoll beside the shore. The knoll, known as An Ealadh (from the old Irish word ailad, a tomb),[1] is still to be seen. When the bodies of King Fergus, Angus Og, and MacBeth were landed here with much lamentation, the sands gleamed white as they gleam to-day. From the heights of Burg, on Mull of the mists across the sound, the lofty waterfalls doubtless gleamed, as they shine this soft evening of July after summer rain, and perhaps Beinn Mhor was wearing the same diaphanous covering of cloud that she wears to-night as I look upon her.

The centuries pass, but the pilgrimage to Iona continues. Each day during the months of summer men and women arrive from all parts of the world to find rest and peace and the benison which Columb of the Cell bestowed on the island long years ago. The pilgrims find on Iona a community well educated and intelligent. The village library, with its store of books, some of them of considerable value, gives profitable reading during the long winter evenings. Iain Mòr of the Staffa ferry is full of information and old lore, and is as skilled a bridge-player as he is a seaman. The men of Iona have made names for themselves in many professions. They are reliable and daring seamen, expert at hand-

[1] For the translation of this unusual word I have the authority of Professor W. J. Watson.

ling a boat in heavy weather when the surf runs high and the south wind rushes across the island. The population of Iona is decreasing rapidly and now (1934) there is only one child of under three years of age on the island. The traveller Pennant mentions that at the time of his visit (about 1770), what he calls the " town " of Iona consisted of some fifty houses thatched with the straw of bere—pulled up by the roots and bound firmly on the roofs with ropes made of heather. I am told that in 1846 Iona had a population of 500 : to-day the number is no more than 132. Formerly Gaelic was universally spoken on the island, and it is only since the war that English is become the language commonly used. Gaelic is still the speech of the older people, but many of the younger generation are unable to converse in it, and yet in the Ross of Mull, a mile across the sound, Gaelic is the universal language.

In any account of Iona the name of Mr. Alexander Ritchie cannot be passed over, for besides having unrivalled knowledge of the old history of the island, he has created the industry of copying (mostly in silver) the ancient Celtic designs. The work, which is highly skilled, enables the present generation to appreciate Early Celtic craftsmanship. Formerly Mr. Ritchie acted as guide to the abbey and to the historic burial-ground, but advancing years have compelled him to remain mostly at home, although he still works at the craft which is peculiarly his own. He is perhaps inspired by his surroundings. Above the white sands sea swallows flit on pointed, shining wings and the oyster catcher, bird of Bride, calls from the low rocks, while on days of wind the raven, croaking with deep cries as he sails on dark wings, battles joyfully with the Atlantic storm. Gannets patrol the green, sun-flooded Sound of Iona, ever scanning the clear deeps. When they see a large sand eel their strong flight on the instant is checked, and, falling like a plummet, they plunge beneath the surface like a white arrow. In the depths they catch and swallow their fish, then shoot buoyantly up to the surface. Here they rest for a moment, shaking out their plumage that glistens like snow, then take wing to continue their fishing. On the green *machair* and white sands ringed plover nest, and a peregrine falcon one summer recently took heavy toll of the crofters' chickens.

Like the Outer Hebrides, Iona has its *machair* and sands mainly on its western shore. Motor-cars have not as yet come to Iona, and it is pleasant to walk on the dry gravelly roads with their centres worn low by many generations of island horses. There is a delightful walk across the island along a smooth road that leads to the western *machair*, where great Atlantic waves roll with thunder in upon a white strand. A few yards to the south of this road, near the centre of the island, is a large green knoll. This is now called Sithean Mór, the Large Fairy Knoll, but is traditionally believed to be the hillock written of in Adamnan's *Life of Columba* as " Colliculus Angelorum," in Gaelic Cnoc Aingeal, the Angels' Knoll. Here Columba communed with angels, and Adamnan, writing of the event, describes how the saint on a certain day assembled the brethren together and said to them with great earnestness, " To-day I wish to go alone to the western plain of our island; therefore let none of you follow me." But a certain brother (" a cunning and prying man "), going by another way, secretly posted himself on the top of a certain hillock which overlooked the plain. He saw Columba standing on a mound on the plain, praying with raised eyes and hands spread out to heaven. The " prying brother " then saw a marvellous sight. Angels clad in white garments flew to the saint with wonderful swiftness and stood around him as he prayed. " But after some conversation with the blessed man, that celestial band, as if perceiving that it was being spied upon, sped quickly back to the heights of the heavens."

Looking west from the Angels' Knoll one sees perhaps thin columns of spray thrown high into the air as the great rollers rush into the Spouting Cave. Beyond this cave is a promontory with a curious history. Here the people of Iona on a certain day of early spring boiled great cauldrons of porridge which they poured into the ocean. This porridge was given as an offering to a sea deity named Shonny. In return for his porridge Shonny arranged that a plentiful supply of seaweed should be washed ashore. Seaweed on Iona was formerly burned for kelp, and is still used as a top-dressing for the fields.

The abbey of Iona is a prominent landmark. It was built by Reginald, Lord of the Isles, in 1203. Little of the original building remains to-day and most of the abbey is late fifteenth or early sixteenth century work. The greater part of the nave is modern and was built in 1905. Beside the abbey stood the Black Stone, on which the most sacred and binding oaths were sworn. Martin mentions this stone, and places it on record that MacDonald, King (or Lord) of the Isles, with uplifted hands and bended knees on the Black Stone, gave his vassals the rights of their lands. The Black Stone has disappeared, and it is believed that it was either broken up or thrown into the sea because men feared it possessed the power of enchantment.

The nunnery of Iona, now a picturesque ruin with many flowers growing from the old stones, is supposed to date from the same period as the abbey. Both were built more than 600 years after Columba's day. Indeed, one cannot imagine that he would have consented to a nunnery being built on Iona, for he allowed no women on the island, nor even a cow. He is believed to have said, " Where there is a cow there is a woman, and where there is a woman there is mischief."

Near the abbey of Iona stand several old Celtic crosses, and it is unfortunate that nothing is known of their history. On the roadside, between the village and the abbey, is MacLean's Cross, an example of the fifteenth-century solid-headed crosses peculiar to the west coast. The schist shaft is carved on both sides with delicate tracery. This cross is apparently fragile, yet it has withstood unharmed the storms of centuries. Outside the abbey stands a great whinstone cross, believed to be very old. This is St. Martin's Cross and experts have dated it from the ninth or tenth century. Spirals formed of intertwined vipers and ornamental bosses decorate the front of the cross, while on the obverse side are Scriptural scenes, the Virgin and the infant Christ and angels surrounding them forming the central panel. In the summer of 1927 Professor MacAlister discovered near the base of St. Martin's Cross an inscription in faint Erse letters which, when translated, read : " A prayer for Gilla Crist, who made this cross." St. John's Cross, which stands before what is known as Columba's Tomb, has now been restored. It is a beautiful cross, and of it the eminent scholar Doctor Joseph Anderson writes : " the cross shaft is decorated in the purest style of Celtic art with such inimitable beauty and intricacy and harmony of design that I am safe in saying of it that no finer specimen of art workmanship exists in Scotland."

Iona, remote as it is, begins to feel the influence of this modern age. The Gaelic language is dying out. No longer does the old ferryman, Coll MacLean, sail out from Fionphort in his well-tried skiff, braving the winter storms with reefed sails and carrying the mails to Iona. Old Coll has gone, and motor boats, without the charm of sail, have taken his place. There is in summer a daily swift steamer from Oban, and at noon one can read one's morning paper. Yet the Atlantic, mother and guardian of the isle, remains unchanged though ever changing. The waves roll into the caverns as they did in the day of Columba, and the great grey seals, which were the saint's special care, still swim in the boiling surf of Port a' Churaich.

CHAPTER XL

COLONSAY

On a quiet July day I left Iona and, sailing between the Torran Rocks, felt the lift of the long westerly swell which broke white on the Erraid shore. From time to time, as the small craft on which I sailed was lifted on the crest of a great wave, I could see the lonely Dubh Hirteach lighthouse rise needle-like on the southern horizon. Little parties of razorbills were flying west with catches of fry for their young on some distant isle—perhaps they were flighting home to Mingulay in the Outer Hebrides, where vast numbers of sea-fowl breed—and other parties, unladen and flying higher, were hurrying east to the fishing grounds.

We sailed along the Mull coast until we were opposite the rocky Ardalanish Point, then steered out into the Atlantic, setting a course for Colonsay, which rose, with dark rocky outline, across the dozen miles of intervening sea. Behind Colonsay was Jura, its high rounded hills that day the home of dense showers of slow-moving rain. But on the Atlantic the weather remained clear, and as we gradually neared Colonsay the golden sands at Killoran Bay each minute became more beautiful. As we approached the island fulmar petrels circled round us inquiringly, and guillemots, kittiwakes and razorbills flew in the direction of the high rocks which rise south of Killoran Bay. The Island of Colonsay was to us an unknown country, and it seemed as though a landing on the western coast would not be easy, for as we approached the shore we could see a heavy swell breaking white on the outlying reefs. But the tide fortunately was low, and beneath Cailleach Uragaig on the north side of Killoran Bay, low tangle-covered skerries broke the force of the swell. In their lee a sheltered bay was formed, with calm water and a good landing-place on a shingly beach. Colonsay, like so many of the western isles, has a Norse name. Professor Watson has no doubt that the original name was Kolbeins-ey, Kolbein's Isle, a name which recurs in the Norse Landnamabok.

The island is one of remarkable contrasts. The Atlantic swell thunders on the golden sands of Killoran, and on the black outlying reefs and rocks on either side of the bay, yet a few hundred yards inland are the thick woods of Colonsay House, where whitethroats sing among the foxgloves (the foxglove here grows to a height of at least six feet), and the wood-pigeon, after filling its crop from the fertile fields, flies back to its nest in the dense woods where semi-tropical plants are sheltered from every wind. The woods which screen Colonsay House were in existence as long ago as 1776, for Pennant mentions them. It might be thought that the trees, growing as they do upon a wind-swept Hebridean island, would be stunted and weather-beaten, but they stand tall and erect, and as shapely as many trees of the mainland. Through these Atlantic woods the swallow flits, and the cuckoo and the redstart call through the long days of early summer.

Colonsay, like Iona, has strong associations with St. Columba. On Oronsay, a separate island at flood-tide but joined to Colonsay at the ebb, Columba, so the tradition goes, landed on his northward journey from Ireland. He had resolved to continue his voyage until his native land was hidden beneath the ocean and accordingly, when he found that Ireland was visible from the small hill of Oronsay, he continued his journey and made Iona his home. It is only in very clear weather that Ireland is visible from Oronsay, and it is probable that Columba stayed here awhile. On leaving Oronsay the saint blessed it, and said that it should be a Sanctuary for all those in trouble—and a Sanctuary it was, through many troubled centuries. The boundary of this Sanctuary is still seen. On the wet, shining sands, midway between Oronsay and Colonsay, there is visible at low tide the foundations of the Sanctuary cross. When a man, fleeing to Oronsay to escape the fury of his enemies, had reached this cross he was safe for the time being, and if he remained on Oronsay for a year and a day he was then a free man, wherever he might go.

Oronsay is now renowned far and wide because of its old Priory. There is a tradition that this Priory was founded five hundred years ago by John, Lord of the Isles. Here is the Great Cross of Oronsay, twelve feet high, and of beautiful design. It is believed to have been erected to the memory of Colin, the prior who died in 1510. At the foot of the cross are the remains of an old sundial, placed upon the top of the pedestal.

Within the old ruined Priory of Oronsay are many gravestones with delicate Celtic tracery upon them. On one of them is seen a galley under full sail, and perched on the top of the mainmast is a bird which appears to be a raven. It is known that ravens were carried in viking galleys, and in the galleys of the old island chiefs on long sea passages, because these wise birds were able to sense the presence of land invisible below the horizon, and by flying towards it to give the mariners their course. On one slab a figure in armour, believed to be MacDuffie, is seen. The MacDuffies of Colonsay were a distinguished island family, and in 1463 one of them witnessed a charter by John, Lord of the Isles. The original name of the founder of the family was MacDubh Shithe, the Son of the Black Man of Peace. According to the *Annals of Ulster* he was head of the school on Iona in 1164. Martin noticed in his time the following inscription on one Oronsay tomb : " Hic jacet Malcolumbus MacDuffie de Colonsay." This writer says that in a stone was fixed the " colour staff " of the MacDuffies. On this miraculous staff depended the fate of the family, and when Murchardus MacDuffie, the last of the clan, died or was slain in the year 1539 the staff disappeared.

Legends of the MacDuffies or MacPhees (as the family clan are now named) are numerous at the present day on Colonsay. In

MacPhee's Cave at Uragaig was enacted a tragedy of old times. MacDuffie was in hiding here from MacLaine of Lochbuie (or, as some say, from MacIain of Ardnamurchan). The cave has two entrances, and MacDuffie, grasping his trusty claymore, stood guard at the larger entrance, while his renowned black hound guarded the second opening. Their bravery for long kept off their enemies, but at last was unavailing, for their foes enlarged a small hole in the roof of the cave near the centre of the tunnel and slew the last of the Lords of Colonsay. Now there are but two families of the name of MacPhee on Colonsay, and it is interesting that they still show the dark complexions noticed by Martin two hundred and fifty years ago. To-day a MacPhee lives near the old cave, and he acted as my guide to it. He was a man of swarthy face and courtly manners, and lived on the croft above the cave where his renowned ancestor met his death.

Colonsay is an island of old ruined churches, sacred wells, and historic *duns*. The most renowned of its wells is perhaps Tobar Chaluim Chille, St. Columba's Well. It is on the north shore of Killoran Bay, where the ground is shaken by the might of the Atlantic swell as it breaks upon the black rocks below. The spring is now known usually as the Wishing Well, and many people journey to it, wish their wish beside its waters, then leave an offering above it. I noticed a small silver *cuach* or cup, with the initials " A. M'N. F. 1894 " on it.

The sands of Iona are white : the sands of Colonsay are golden. I can imagine no more beautiful place than Killoran Bay, where is the Wishing Well. The black rocks which rise on either side the bay are a foil to the golden sands. On dark days of mist and rain these sands appear to hold sun-fire in their depths. At the edge of the sands a viking prince lies buried with his horse beside him, and as dusk falls on land and sea there is a feeling here of old things that wander abroad on the night wind.

The hills of Colonsay are small : there is none so high as 500 feet, and Carn Mór, the Great Cairn, which I shall describe, is but 428 feet above the Atlantic, and yet this small hill gives a wider view than many mainland hills five times its height. It was on a summer day with the north wind blowing fresh from Mull that I climbed Carn Mór. Days of rain and mist and strong winds from the south-west had made Colonsay a gloomy isle. During this time it might have been an island in mid-Atlantic, for on the horizon north, south, east and west, no land was visible. Then came the welcome north wind, dispelling the low-drifting clouds, drying the sodden ground, and bringing back the glorious weather of the earlier summer months. My way to Carn Mór led near Dùn Eibheann, where in Martin's day a tradition lingered concerning a race of pigmies or *lusbirdan* who were said to have lived in that *dùn* at a still earlier time. On the shore the old fortress of Dungallan was in bright sunshine.

I crossed the pleasant *machair* at Machrins, where the celebrated Lifting Stone stands. This large rounded stone rests by itself upon the green *machair*, and for the last century at least has been the test of a man's strength. A distinguished Professor of Celtic, who represented Oxford at " throwing the hammer " in his undergraduate days, has confessed to me that he essayed to raise the Lifting Stone, but in his own words " failed to put wind between it and earth." Neither I, nor those with me, had more success, but I am told that the raising of this stone is partly a knack. On the *machair* I spoke with a stalwart son of the island, who assured me that in the prime of his manhood he had been able to lift the great stone into a farm cart with the back out, and that in those days a number of the islesmen had been able to lift the stone from the ground with ease. The tradition was (he told me) that the Lifting Stone had been carried, perhaps from the seashore, wrapped in a plaid to its present resting-place on a man's back ! This says much for the strength of the man, and the strength of his home-spun plaid, but plaids were woven very hard and fine at that time, and were much stronger than plaids of the present day. The Lifting Stone, however it may have come there, is certainly foreign to the ground on which it now lies.

From the *machair* at Machrins where green plover called it is no great distance to Carn Mór. The bell heather was in flower; the ling was green and full of sap. Immediately below the summit of Carn Mór is a small loch where water-lilies grow and herons nest. The herons of Colonsay are unusual in their nesting habits. On the mainland these long-legged birds nest on the highest trees, where they are safe from all but the most expert climbers, but on Colonsay they make their nests on the ground, among the reeds near the margins of the lochs. Can it be that the heron, like the bittern, was originally a ground nester, and because of the unwelcome attentions of mankind has retreated to the greater safety of the highest tree-tops?

As I reached the top of Carn Mór all the high ground of the great Isle of Mull appeared to the north. On Beinn Mhór lay a delicate cloud : to the right of that hill rose the lesser peaks of Creach Bheinn and Beinn Bhuidhe. Beyond, the long low line of the Ross of Mull, showed Dùn I, the hill of Iona, and on the far horizon were the hills of Rhum, delicately outlined. To the north-east of Mull I could see the hills of the mainland. The two tops of Cruachan were clear, but mist lay on the hills of Glen Coe. Nearer at hand the sun shone upon na h-Eileacha Naomha, the Holy Rocks, or, to give them their modern name, the Isles of the Sea. Far out on the western ocean rose the lonely lighthouse on Dubh Hirteach, which I had faintly seen from the crest of a wave on the crossing from Iona some days before. The form of the lighthouse reminded me of one of the old Celtic crosses which beautify Iona. Dubh Hirteach[1] lighthouse is old and well-tried. It has matched its strength with the Atlantic times without number, and one memorable winter's day the seas were so heavy that they actually smashed the windows of the lantern at the top of the tall tower. Some of my readers may remember the difficulties of the relief vessel in the early days of 1934 in taking off one of the lighthouse-keepers

[1] This name is sometimes incorrectly spelled on maps and charts as Dhu Artach.

who had his leg crushed by a great wave. Dubh Hirteach (the Black Deadly One) was given its name because of the reefs which were a menace to shipping here in the days before charts and lighthouses were known. Its name was (and perhaps still is) used on Colonsay to frighten a disobedient child, who was told " If you are not good you will find yourself on the Dubh Hirteach."

Far beyond that lonely lighthouse and to the north of it rose the hills of Tiree, and my mind turned to the tragedy of one late autumn day when a fleet of Tiree fishing boats were caught and overwhelmed by a sudden storm. The boats were scattered. Many of them never saw land again. One or two, with torn sails, reached the Bay of Kilchattan, beneath where I stood, and I believe that one gained the shelter of an Islay harbour. It was long before Tiree recovered from that disaster, when the gale must have rivalled in fury the historic storm during the battle of Largs in 1263, when King Haco's galley, with seven anchors out, found herself drifting towards a lee shore and dropped her eighth and last anchor which averted disaster.

Out on the ocean beyond Dubh Hirteach was a trawler. At that great distance it appeared no larger than a toy vessel : it rose and fell on the great Atlantic swell which had travelled east perhaps a thousand miles from some storm on mid-ocean. How sheltered in comparison was the tidal stream flowing, with the sun sparkling upon it, in between Colonsay and Oronsay !

Colonsay at different parts of its rugged coast-line possesses sea cliffs of a considerable height. The greatest of these sea cliffs is at Aonaidh nam Muc,[1] which receives its name from the fact that in former times the pigs of the island used to be kept on the hills here during the summer months. On the cliffs a large colony of sea-birds nest. Innumerable guillemots, razorbills and kittiwakes dispute for suitable ledges, and fulmar petrels have recently appeared. North of Aonaidh nam Muc and the Bay of Killoran, a short distance beyond the farm of Baile na h-Aird, are the ruins of a church of great antiquity, Cille Cha-

[1] The Pigs' Hill.

triona, or Catherine's Church. Beside it stands Clach a' Pheanais, the Stone of Punishment, where the prescribed penance was performed after confession.

On Colonsay there are no motor-cars and no motor bicycles. The island is therefore a pleasant place for him who seeks a restful holiday. The people of the island are contented and prosperous. It is a fine tribute to its public-spirited proprietor that the spectre of unemployment is non-existent here. There is an atmosphere of friendliness on the island : the collie dogs are friendly. They do not rush, barking furiously, upon the visitor ; they cannot conceive that he may have unfriendly intentions towards their household. Even the midges are less persistent and annoying than on other less-favoured isles. It was with feelings of regret that I left Colonsay and through the kindness of my host was landed after an hour's sea passage at the little Islay seaport known as Port Askaig.

x

CHAPTER XLI

ISLAY

I LANDED at Port Askaig on a perfect afternoon in July.

As I sailed across from Colonsay I saw the lighthouse upon Rudha Mhàil, where in the old days the people assembled to pay their rents, gradually grow in size, and soon I had reached the entrance to the Sound of Islay, that narrow strait which divides Jura from Islay. From the east shore of the Sound the Paps of Jura rose, clear and green. West was the less hilly island of Islay. Port Askaig nestled beside the tide that flows so swiftly here that a slow steamer has difficulty in making headway against it. Trees grew to the water's edge, and at first sight Islay seemed to resemble the mainland rather than the Hebrides, but I was to learn later that this first impression is a misleading one. From Port Askaig I travelled by an excellent road, passing near Loch Finlaggan, and reaching Bridgend on the upper reaches of the broad bay known as Loch in Daal. Thence I journeyed west and north-west, by Loch Gruinard and Loch Gorm, to a beautiful sandy bay on the western coast, named Sanaigmore, where my wife and I pitched our tent our first night on the island. Each Hebridean island has its own distinctive charm, and Islay is no exception. It is large, with a coast-line that is partly rocky, partly sandy, but never monotonous. The fertility of Islay is proverbial. She was known in the Hebrides as the Queen of the Isles. The farms are larger than in Mull or Skye, and the crops ripen earlier. Strawberries are gathered before the longest day, and by mid-July turnips are meeting across the drills. The character of the island is so varied that in places (as on the *machair* of Loch Gruinard) one is reminded of the Outer Hebrides, and sometimes, in the more central parts of the island, the countryside suggests Ireland. Until recently there was a considerable amount of trade between Islay and the north of Ireland, but there is none at the present day.

Islay, even in Ptolemy's time, was celebrated for its horses, and there is an old Gaelic saying that an Islay man would carry a saddle and a bridle a mile in order to ride half a mile. To-day, in Islay as elsewhere, the motor-car has largely superseded the horse. The visitor to Islay cannot fail to be impressed by the excellence of the roads. Islay (unlike Skye) is as yet undiscovered, or perhaps it is that the longer sea passage is a deterrent to motorists. At all events it was a relief, after being covered with mud from heavy charabancs and fast touring cars on the narrow and rough roads of Skye, to find in Islay broad roads with a fine surface, and few cars on them. Islay has many old Celtic crosses and chapels. There is an island tradition that St. Columba on leaving Ireland landed at Kildalton at the south end of Islay. Beside the ruins of an old church here the Sanctuary Cross stands, marking the limits of an ancient Sanctuary such as I have described in the chapters on Colonsay and Applecross. In the churchyard is the beautiful Kildalton Cross, resembling in form St. John's Cross on Iona, and around it lie delicately carved gravestones of great age, each showing a warrior grasping the two-handed sword which he doubtless wielded powerfully during his life.

Near Kildalton, upon a bare promontory, are the dark ruins of the castle of Dùn Naomhaig, sometimes anglicised as Dunnyveg, where the great MacDonalds, Lords of the Isles, had a stronghold. After the glory of the Kings of the Isles had departed this grim old ruin saw troublous days. In 1519 it was in the keeping of the Earl of Argyll. In 1586 it was besieged by MacLean of Duart, but the MacDonalds maintained a footing in it (although from time to time they were temporarily driven out by superior forces) until the year 1615, when it was delivered up to Campbell of Calder. After the year 1647 the castle became a ruin. Pipers will recall the beautiful *piobaireachd* known as the "Lament for the Castle of Dùn Naomhaig." Another tune, "Colla mo Rùn," was, according to the Islay tradition, composed and played for the first time at a window in the castle by MacDonald's piper. The castle was captured during the absence of the chief, Coll Ciotach, and Coll's piper fell into the hands of his master's enemies, who planned to capture Coll also. The chief, on his return from some expedition, approached his castle unsuspectingly, and would have walked into the trap had not the piper played a warning tune which his master was quick to understand.[1] The son of Coll Ciotach at the battle of Auldearn was entrusted by Montrose with the Royal Standard, and we are told " the pikemen were so close upon him as to fix their spears in his target,[2] which he cut off with his broadsword in groups, at a stroke." Surely a very graphic description, this, of a brave man in a tight corner.

The MacDonalds, in the height of their power as Lords of the Isles, considered themselves equals with the kings of Scotland. The Kingdom of the Isles, as it was sometimes called, extended from Islay southward to the Island of Rathlin and northward to Skye and even beyond that island. On Loch Finlaggan in Islay the Lords, or Kings, of the Isles were proclaimed. The ceremony took place on an island of the loch in the presence of a bishop, seven priests, and the chiefs and chieftains of all the leading highland families. On the island was a square stone seven or eight feet long, and in this stone a hollow of the shape of a man's foot had been cut. Wearing a white robe, and with one foot in this hollow, MacDonald stood while a white rod was placed in one of his hands. This white staff was his pledge that he was to rule in a Christian manner, without tyranny or oppression. His father's sword was then placed in his other hand and he was anointed by the bishop while those present offered their prayers for the new King of the Isles.[3]

[1] A different version of the same story is told of Duntroon Castle, which I have described in Chapter XLII.

[2] Targe or shield.

[3] Compare this with ceremony at Dunadd, *vide* Chapter XLII.

Hugh MacDonald of Sleat, writing of the constitution or government of the island-kingdom, says, " MacDonald had his council at Island-Finlaggan in Isla, to the number of sixteen, viz. four Thanes, four Armins, that is to say lords, or sub-thanes, four Squires, or men of competent estates, who could not come up with Armins or Thanes, that is freeholders or men that had their lands in factory, as Magee of the Rinns of Isla, MacNicholl in Portree in Skye, and MacEachern, MacKay and MacGillivray in Mull, Macillemhaoell or MacMillan, etc. Moreover, there was a judge in every Isle for the discussion of all controversies, who had lands from MacDonald for their trouble and likewise the eleventh part of every action decided. But there might still be an appeal to the Council of the Isles. MacFinnon [1] was obliged to see weights and measures adjusted, and MacDuffe or MacPhie of Colonsay kept the records of the Isles." (*Collectanea de Rebus Albanicis*, p. 297.)

The ruins of a chapel and old buildings are to be seen to-day on this historic island of Loch Finlaggan. Fifty yards distant from it is a smaller grass-grown island known as Eilean na Comhairle, the Isle of Council. Here was the seat of government in the Isles : here MacDonald with his Council of sixteen sat in judgment, the king seated upon a stone by himself, his knights grouped around him. There are to-day no traces of the stone table and the seat, but there is a tradition that they were carried away by one of the Earls of Argyll. On the larger island of Loch Finlaggan are a remarkable number of old recumbent gravestones, rivalling those of Iona in the beauty of their design. It is believed that the wives and children of the Lords of the Isles were buried on this island, whilst the chiefs themselves were borne to Iona for burial. But from the effigies of warriors engraven on the old stones it would seem that certain of the Lords of the Isles had been buried here.

On a summer day it is easy to see in the clear waters of Loch Finlaggan the large stepping-stones which formerly joined the

[1] Now written MacKinnon.

Island of Council with the larger isle on which MacDonald's castle and chapel stood. The view from the island is a fine one. Against the east horizon the hills of Jura stand; the air is scented with meadowsweet; above the loch swallows flit. No longer does MacDonald rule on Islay, nor do those galleys which, with sails unfurled, are depicted on the old tombstones, steer proudly across the seas to Ireland, to Mull, or to Skye. But the memory of this imperious family remains, and will remain for all time in the isles of the west.

I have mentioned the Cross of Kildalton. There is another old cross of equal beauty and historical interest at Kilchoman on the western side of Islay. Here is a view across green *machair*, golden sands, and the blue ocean, to Ireland on the horizon. The Cross of Kilchoman is of great age, and little is known of its history. On the pedestal of the cross is a round stone in a hollow. For many centuries this stone has been turned *deiseil* or sunways by the faithful who have offered up a prayer at the cross. In Oronsay, and other districts of the west, are traditions of similar stones set in the pedestals of old crosses, but the stones themselves have been lost, or perhaps have been removed by those who looked severely upon such practices. Kilchoman (Cill Chomain or St. Comman's Church) had, like Applecross, Oronsay and Kildalton, its Sanctuary, and it is of great interest to see that two of the Sanctuary Crosses of Kilchoman are still standing intact. I was shown one of these crosses. It is of simple and austere design, and appears to be of great antiquity. It stands some hundred yards west of the burial-ground.

Near Kilchoman are the ruins of the ancestral home of the MacEacherns, hereditary sword-makers to the Lords of the Isles. The name remains on Islay, but the family to-day are more skilled as pipers than as sword-makers. Doubtless the MacEacherns had much work to do after the historic battle of Gruinard, fought on the shores of Loch Gruinard in the year 1596 between the MacDonalds of Islay and the MacLeans of Duart. Sir Lachlan of Duart landed on the Islay coast with a large force, hoping to take possession of the whole of the island. After heavy fighting he was killed, and many of his men fell. A man of the name of Maccafer on the shore of the loch has to-day in his possession an old sword believed to have been wielded with effect at this battle. The spot where Sir Lachlan MacLean fell is marked by a stone. Near the old battle-field is pleasant *machair* land, and here a fine herd of pedigree Highland cattle owned by the Laird of Islay House pasture quietly on summer days. Where men fought in deadly strife terns now flit on delicate wings, and the flowers of the centaury glow like hidden fires where the sweet-scented dog rose creeps prostrate over the sandy wind-swept ground.

Loch Gruinard and its shores are a pleasant country, but upon the wild rocky coast of the Mull of Oa, at the south-west end of the island, there is a sense of sadness and gloom, even in calm summer weather when the ocean is undisturbed by storms. Perhaps an echo remains here of that night during the Great War when disaster overtook the liner " Tuscania " while she was conveying American troops to France. No more inhospitable shore for a wreck can be imagined. Great precipices overhang the sea. Jagged rocks project hungrily from the water's surface beyond the cliffs. It was little wonder that hundreds of American soldiers, and many British seamen also, met their death in that great disaster. Here and there, in rocky coves above the reach of the tide, the " Tuscania's " life-boats lie, their wood bleached and splintered by the rocks. Could they speak they might tell of a dark night of heavy seas and the black fangs of merciless rocks rising up in their path, to overwhelm them and those who crowded them. On the high ground overlooking the sea here is a great tower, erected by the American Red Cross to the memory of those who had journeyed across the ocean to fight in France, and had lost their lives in that sea disaster before they had reached the land they had sailed overseas to defend. It was in keeping with the sadness of the place when a grey seal, lying on a skerry out to sea, lifted up his head and howled mournfully from time to time. His cries, sung as a *coronach* or dirge, carried a full mile inland over the heather. Of seals, Dean Monro, writing in 1542, says that an infinite number lie on the sandy banks of the sea on this land and that they are "slaine with dogges learnt to the same effect." I have not heard elsewhere of dogs being used to kill seals.

Each district of Islay has its own peculiar atmosphere. Sanaigmore, where I stayed during my visit to the island, is a place of free, vital air, where fulmars, razorbills and guillemots have their home on the rocks. Oyster catchers bathe in the sandy bays, and proud mother eider ducks shepherd their small families through breaking seas. At night sunset and afterglow redden the northern sky and the two rhythmic flashes of light from Dubh Hirteach lighthouse pierce the twilight. Before sunrise the hills of Mull rise dark on a rosy horizon and beyond them is the country of Morvern and Ardgour, scarcely mounting above the sea horizon. On days of great clearness the twin tops of Cruachan rise, ethereal and very faint, to the blue of the distant sky.

Islay has a daily mail steamer sailing to West Loch Tarbert on the mainland of Argyll. The boat does not sail each day from the same port. Three days a week she makes Port Askaig her harbour for the night; three days a week she lies at Port Ellen. It was from Port Ellen that I sailed, on a warm sunny morning of summer. Port Ellen, which may be called the capital of Islay, was a place of great stir that morning, for many people were returning to the city after the Glasgow Fair holidays. As we crossed the open sea to Gigha, Ireland and the Mull of Kintyre were clear. We put in at Gigha, a low pleasant isle, very green that summer morning, and then entered West Loch Tarbert, a long narrow loch with great numbers of mute swans swimming upon the brackish waters near its head. At West Loch Tarbert pier the boat was met by a fleet of motor-cars ready to take the passengers across the isthmus to Loch Fyne to catch the steamer for Glasgow, and we at once entered a country where life is not taken so easily and so calmly as in the Isles.

CHAPTER XLII

JURA

" Jura, a horrid ile and a habitation fit for deere and wild beasts."
—Sir James Turner (1646).

More than one thousand years ago Norsemen hunted the red deer on Jura. Dýrey (Deer Island) they named it, and that name, in a somewhat altered form, persists to the present day. Jura is visible from afar. Its high and shapely bens are a landmark for mariners while yet no other land of Scotland is seen. I have looked across to the Paps of Jura from the Cuillin hills of Skye, just over one hundred miles distant, and I have seen them from misty Hecla of South Uist in the Outer Hebrides, and always, from whatever quarter they were seen, the hills of Jura were graceful and distinctive.

Although I had looked upon Jura from Skye, Mull and Iona to the north, and from the hills of the mainland to the east and north-east, it was long before I set foot upon its pleasant shore. But at last came a July day of brilliant sunshine when I stood beside the fast-flowing tide at Port Askaig on the Sound of Islay. A few minutes later I was crossing the narrow sound of eager, sun-kissed waves to Jura of the Bens.

There are less than half a dozen motor-cars on Jura, and because of this absence of motor traffic the roads of the island are surprisingly good, although in places they are inclined to be grass-grown. On the afternoon of my arrival I was able, through the kindness of my host, to climb Beinn an Oir, the Hill of Gold, the highest of the Jura peaks. The hill received its name in the distant past from fancied treasure buried near it. Those were the times when the MacDonalds owned the island (they subsequently shared it with the MacLeans of Mull), and a memorial of the days when the great MacDonald, Lord of the Isles, ruled on Jura is a small island called Fraoch Eilean,[1] the Heathery Isle, for here the great man's prisoners were kept. The battle-cry of the ClanDonald was " Fraoch Eilean," so the isle has become intimately bound up in clan history. In 1690 a charter was granted to the Earl of Argyle of the island of Jura, which was forfeited by Angus MacDonald. By this charter the legal right passed from the ClanDonald who had held these lands for many centuries.

Pennant, during his tour in Scotland more than 150 years ago, climbed Beinn an Oir (2,571 feet in height). He was rewarded by a magnificent view, which he vividly described in his *Tour*, written in 1769. On the day when I set out to climb Beinn an Oir the view at first was so clear that, even from near the shore, the distant hills of Ireland were seen. With a stalker as my guide I climbed by way of a green grassy glen near the head of which was a hill loch, ruffled by the fresh and increasing north wind. Looking back, we saw that the view south was unusually clear. Across the sea were the hills of Arran, rising above the heights of Kintyre. They recalled the Cuillin of Skye, their crowded summits gracefully pointed and clear-cut. But they were more smiling, and less austere, than the Cuillin. The stalker told me that he sometimes fancied, when out on the high ground of Jura in very clear weather, that through his telescope he could see deer on the high ridges of Arran. Nearer at hand was the coast of Argyll—Kilberry, Loch Caolisport where the sun shone brightly on golden sands, Loch Sween, and Knapdale. In the Sound of Jura the north wind was sending white-capped waves to break against the tall tower of Pladday lighthouse. Through the Sound two graceful yachts steamed north, one leisurely, the other so fast that her white bow-wave glistened in the sun's rays.

We reached Loch an t-Siob, and looked up to the graceful

[1] Not to be confused with Fraoch Eilean on Loch Awe.

slopes of Beinn Siantidh, the Bespelled Hill. The sky above our heads remained blue, but thin mists began to race across the high tops. Sun and mist strove for the mastery as we reached Beinn an Oir. The warm summer sun contended with a chill north wind which condensed its moisture on the sun-warmed hills. On the warm dry earth heather and milkwort were flowering, while beside icy springs, bright with mosses, the flowers of the starry saxifrage opened white petals. Around us were precipices where the golden eagle sails, and I was interested to hear of an experiment made here which other landowners might do well to copy. The eagles of Jura were preying on grouse, and were becoming deservedly unpopular. There were no mountain hares on the island, and so the owner of the ground introduced a number of blue hares for the benefit of the eagles. The eagles turned their attentions to the hares in preference to the grouse : the hares maintained their numbers, but did not unduly increase : the grouse became more plentiful and harmony was restored. We entered the eddying cloud, and a pair of ptarmigan, mysterious on white wings, rose from the hill-side and were lost to sight on the instant in the mist. Jura is, I believe, the most southerly haunt of the ptarmigan in Britain to-day, although (as I have mentioned in my account of Arran) they were found in Pennant's time on that island.

When the Sappers were surveying the west coast some ninety years ago, Beinn an Oir was one of their headquarters, and at a height of 2,000 feet above the sea we passed a ruined bothy where these surveyors lived, and from the bothy to the hill-top followed their track, which is still in good order. During the climb we had been in shelter, but when we gained the ridge we were at once buffeted by a bitter wind. From the summit ridge to the hill-top the ground is rough and stony, but the track made almost one hundred years ago is still broad and even. This path leads straight to the cairn—surely the most massive cairn on any highland hill—and in its lee there was shelter from the wind. Here we sat awhile, hoping for an improvement in the weather.

The clouds drove past us, swirling and eddying. Sea thrift was flowering on the hill-side near us, very sturdy and indifferent to the cold. Through the enveloping cloud the sun shone pale, and despite the mist there was a strong light on the hill-top. From time to time the mist curtain drew partially aside, and we saw the Sound of Islay far below, and the sunlit country of " green, grassy Islay " beyond it. But before our eyes had time clearly to take in the view the clouds had again closed on us. Even the surrounding hills of Jura were invisible.

Somewhere below us was Loch a' Bhaile Mhargaidh, where Islay cattle destined for the mainland markets of the south were rested the first night after they had crossed the Sound of Islay. The second day the animals were driven to Lagg and thence, after a night's rest, were ferried across to the mainland of Argyll at Keills, which I have described in another chapter. Somewhere beneath us, too, was the burial-place of Earnadail, one of the early Celtic saints. He lived on Islay, and during his last illness requested that after his death his followers should carry his body to Jura and should bear it forward until they should see a mist enfold the hill-side ahead of them. They obeyed the instructions of the saintly man, and in time saw the guiding mist, and where it rested on the hill they buried their charge. The grave is not far from the road, a mile or thereabouts north of Craighouse.

Jura has been called an t-Eilean Bàn, and the Gaelic word Bàn is here used in its secondary meaning of " Blessed." On its lonely shores are a number of caves. In certain of these caves the illustrious dead were rested, sometimes for many days, until winter storms subsided, on their journey to the holy isle of Iona. In the cave at Corpach there was an altar in Martin's time, but this has long disappeared. One of the caves has the interesting name of Uaimh Mhuinntir Idhe, the Cave of the Folk of Iona.

Old writers have put on record the healthy climate of Jura. Its people were unusually long-lived. In the old burying-ground at

InverLussa, near the north end of Jura, is a stone with the following interesting inscription :

> " Mary MacCrain, died 1856, aged 128.
> Descendant of Gillour MacCrain,
> who kept 180 Christmases in his own house
> and who died in the reign of Charles I."

In the time of Mary MacCrain Jura was a more populous isle than it is to-day. In the glens, now desolate, are the ruins of many summer shealings. Pennant vividly describes them in his *Tour*. Beside the shore he found, on landing upon the island opposite Port Askaig, the shealings of goat-herds who kept a flock of eighty goats for the sake of their milk and the cheese which was made from it. Besides these he found other shealings near the same place. They formed " a grotesque group, some oblong, many conic, and so low that the entrance is forbidden without creeping through the little opening. A shealing has no other door than a faggot of birch twigs placed there occasionally. The shealings are constructed of branches of trees, covered with sods. The furniture is a bed of heath, placed on a bank of sod ; two blankets and a rug, some dairy vessels, and above certain pendent shelves made of basket-work, to hold the cheese."

The island road is on the east side of Jura. The west side is as primitive, and even more lonely than in Pennant's time. Here is a land of lochs, bogs and rough moorlands, and one fine sea loch—Loch Tarbert by name—where many yachts anchor because of the beauty of the scenery and the excellent anchorages which the loch affords. A mile north of Jura is the hilly island of Scarba which holds many red deer. Scarba is separated from Jura by the Gulf of Corryvreckan, in Gaelic Coire Bhreacain, through which strong tides race. With westerly winds a very heavy sea runs here, and the place was one of great peril for sailing vessels.[1]

The old *Statistical Account* (Vol. VI, p. 260) has the following vivid account of Corryvreckan : " Between Jura and Scarba the

[1] Also described in Chapter XXXIX.

space is about one mile over, in this narrow strait. Three currents formed by the islands and mainland meet a fourth, which sets in from the ocean. The conflux is dreadful and spurns all descriptions. Even the genius of Milton could not paint the horror of the scene. At the distance of 12 miles a most dreadful noise, as if all the infernal powers had been let loose, is heard. By the conflict of these inanimate heroes, who will not yield, though fighting twice a day since the foundation of the world, an eddy is formed, which would swallow up the largest ship of the line. But at full tide these combatants take a little rest, and when they are asleep the smallest bark may pass with impunity."

The name Coire Bhreacain was in earliest times applied to the whirlpool between Rathlin and Antrim, now called Sloc na Mara. When St. Columba sailed north to Iona he took with him a little earth from the grave of Ciaran of Saigir, " the senior of the saints of Ireland." This earth, like the earth from Maol Ruibhe's grave in Applecross, had miraculous properties, and when Columba's galley was in danger from the steep waves while passing through Coire Bhreacain at Rathlin, he cast some of the saintly earth on the sea. The waves fell, and his ship passed through the strait in safety.[1]

It was late in the evening when we descended Beinn an Oir. The cloud had reached almost to the shore. A soft blanket of white mist closely covered the Mull of Kintyre. Gone was the outline of the Irish coast. The air was damp, and rain was near. Many broods of grouse rose at our feet. Grouse on most western moors are decreasing, but of late years fresh blood has been introduced into Jura from Yorkshire, and now grouse prosper on the island. Blackgame also are increasing on this favoured isle.

Beside the shore we passed straggling woods where heavy stags have their home, and as dusk fell reached the rose-scented gardens of Jura house.

[1] For another story of Columba in Coire Bhreacain *vide* Chapter XLIV.

CHAPTER XLIII

THE HOLY ROCKS: OR THE ISLES OF THE SEA

BETWEEN Mull and the mainland of Lorne in Argyll a group of rocky islands rise from the ocean's floor. In most maps they are named the Garvelloch Islands, a name that is taken from one of their number, Garbh-eileach, the "rough rocky place."

The Garvelloch Isles are four in number. From north-east to south-west they are Dùn Chonaill, Garbh Eileach, Cuil Bhrianainn and na h-Eileacha Naomha. These names in English would be, the Fort of Conall, the Rough Rocky Place, Saint Brendan's Retreat and the Holy Rocks.

Skene, following Reeves, identified Hinba, the island mentioned in Adamnan's *Life of Columba*, with na h-Eileacha Naomha, but Professor Watson the Celtic authority is of the opinion that the evidence points rather to Jura as the Hinba of old. But he believes that na h-Eileacha Naomha is beyond reasonable doubt the site of Brendan Moccu Alti's monastery of Ailech, founded probably some time before Columba reached Iona.

No island group is richer in spiritual associations of the past than these small islands, and on the most southerly of the group are the remains of what is perhaps the earliest Christian settlement in Scotland. The ancient buildings of Iona, built as they were of turf and wattles, have entirely vanished; the old buildings of Ailech, fashioned of stone, remain to bring before us the life of an early Celtic saint.

But it is not only na h-Eileacha Naomha and its monastery of Ailech that are full of historical associations, for on the adjacent island of Cuil Bhrianainn, Saint Brendan had his retreat, and on the most northerly member of the island group is Dùn Chonaill, an old fortress to which the kings of Dalriada retired when hard pressed. That early writer Dean Monro mentions that this *dùn* was named after the great Irish warrior, Conall Cearnach, the companion of Cuchulainn in many a hard fight. Lachlan MacLean of Duart received the charge of this old fortress from King Robert III, but to-day there is little to show that a strong castle once stood here; the isle is grass-grown to the summit and sheep pasture where kings trod.

The pilgrim who seeks to land on na h-Eileacha Naomha, the isle of Saint Brendan's monastic settlement, must first propitiate the Atlantic swell, for the small rock-girt bay has little shelter and is swept by great combers during stormy weather. But if the spirit of ocean smiles upon him and he is able to set foot ashore he sees, beside the tide, the clear waters of Columba's well sparkle in the sunshine, and, a short distance above the well, the ruins of Brendan's settlement of Ailech. The drystone walls of these small buildings remain wonderfully preserved to show the master craftsmanship of the sixth century. In the small settlement are the chapel, the monastery (a many-chambered dwelling), and a curious building having a deep oven-like hole with a fireplace and flue below it. This is believed to have been a kiln for drying the monks' corn. To the east of these ruins are the remains of two *clochain* or bee-hive cells connected to one another by a small passage. A few yards from these cells is an isolated natural rock known as a' Chrannag, or in English the Pulpit.

If this isle be indeed Hinba, it was perhaps in one of these bee-hive cells that Columba had his holy vision, described by Adamnan, Abbott of Iona in 679. Adamnan was almost a contemporary of Columba, for he was born only twenty-seven years after the death of the saint. Adamnan describes Columba receiving on Hinba the gift of holy inspiration, " so that he remained three days and as many nights, neither eating nor drinking, within the house which was locked and filled with celestial brightness, and he would allow no one to approach him.

And from this same house rays of intense brilliancy were seen at night bursting from the chinks of the doors and the keyholes. And certain hymns which had not been heard before were heard being sung by him. But he himself, as he afterwards declared in the presence of a very few persons, saw openly manifested many secrets hidden since the beginning of the world. And some obscure and most difficult passages of the Sacred Scriptures became plain and clearer than the light to the eyes of his most pure heart. He complained that his foster-son Baithene was not present, for if he had chanced to be there during those three days, he might have written down many things from the lips of the blessed man unknown by other men—mysteries either concerning past ages or those which were to follow after, and also some explanations of the Sacred Volumes. Baithene, however, could not be present, detained as he was by a contrary wind in the isle of Egea, until those three days and as many nights of that incomparable and honour-conferring visitation came to an end."

Many sculptured stones were formerly to be seen in the old settlement of Ailech, but to-day a single stone, and that broken in half, is all that remains. Perhaps a hundred yards south of the settlement, and close to the sea, is the old burial-ground surrounded by a low wall gracefully curved at its four corners. Yet the most remarkable grave is not here (where blackberry stems twine with friendliness over unknown graves), but on a small eminence a short way up the hillside. Here stand two old stones—one with a cross incised on it—surrounded by a circle of small stones. These stones mark, if the old tradition of the district be credited, the grave of Eithne, mother of Columba, who was buried where she could look on to Scarba, frowning immense across the sea, and the long coast-line of Jura, half hidden in soft autumn haze when I stood beside that sacred grave and looked across to sunny isles set in a deep blue smiling sea. Stonechats flitted happily beside that grave, a wee wren flew shyly off, and high overhead a passing raven somersaulted

Y

on care-free wings. The *seilisdeir*, or yellow iris, held its full seed heads to the autumn sun, and the lesser crane's-bill spread a pink carpet of flowers over the grey ruins of Ailech.

I climbed the sun-warmed grassy slope above this old grave, which lies north-east and south-west, and from the highest point of the small hill looked across the broad ocean sound to the great Island of Mull, where Beinn Mhor stood with sun and shadow upon its slopes and rocky Creach Bheinn and dark Beinn Bhuidhe rose in grandeur. Further north Dun dà Ghaoithe mounted from Craignure to the blue sky. There was sun on the peaks of Morvern and on the white lighthouse on Lismore, while in clear sunlight far up Loch Linnhe rose the hills of Ardgour and Glen Coe, with the mighty ridge of Ben Nevis towering above them all. Often must the monks of Ailech have climbed this small grassy hill, where late-flowering honeysuckle scented the still October air, and have seen cold sunrise and warm sunset glow, and heard the cries of passing curlew in the darkness of night while listening to the voice of mother ocean beneath them. Sometimes, perhaps, they wandered to the north end of the island and sat beside the curious arch in the solid rock known as the Clarsach or Harp and watched the solans diving in the flashing tidal streams past Geodha Bhrìde (Bride's Creek) and Geodha Bhrianainn (Brendan's Creek).

Time slipped by as I sat on the small lonely hill of Ailech. The flood tide increased in power, and Coire Bhreacain, that great river and whirlpool between Scarba and Jura, poured out a flood which spread like some vast river across the tranquil face of the Atlantic. Coire Bhreacain, a dreaded gulf in the days of sailing ships, received its name, according to an old tradition of the district, from Breacain, a prince of Norway, who sought the daughter of the Lord of the Isles in marriage. The Lord of the Isles imposed on him the hard condition that he must remain at anchor in the Gulf of Coire Bhreacain [1] in his galley for three

---

[1] For the history of Coire Bhreacain, see *Celtic Place-Names of Scotland.*

days and three nights. Breacain returned to Norway, and asked the advice of the sages of that northern land. They told him to take with him three ropes, one of wool, one of hemp, and the third of hair of maidens of spotless fame. The daughters of Norway willingly surrendered their tresses, but, unknown to Breacain, one of the girls had succumbed to temptation, and her hair in the rope cost him his life. Breacain sailed for the Hebrides in his galley. He arrived at the dreaded gulf beneath the frowns of Scarba, and anchored in the tidal river. The first night the woollen rope broke. On the second night the hempen rope was unequal to the strain. The galley was now held only by the rope of hair, and this held until the end of the third night, when a storm so furious arose that the strand of hair of the erring maiden parted. This weakened the remaining strands of the rope of tresses, and just before daybreak they also broke and the hero and his ship were carried away and engulfed in the raging flood. His faithful black dog fought his way, dragging his master's body with him, to the Jura shore, and Breacain was buried in the cave which still bears his name.

The flood tide was almost spent as we sailed out from the Holy Rocks of Ailech and steered on Coire Bhreacain, faint in sun-lit haze. We reached the entrance to the gulf and saw Scarba loom gigantic above us, with steep rocky slopes which reached almost to the clouds. There were many caves along its lonely shore, and in a warm sunny corrie stags were grazing. The tide was slack. A' Chailleach, the Water Hag of the Whirlpool, slept. No waves broke the blue surface of the gulf, where many gulls and guillemots fished. Soon we had passed beyond the frowns of Scarba, and before the moon heralded a night of beauty had dropped anchor beneath the old castle of Craignish, sheltered by its kindly trees from the strong winds of ocean.

CHAPTER XLIV

LOCH AWE

Loch Awe is a long and comparatively narrow loch in mid-Argyll. It is 20 miles distant from Oban, and the main road from Oban to the east passes along its north shore. Loch Awe is one of the five streams mentioned by Adamnan. He writes of it as Stagnum fluminis Abae, the Lake of the River Aba. Professor Watson, the Celtic scholar, in his fine work, *Celtic Place-Names of Scotland*, mentions that in the word " Aba " we have a Latinised form of the old Irish word " ab," a river. The same word is found in Loch Abhaich (anglicised into Lochavich) on the north-west side of Loch Awe. On an island of Lochavich is a ruined castle to which a secret subterranean causeway formerly led. The tradition of the place is that the architect who planned this secret means of approach had his head cut off afterwards, in order that no information might be given as to the position of this causeway. On Loch Awe are a number of islands rich in old traditions and history—Innis Chonaill and Innishail, Fraoch Eilean and Innis Chonnain—their very names full of beauty.

On Innis Chonaill is a ruined castle, the oldest castle of the Argyll family. Innishail has spiritual associations with the past and on it are the ruins of Saint Findoca's chapel. Findoca and her sister Fincana were two holy virgins, and their day is October 13. Innishail was evidently old MacNachtan territory, for there is a record that in or about the year 1257 Ath Mac-Nachtan with the consent of his brother Sir Gilbert made a grant of the church of " St. Fyndocha on Inchealt." In certain works it is stated that a Cistercian nunnery stood on Innishail,

Loch Awe.

but the Duke of Argyll informs me that he believes this statement to be incorrect. He considers that the convent was an early Celtic one, and that as the nuns probably wore undyed woollen garments the tradition of this colour in later times would have been confused with the Cistercian habit. On a promontory of the mainland immediately south of Innishail was a small monastery, but the records of the monks were destroyed by the Atholl raiders in the year 1685. The name of the promontory is Innis Draighnich, a name which Professor Watson considers to mean the Island (it is now a peninsula) of the Blackthorn-shrubbery.

An east wind was sweeping across Loch Awe from the chilly heights of Ben Lui when a friend and I left the sheltered bay to the leeward of Innis Draighnich, but our boat, rowed by a smiling strong-armed islesman, soon crossed the turbulent water and we found ourselves on the south shore of Innishail, where we landed at an old jetty which may well have been used at the time of Findoca. But before landing on the island we passed two curious rocks, which dragon-like rose from the water a short distance from the shore as though on guard. In recent times Innishail was a rabbit warren, but now a large part of the isle has been planted with coniferous trees, which are already of considerable size. We fought our way through withered bracken at least six feet high, and climbing to the low crown of the island came upon one of the iris-grown fish-ponds of the convent and saw the venerable chapel and many old graves. On one moss-grown recumbent stone are three small crosses (each surrounded by a circle) with a common shaft. Another stone shows an angel offering Christ on the Cross drink from a cup, while Roman soldiers stand smiling on either side. Within and around the crumbling chapel, which pilgrims have visited through the centuries, are many beautiful old Celtic gravestones, some entirely covered with grass and moss, others partly visible. The wind sighed through the trees, but the air was quiet beside the old chapel: an atmosphere of sadness and resignation is to be experienced here. But in spring hope is personified in the daffodils which spring to life amongst the withered fronds of the bracken, and at this season the slopes of Innishail are golden with flowers that are the descendants of bulbs set in the ground by the delicate hands of the nuns many centuries ago. The daffodils of Innishail are in flower at a time when those of the mainland are still in bud, for the slopes of the isle lie full open to the sun.

Long after the chapel of Innishail became a ruin the bell remained on the island, but it has now been removed to the church of Innishail, on the mainland opposite. That bell perhaps saw the suppression of the house of nuns, " memorable," says the new *Statistical Account*, " for the sanctity of their lives and the purity of their manners." At the Reformation, when the innocent were involved equally with the guilty in the sufferings of the times, the nuns were driven from their island home and the isle was granted to Hay, Abbot of Inchaffray who, " abjuring his former tenets, embraced the cause of the Reformation." At a later period an inn was built on Innishail, for in coaching days travellers crossed Loch Awe here in order to save the long detour round the eastern shore.

To the east of Innishail rise the small island known as Fraoch Eilean and the larger isle of Innis Chonnain. It is believed that Innis Chonnain takes its name from Connan, the saint of the *Diseart* or Hermitage at Dalmally. In the old *Statistical Account* mention is made of Saint Connan's Well, " a quarter of a mile eastward from the inn of Dalmally : memorable for the lightness and salubrity of its waters."

On the small Fraoch Eilean stood a castle of the MacNachtans, built by Sir Gilbert MacNachtan in the reign of Alexander III. In an old charter signed by the Scottish king are the words, " Concessimus Gillechrist MacNachdan . . . custodiam castri nostri et Insulae de Frechelan." It is alleged that Sir Gilbert and his heirs held the castle from the king on the condition that they should entertain the sovereign if ever he should pass that way and should not fail to give the king a bed of clean straw. The key of this old castle, in later years the residence of MacDonnachaidh [1] of Inverawe, was, *vide* the new *Statistical Account,* " picked up among the ruins not so many years ago by a gentleman of the neighbourhood, who handed it over to Campbell of Monzie, the present proprietor, who has it now in his possession."

Pennant describes a curious tradition concerning Fraoch Eilean, namely, that the island is the Hesperides of the highlands. " The fair Mego longed for the delicious fruit of the

Pass of Brander.

isle, guarded by a dreadful serpent. Fraoch, who had long loved the maid, goes to gather the fruit. By the rustling of the leaves the serpent was awakened from his sleep. It attacked the hero, who perished in the conflict. The monster was also destroyed. Mego did not long survive the death of her lover."

In the old Celtic sagas, Fraoch or Fráech was contemporary with Cuchulainn, and he is commemorated in the ancient tale of Táin Bó Fráich, the Driving of the Cattle of Fráech, but it seems probable that the derivation of Fraoch Eilean is a more prosaic one and that its meaning is Heather Island.

Of Fincharn, near the farther end of Loch Awe, little is

[1] The patronymic of Campbell of Inverawe.

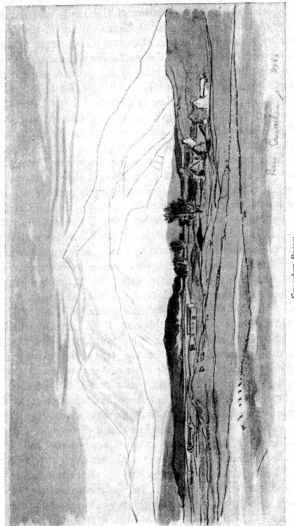

Cruachan Beann

known. It was the main fortress of the Lords of Glassary, and the oldest known Charter of Lands in Argyll, namely a charter by Alexander II dated at Strivelin on August 1, 1240, to Gillascop MacGilchrist, grants him for his homage and service " in Erregaythil " the 5 pennylands of Fincharn except the ½ penny land which Eugenius (Ewen) his brother holds. At a later time the Scrymgeour family became Lords of Glassary, and Dugald Campbell of Argyll, *circa* 1315, with his wife Margaret de Glassereth had a charter from John de Glassereth, Lord of that Ilk, of various lands including Cairnfin—which from the context is the place that is now known as Fincharn.

Near the lower reaches of Loch Awe is the old chapel of Killineuer, in Gaelic Cill an Iubhair, the Church of the Yew. The stones for this chapel were dressed in a quarry close to Killevin of Loch Fyne, and if we believe the narrative of the parish minister in the new *Statistical Account*, " on a particular day appointed the people attended in such numbers as to form one close rank from Killevin to Kilneuair, a distance of twelve miles, and each stone as raised at the quarry or hewing station was handed from one man to another along the whole rank until it was fixed by the last of them in its place in the building." There is a curious old story told of this chapel. A ghost was said to haunt the place, and a daring tailor ventured to bet that he would make a pair of trews within the walls of the chapel during the midnight hours. Carrying a torch, he arrived at the ruin and set about his task as boldly as possible, but he had not sewn long when a hollow voice directed his attention to a hand of gigantic size rising from one of the graves within the chapel. He then heard the words " Am faic thu a chrog mhor liath so a' thailleir? " (" Do you see this great hoary hand, tailor? "). The tailor valiantly made answer, " Chi mi sin 's fuaighidh mi so " (" I see that, and I will sew this "). A skelton head then appeared from the grave and the voice, again speaking in blood-curdling tones, said, " Am faic thu an ceann mór liath so a' thailleir? " (" Do you see this large grey head, tailor? ")

Less boldly the tailor this time made answer, " Chi mi sin 's fuaighidh mi so " (" I see that and will sew this "). The conversation proceeded on the same lines as each fresh member of the skeleton's anatomy appeared. At last the whole skeleton stood immense before him and the poor tailor fled in terror. He was only just in time, for even as he dashed from the chapel a huge bony hand was stretched out to seize him, and failing to grab the tailor left its impression on the wall. If the truth of this story be doubted the ghostly hand-mark remains to this day on the chapel wall for all to see.[1]

Although Loch Awe is the home of old castles and of still older traditions, there is none so old as Beathach Mór Loch Obha, the Big Beast of Loch Awe. He may be more venerable than the Monster of Loch Ness; some say he was like a horse, others, like a great eel. It was known that he had twelve legs, and when the bays of the lochs were frozen in winter, cracks and rumblings were sometimes heard, and the people with a shiver would say one to another, " That is the Big Beast, breaking the ice."

[1] A similar tale is told of the tailor of Beauly.

CHAPTER XLV

In early times the name Argyll was given to all the western coast of Scotland from the Mull of Cantyre to Loch Broom in Western Ross-shire. North of Ardnamurchan the country of Argyll was then called Oirer a Tuath (the North Coast) and to the south of that promontory Oirer a Deas (the South Coast). Argyll itself in its original form is Oirer Ghàidheal, the coast-land of the Gael.

From Oban (the Little Bay) the road winds southward through mid-Argyll. It skirts Loch Melfort, and in the neighbourhood of Loch Craignish passes near the old battle-ground of Druim Righ where a body of Norsemen, landing from their galleys unexpectedly, attacked the people of the district. The Gaels put up a stout resistance, and one of the leaders of the North-men, Ulrick by name, was slain at Sluggan, where a grey stone stands as his memorial. It is narrated that the Norse leader Olave and the leading prince of Argyll fought in single-handed combat, and that Olave was killed and was buried at Dùn Aula, about half a mile from Druim Rìgh. There is here a rough stone set up by the people of the district as a memorial to the chivalrous Norsemen.

At the mouth of Loch Craignish stands the old castle of Craignish. It is believed to have been first a stronghold of the MacEacherns, and in late times was held by the Campbells of Craignish. It is on record that Alasdair MacDonald (Alasdair mac Colla Ciotach), who led fifteen hundred Irish to the aid of Montrose in 1644, invaded the lands of Craignish, but Campbell of Craignish moved his cattle to one of the islands of the Sound and reinforced his castle garrison to such purpose that after a siege of six weeks the besiegers were obliged to withdraw.

To the north of the Craignish promontory are the islands of Shuna, Luing and Torsay, and on the latter isle is an old ruin named Caisteal nan Con, which may have been at one time in the possession of the MacLeans. The island of Luing is celebrated for its quarries of slate. Far out to sea rise na h-Eileacha Naomha, the Holy Rocks [1] (in the maps sometimes named the Garvelloch Islands), and the mighty isle of Scarba. The *Statistical Account* narrates that about half a mile to the northwest of the southern point of Craignish peninsula is a small bay known as the Port of the men of Athole. Here some of the Marquis of Athole's men were defeated during their great raids on Argyll in the latter part of the seventeenth century, and were drowned in the bay while endeavouring to escape.

A few miles south of Craignish, on a promontory of Crinan Loch, is the old castle of Duntroon, still used as a residence. It is commemorated in a classical piece of pipe music called " The Sound of the Waves against Duntroon Castle " and was the scene of a romantic and tragic episode in the seventeenth century. The story is somewhat as follows. Colla Ciotach (Left-handed Coll), with his followers, had invaded Argyll and, intending to attack Duntroon Castle, sent his piper forward by land in order to procure information. The piper was admitted to the castle, and perhaps delighted its inmates by his playing. He found that the stairway was so narrow that only one person could climb it at a time to attack the place. His actions having aroused suspicion he was imprisoned in one of the turrets of the castle. From his small window he observed the galleys of Colla Ciotach approaching, and fearing lest they should fall into a trap he played on his pipes the tune which is known as the " Piper's Warning to his Master." The words of the air are as follows :

> " A Cholla mo rùin seachan an tùr, seachan an Dùn,
>   A Cholla mo ghaoil seachan an caol, seachan an caol.
> Tha mise an làimh, tha mise an làimh."

---

[1] Described in Chap. XLIII.

"Coll my beloved, avoid the tower, avoid the dun,
Coll my beloved, avoid the Sound, avoid the Sound.
I am in their hands, I am in their hands."

The piper made his pipes speak, and Colla Ciotach, understanding the piper's message, did not attack, but the player had his fingers cut off and succumbed from shock and loss of blood. He was buried beneath a large stone slab in the castle kitchen; his grave is still to be seen, and his ghost is said to haunt the castle.

Duntroon Castle was bathed in soft autumn sunshine on the golden afternoon when I visited it. A gentle breeze ruffled the blue waters of the sea loch on which it stood, and a wandering solan passed up the loch in search of mackerel. Surely in the air was the echo of faint pipe music, and I could visualise that day of long ago when the piper stood in the castle turret and as he played anxiously watched, unmindful of his own peril, the course of the approaching galleys, and finally saw with relief that they had understood the message he had sent out on the air with all the intensity of his feeling.

The district is the home of many antiquities. In the old churchyard at Kilmartin are sculptured stones, and in the neighbourhood of Poltalloch are old *dùns*, burial chambers, and cup-marked rocks. On a slab near an early Christian grave, discovered near Poltalloch in 1928, an inscription in Ogham characters was found, a relic of the early Dalriadic settlers in the place. Between Kilmartin and the Crinan Canal is a stretch of level boggy country known as Mòine Mhór, the Great Moss. Just to the north of the moss is Dunadd, a place of much historical interest, and believed to have been the seat of the kings of Dalriada. The small hill rising from green grassy country reminded me of Beregonium (which I had visited the previous day), except that there was no friendly ocean beside it. As at Beregonium, several passes lead up to the *dùn*.

We know little of Dunadd. In the year 736 Aengus, king of the Picts, from his fortress beside Loch Etive made an attack

upon Dunadd, which he captured, and bound with chains two
sons of the king of Dalriada, Selbach by name. Five years
later Aengus again dealt Dalriada a " smiting " from which she
did not recover for long.

Near the summit of Dunadd, on a level surface of rock surrounded by short grass, can be seen the spot where the kings of
Dalriada were crowned. A wild boar is incised in the rock
here, and beside it the print of the human foot is carved out of
the rock. The footmark is facing north-east. On the farther
side of the figure of the boar is a circular hollow or *ballan* in
the rock. It is thought that the kings of Dalriada were crowned
as they stood with the left foot forward and placed in the footmark, and that they were anointed with holy water taken from
the round hollow. But there is another fanciful tradition to
account for this old footmark. It is said that the witch of
Cruachan, landing after a great leap from the mighty hill above
dark Loch Awe, landed here and left the mark of her foot. If
this indeed be true the witch must have had small feet, for the
footprint is rather small for even a mortal man to place his
foot in.

From Dunadd in clear weather Cruachan is visible, and the
hills of Mull. Behind Duntroon Castle rises Jura, outlined in
glory against the sunset of a summer's night.

The footprint of Dunadd is world famous. Less well known are
the two footprints in a rock at Kilmichael, a couple of miles
distant. Above the churchyard with its old recumbent sculptured stones is a large flat rock, from which the grassy layer
has recently been partially removed. Here are many cup marks
and circles, and near them are two footprints, smaller than those
at Dunadd, and also facing north-east. Is it possible that the
queens of Dalriada were crowned here? We read of the importance of the queens in early Celtic literature, and it seems
only natural that some religious ceremony should have marked
their rise to queenly station. Midway between Dunadd and
Kilmichael is to be seen on the hill-side the hole for a flagpost,

perhaps a relic of the days when the kingdom of Dalriada flourished.

These footprints at Dunadd and Kilmichael were the more interesting to me as the previous day I had seen, at Dunollie Castle, Oban, the print of a human foot on a large stone. This stone has been taken across to the mainland from the island of Kerrara, and it is traditionally believed that the MacDougall chiefs when they succeeded swore on that old stone honourably to serve their clansmen in war and peace.

Across the southern margin of Mòine Mhór is the Crinan Canal, which enables vessels of small size to cross to Loch Fyne and the waters of the Clyde area without taking the long and exposed passage round the Mull of Cantyre. Many of the smaller vessels engaged in the herring fishing avail themselves of this sheltered waterway.

South-west of Crinan is the interesting country of Loch Sween and Knapdale. There are two roads, one on the north, the other on the south of the loch. At Keills, where the more northerly road ends, was in former times the ferry to Jura, and the older generation of the district still remember cattle being ferried from Islay and Jura and landed at Keills on their way to the markets of the south. Beside the old ruined chapel at Keills stands a Celtic cross of remote antiquity. On the cross is shown an angel carved above what appears to be a bird's nest containing three eggs. Another group portrays two otters above and two dogs below holding converse with a short cloaked figure. There is Celtic tracery beneath the figures. In the burial-ground within the ruined chapel are many old recumbent stones. One of them marks the grave of a Graham of Claverhouse, and at the head of this stone is a small circular hole so that he who is buried here may see through the small window of the chapel to the countryside beyond it. I was informed that there is an old woman still alive in the district who is a descendant of Graham of Claverhouse and has the right of burial here.

It is necessary to return along the shore of Loch Sween almost as far as the Crinan Canal before visiting the opposite shore of the Loch, and at one point the road passes within two miles of Kilmahumaig, where is a mound called Dùn Domhnaill. Here, if local tradition is accurate, the Lords of the Isles were accustomed to hold their courts of justice, and it is narrated that on one occasion a man who had been condemned to death succeeded in making his escape. The Lord of the Isles, greatly annoyed, ordered one of his vassals, a man remarkable for strength and fleetness of foot, to pursue the fugitive and bring him back, either alive or dead. He was overtaken, was overpowered after a short and desperate struggle, and was carried back to the place of execution, where he was quickly hung. The Lord of the Isles, to mark his appreciation of his vassal's bravery, there and then gave him a charter of the lands of Kilmahumaig in the following words :

" Tha mise, Domhnall nan Domhnall,
  Am shuidhe air Dùn Domhnaill,
  Ag tabhairt còir o'n diugh gus a màireach
  Is mar sin gu latha bhràtha
  Dhuitse, Mhic Aoidh bhig,
  Air Cill Ma-Shumaig
  Suas gu flaitheas Dé
  Agus sìos gu h-Ifrinn
  Fhad 's a shéideas gaoth
  'S a ruitheas uisge ;
  Agus so an làthair Catriona mo bhean
  Agus Airig bheag mo Bhanaltrom."

" I Donald of the Donalds,
  Seated on Dundonald,
  Give title from to-day till to-morrow and so on till the day of doom
  To thee, Little MacKay
  Of Cill Ma-Shumaig
  Up to God's Heaven
  And down to Hell
  As long as wind blows
  And water runs ;
  And this in presence of Catriona my wife
  And of little Airig my nurse."

On the south shore of Loch Sween are the ruins of Castle Sween, known in early times as the Key of Knapdale, and

z

beyond it is the ruined chapel of Kilmory, with the MacMillan Cross beside it. At the Point of Knap, on a low sunken rock visible only at very low tides, was carved (so says tradition) the charter of the MacMillans to the lands of Knapdale. The building of Castle Sween (more correctly Suibhne) is lost in the mists of antiquity. According to one tradition it was built by Suibhne mac Righ Lochlann, Suine, son of the King of Norway.

Mrs. Rogers of Ellary informs me that the oldest records in her family, the MacNeills of Colonsay, ascribe their descent from Suibhne Ruadh or Swenus de Ergadia, who was Thane of Knapdale in the thirteenth century, and Castle Sween remained in the hands of the MacNeills until it passed, in the sixteenth century, to a MacMillan through his marriage with the MacNeill heiress. At a later date the castle was again in the hands of a MacNeill.

A very old poem on Castle Sween is in existence. It begins " Dàl chabhlaigh ar Chaisteal Suibhne," and it is the work of one Artur Dall mac Gurcaigh. The poem is addressed to Eoin mac Suibhne on his setting out from Ireland to recover his ancestral lands in Knapdale in 1310. The poem was showed me by Professor W. J. Watson.

The part of the castle now known as MacMillan's Tower was built much later, and is ascribed to the great chief known as MacMillan Mór, in whose memory the MacMillan Cross was set up.

Robert the Bruce besieged Castle Sween—which was at that time a residence of the Lord of the Isles—took the great Mac-Donald prisoner, and imprisoned him in Dundonald Castle, where he died. The new Lord of the Isles—Angus Og—became a strong supporter of Robert Bruce, and because of his bravery and his clansmen's valour upon the battle-field of Bannockburn the king granted them in perpetuity the privilege of fighting on the king's right hand in every battle. The MacDonalds greatly prized this distinction and the failure to assign to them their rightful place on the battle-field of Culloden may well have turned the fortunes of the day.

In the year 1644 the castle was besieged and burnt by Sir Alexander MacDonald, better known as Alasdair mac Colla Ciotach.

Beyond Castle Sween, and near the Point of Knap, is the ruined chapel of Kilmory, and here are a great number of recumbent Celtic gravestones, many with delicate patterns and beautiful tracery. Standing as though on guard at one corner of the graveyard is the MacMillan Cross. At its base are the words *Haec est Crux Alexandri MacMulen.* On the west face Christ is seen on the cross, with a smaller figure on either side of him. Below are a claymore and further Celtic tracery. On the east face of the cross dogs are seen hunting a stag : below this group stands a figure with hunting horn and Lochaber axe held aloft—perhaps to administer the death-blow to the stag.

Leaning against the chapel of Kilmory I noticed an old stone with a cross within a circle upon it. It resembled some of the Sanctuary crosses I had seen on Islay, and in its original position it may have been one of a circle of crosses set to mark the " girth " or Sanctuary of the chapel of Kilmory. Beside the cross is a prayer ball in a cupped stone. The pilgrim after his prayer was accustomed to turn the stone *deiseal* or sunwise, and this action rendered his prayer more efficient. A few yards distant from the MacMillan Cross lived until recently the Mac-Taggarts, hereditary weavers of Knap. In the house stood two looms at least 300 years old. The last of the weavers was a man of over ninety when he died, and with him has passed from Knapdale the art of weaving.

CHAPTER XLVI

KNAPDALE AND THE COUNTRY SOUTHWARD

Two miles seaward of Kilmory stands the island which is marked on present-day maps as Eilean Mór, but which is more correctly Eilean Mór mhic O' Charmaig. Cormac, the saint from whom the island derives its name, may be either Baetan Maccu Cormaic, abbot of Cluain mac Nois, who died on March 1 in the year 664, or Abban Maccu Cormaic of Magh Arnaide. Professor Watson in his *Celtic Place-Names of Scotland*, explains that the ancient Irish gentilic term *maccu* became later *mac ui* or *mac O'*. Cormac's church—Cill mo-Charmaig—was at Keills, and the small church or chapel on Eilean Mór is also ascribed to him, but would seem from its appearance to be of a later date. In the new *Statistical Account* we read : " Within this chapel, in a recess in the wall, is a stone coffin in which the remains of the priests are said to have been deposited. The figure of a naked man is cut on the lid of the coffin. The coffin also for ages served the saint as a treasury. Till of late not a stranger set foot on the island who did not conciliate the favour of the saint by dropping a small coin into a chink between the lid of the coffin and its side."

It was a grey morning of autumn when I sailed out from sheltered Loch Sween and saw Eilean Mór rise from the sea. The flood tide was sweeping in from the Atlantic with irresistible might, and when the launch had crossed the tidal river and had dropped anchor in a small sheltered loch on the north-east side of the island we landed at the rough stone jetty where pilgrims and holy men had landed from their *curachs* in earlier times.

It is sad to chronicle that the fine old cross which formerly stood beside the chapel here has been wantonly destroyed. The head was broken off and carried away some years ago, and efforts to trace it have been without result. Happily the old crosses at Keills and Kilmory are still unharmed. A short distance from the island chapel is a small cave where Cormac had his cell, and beside the cave is a small ruined dry-stone building not unlike the ruins on the Garbh Eileach [1] group of islands. From the aperture of the cave is a drop of some eight feet to the earthen floor, where there is space for one man to sleep. On the stone wall are incised a circle, emblem of eternity, and a small cross delicately carved. There is a tradition that no married couple may enter this cave, and that if they do they will be childless. (The cell of Saint Fiacre, a Celtic missionary to France and whose birthplace was Dunstaffnage, was also strictly forbidden to women.)

The October sun shone warm at the entrance of Cormac's cave on Eilean Mór. Brambles twined about the old ruins at the cave's mouth. Here was a sense of tranquillity and sanctity— the impress of a saintly life upon its surroundings.

Beyond the rocky shore the tide increased in power, and flowed mightily past low tangle-covered skerries which thrust dark heads above the tumultuous waters. Solans diving here for fish sent clouds of shining spray into the sun-lit air and black guillemots, already in winter plumage, rode the waves buoyantly. Across the green sea and golden sunlight rose the long hilly island of Jura, its slopes russet, its high tops still veiled by the fast-melting clouds of morning. On the distant southern horizon were the low island of Gigha and the high coast-line of Cantyre. The grass of Eilean Mór was warm and dry and the last of the summer flowers opened to the autumn sun. A snipe rose from the long grass and on the rocks stood dark-plumaged shags as though on guard over this old sanctuary.

The evening light was soft on land and sea as I reached the mainland. Beinn an Oir of Jura had freed herself of cloud and rose in beauty to the quiet sky. The breeze had fallen light,

[1] Described in Chapter XXXIX.

and pools of colour lay on the sea beyond a narrow belt of white sand. Already the tide had turned, and was streaming tirelessly west as it had done each day since the time of Saint Cormac and of MacMillan Mór of Knap, whose noble cross reflects the last rays of the sun as it dips behind the kindly hills of Jura of the red deer.

From Kilmory beside the Point of Knap a rough track leads across the hill to Ellary on Loch Caolisport. Near the shore of this loch, at a place called Cove, are a ruined chapel and a cave in which it is traditionally believed Columba lived for a time on his way from Ireland to Iona. Some authorities are inclined to doubt whether indeed Columba made his way leisurely along the coast of Argyll before reaching the island with which his name is so closely associated, but it seems only natural that in those days of open *curachs* a traveller setting out northward from Ireland would hug the land, and would thus sail first across the Strait to the Mull of Cantyre, and would then continue along the Scottish coast to a point opposite the south end of Jura, and, crossing the sound here, would reach Iona by way of the Sound of Islay with a halt at Oronsay on the journey.

The cave on Loch Caolisport where Columba is traditionally believed to have celebrated the Sacrament is in surroundings of great beauty and restfulness. The old altar remains ; in the rock near it are two circular hollows, one small, the other larger. The holy water was kept in the smaller hollow ; the larger was for the washing of the pilgrims' feet. On the wall of the cave above the altar is carved a small cross, thick, sturdy and shapely —the work of master hands. High on the opposite face of the cave is incised a cross within a circle. Near the old altar ivy and ferns grow in a subdued light, and the crane's-bill flowered red here on the autumn day when I visited the cave. Further along the shore of the loch, in a sheltering wood, is a grassy burying-ground, believed to be one of the oldest in Scotland and to date back to the fire age. I recall the wealth of blossom in the Ellary garden on the day when I visited Columba's Cave and the old burial-ground, and the quiet atmosphere of the place. Although the season was October sweet peas and dahlias were in full bloom, and many fine trees protected the garden from the ocean winds.

There is a road across the hill from Ardrishaig (the port of the steamer from Glasgow) to Loch Caolisport, and this road travels south-west along the south shore of the loch past Kilberry and Dunmore to join the main Campbeltown–Ardrishaig road at Tarbert. At Kilberry there is a fine view over the sea to Ireland, and large fields (where many grouse and blackgame were feeding on the day when I passed that way) alternate with stretches of rough and rugged moorlands. Kilberry is named after Saint Berach, who visited Columba at Iona. Adamnan relates the adventure of Berach with a sea monster on crossing from Iona to Tiree. Kilberry (in Gaelic Cill Bhearaigh) was formerly a monastery, and the fish-ponds of the monks are still to be seen here. Near these ponds stands a curious old Celtic cross. The shaft has evidently at some time been broken, and the head of another cross placed upon it.

South of Kilberry, beside Loch Stornoway, are some fine standing stones, and now the road leaves the coast for several miles and returns to the sea again near Dunmore, on West Loch Tarbert. Dunmore, a large *dùn* hidden in the woods, appears to have been an important structure in early times. Not far from it is a large stone of unusual shape marking, according to tradition, the grave of Diarmid. The Gael carried the tale of Diarmid's death to Scotland, and the scene of his hunting the wild boar and of his tragic death is associated with many districts. Beyond this stone, and built in a prominent position, is the Fort of the Black Dog. It was an October evening when I stood here. To the south was Arran in deep shadow, clouds resting on its hills. But on the nearer hills the setting October sun shone bright, and above the long golden bracken greyhens sailed swiftly to their evening feed.

The road that winds beside West Loch Tarbert passes through scenery of great beauty. In autumn the woods of oak and hazel are full of colour, and many birds have their home here.

Each day the mail boat from Islay may be seen to steer up the narrow loch to her moorings at West Loch Tarbert pier, and after a short stay to return westward to her ports of call on the misty islands of Islay and Jura. Communication between Islay and the mainland has been greatly improved of late by a daily aeroplane service, which enables the traveller to spend some hours of the day in Glasgow and to return to Islay the same evening.[1] Across the isthmus of Tarbert the Norse King Magnus caused his ship to be dragged, the king himself on the poop holding the tiller, and it is perhaps from this event that the district south of the isthmus is still called the *island* of Cantyre by some of the old people. Although the distance from West Loch Tarbert across the isthmus to Tarbert in the east loch is less than a mile, the two districts are very different in character. One leaves a lonely country with an atmosphere of early times, and reaches suddenly the busy fishing village of East Loch Tarbert on Loch Fyne, where boats of all kinds ride at anchor in the harbour. An old ruined castle stands here, and is said to have been built by King Robert the Bruce.

At the entrance to Loch Fyne, and within four miles of the Isle of Arran, stands the old castle of Skipness. To reach Skipness (a Norse word, signifying the Ship's Point) it is necessary to skirt West Loch Tarbert to Redhouse and cross the high ground to the Claonaig Water, which flows into the strait known as Kilbrennan Sound, separating Cantyre from Arran. From the highest part of the road I had an unusual view of the hills of Arran. They rose dark from the Sound, which was covered by a low haze of a brown colour, and so thick that the sea was scarcely visible. On Goat Fell dark clouds rested, but the surrounding peaks were clear.

Skipness and its old castle are beside the Sound and Skipness Castle stands back from a shore of shingle. It is a large and stately ruin, and creepers showed warm tints about the walls on the

---

[1] It has unfortunately been decided to discontinue this service after the present (1934) autumn.

autumn day when I saw it. Little is known of the history of Skipness Castle. It has been added to at different periods, but does not appear to have been built for defence, for it stands on no rocky eminence like most of the old castles of the west, but is approached across level ground. It is built partly of red sandstone, which is not found in the district and which is believed to have been brought over the Sound from Arran. From Skipness, Arran appears as the most mountainous of all the western isles. I was told that the sunrises and sunsets on this island as seen from Skipness were of remarkable beauty, especially in winter when the higher reaches of the Arran hills were snow-clad.

From Skipness a road passes along the eastern shore of Cantyre to Campbeltown. Midway between Skipness and Campbeltown stands Saddell Abbey, believed to have been founded by Somerled, first Lord of the Isles, that great chief who was assassinated at Dunbarton and who is said to lie buried within the abbey walls. The *Statistical Account* has the following curious remarks on the Abbey of Saddell: " After it had for centuries withstood the violence of the solstitial rains and equinoctial gales the hands of a modern Goth converted it into a quarry out of which he took materials to build dykes and offices—paving some of the latter with the very gravestones. He did not, however, long survive this sacrilegious deed, as he soon afterwards lost his life by a trifling accident, which the country people still consider a righteous retribution."

Tradition affirms that Reginald of the Isles after his father's death sent to Rome for a quantity of consecrated dust and " made the building commensurate with the extent to which it could be scattered." The abbey was built in the form of a cross, which lay towards the four cardinal points of the compass. The monks of Saddell were Cistercians, and during King Haco's great expeditions they asked and obtained of the Norse king protection for their abbey. Saddell was richly endowed by Angus of the Isles and his successors. Its lands extended to Arran and even to Bute.

The *Statistical Account* mentions that the most conspicuous of the old tombstones here is " one of the Lord of the Isles himself in the character of a warrior, sculptured upon the stone as large as life, with the two-handed sword lying sheathed by his side. Others of the same kind have a monk in miniature beside them, to recommend them, it is thought, to the keeper of the keys. The Abbot's tombstone, which lies somewhere among the ruins, has been described as a remarkably fine one. He is drawn at full length—his head shaven, and his pontifical robes reaching to his heels. His hands are closely clasped, raised very high, and resting on his breast, as if in the attitude of prayer. On the lower part of his breast is the seal of the monastery, resembling not a little the arms of Canterbury, the sand-glass and the trumpet to represent the lapse of time and the approach of judgment. On the lower part is a label filled with Saxon or Runic characters, but so effaced as to be almost illegible. A gravestone close by that of the chieftain MacDonald himself contains the figure of a warrior, said to represent one MacKay, to whom Robert Bruce made a grant of the lands of Ugadale. Here is also the grave of Archibald Campbell of Carradale, who was killed at the battle of Inverlochy."

Saddell Castle and the abbey must have been the scene of many raids. An insight into the life of those early times is contained in a letter written by the Irish deputy Sussex on board his ship the " Mary Willoughby," at anchor in Loch Kilkerran in the autumn of 1558 : " I landed and burned eight myles of length and therewith James M'Conell's chiefe howse callit Saudell, a fayre pile and a strong." MacDonald had obtained the lands of Saddell shortly before that date from the Earl of Arran, on condition that he gave up his claim to certain of the lands of Arran, and that he would assist the bishop of Argyll, the king's brother, in levying his tiends throughout Cantyre. As I have mentioned elsewhere,[1] Angus Og, Lord of the Isles, concealed Robert the Bruce at his castle of Saddell after the king's defeat at Methven in Perthshire.

[1] Chapter XLIV.

CHAPTER XLVII

THE COUNTRY OF THE MULL OF KINTYRE

THE long peninsula of Kintyre or Cantyre (in Gaelic Ceann Tíre, the Head of the Land) which terminates in the wild headland of the Mull has long associations with its sister country of Ireland over the sea. On Kintyre landed Fergus Mór, first king

Atlantic Waves, Kintyre.

of Dalriada (whose name is present in the burn of Tirfergus), and Adamnan relates that Columba on a visit to Kintyre spoke with the captain and crew of a vessel newly arrived from France. On that occasion Columba had come from Iona, but there is a tradition of the country that the saint originally made his way from Ireland to Iona by way of the coast of Kintyre and stayed there awhile, before residing for a time in the cave at Ellary on the shore of Loch Caolisport.[1] At a later date King Haco's fleet

[1] *Vide* p. 342.

rounded the Mull and captured the strong fortress of Dunaverty, compelling the Scottish knight who held it for Alexander III to surrender the castle, and appointing Guthorn Bakkakoff as governor in his place. The oldest name for the Mull of Kintyre is Epidion Akron (Greek—Ptolemy), the Epidian Cape, from the Epidii, the Celtic folk who inhabited Kintyre. The name became in Old Irish Ard Echde. In Adamnan it is Caput Regionis, a literal translation of the Gaelic name Ceann Tire. In the Norse Sagas it is Saltire or Satiri, the Land's Heel.

The traveller making his way to the Mull of Kintyre from the north, passes along a stretch of wind-swept country, level and productive, at the edge of which the long Atlantic swell breaks white even in calm weather. On the grey autumn day when I wandered south along this beautiful coast-line I could see Islay and Jura on the horizon to the west. There was a deep blueness on those island hills, and heavy shade was on them except for one small pool of golden sunshine on the heathery coast of Jura. In the middle distance rose the long island of Gigha with its small neighbour Cara, and on the far horizon lay Rathlin with the hills of Ireland beyond it. I passed the castle of Largie, where the MacDonalds still hold their old lands, and even in the most wind-swept places saw many small gardens bright with flowers. It was delightful to me, coming from the garden-less district of northern Skye, to find that the people of Kintyre had so great a love of flowers. Within a stone's throw of some of these cottage gardens creamy seas broke lazily upon the low sandy shore, where oyster catchers were feeding and bathing, and lapwings were circling in great flocks high overhead. Here was the Spirit of Ocean—of the open unbridled Atlantic—and a Hebridean atmosphere. Yet here were no small crofts, as in the Hebrides, but large farms with well-filled stackyards. The potato crop was being lifted, and so many weeks had passed without rain that clouds of dust rose and were suspended on the quiet air as the work proceeded. To reach the Mull of Kintyre it is neces-

Davarr, Kintyre.

sary (if one is to keep to the road) to pass through the town of Campbeltown. The old name of the place is Ceann Loch Cille Chiaráin, the Head of St. Ciaran's Loch, and the old name of the parish is Kilkerran.

In the new *Statistical Account* mention is made of " St. Kiaran, the apostle of Kintyre," whose cave is situated four miles from Campbeltown. " In the centre of the cave is a small circular basin, which is always full of fine water, supplied by the continual dropping from the roof of the cave. There is also a rudely sculptured cross on a stone, upon which the saint is said to have sat and prayed. This St. Kiaran was highly esteemed by his contemporary, St. Columba, who wrote a sacred ode upon his death, in which he celebrates his virtues. The ode is still extant; it commences, ' Quantum Christe ! Apostolum Mundo Misisti Hominem. Lucerna hujus insulæ.' "

In the same account, written in the year 1843, is the following : " In the centre of the main street of Campbeltown an ancient cross forms a principal feature of attraction. It is richly ornamented with sculptured foliage. It has on one side this inscription : ' This is the cross of Mr. Ivar M. K. Eachran, once Rector of Kyregan, and Master Andrew his son, Rector of Kilcoman, who erected this cross.' "

Near Campbeltown is Machrihanish, where a celebrated golf course has been laid out on the sandy *machair* : the road to the links branches off about a couple of miles south of Campbeltown from the road which leads to the Mull.

Near the Mull of Kintyre the character of the land changes. Here are wide moors with small glens leading down to the sea, and many hills, some of them rising steeply from the ocean. The narrow road to the lighthouse on the Mull winds through this hilly country and it is now possible to drive a car all the way to the gates of the lighthouse. At the highest point of the road, which must be a full thousand feet above sea level, I left it and turning to my right climbed Beinn na Lice, a hill of 1,400 feet which rises here. Crossing green slopes of crowberry, where blue hares fed, I soon reached the cairn on the hill-top. There was a profound silence on the hill and a soft grey light was over land and sea. Rathlin, blue and mysterious, rose across the calm ocean strait named of old Sruth na Maoile, where the children of Ler were compelled by witchcraft to remain in the shape of swans during 300 long years. Rathlin lies so close to the Irish shore that it is interesting to remember it was for long reckoned as one of the Hebrides, and was a part of the kingdom of the Isles. On Rathlin Robert the Bruce was concealed by his ally Angus Og, Lord of the Isles, and when the kingdom of the Isles was surrendered to the Scottish Crown in 1476 the island became a part of the lands of MacDonald of Islay. Rathlin is mentioned by Adamnan, who writes of it as " insula quæ vocatur Rechru," and the Isle was known as Rechrin before the variant Rathlin was used. Between Rathlin and Ireland I could see no waves on that great tidal stream known in early times as Coire Bhreacáin (not to be confused with the strait of the same name between Jura and Scarba) and written of by the learned Adamnan as Charybdis Brecani. The tale of Breccán who was drowned in this whirlpool with all his company of fifty ships, is told in the Book of Ballymote. Breccán lived before Columba's day, and it is recorded that Columba was once in peril from the whirlpool, and when the *curach* appeared likely to be overwhelmed Breccán appeared in friendly greeting and the coracle safely crossed the steep waves of the tidal stream.

A haze was now spreading fast northward over the ocean, but I could see the high rocks of Fair Head behind Rathlin and the misty outline of the Antrim mountains to the south. Jura and Islay were now faint on the horizon, while to the east Ailsa Craig was a dim cone rising from an invisible sea. North-east were the hills of Arran, now seen with difficulty in increasing mist and haze. More than a thousand feet below me was the lighthouse, beyond which gannets from Ailsa Craig could be seen travelling out to sea in the direction of Islay, flying very low above the tidal stream that was flowing north. When I had almost reached the lighthouse I saw many grouse flying over the steep heather-covered hill-side; it was unexpected to find them so near the open Atlantic. A friendly wheatear, on migration perhaps, flitted from stone to stone. I had a kindly welcome from the head lighthouse-keeper, who told me that he had, a few months before my visit, been transferred from Barra Head to this station. He said that the bird life on the Mull was disappointing after Barra. The lighthouse on the Mull of Kintyre is one of those stations sending out directional finding wireless waves to shipping in time of fog, and two powerful wireless aerials stand close to the lighthouse.

As I reached the top of the hill road once more I looked back over the ocean and saw pools of soft sunlight which relieved the haze that was momently thickening. Soon the coast of Ireland was hidden from view and even the island of Sanda, a few miles off the shore of the Mull and the most southerly point of Argyll, was scarcely seen against gathering clouds. On Sanda are the ruins of a chapel dedicated to St. Ninian.

I returned to Campbeltown by way of the village of Southend and passed, perhaps a mile before reaching it, a pleasant sandy bay flanked on the east by a small rocky peninsula. On this peninsula are the remains of the old fortified castle of Dunaverty. As early as the year 710 there is a record of this *dùn* having been besieged, but it will be known to posterity as the site of " as disgraceful, bloody, and indiscriminate a massacre as the pen of history has ever recorded." It was in the year 1647. The power of Montrose had been broken and at Dunaverty almost his last adherents were besieged by Leslie's army. The garrison of the castle consisted of MacDonalds and MacDougalls under the leadership of Archibald MacDonald of Sanda. The garrison held out until their water supply was cut off by the besiegers, and when a party from the garrison attempted to supply themselves from a stream near the base of the rock they were all slain. A flag of truce was then sent out, and the garrison surrendered to the mercy of the kingdom.

" General Leslie," says the new *Statistical Account,* " afterwards made a nice distinction, that the besieged had yielded themselves to the kingdom's mercy and not to his, and, availing himself of this infamous casuistry . . . the whole garrison were put to the sword except one young man." That young man's name was MacDougall, and he owed his life to the good offices of Sir James Turner, adjutant in Leslie's army. The episode I have mentioned in my chapter on the " Country of Lorne." But before the garrison of Dunaverty surrendered, the infant son of Archibald MacDonald of Sanda was carried secretly by his nurse from the fortress under cover of darkness and the baby was hidden in a cave that to this day is known as MacDonald's Cave. The nurse was Flora MacCambridge and the baby's name was Ronald.

Little remains to-day of the old fortress of Dunaverty on the grassy mound overlooking that broad bay with its red sandy shore. It was October when I visited the place, but the late summer had been unusually fine and warm and the sea rocket still flowered at the edge of the sandy shore while, to complete the illusion of summer, eider drakes called from the waters of the bay. I spoke with a fisherman who told me that he had often come across human bones in the sand here, and that he had also found old bullets. He said that when the foundations of the house which stands immediately beneath the castle were being laid, many human bones were unearthed. But before that, in the year 1822 after an unusually high tide, accompanied by a gale of wind, the sand was drifted from a bank near the ruined castle, and an immense number of human bones and skulls were laid bare.

A few hundred yards from Dunaverty, and near the public road, is to be seen a small enclosure. Here are buried Archibald Mór and Archibald Òg of Sanda, the leaders of the force who were massacred and who shared the fate of their men. It is narrated that MacDonald of Largie was also murdered in cold blood and is buried here. As though ashamed of that disaster which overtook its inmates the castle of Dunaverty has almost entirely vanished. When Robert the Bruce passed some nights here on

A A

his way from Saddell to Rathlin the fortress was considered well-nigh impregnable, for the sea almost surrounds the *dùn*, and on the landward side was a fosse, covered with a drawbridge. The district shortly after the massacre was visited by the plague, so that the whole countryside was depopulated.

It was evening when I passed again through Campbeltown—now a changed place to what it was in the days when the great MacDonald had a castle here—and the sun was sinking as I

Old Houses, Campbeltown.

arrived at the western seaboard of Kintyre. From a sky overspread by soft cloud a shaft of glowing light shone on sea and land, suffusing the long Atlantic combers that broke upon the shore where perhaps the great Fergus, first king of Dalriada, landed from his *birlinn* or galley. Faintly across the sea was Gigha, mysterious across drowsy waters, and as darkness settled on the coast the tremulous uncompleted autumn songs of wandering curlews mingled with the low murmur of advancing seas.

CHAPTER XLVIII

THE LOCH FYNE COUNTRY

THE Atlantic, flowing north-east past the Mull of Kintyre, fills at its flood tide two broad sea lochs. The more southerly of these lochs is known as the Firth of Clyde, the more northerly as Loch Fyne, in Gaelic Loch Fìne, the Vine Loch. Past Skipness Point and Tarbert, past Lochgilphead and Shirvan the tide sweeps, then flows north-east through a narrowing loch beside Minard and Crarae (where the Scrymgeours, hereditary standard-bearers to the Scottish kings, were superiors in early times) and sees the old grey walls of Castle Lachlan rise in the soft western sunlight. Beyond Furnace, with its old smelting works and great quarries, the Atlantic waters flow, and now have reached the head of the loch and are washing the shores of Inveraray and the old MacNachtan stronghold of Dùn dà Ràmh.[1] At last they reach the estuary of the river Fyne, and receive the consecrated waters of Kilmorich into their keeping.

Inveraray is the capital of the Loch Fyne country and no one who enters the town can fail to be impressed by the old-world atmosphere of the place. The town is built at the edge of the sea loch, and in earlier times the county families of Argyll were in the habit of spending their winters in their town houses in Inveraray. Here are to be seen the parish church, divided into two parts so that two services, one in Gaelic and the other in English, could be conducted at the same time, and near the church a memorial to a family of Campbells massacred during the hard rule of the men of Atholl. In Inveraray stands the

[1] Spelled in modern maps as Dundarave.

Crarae Quarry, Loch Fyne.

house where that great Scottish writer, Neil Munro, was born.[1] Perhaps the most interesting building in the town is the old court-house, where James Stuart of the Glen was tried for the murder of Campbell of Glenure in 1752, was convicted by a Campbell judge and jury, and was hung in his own country at Ballachulish.[2]

As I stood in the room where the trial was held I wondered that the judges and witnesses could all have been accommodated there, for it is not a large room, although comfortable and sunny. On one of the small windows, written perhaps with a diamond, are the words, " Inveraray Town House, 25th May, 1765," and, beneath them, in a different handwriting, " Charming Miss Tibby Dunstafnage." The writing in the first sentence is exceedingly good; in the second the writing begins carefully but appears hurried at the end—perhaps the writer heard footsteps approaching before he had finished his remarks on a charming girl.

On one of the windows of the Argyll Hotel at Inveraray the poet Robert Burns wrote these lines :

> " There's naething here but Hielan' pride,
> An' Hieland scab, an' hunger;
> If Providence has sent me here,
> 'Twere surely in his anger."

The tradition is that the good people of the hotel were making preparations for the arrival of the Argyll family, and that the wandering poet failed to impress on them the importance of his own wants.

On the sea front stands the Inveraray Cross, believed to have been carried away from Iona and to date from the early fifteenth century. There is a Latin inscription on the cross, stating that it commemorates Duncan MacGille Comghan, his son Patrick, and MacGille Muire, the son of Patrick. On the opposite side of the road, within the castle grounds, is All Saints Episcopal

[1] His great novel *John Splendid* describes vividly the Inveraray country at the time of the Battle of Inverlochy.

[2] See Chapter XXIX.

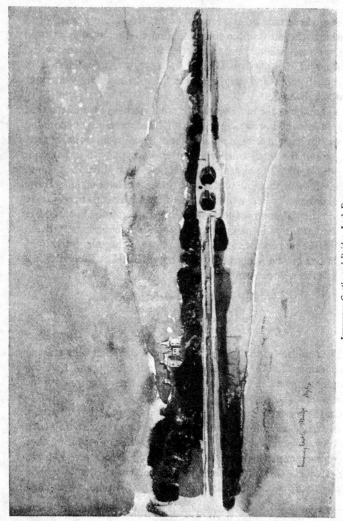

Inveraray Castle and Bridge, Loch Fyne.

Church. The tower, which was recently completed and is 126 feet high, contains one of the finest peals of bells in Scotland.

The present town of Inveraray dates from 1745. When MacCailein, Duke of Argyll, decided to build himself a new castle he considered the town, as it then stood, was too near the new castle for his liking, so he had the town pulled down and rebuilt where it now stands. The present Inveraray Castle is, I believe, the third, and the gate of one of the earlier castles is mentioned by an old Celtic writer as one of the seven wonders of the world.

As I approached Inveraray after sunset by way of Glen Aray from the high ground south of Loch Awe, a slender moon shone upon the flaming gold of old trees in the full beauty of autumn foliage. Beneath me were the waters of Loch Fyne—silent and calm, and reflecting the golden lights of Inveraray. High above the castle idly floated the flag of MacCailein Mór, the Galley of Lorne worked upon it dimly seen in the half-light of a closing day. There is an air of old times in the castle grounds and the birds here are unusually tame. Tall and stately trees grow here. One of the most notable is a Scots pine 245 years old, the tallest of its kind in Britain. Its height is 128 feet and its girth 15 feet. There is a curious tradition that this tree as a seedling was dropped where it grows by the men of the Atholl country about 1689 as they set out northward from Inveraray to their own district, carrying what spoil they could. Not far from this tree are three splendid larches, while along the shore of Loch Fyne to the south-west stands what is believed to be the largest conifer in Britain to-day. It is a silver fir (*abies pectinata*), and its age is reckoned to be 253 years, its height 168 feet, and its girth 20 feet 7 inches—a truly magnificent tree, graceful, upright, and still full of vigour.

One old tree in the grounds of Inveraray Castle is known as the Marriage Tree, and it was considered a happy augury before marriage to go round the tree blindfolded three times without touching its trunk or any of the low-spreading branches. Less cheerful is the history of the two beeches which grow side by side

Tarbert, Loch Fyne.

near the high-road.   These are the Hanging Trees, and I am told
that in the ground beneath them are many human bones.   But
in earlier times the rule of a great highland chief was of necessity
severe, and a reminder of these stern times is seen in the watch-
tower upon Dùn Cuaich, the steep hill which Sir Walter Scott
describes as "a picturesque peak starting abruptly from the lake,
and raising its scathed brow into the mists of middle sky, while
a solitary watch-tower perched on its top like an eagle's nest
gave dignity to the scene by awakening a sense of possible
danger."

Beyond Inveraray, and near the head-waters of Loch Fyne, is
the castle of Dùn dà Ràmh (Dunderave), the Fort of the Two
Oars, and on the road from Inveraray to this castle one passes
not far from the Boshang Gate, at the entrance to Glen Shira.
There is an amusing story to account for the unusual word
Boshang.   It is said that a distinguished Frenchman was once
the guest of the Duke at Inveraray Castle.   In this wild country
of the west, with its moors and mists and dark sea lochs, he had
a great longing for the verdure of his native land.   When he
walked one day to the level country at the entrance to Glen Shira
and saw the fresh green grass he was delighted, and exclaimed,
" Quel beau champs ! "   And ever since then the gate has been
known as the Boshang Gate.

As I approached Dunderave (where, on either side of the castle,
is a shelving shingle shore over which the MacNachtan galleys
could be drawn beyond reach of the tide) a bitter squall, driving
up Loch Fyne, shook the beech trees that surround the castle,
sending their brown leaves on the late autumn air thick as a
shower of driven snow.   I looked across the loch to Ardkinglas
where Sir Colin Campbell, Sheriff of Argyll, had his home that
winter day of long ago when MacIain of Glen Coe came to him to
be sworn.   When the Campbells left Ardkinglas and the property
passed into other hands, ghostly drums were heard sounding
imperiously on the quiet night air.

Dunderave was the home of the MacNachtans (later spelled

MacNaughtons), a very old highland family who trace their descent from Nachtan, a son of the family of Lochow, before ever that great family assumed the surname of Campbell. About the year 1246 Gillechrist MacNachtan made two grants of the church of Kilmorich, in which he referred to his wife Bethoc and his father Malcolm. Of the old church of Kilmorich at the head of Loch Fyne little or nothing remains to-day. MacNaughton of

Dunderave, Loch Fyne.

Dunderave accompanied the Earl of Argyle to Flodden, where he was slain, and in later times Colonel Alexander MacNaughton in the year 1627 raised a company of 200 highland bowmen for service in the war with France.

The NacNaughtons no longer live in their old castle of Dunderave, but another ancient family of Loch Fyne, the MacLachlans, still hold their stronghold of Castle Lachlan. This is the more surprising because the MacLachlan of the day rose (although he was obliged to cross Campbell country to do so) for Prince Charles Edward in 1745. There is a tradition in the Loch Fyne country that MacLachlan started out to join the Prince with only 20 men. They crossed Loch Fyne and landed at Crarae. Here an ill omen discouraged them—the chief, on mounting his horse, was turned thrice widdershins by his restive steed. Perhaps MacLachlan paused for prayer and meditation before the old chapel of Killevin and its ancient cross. Eibhinn or Aibind was one of the holy maidens who attended Bride. Her name means Delightful, and her chapel was deeply venerated. Before he joined the Prince at Holyrood on September 18, Lachlan MacLachlan, chief of his clan, rode at the head of 180 men. At Culloden the MacLachlans and the MacLeans together formed one regiment and fought on the right wing of the army. MacLachlan met his death on the field, and one of his sons, who was acting as aide-de-camp to the Prince, was killed also.

It is said that one of the MacLachlan chiefs paid his feu-duty to the Crown by placing a pair of gloves on a stone near Strachur, called Capull Cruaidh. He took his servant with him as a witness that the feu-duty had been paid, and when the chief had turned his back the servant would pick up the gloves and take them back to the castle, where they would remain until the following year, when the same little ceremony would take place ! Like other old highland castles, Castle Lachlan had its fairy or brownie. This little brownie was naked, and one year, as the winter was very cold and frosty, it was thought to please him and do him a kind action by making a pair of trousers for the elf.. One night the trousers were flung over the back of a chair in the kitchen, where the brownie usually spent the night hours enjoying the grateful warmth of the fire. The brownie was called Munn, and in the dead of night a small petulant voice from the kitchen was heard to complain, " Oh ! oh ! trousers about his backside without his measure. It is time that Munn was going." And he went !

Earlier in this chapter I have mentioned the Boshang Gate.

The glen at the entrance to which it stands is Glen Shira (in Gaelic Gleann Siara), a fertile and wooded glen which leads away

Glencroe, Argyll.

north-east into the hills. In this glen is the Dubh Loch, where was an early fortress of the MacNachtans, but perhaps the most interesting ruin in the glen to-day is a small house (now roofless) about five miles from the sea and built beneath the grassy slopes

of Beinn Bhuidhe. This is Rob Roy's house, where that celebrated MacGregor lived for ten years before the first Jacobite
rising of 1715. Some years ago a dirk, having Rob Roy's
initials engraved upon it, was found on a ledge above the river
not far from this ruin, and in Inveraray Castle is to be seen Rob
Roy's sporran. At one time the MacGregors owned wide territory in the highlands, and a part of their lands was the district of
Glen Strae and Glen Orchy. It is said that they held the old
castle of Kilchurn at the head of Loch Awe before it passed to
the Breadalbane family.

Glen Shira is a comfortable, well-wooded glen. The late
autumn sun shone on the oaks that clear morning when I walked
up the glen, so that they were alight with many bright colours.
On one of the trees a buzzard was sunning himself, and was
reluctant to take wing. When he did so he rose in spirals a
little way on the north wind, then alighted once more on a tree
farther up the slope of the hill. Near Rob Roy's house, at the
confluence of the Shira and the Brannie Burn, is a *grianan*,
sheltered from the wind and full open to the sun, where the dried
bracken was crisp on the warm slope, the hiding-place of woodcock during the daylight hours. I entered Rob Roy's house
through the opening which had once been the door and examined
the well-built wall which, could it but speak, might tell stirring
tales of an era when violent death in the highlands was an everyday occurrence and when men lived dangerously, trusting to the
keenness of their vision and of their hearing, and to the strong
blade of their claymore.

I left Rob Roy's house and climbed the slopes of Beinn Bhuidhe.
In places the grass was green, but here and there it had already
turned to a flaming orange. A bitter wind swept the hill, yet
on the sheltered bank of a clear streamlet, a single flower of the
yellow saxifrage (*saxifraga azoides*) was open to the low sun. On
the spur of the hill a pair of golden plover were standing. They
showed no fear as my companions and I approached them and
we had almost reached the birds when they rose and disappeared

with swift flight across the side of the hill. They had perhaps newly arrived from northern Scandinavia and we may have been the first human beings they had ever seen.

As we climbed the shoulder of Beinn Bhuidhe and approached the outpost summit of Stac a' Chuirn (2,679 feet) we had risen above the lesser hills and now looked across the heights of Cowall on to the hills of Arran, while more to the north we saw the faint outline of Jura and the hills of the Isle of Mull. The breeze was freshening : on Loch Fyne, far beneath us, were dark flurries of wind on the water off the Inveraray shore where a Britisher destroyer swung at anchor, and on Loch Awe with its isles small white-capped waves were springing into life. Innishail and Innischonnan, Fraoch Eilean and Innis Chonaill—what group of islands in all Scotland have more remarkable historical associations than these?

From the icy spur of Beinn Bhuidhe I looked across Loch Awe and saw the Pass of Brander dark beneath the sunset sky. In this dark pass was fought a desperate fight between the MacDougalls of Lorne and Robert the Bruce. Here the Bruce, avenging Dalrigh, defeated the men of Lorne with great slaughter and old cairns to this day mark the battle-field and perhaps the burial-place of the slain. The clouds sailed across the wide corries of Cruachan, and a bitter wind blew from the hills of the Black Mount Forest, grey with the first powdering of autumn snow. North-east, east and south-east were many great hills— Ben Lui, Ben Vorlich of the MacFarlane country, Ben Lomond and Ben Ime. Against a steel-blue sky the outline of each was sharp-cut and very clear. For a short time we sat in scant shelter immediately beneath the hill-top and watched more than one herd of red deer feeding in the grassy corrie below. An icy wind eddied about the rocks, and as daylight ebbed we hurried, numbed with the cold, to the warmth of the lower grounds and saw grey crows flying fast down-wind from their feeding-places in the hills to the trees near the old cottage of Rob Roy, where they roost.

CHAPTER XLIX

ARRAN

EMIGRANTS leaving the Clyde on a transatlantic liner bid farewell to Scotland as they gaze, longingly and wistfully perhaps, upon the hills of Arran. What inspiring hills they are! I can imagine nothing finer than the bens of Arran when seen

Standing Stones on Machrie Moor, Arran.

against the last of the sunset. Even the Cuillin of Skye are not more imposing. Goat Fell, Beinn Tarsuinn, Ard Bheinn, Beinn Bhreac and other peaks rise dark and massive against the bright horizon.

Little wonder is it that, according to one Irish tradition, Arran was the home of Manannan mac Lir, the God of the Sea. In the old writings of Ireland Arran is sometimes referred to as

Emain Ablach, Emain of Apples, and perhaps in the old days it was considered to be, like Tir nan Og, the Land of Youth and Happiness. In Irish literature Arran is often mentioned. The short poem in the *Acallamh* beginning " Arann na n-aighedh n-imdha," " Arran of the many stags," is considered by scholars to be one of the finest pieces of nature poetry in the Gaelic language.

Arran to-day has little or no communication with her sister isles, Islay and Jura, lying farther out in the ocean beyond the

Drumadoon Point and Pulpit Rock, Arran.

Mull of Kintyre, but Professor Watson, in his *Celtic Place-Names of Scotland*, mentions that he has heard in the west the combination " Bód is Ile is Arainn," " Bute and Islay and Arran," and puts it on record that Irish tradition joins Arran, Islay and Rathlin. He considers it possible that here we may have an indication of an old island group corresponding to the Eboudae or Hebrides.

The derivation of the word Arran is obscure. The isle is kidney-shaped, and it might be thought that, like the island of Aran off the Connemara coast, the name had arisen from *Àra*, genitive *Àrann*, a kidney. The stumbling-block is that the initial vowel in our Scottish Arran is short. In the *Acallamh* " Arainn " rhymes with " Manainn," and " Arann " with " abann."

From Bennan Head in the south to the Cock of Arran in the north is a distance of just under twenty miles; from Holy Island in the east to Drumadoon Point in the west is between eleven and twelve miles. There was an old Gaelic saying that to see the Hen of Lewis (Chicken Head), the Cock of Arran,

Glen Rosa, Arran.

and the Pullet of Man (the Calf) in one day's sailing was a swift journey indeed.

Arran in these days of fast steamers has been brought so near the lowland coast of Ayr, and the great city of Glasgow, that it is not surprising to find the old Gaelic language disappearing from the island. Indeed it is a matter of surprise that there should be any Gaelic-speaking people left. There are a few enthusiasts on the island who do their best to foster the language of their forefathers, and the Lady of Arran (the Duchess of Montrose) and her eldest son the Marquess of Graham are both able to converse in Gaelic and encourage those around them to

B B

speak it. The Gaelic-speaking families live mostly in the north and west of Arran, for these districts lie near to the highlands of Kintyre. The south end is more lowland, and for many years there has been a good deal of inter-communication between it and the Ayrshire coast, some twelve miles distant.

The visitor to Arran probably lands at Brodick. He sails in to the Broad Bay,[1] named by the vikings a thousand years ago, and sees, standing above stately trees, the Castle of Brodick. Here are relics of old days—the table at which Robert the Bruce sat, and the room in which he slept.

The village—or should it be called the town?—of Brodick stands beside a pleasant shore. Three fine glens—Glen Rosa, Glen Shurig and Glen Cloy—lead away into the heart of the hills here. There is a Right of Way along Glen Rosa, across the pass below Cìr Mhór, then down a steep face to Glen Sannox. I crossed the *bealach* or pass on a dark day, in keeping with the austere hills which rose around me to the drifting clouds. In the high corries stags were feeding, their warm red coats contrasting pleasingly with the dark green of the grass. The water of Glen Sannox is as clear as the young Dee on Braeriach, or the river at Sligachan in Skye. It flows away northward between that steep and delicate peak Cioch na h-Oighe (the Maiden's Breast) and those two formidable hills, Caisteal Abhail and Ceum na Cailliche (the Step of the Carlin). Who the *cailleach* was who took that stupendous step is not known. Perhaps she was the same as the *Cailleach* of Beinn Bhreac, who forded the Sound of Mull with the water reaching only to her thighs. But the *Cailleach* who named the hill had her rival in size in the *gruagach* or fairy who tended the cattle of the people of Arran. Being offended, this *gruagach* determined to leave the district. She placed her left foot on Beinn Bhuidhe in Arran and her right foot on Ailsa Craig, making the Craig the stepping-stone to cross to the mainland. But the poor *gruagach* was vulnerable although she was so huge.

[1] Brodick is really the Broad Bay.

When she was moving her foot a three-masted ship passed below her, and its mainmast, striking her in the thigh, threw her into the sea, where she was lost. The people of Arran long mourned their friend. This quaint tale is found in *Carmina Gadelica* by the late Alexander Carmichael.

The Fianna of Ireland hunted the red deer on Arran. The name of at least one hill is their memorial to-day. Suidhe

Glen Sannox, Arran.

Fhearghais (the Seat of Fergus) is one of the peaks which rise from Glen Sannox. Fergus of the True Lips was the poet of the Fianna. It was he who in the brunt of battle incited the heroes to perform deeds of still greater valour. Glen Sannox leads down to the sea at Sannox Bay. Sannox is in Gaelic na Sannagan (the Sandy Bays), whence the English plural form. From Sannox Bay to Brodick along the excellent coast road is no more than six miles. The road passes the village of Corrie, with its hotel, and here a ferry boat puts out from the shore to

Arran Peaks from North Glen Sannox.

convey passengers alongside the afternoon swift steamer to the mainland. On the day when I left Arran, Corrie was our last call, and as the ship " lay to " awaiting the ferry I was strongly impressed by the resemblance of this part of the island to some northern district of Norway. From the tide the hills seemed to rise almost sheer, until they were lost in the fast-moving clouds.

From Brodick a good road leads by way of Glen Shurig across to Machrie on the west side of the island, and to Drumadoon. Leading away south-west from Brodick is another delightful glen, named Glen Cloy. In this glen, at Kilmichael, is the ancestral home of a very old Arran family, the Fullartons. Of this honourable family Martin, writing just before the year 1700, mentions that they are of French parentage, and that their Gaelic name is Mac Louis. He mentions that, if tradition be true, this little family was, even in his time, of seven hundred years standing. " The present possessor obliged me with the sight of his old and new charters, by which he is one of the King's Coroners within this island and as such he hath a halbert peculiar to his office. The perquisites due to the Coroner are a firlet or bushel of oats and a lamb from every village of the isle, both which are punctually paid him at the ordinary terms." Pennant, writing in 1774, amplifies Martin's statement. He mentions that King Robert the Bruce, out of gratitude for the protection which he received from Fergus Fullarton, gave him a charter, dated " at Arnele, Nov. 26 in the 2nd year of his reign, for the lands of Killmichel and Arywhonyne, or Strathoughlian, which are still in the family."

It was on a fine summer's day that I passed up Glen Cloy and saw the simple white-harled house surrounded by many trees with its old motto " Lux in tenebris " above the door. The burn was in spate, for heavy rain had fallen through the night. I continued my way up Glen Dubh (the Black Glen), for I wished to see the ruins marked on the map as Bruce's Castle. By means of a large-scale map it was not difficult to find the presumed site of a king's castle. A *sithean* or fairy mound rises beside the burn, but my friend and I could see no traces of any building here, and surely the place is a most unlikely one for any strong castle, for it is far from the sea, and could be overlooked from the rising ground on either side of the glen. It is possible that the maps are now inaccurate, and that Bruce's Castle originally stood on a site which is to-day unknown.

Almost as popular as Brodick are Lamlash and its bay, some six miles to the south. The name Lamlash, crude and unattractive in its present-day form, has a history of considerable interest. The name is really Eilean Mo-Laise, or St. Molaise's

Imachar, Arran.

Island. "It is clear," writes Professor Watson, "that Lamlash is for '*lean-M'Laise*, the first syllable of *eilean* having been elided in unstressed position, and that the name was primarily that of the island now called Holy Island."

Many people must have looked across to Holy Island from Lamlash, that tall and majestic island which rises across the bay at a distance of perhaps a mile from the mainland. The early name—Eilean Molaise or St. Molaise's Isle—originally applied to the island and not the town. Saint Molaise, a contemporary of Columba, lived on the island and his cell was in the cave which was excavated recently. Like Columba, Molaise

is traditionally believed to have been of Royal Irish race, and
he travelled across the sea to live and meditate upon a lonely
island. His cell is close to the western shore of Holy Island.
It is a low and shallow cave, small and humble compared with

The King's Caves, Drumadoon, Arran.

the great King's Cave on the western shore of Arran. A few
years ago, when the cave was excavated, a large heap of shells
was found—the remains of a saint's simple fare. The small altar
is now scarcely seen, and the wall of the cave is being defaced
by the unsightly initials of thoughtless sightseers. On the wall

are old runic inscriptions, now read with difficulty, which experts have pronounced to be Norse. These inscriptions are believed to have been cut in the rock by vikings from King Haco's fleet, anchored in Lamlash Bay before the battle of Largs in 1263. The names of these hardy vikings have been of late deciphered by Norse scholars.

Below Molaise's Cave is a curious stone, known to the old people as the Stone of Judgment. At each of the four corners of the stone a rude seat is carved out of the solid rock, and stone steps lead to the level top of the boulder. Beside the Stone of Judgment is Molaise's Well, clear and pure, and, so it is said, possessing miraculous properties.

The Celtic saints, living austere and simple lives near to the heart of nature, left a benign influence upon the isles where they lived. That influence persists to the present day. It is found on Iona and upon Oronsay, and here on Molaise's Isle I experienced its peace and restfulness.

This island, now known as Holy Island, rises to a height of over 1,000 feet above sea level. Upon its rocky eastern slopes a race of wild goats live, and on the quiet summer day when I visited the isle house-martins circled low above the blossoming heather like stormy petrels. I climbed to the summit of the island, and sitting beside the cairn, watched gannets a thousand feet beneath me making their way singly or in small parties towards Ailsa Craig which rose, delicately cloud-capped, to the hazy horizon southward. Snow-white, small and singularly beautiful were the gannets when seen from this height. Heedless of the clamouring flocks of lesser black-backed gulls which sailed uncertainly high above the sea in the shelter of the island they steered a steady and unerring course to their distant nesting rock. Molaise perhaps sat here, and watched the gannets and was inspired by the beauty of their flight and by their snowy plumage. I can picture him climbing the steep slope, and then returning serenely to his cell with its altar hallowed by prayer, and its little heap of shells.

Ailsa Craig, from Arran.

Arran from Kintyre.

There was, according to Dean Monro, a monastery of friars
founded by John, Lord of the Isles, on Holy Island. At the
present time the island is uninhabited, except for a farm built
on the side of the friary, and the lighthouse-keepers' buildings
at the farther end of the island. The ling on this island is
exceptionally fine, and appears to flower several weeks earlier
than in most parts of Scotland. Bird life on the isle is numerous

Cìr Mhór; the Heart of Arran.

and varied. During the hour I spent here I saw a brood of
grouse, a snipe, and a flock of twites on the north side, and a
colony of lesser black-backed and herring gulls nesting on the
screes of the steep east face. The character of the isle in one
respect must have altered since Pennant's day, for he writes:
" The walk is far from agreeable, as the island is greatly infested
with vipers."

On the mainland, opposite the south end of Holy Island, is

King's Cross. The place receives its name, according to island tradition, from Robert the Bruce. The story goes that Bruce had sent one of his chief men across to Turnberry to see how the land lay. The arrangement was that the messenger, Cuthbert by name, was to kindle a fire near the shore if the occasion were propitious for Bruce to cross with his army to the mainland. Bruce, from his castle at Brodick, saw on the prearranged

Kildonan Castle, Arran.

night a welcome beacon shine more and more brightly, and crossed with his men, embarking at the promontory which now bears the name King's Cross. But when he arrived at Turnberry the king was disillusioned. This was no welcoming beacon which he had seen, but either an accidental fire, or perhaps a deliberate attempt by his enemies to entice him across from his island stronghold. The lion-hearted Bruce refused to be discouraged by the tidings which he received on landing. He and his small army, battling valiantly against great odds, passed on from success to success, until the final victory at Bannockburn crowned their courageous efforts. The king doubtless added many fighting men to his standard during his victories—Angus Og [1] alone brought 10,000 men into the field. It will be recalled that previous to his arrival at Arran, Bruce had been concealed on Rathlin by the Lord of the Isles. That spring the Bruce had crossed to Arran with thirty-three galleys and three hundred men, and had captured the castle of Brodick where (as I have mentioned) his table and his room are still to be seen.

From Lamlash a hill road crosses to the south-west of Arran by way of Glen Corrodale and the Sliddery Water. From the road at the watershed (1,000 feet above the sea) a fine view is seen to the south-west. The traveller may take the coast road, which follows the shore of Whiting Bay and, at the south end of the island, passes near Kildonan Castle—named after the martyred St. Donnan of Eigg—and then leads westward, past Kilmory and Sliddery, to Drumadoon. Near Drumadoon are a number of caves. The shore here is lonely and the ground is now uncultivated, but the remains of old " lazybeds " can be seen on the pasture land. The largest of the caves is one of renown— the King's Cave. Arran tradition records that Robert the Bruce hid in this cave, and here watched the persevering spider which gave him fresh heart. (It should be noted that another tradition places the spider episode in a sea cave of Rathlin.)

Curiously enough I can find no mention of the King's Cave under its present name in any of the old books on Arran. Martin calls it the Cave of Druimcruey and gives the tradition of his day. He writes that the cave was formerly the dwelling-place of Fin mac Coull (Fergus, another of the Fianna, it will be remembered, had his seat on a high hill above Glen Sannox) when he and his warrior band hunted the red deer of Arran. There is here no mention of Robert the Bruce, but whether the cave be rightly or wrongly associated with Bruce, it is likely

[1] Lord of the Isles.

to retain its royal name. This great cave is remarkable because of the carvings which adorn its walls. The interior is so ample that, according to Martin, " a hundred men may sit or lie in it." The roof is high, and a great pillar or buttress some way in divides the cave into two arms at its upper end. The buttress, and the cave walls on either side, are adorned with quaint and sometimes beautiful figures belonging to a past age but singularly well preserved. The most remarkable is a delicately fashioned claymore or two-handed sword cut on the buttress of the cave. That claymore was old even in Martin's day, although it is nearly two hundred and fifty years since the writer from Skye visited the cave. Perhaps Bruce from his hiding-place within the cave looked across the sea to Kintyre, the home of the friendly MacDonalds, and saw the sands of Carradale and of Saddell gleam across cobalt waters, and shoals of herring play near to the cave as dusk approached from the east. He saw perhaps the island of Sanda on the south-west horizon, and on very clear days the distant island of Rathlin, on which he had passed a winter in concealment.

I like to picture that old claymore on guard, facing watchfully seaward through the centuries. It has seen galleys, under full sail or driven by the oars of many powerful rowers, pass by on some foray. It has watched the larger, but not more sea-worthy, vessels of a later date. It has seen the coming of the steamship, and to-day from its twilight wall the claymore still looks out towards the friendly sea.

Beside the old sword is the figure of a man in saintly attitude with hands upraised above his head. On the wall of the cave, near the buttress, a group of red deer are to be seen, a young fawn among them. Upon the opposite wall, near the cave's entrance, is a finely carved family of serpents, coiled and asleep. Besides the claymore, the figure of the saint, the deer and serpents in a friendly gathering, there are curious symbols incised upon the walls. One is apparently a galley under sail; another may be a shield. At the entrance to the cave is a seat,

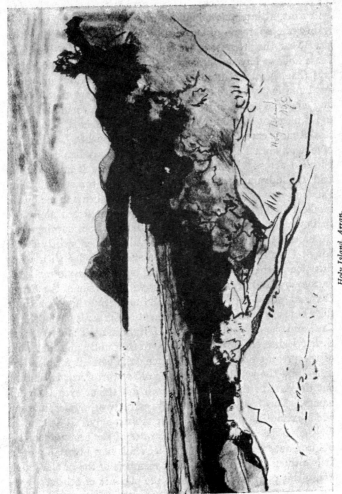

Holy Island, Arran.

cut out of the solid rock. It was here that the watchman or sentry sat, at intervals taking a turn outside the cave to guard against the approach of enemies by land, or hostile galleys by sea. Near the stone seat are hollows in the wall of the cave. These hollows have apparently been made by hand, and Martin says that they were used as supports for the beams on which was hung Fionn's huge cooking pot—a pot so vast that a whole stag could be boiled in it. The King's Cave is roomy and dry, and is pleasant to wander through, for it has none of the airlessness of most caves. It was a clear July day when I visited the cave, and when I left it and climbed the grassy bank behind it I looked across a country of beauty to where Beinn Bharrain held the advancing thunder-clouds on his brow and Beinn Tarsuinn rose blue to the sky. On the rocks beneath me oyster catchers stood, and terns with graceful flight fished along the shallows. In the air was the pleasant aroma from burning peat.

Through the kindness of my hosts I had sailed swiftly to the King's Cave from Dougrie Lodge, a shooting lodge with a fine situation at the mouth of Glen Iorsa, but it is easy to make the journey by land, for the road passes within a mile of the King's Cave. I would beg of all those who may read this book to do their best to prevent the disfigurement of the walls of the King's Cave and the cave of Molaise on Holy Island. The caves, with their priceless old carvings, are free to the public, and the public of the present day are not " playing the game," for they are disfiguring the walls, and even the old works of art, by cutting out the date of their visit, and their initials, or even their full names. This is a thoughtless and destructive practice, and one which cannot be protested against too strongly. It says much for the public-mindedness of the owner of the ground that the old iron gate which was formerly locked is now invariably open. It is a thousand pities that a few members of the public should abuse this privilege, and destroy the pleasure of others.

CHAPTER L

THE HILLS OF ARRAN

ARRAN is a frontier isle. It is not one of the Hebrides, although on its western fringe one feels the Hebridean atmosphere. It has nothing in common with the Ayrshire coast which is clearly seen from its shores in fine weather. Arran is

Lochranza, Arran.

the last of the highlands which stretch south, many a long mile, from Cape Wrath and the Butt of Lewis by way of Skye, Mull, Jura and Islay, and Loch Inver, Gairloch, Ardnamurchan, Lorne and Kintyre, to the mountainous island which rises from the sea at the entrance to the Firth of Clyde. The hills of Arran bring climbers to them from all parts of Europe. A few days before I crossed to Arran from Jura (making my way by West Loch Tarbert and Campbeltown and being most fortunate in finding an excursion steamer at the latter port leaving at once for Brodick) I had looked from Jura to the Arran heights, and had been impressed by their resemblance to the Cuillin of Skye. When the Arran hills are seen from their own island this resemblance is scarcely so striking. The bens of Arran are less sombre than the Cuillin and, with a few exceptions, they are much easier to climb. Goat Fell (Geita Fjall or Goat Hill), considering that its summit reaches a height of almost 3,000 feet above sea level, is a very easy ascent.

On the early morning when my host led me from the Castle of Brodick to its braes the sun was shining warmly and a thin wisp of mist floated airily to leeward from the summit. Early as we were, the Arran house-flies were ready and eager to form our escort, and swarmed about our heads, pressing upon us their unwelcome attentions. Our way was first through young plantations, and I was told how in Arran the rhododendron had become the very worst of weeds. It spreads so quickly that it cannot be kept in check, and crowds out the young trees, forming an undergrowth so dense that a man can scarcely fight his way through it. How I longed for a few thousand of those precocious rhododendrons to shelter my own treeless and windswept home in the north of Skye! As we climbed the clouds thickened. The Ayrshire coast was still in bright sunshine, but the mist was already dropping low upon the western peaks of Arran. There were many grouse on Goat Fell that summer day, but no ptarmigan. In Pennant's time ptarmigan were to be found on Goat Fell, but the stock has long since disappeared. The birds may have become inbred, or their numbers may have been thinned to vanishing point by too eager sportsmen. At the present day Ben Lomond is probably the furthest south hill in Scotland where ptarmigan are still to be found. Several hundred feet before reaching the top of Goat Fell we entered the

cloud, and although we remained for more than an hour on
the summit the mist never lifted, and a drizzling rain fell. A
mountain indicator on the hill-top made us realise the extent
of the view, for on a clear day such distant hills as Skiddaw
in the Lake District and Creach Bheinn near Ballachulish, are
to be seen, and even the Isle of Man is visible at times. The
high hills of north-west Ireland are prominent also.

The day on which I climbed Beinn Bharrain (2,345 feet) on
the north-west seaboard of Arran, I was more fortunate. A
north wind was herding white wavelets across the Sound from
Saddell and Carradale as I left the road at Pirnmill. Ahead of
me dark clouds shrouded Beinn Bharrain, but the weather to
windward was fine, and I had hopes of the mist lifting towards
midday. I had climbed only a few hundred feet when, looking
back across Kintyre, I saw the Bens of Jura, shapely and mist-
capped, on the northern horizon. Only a few days before, I
had stood on the highest of them, Beinn an Oir, and it was
pleasant to see them rise across the intervening hills and sea.
Campbeltown with its island of Davarr, Ugadale, the outlying
isle of Sanda—all were distinct, and beyond them and more to
the south, the long hilly outline of the Irish coast and of the
island of Rathlin or Rechrain. As I reached the upper slopes
of Beinn Bharrain the wind freshened, and cold showers formed
on the hill. A raven, croaking and somersaulting, warned me
in unmistakable bird language from his beat, a pair of golden
plover passed high overhead looking no larger than swifts, and
a red-throated diver flew strongly across the hill, steering a
course for the sunlit sea two thousand feet below.

At the fringe of the mist cap I waited in the shelter of a
rock. Gradually the cloud lifted, and the sunshine crept upwards across the face of Beinn Bharrain. I followed the retreat-
ing cloud, and when I reached the hill-top the mist had left it.
The view amply repaid the climb. Northward the horizon was
very clear. The mist cap had lifted from the Jura hills, and
beyond Jura, showing across its lowest ground, the high land

of distant Colonsay could be seen. North-east of Jura rose the hills of the Isle of Mull, and I recognised massive Beinn Mhór, and the Hill of the Two Winds which rises from the waters of the Sound of Mull. Islay was so distinct that through a telescope the houses beside Port Ellen were visible. Many of the hills of the Scottish mainland were hidden by showers, but the twin peaks of Cruachan from time to time showed themselves. It is a far journey from Arran to Jura, and yet, as the raven flies, the two islands are no great distance apart. Through my telescope I could see the waves breaking white before the north wind on Jura Sound, and the paddle mail-boat from West Loch Tarbert churning her way towards Jura. Across the thirty miles of land and sea I saw her white wake disappear as she made fast alongside the pier at Craighouse. I saw, too, the white pillar of Pladday lighthouse and the white-washed wall which surrounds the lighthouse buildings on MacArthur's Head on Islay. Eastward over Arran was a striking picture of sun and shade. In a deep ravine almost 2,500 feet below me Glen Iorsa lay in gloom, swept by a succession of showers driving across it from the north-east. On Beinn Tarsuinn and Beinn Nuis hurrying mists rested lightly, and beyond them Goat Fell, the highest peak of Arran, was flooded with strong sunshine to the summit. The path of these passing showers was narrow, yet they crossed all Arran, and spread their net out over the sea to the leeward of the island, veiling the cone of Ailsa Craig in that direction. Late in the afternoon the wind dropped, and in warm sunshine I made my way through pleasant Glen Iorsa and saw herds of cattle feed beside the lodge of Dougrie. The scent of hay was on the summer air, and the evening was peaceful beside the clear river and the pleasant bay where red-throated divers called on the ebb tide.

The fine weather was of short duration. A few days afterwards I shivered on the summit ridge of Beinn Tarsuinn in an increasing west wind which was driving in the Atlantic clouds. Below me, sometimes hidden, sometimes revealed for a few seconds, was the fine Coire Bhradain, where many stags were feeding. Below me, too, was an invisible precipice. Across the glen the clouds dropped lower on Goat Fell. Rain began to fall, at first gently, then in such downpours that the rock behind which I cowered literally ran water.

Arran in summer is the holiday resort of thousands of people. I believe that nowhere else in Scotland is there such freedom allowed. There is scarcely a restriction in the whole island. Scores of people each day climb Goat Fell, a fine hill which to-day is in danger of being spoiled because of the carelessness of those who litter the slopes with their discarded debris. On the day when I climbed that hill the path leading to the summit was an eyesore. Paper of all kinds, orange-peel, banana skins, broken bottles, cigarette packets—all these things lay on or beside the path. I would beg of climbers that, in return for the freedom of the hill, they should bury or hide their litter and keep unspoiled the beauties of nature.

CHAPTER LI

THE LAND OF COWALL

BETWEEN Loch Fyne and the busy estuary of the Clyde is a region of hill and glen, deeply indented by sea lochs. This district is Cowall, and its name is derived from Comgall, the chief of one of the four tribes of the ancient Kingdom of Dalriada. As the crow (or shall we say the eagle) flies there is no district of Cowall that is more than half an hour's distance of Greenock, or even Glasgow, and yet the land of Cowall is less affected by modern civilisation than many more remote districts of the highlands. It is true that at Dunoon one finds the bustle and stir of a popular seaside town, yet in a very few miles one reaches, at Loch Striven, a land which has changed little since the days of more than six centuries ago when the Lamonts were Lords of Cowall, and the Argyll family had scarcely obtained a footing here.

At the entrance to Loch Striven stand the ruins of Castle Toward, the ancestral home of the powerful Lamont chiefs. The castle has been deserted since the tragedy of the year 1646 when the Lamonts were besieged by a strong Campbell force and on surrendering were killed in a manner which recalls the crime of Dunaverty in Kintyre during the same troubled period.

Of the Toward massacre there is the following in the new *Statistical Account*:

" The indictment of the Marquis of Argyll bears, that certain of his clan having besieged and forced to a surrender the houses of Toward and Escog, then the property of Sir James Lamont, having violated the terms of the capitulation on which the surrender was made, ' did most treacherously, perfidiously, and traitorously fetter and bind the hands of near 200 persons of the said Sir James' friends and followers, who were comprehended within the said capitulation, detaining them prisoners with a guard, their hands being bound behind their backs like thieves within the said Sir James' house and yards of Towart, for the space of several days, in great torment and misery, and in pursuance of their farther villany, after plundering and robbing all that was within and about the same house, they most barbarously, inhumanly, and cruelly murdered several, young and old, yea, sucking children, some of them not one month old, and that the said persons, defendants, or one or others of them, contrary to the foresaid capitulations, our laws, and acts of Parliament, upon the — day of June 1646, most traiterously and perfidiously did carry the whole people who were in the said houses of Escog and Towart in boats to the village of Dunoone, and there most cruelly, traiterously, and perfidiously, cause hang upon one tree near the number of thirty-six persons, most of them being SPECIAL GENTLEMEN of the name of Lamont, and vassals to the said Sir James. . . . Insomuch that the Lord from heaven did declare His wrath and displeasure against the foresaid inhuman cruelty, by striking the tree whereon they were hanged in the said month of June, being a lively, fresh-growing ash tree at the kirk-yard of Denoone, among many other fresh trees with leaves—the Lord struck the said tree immediately thereafter, remaining so for the space of two years, which, being cut down, there sprang out of the very heart of the root thereof a spring like unto blood, poppling up, running in several streams all over the root, and that for several years thereafter, till the said murderers, or their favourers, perceiving that it was remarked—by persons of all ranks (resorting there to see the miracle), they did cause howk out the root, covering the whole with earth, which was full of the said matter like blood.' "

Even when allowance has been made for possible exaggeration in this quaint indictment, there appears to be no doubt that an infamous massacre did take place after the surrender of the castles.

It is said that the Campbell castle of Dunoon (beside which the Lamonts were hung) was not inhabited after that time, and to-day there is little remaining of its ruins, which stand beside the pier at Dunoon. The castle of Dunoon, a royal fortress, must have existed early in the thirteenth century, for between the years 1230 and 1246 John, the Constable of Dunoon, witnesses a charter of Lauman, the son of Malcolm. In 1334 the castle was surrendered to Edward Balliol, in token of which the keys were delivered to him at Renfrew. Soon afterwards " Dougall Campbel, lord of Lochow, and Robert the Steward of Scotland, landed in Cowaill with their galleys and engines of war and besieged and took the castle of Dun Dounhone." [1]

[1] *Orig. Paroch.*

In the year 1460 the lordship of Cowall and the castle of Dunoon were annexed to the patrimony of the Prince of Scotland, and James III granted to Colin, Earl of Argyle, the heritable keepership of the castle, with the power of making constables and other necessary officers. In 1544 the Earl of Lennox, with a number of highlanders, and assisted by some Englishmen, burnt the town of Dunoon, and defeated the Earl of Argyle, who attempted to oppose their landing. This attack was only temporarily successful, and in the year 1546 " Walter Macfarlane of Ardleische, Andro Macfarlane his son, John Maknewar, Robert Buchquhannane Thomassone his servant, Johnne M'Henry, and Donald Hegy ' Pypar ' had a remission from Queen Mary for assisting the English in burning the town of Dunnone and besieging the castle." [1] The Argyll family were apparently keepers of the castle of Dunoon from the year 1440 almost continuously until it was abandoned, their rights as the keepers of the castle being confirmed by successive Scottish kings.

It was on a spring day of storm and sun when I reached Dunoon and its sheltered bay of Sandbank, where a large liner and many yachts were anchored at their winter quarters. Earlier in the day I had passed along the shore of romantic Loch Eck, near to Inverchapel, a district of much old lore. In *Origines Parochiales* it is written that in the year 1497 " John Culquhone of Lus sold to Archibald Earl of Ergil a half markland in the territory of Inverquhapill [this is Inverchapel at the foot of Loch Eck] occupied by a certain procurator with the staff of Saint Mund (cúm baculo Sancte Munde), called in Scotch Deowray (Deòradh, the Pilgrim)."

In a foot-note to this passage occurs the following : " The tenure of this land in right of the crosier of Saint Mund is not quite singular. A similar tenure existed in Glen Dochart and also in Lismore. It may be observed that the hereditary keepers of the relic of Saint Fillan of Glen Dochart bore a name running

[1] *Orig. Paroch.*

through Jore and Deor of the fifteenth century to the modern Dewar."

The Cobbler, Loch Long.

On the day when I explored the ruins of the castle of Toward with its venerable Norman doorway and its strong walls which still defy the Atlantic storms, the west wind was sweeping into

Loch Striven and the hills of Arran rose dark and cold against the sunset. But there was shelter in the trees which now surround the old castle, and as I stood beside the ruin, I remembered the old story of the sacredness of highland hospitality which is connected with the place. Young Lamont and the son of MacGregor of Glen Strae were hunting together near the head of Glen Coe, and a quarrel having arisen between them, Lamont killed young MacGregor with his *sgian dubh*.[1] Horrified at his sudden hot-tempered act, and fleeing from MacGregor's attendants who were close on his heels, young Lamont at nightfall arrived at Stronmiolchoin, the home of MacGregor of Glen Strae and, unaware that the father of his victim lived here, knocked at the gate and claimed the right of highland hospitality and shelter against his pursuers. His request was granted, and when those who sought him arrived a few minutes later and pleaded with MacGregor that the slayer of his son should be given up to them, the chief remained true to his pledged word and later saw young Lamont safely across Loch Fyne into his own country of Cowall.

Years passed, and then came the fight at Glen Fruin when the MacGregors became a hunted clan, their lands, and even their name, being taken from them. MacGregor of Glen Strae, now an old man, arrived as a fugitive in Cowall, and was given a welcome by Lamont and shelter and hospitality at his castle of Toward. It is said that MacGregor ended his days here, and that his gravestone was formerly to be seen in the old burying-ground of Toward an Uillt on the hillside above the castle.

It is now many centuries since the Lamonts were Lords of Cowall, and after their time the Argyll family for long were powerful in the district. Not far from Dunoon, on the shore of the Holy Loch, are to be seen the site of the old chapel [2] and the burial-ground, sacred to Saint Fintan who died in the year 635. Here is the burying-place of the Argyll family: Earl

---

[1] Hunting knife.   [2] Kilmun.

Archibald who fell at Flodden and Earl Colin, who died in the year 1529, are buried here.

It is said that the first member of the Argyll family to be buried on the shore of the Holy Loch was Celestin, son of Sir Duncan Campbell, Black Knight of Lochow. The lad was being educated in the lowlands, and died there. A snowstorm of such violence was raging at the time that it was found impossible to carry the body nearer to his home than Kilmun, and the Black Knight asked of Lamont that his son might be buried at Kilmun. The request was granted in these words : " I, Great Lamont of all Cowall, do grant unto thee, Black Knight of Lochow, a grave of flags, wherein to bury thy son in thy distress." The Black Knight shortly afterwards in gratitude endowed the church of Kilmun, and in 1442 founded a college there.

A few miles distant from Dunoon and Kilmun is Glen Masan, associated in the minds of Celtic scholars with what is known as the Glen Masan MS. This MS. was in the possession of the Rev. John MacKinnon, Minister of Glendaruel at the end of the eighteenth century. It is the property of the Highland Society of London, and is now in the National Library, Edinburgh. The age of the MS. is uncertain, but it is very old. It deals with the favourite tale in the Three Sorrows of Story Telling— the Tale of the Sons of Uisneach, which has been told by the glow of peat fires in Ireland and Scotland from time immemorial. In this old MS. is the lament of Deirdre, in which she sings of the western glens which she is leaving with forebodings of disaster in order to return with Naoise to Ireland.

> " Glen da Ruadh !
>   Dear to me each of its native men,
>   Sweet the cuckoo's note on bending bough
>   On the peak above Glen da Ruadh."

It is generally believed that the Glen da Ruadh of the Lament is the glen which is known to-day as Glendaruel in Cowall, but a correspondent in the *Oban Times* has recently advanced the opinion that Glen da Ruadh is in reality on Loch Etive-side, and is a small glen on the side of Ben Starav, well known to the old people. Subsequent inquiries, however, from a man who had been all his life in the district, seemed to cast doubt on this suggestion, for he had never heard of the glen. I thought it possible that the name might appear in the original Six-inch Ordnance Survey of Loch Etive, and wrote the Director of the Ordnance Survey on the matter. He replied that no Glen da Ruadh was marked on the map. This map was made in 1870 when the old families must still have been in the glen and would, one might have thought, have given the name to the surveyors.

When spring comes to Cowall of the green glens and grassy hills, the cuckoo sings in Glendaruel and the solans arrive from the ocean on the sheltered waters of Loch Fyne and Loch Riddon. Many centuries have passed since Deirdre of the dark beauty sang of the charm of Glendaruel, but the glen remains untouched by the unrest of modern civilisation. In the church-yard of Kilmodan are many old graves. One gravestone is to the memory of An Taillear Luath, the Swift Tailor, who died in 1781. There is a Gaelic inscription on this stone, of which the following is a translation :

> " Stranger who passes by my gravestone,
> Look now at and consider the past days of your life.
> Short is it since the time has flown
> When I could run as swiftly as yourself."

But the oldest grave, if the tradition of the glen be credited, is not in the burying-ground of Kilmodan but on the shore of Loch Riddon. It is said that a Norse chief named Mechan was slain by the natives in a fight which was fought there in the year 1263. In the new *Statistical Account* is the following :—

" The most ancient name of this parish is said to have been Glenduisk, signifying the Glen of the Blackwater. A battle was fought between Mechan, son of Magnus, King of Norway, and the Albuns or Gails, where it is said the Norwegians were slaughtered on each side of a river called Ruail, which runs through the middle of the glen, and their bodies being thrown into the river gave the colour of blood to it. Hence the parish got the name of Glendaruel, which signifies the Glen of Red Blood."

The river which flows through Glendaruel empties itself into Loch Riddon, and on this loch, not far from where the pier of Craig now stands, is the historic island of Ellengreig. To-day Ellengreig is a small grassy island on which are ancient ruins, now barely visible. But in Fordun's time (1400) there was on the isle " an impregnable castle belonging to the lord of Lauquhaw (Loch Awe)." [1] In the year 1685 the castle, which was then a ruin, was restored and fortified by Archibald, Earl of Argyle. To-day one solitary oak stands sentinel upon Ellengreig. It is not a large tree, but must be of a great age for in an old sketch

Gareloch, near the Clyde.

made eighty years ago which Mrs. Burnley Campbell of Ormidale has shown me the tree appears almost as it does to-day. There is a tradition in the glen that even before the time when the castle was first built St. Aedan (who named Kilmodan) and St. Finan (who named the neighbouring chapel of Kilfinan) landed on Ellengreig as they approached the shores of Cowall from the south-west and rested awhile here. Perhaps St. Finan crossed over to Kilfinan by way of the hill track which links Glendaruel with Otter Ferry. If he did travel that way he rested no doubt at the watershed, and looked upon the hills and the sea and distant islands.

[1] Apparently a description by Fordun's continuator and interpolator, Bower, Abbot of Inchcolm, in the Firth of Forth, born 1385, d. 1449.

When I crossed that road on a day of late April the north wind had cleared the air and to the south-west rose the hills of Arran, sharp-cut and powdered with snow. The bens of Jura were almost hidden in cloud, but Scarba was clear and blue and the hills of Mull were beautiful in sun and shade. Mountain hares raced across the hill; in the distance a kestrel hovered, and grouse were calling in the sun. From the watershed is a descent of rather more than 1000 feet to the waters of Loch Fyne. Here the long sandy spit known as the Oitir was submerged. Above the shoal the water of the sea was pale green; beyond it the deep waters were cobalt. In the air beside the loch was the scent of whins and of young larch needles, swaying like feathers in the wind. Beside the pleasant house of Ballimore wild hyacinths beneath the spreading trees had formed a carpet as closely woven as of young grass, and of a still fresher green. The first swallow of spring glided easily through the tree-tops, where the first of the leaves of the sycamore trembled in the rude north wind.

A couple of miles down Loch Fyne from Ballimore is the old castle of the MacEwens, built on a grassy terrace above a small sandy shore. Little remains of this castle; even the walls are seen with difficulty. It is on record that the castle was in ruins as early as the year 1700 and it was probably abandoned considerably before that time. The MacEwens were known as Clann Eoghain na h-Oitreach, and in a MS. of 1450 it is stated that the clan are descended from Anradan, the common ancestor of the MacLachlans and the MacNeils. There is a record of MacEwen of Oitir about the year 1200. After the middle of the fifteenth century the barony and lands passed to a branch of the Campbells, who became from that time the Campbells of Otter. Like the MacLachlans, the Campbells of Otter had their friendly fairy who lived with them and watched over their fortunes. When the family left Otter and moved farther down the loch the fairy accompanied them, and made himself unpleasant to those whom he considered had no business about the place !

On Loch Fyne, as elsewhere in the west, the population is decreasing, and the Gaelic language is disappearing. At Kilfinan I conversed with an old man who told me that when he was a boy 100 pupils attended the local school, and all of them were able to converse both in Gaelic and English. Now, he said, there were no more than seven pupils at the school, and none of them was able to speak Gaelic.

Higher up Loch Fyne, on the same side of the loch as Kilfinan, is the ancient parish of Strathlachlan, which was united to the parish of Strachur about the year 1650. There was an old custom quoted in *Origines Parochiales* that " on the death of the laird of Strathlachlan or the laird of Strachur the survivor lays his neighbour's head in the grave. Its origin is dated by tradition at the period of the Crusades, when it was said that the heads of those two families went together to the war, and each solemnly engaged with the other to lay him in his family burying-place if he should fall in battle."

The MacLachlans of that Ilk are believed to have been in possession of the lands of Strathlachlan before the eleventh century. Castle Lachlan, a high, square tower, appears under its present name in the reign of King Robert the Bruce. The castle was deserted by the family rather more than a century ago.[1] On a night of rain I passed by Castle Lachlan, which rose dark and strong beside the storm-vexed waters of Loch Fyne where a solan fought the tempest, and I thought of that day in the year 1745 when MacLachlan, chief of his clan, crossed the loch with his clansmen to place himself at the service of Prince Charles Edward and like the immortal Mac-Crimmon returned no more to his beloved western land.

[1] They still live beside the old castle.

CHAPTER LII

THE COUNTRY OF LOCH LOMOND

FROM the misty winter sky the low sun shone like a ball of fire. Around Buchanan Castle the last of the leaves were slowly falling from the trees to the damp earth, but the proud Douglas fir—the first, or one of the first, of these conifers to be planted in the highlands of Scotland—was dark green as at midsummer. Below the castle were the ruins of the old house of Buchanan, destroyed by fire in 1870, and beyond lay Loch Lomond with its islands.

Loch Lomond takes its name from Ben Lomond, the Beacon Hill, which rises near its upper end. The lands on the south side of the loch were held by the Buchanans, and in the year 1282 Sir Maurice de Buchanan obtained from Donald, sixth Earl of Lennox, a charter of the lands of Buchanan, on condition that any man sentenced to death should be hanged upon the Earl's gallows at Cator. In, or about, the year 1682 the Buchanan estate was acquired by the third Marquis of Montrose (grandson of the Great Montrose) and in the Montrose family the property has remained.

The Endrick Water flows windingly near the old house of Buchanan to Loch Lomond. The country here is almost level, and the marshy fields are the winter haunt of many wild-fowl. Professor Watson believes that Endrick is from the Gaelic word " Eunarag," the snipe, because of its twisting course. I followed the Endrick to Loch Lomond and saw mallard, teal and wigeon rise into the winter haze, and a sluggish salmon or sea trout from time to time break the glassy surface of the quiet pools of the river. On Loch Lomond many duck of all kinds were assembled. Some were swimming, others were flighting low above the surface of the loch. High overhead a shoveller passed, his broad flattened bill identifying him at a glance, and a sentinel redshank rose with loud cries from that silent shore.

Beyond Inchmurrin, dim in haze, were the hills of Glen Fruin. The desperate battle of Glen Fruin was fought in the year 1602 between the MacGregors and the Colquhouns, and was one of the last clan fights in the highlands. In this engagement the Colquhouns fared disastrously, for most of them were killed and the remainder were pursued to the gates of their castle. The MacGregors burned and plundered the houses of their enemies, and drove off 600 cattle, 800 sheep and goats, and some 300 horses. But this bold victory against a superior force was to bring swift and terrible punishment upon the clan. After the battle sixty Colquhoun widows appeared before James VI at Stirling, each carrying on a pole the bloodstained shirt of her late husband. They called for justice, and the king, greatly moved, gave orders that the " viperous " MacGregors should be exterminated by fire and sword, that their lands should be taken from them, and that the very name of MacGregor should be proscribed. It was even decreed a serious offence to shelter a MacGregor; the clan were hunted on foot, on horseback, and with bloodhounds. They had little chance of defending themselves, for no MacGregor was now permitted to carry a weapon " except a pointless knife for eating his victuals." This persecution long continued, and it was not until 1795 that the laws penalising the clan were abolished. There is a fine wild *piobaireachd* which commemorates that fierce fight of long ago. Its name is " The Rout of Glen Fruin " and the tune is probably almost as old as the fight. It may have been composed by a MacGregor piper, but the history of many of these old pieces of *ceòl mór* is unknown. All that can be said is that the composer has caught the spirit of that fateful February day when the Clan Gregor by their victory brought destruction on them-

D D

selves and namelessness upon their children and their children's children.

Loch Lomond was high this winter day, but the flood water was slowly ebbing. The sun had set when my host and I reached Balmaha and looked out over the loch to the wooded island of Inch Cailleach. We launched a boat and rowed across the darkening waters, and as we approached the island felt a cold breeze drift out from its frosty banks. This icy current of air, breathing upon the relatively warm water of the loch, caused clouds of vapour to rise. We landed on the island and drew our boat up on the shingle. In the silence of dusk we made our way through the trees to the ruins of a chapel and an old burial-place. Some interesting recumbent stones are here. The Templar's Grave (the history of which is, I believe, unknown) bears on its ancient stone a carved sword with the much-worn letters I.H.S. on the hilt. Near it is a large stone bearing the date 1623. This stone stands on six pillars, bears the MacGregor coat of arms and is placed to the memory of Gregor MacGregor. It is interesting that the proscribed name should appear on the stone; can it be that the MacGregor chiefs had their name restored to them after death? The island is the burial-place of the MacGregors and the MacFarlanes, and close to this MacGregor stone is one with the writing almost worn away by the hand of time. I could see nothing on this flag in the fading light of a winter's afternoon except the words Loch Sloy, which stood out with clearness. "Loch Sloy" was the MacFarlane rallying cry, and so I knew that this must be a MacFarlane stone. I later ascertained that the stone was to the memory of Duncan MacFarlane, who died in 1783. Mac-Farlane and MacGregor sleep side by side on that pleasant isle of Loch Lomond which is as quiet and unspoilt to-day as it was when they were laid to rest there. Each night capercaillie fly from the mainland to roost on the large Scots firs which grow on Inch Cailleach. We stood beneath the stars and awaited the coming of these great birds as the moon grew brighter and the last of the sunset faded from the west, but the capercaillie came not, and at last we groped our way down a steep bank to the shingly bay and rowed out into the loch. In the water the moon was faultlessly reflected and seemed to shine up at us from a great depth : as we landed at Balmaha she was bathing the old trees in a mellow light, and the black waters of the loch, roused to life for a few moments by our oars and the small bow wave from our boat, had gradually fallen into the long sleep of a windless winter night.

The weather remained so fine that my host decided that we should climb Ben Lomond, a fine bold hill which rises from the shore of its loch to a height of 3,192 feet above sea level, and stands amid beautiful and romantic scenery. The climb from Rowardennan is an easy one, and on the November morning when we set our faces to the hill the track was deserted, for the last of the autumn climbers had left the district. The drive from Buchanan along the shore of Loch Lomond that morning of early winter was through a land of beauty. Loch Lomond, with the deep blue of the north wind in its waters, was smiling beneath a cloudless sky. On the banks and islands of the loch the oaks and birches were of shining gold. Here and there wandering breezes played upon the waters, then left them to dream away the hours of sunshine. Blackgame flew across the road from one birch wood to another above golden bracken and grass lightly powdered with frost : the sun was bright on Ben Lomond and the veins of quartz near the summit gleamed like snow wreaths.

As we reached the shoulder of the hill a pair of ravens rose ahead of us and, soaring lazily, were our escort almost to the hill-top. Rather more than half-way to the summit the track reaches the south ridge of the hill and it was here that we first realised that fog bound much of the low country. Eastward, the Wallace Monument at Stirling rose against a misty horizon. Glasgow was hidden by a grey motionless pall of fog, and this cloud appeared to extend eastward and join a great bank of fog above Edinburgh. But where we stood on Ben Lomond the air was unusually clear and as we neared the hill-top a wide and romantic view opened out. The extremes of temperature at the hill-top were remarkable. We sat at the cairn for almost two hours in warm sunshine, but we had only to step a yard across the hill to the steep north-east slope in order to enter a sunless, frost-bound land. Here the ground was iron-hard, the air was icy cold, and puffs of frigid wind rose from a dark and sunless corrie. The view from the summit of Ben Lomond was new to me, and it was interesting to recognise old friends among the hills from a new view-point. The sharp peaks of Arran, etherealised by distance, formed the horizon to the south-west. We saw the Arran mail boat cross quickly to the mainland, and a large two-funnelled steamer towered above the smaller craft.

The low November sun threw a golden path, glittering with countless small waves, on the sea near Arran, and as the sun moved slowly towards the west the pathway followed it faithfully. On the far western horizon the bens of Jura rose cone-like across the intervening hills of the mainland. Mystic yet clear were these far peaks—they might well have belonged to the immortal isles of Tir nan Og, or I Breaseal, on which are to be found perpetual youth and joyfulness. I Breaseal has usually been considered as a Celtic isle of the spirit, yet in a sixteenth-century map the island is drawn far out on the western ocean. It is a large island, and its shape is drawn as though the map-maker had indeed visited it. Near Jura was the high ground of Islay, and north-west of that island the hills of the Isle of Mull could be seen towering into the grey haze of ocean. The outline of Mull could be followed as far south as the rocky heights of the Wilderness which drop abruptly to Loch Scridain and Loch nan Ceall. North of Mull was the high ground of Ardtornish and Kingairloch. North-west, north and north-east, hill upon hill rose clear and inviting to the blue sky. Each was sharp-cut, and in the crisp air appeared deceptively close. On Cruachan a soft pearly cloud rose and fell, assumed many fairy-like shapes, then dissolved. With the passing of that small cloud the sky was clear above each hill in all that wide country. Ben Nevis, massive rather than inspiring, carried scarcely any snow. In the middle distance rose Ben Lui and the high tops of the Black Mount forest with Ben Dobhran, immortalised by Donachadh Bàn in his hunting song, standing a little apart from them.

On the far northern horizon was a high hill. Unlike its fellows this hill was heavily snow-covered and resembled a distant white cloud. It may have been Ben Alder, which rises in a snowy country near the heart of the central highlands. To the north the air was clearest and Ben Lawers, beside Loch Tay, appeared to be almost within a stone's throw from us. Far beyond Ben Lawers, and rather to the right of it, were distant hills, deep blue and snow-splashed. They may have been the hills of Glen Shee—perhaps even Lochnagar in the king's forest of Balmoral. Loch Sloy, beneath Ben Vorlich of Loch Lomond (there are two hills with the name of Ben Vorlich at no great distance from one another) reflected the blue of the sky. Loch Sloy is in the MacFarlane country. We looked across the narrow isthmus of Tarbet to Loch Long, and thought of a day seven centuries gone by, when the galleys of Angus Mór of Islay, Lord of the Isles and one of the leaders of the great fleet under King Haco, were dragged across this isthmus by strong men to the waters of Loch Lomond. Those galleys harried the islands and mainland of Loch Lomond, and the islesmen "lifted" the cattle of a startled populace who imagined themselves safe from a sea raid on their fresh-water inland loch.[1]

The sun was sinking and the line of haze which had lain throughout the day on the horizon was now silvery in its light. Far below us the vast shadow of Ben Lomond was thrown on the moors. The edge of the shadow of the hill-top on the low country some miles away was a warm brown colour, while the shadow-edges of the flanks of the hill were of a cold blue-grey tinge.

[1] Compare this with a somewhat similar tale in Chapter XLIII.

We had scarcely left the hill-top when we came upon a family party of ptarmigan. They were sun-bathing, and allowed us to stand and watch them at a distance of a few yards. Some of the birds were in full winter plumage of white, others were still in the speckled dress of autumn, and harmonised in a remarkable way with the brown grass and white quartz stones of the hillsides where they were. After a time the birds took wing and the old cock, who had been standing on guard on a rock by himself, swung out fast over the hill-side and overtook his mate and the family. A few minutes before seeing the ptarmigan we had found on the hill-top an unexpected thing. It was a golden birch leaf, and lay on the hard-frozen surface of a wreath of snow. That small leaf must have been carried up from the birch woods at the foot of Ben Lomond, three thousand feet beneath, on a strong up-rushing wind current and now it lay in the land of the ptarmigan—a land where no tree could exist.

The edges of the fog cloud began to pour slowly in upon the southern shore of Loch Lomond and before we left the hill-top we looked again upon the great company of peaks, blue and watchful beneath that cloudless November sky. When, at sunset, we reached the low ground we saw the shades of night begin to gather over Loch Lomond. The moon rose, the sunset faded, but the last of the sun-fire lingered upon the brow of Ben Lomond as a frost-laden dusk came to the glens.

HINTS ON GAELIC PRONUNCIATION

By Professor W. J. Watson

The Gaelic system of spelling has the great merit of being consistent and fairly complete. It has behind it a continuous tradition of over twelve hundred years. Differing greatly from English, it is not hard to master, and once mastered—a matter of a dozen lessons or fewer—it will prove a reliable guide. The hints here given are incomplete, and in any case printed directions require to be supplemented by the living voice.

Stress.—The stress, which is vigorous, falls uniformly on the first syllable. This applies both to uncompounded words and to "strict" compounds, in which the qualifying term comes first; *e.g.* Conghlais, "hound-stream." "Loose" compounds, where the qualifying part follows the "generic" term, are stressed on the second part, which should be separated by a hyphen; *e.g.* Port-righeadh, Portree. One consequence of the vigorous stress is shortening of a long vowel in the unstressed part of a compound; *e.g.* àird, a cape, with long *a*; but Dubhaird, "black cape," with *a* shortened. Another is the extremely light, indefinite quality of final vowels; *e.g.* coire, a cauldron, corrie, pronounced *kor*ᵉ—two syllables, however.

The letters.—Vowels are sounded much as in Latin (reformed pronunciation) and in German: *i* is always as in Germ. *bin*, Lat. *si*; (not as in Eng. *sin*); *a* stressed is as in Germ. *Bach*, Lat. *an*; but unstressed *a* is dulled, somewhat like Eng. *u* in *burn*—except when originally long; *e.g.* clachan, stones, has first *a* open, the second dull; but clachan, a stone cell, has both vowels open (the *-an* being originally long).

Broad vowels are *a, o, u*; *slender* vowels are *e, i*. Long vowels are *long*; they bear, or should bear, an accent.

Some diphthongs, etc.—*ia* : grian, sun : gr(*eea*)n. *ua* : gual, coal : g(*ooa*)l; both with *a* open. *ao* : g*a*oth, wind : one vowel sound, like Fr. *cœur*. *aoi* : as *ao* followed by Lat.-Germ. *i*. *eo*, short; *eò*, long : usually palatalised, like Eng. *yŏ, yō*. *eoi* : always long, as long *eo* followed by Lat.-Germ. *i*.

eu, é : one long vowel sound, as in Fr. *dé*. But *è* is as in Eng. *where* lengthened.

Of the consonants, *b, f, m, p* have one uniform sound, except that after a vowel *b* sounds like Eng. *p*, while after a vowel *p* is preceded by a " puff " (somewhat like Eng. *h*) : so, too, are *c* and *t*. The others have two sounds, according as they are in contact with (*a*) a broad vowel, (*b*) a slender vowel.

Broad.	*Slender.*
c, always hard, as in *cat*.	*c*, always hard, as in *keep*.
g, always hard, as in *got*.	*g*, always hard, as in *get*.
d, no Eng. equivalent; tip of tongue projects well beyond the upper teeth.	*d*, usually like Eng. *j* in *jewel*.
t, no Eng. equivalent; tip of tongue pressed firmly against upper teeth.	*t*, like Eng. *tch* in *ditch*.
n is nasal.	*n*, nasal, and usually like Eng. *n* in *knew*; *i.e.* palatalised.
l, no equivalent Eng. sound.	*l*, like Eng. *l* in *billion*; *i.e.* palatalised.
s, much as Eng.	*s*, as Eng. *sh*.
r, no Eng. equivalent.	*r*, much as in Eng. *rest*.

" Aspiration " resulted from a weakening of the consonantal sound when the consonant was originally flanked by vowels; in Sc. Gaelic it is indicated by *h* after the consonant, except *l, n, r*.

Broad.	*Slender.*
ch, as in Germ. *Bach*; Scots *teuch*. Never as in Eng.	*ch*, as in Germ. *ich*; Scots *laich*. Never as in Eng.
gh, dh, no Eng. equivalent. Like *g* of Germ. *Tag* (*g* soft).	*gh, dh*, like Eng. *y* in *yea, yet*. Silent after slender vowel.
sh, th, as Eng. *h*.	*sh, th*, as Eng. *h*.
fh is silent, except in fhuair, " got," fhathast, " yet," when it is like Eng. *h*.	*fh*, silent except in fhéin, " self "—sounded as *h*.
bh, mh, as Eng. *v*; *mh* nasal.	*bh, mh*, as when broad.
l, somewhat like Eng. *l* in *hull*.	*l*, much as in Eng. *let, MacLeod*.
r, much as in Eng. *rash*.	*r*, much as in Eng.

GLOSSARY OF PLACE-NAME ELEMENTS,
NORSE AND GAELIC

NORSE

a, river, stream; terminally -a :
Ranza, in G. Raonasa for reyni-s
-*á*, rowan-tree water (the *s* is
either irregular or due to a third
element, *e.g.* áss, rocky ridge);
Calda, kalda-á, cold stream.
Genitive *ár* in *Aros*, Mull, for
ár-óss, river's mouth.

ból, farm, abode : *Ullapool*, Ulli's
farm ; *Resipol*.

bólstaðr, a homestead : *Húsabost*,
húsa-bólstaðr, house-stead.

borg, a fort, small dome-shaped hill.
Genitive borgar : *Borreraig* for
borgar-vík, fort bay; *Borreray* for
borgar-ey, fort isle; *Carnaburg*,
in G. Cearnaborg, possibly for
kjarnaborg, churn-shaped height
or fort.

brekka, a slope : *Clibrick*, G. Clìbric ;
first part prob. klif, cliff.

dalr, a dale : *Armadale* from armr,
an arm, a bay; bay-dale;
Arnisdale, Arni's dale ; *Barris-*
dale ; Bracadale, G. Bràcadail, first
part uncertain; *Corodale*, Kóri's
dale ; *Rodil*, G. Roghadal, perhaps rauði-dalr, red dale; *Sad-*
dell, G. Saghadal, probably saga-
dalr, saw-dale.

dýr, a wild beast, fox, deer : *Dur-*
ness, G. Diùranais, for dýra-nes,
deer cape, or possibly wild beast
(wolf) cape ; *Durinish* in Skye is
the same ; *Jura*, G. Diùra, for
dýra-ey, deer isle (see Dean Monro's account of 1549).

erg, a shieling, borrowed from Early
G. airge, now àirigh : *Scourie*,
G. Sgoghairigh for skóga-erg,
copse shieling (Eng. shaw); for
other examples see G. Henderson's *Norse Influence*, p. 164.

ey, an island : *Berneray*, Bjarnar-ey,
Björn's isle (Björn means bear);
Borreray, borgar-ey, fort isle;
Canna, can isle; from the shape of
a prominent rock; cf. *Dun-can*
[*Raasay*]; *Eriskay*, Eric's isle;
Fladday, flat isle; *Handa*, sand-
ey, sand isle (with *s* aspirated to
sh, sounded *h*); *Kerrera*, in
Norse Sagas, Kjarbar-ey; in G.
Cear(bh)ara, first part doubtful;
Pabbay, priest isle; *Mingulay*,
doubtful; ‘*Raasay*, G. Rathar-
saidh, perhaps for rár-áss-ey, roe-
ridge isle; *Ròna*, hraun-ey, rough
isle; *Torsay*, Thori's isle; *Trod-*
day, Thrond's isle; *Gigha*, in
Hakon Saga Guðey; G. Giogha,
Gioghaidh. The N. Guðey means
god-isle, possibly good isle; the
G. form should come from a word
beginning with *gj-*. *Lunga*, lung-
ey, ship isle (N. lung, ship, is
borrowed from G. long). *Oron-*
say, G. Orasa, is for orfiris-ey,
ebb-tide isle, *i.e.* an island which
at low water is joined to the mainland by a reef or ford, covered at
high water; the G. equivalent is
Eilean Tioram, dry island. *Taran-*
say, Taran's isle, Taran being the

short form of Torannan, an early Irish saint. On the island are the remains of a small church called Teampull Tharain, Taran's Temple, and a graveyard called Cladh Tharain, Taran's cemetery.

eyrr, a gravelly bank or beach: *Erradale*, gravel beach dale; *Eribol*, gravel beach farm.

fjall, a hill, fell: *Eaval*, Euval, ey-fjall, island hill; *Goatfell*, geita-fjall, goat hill (G. Gaodabheinn, where fjall is translated by G. beinn. peak, hill; so *Blāven* for blāfjall, blue hill; cf. blae-berry); *Loyal*, in G. Laghal, for laga-fjall, law hill, or laga-völlr, law field; cf. *Dingwall*, Thing-field; *Stula-val*, doubtful.

fjörðr, a firth, bay: *Ailort* for áll-fjorðr, eel bay, or, deep channel bay (*áll* has both meanings); *Ainort* or *Eynort*, perhaps Ey-vind's bay; *Eiseord*, doubtful; *Gruinard*, G. Gruinneard, grunna-fjorðr, shallow bay (several bays so named); *Inchard*, doubtful; *Kanaird*, can bay; cf. Canna; *Knoydart*, G. Cnòideart, Knút's bay; *Melfort*, mel-f., bent grass bay; *Sunart*, G. Suaineort, Svein's bay.

hóp, a small landlocked bay or inlet: *Obbe*, G. Òb; *Oban* is its diminutive (Argyll O. is in G. An t-Òban Latharnach, the Oban of Lorn).

nes, a cape, point, promontory: *Ness* in Lewis; usually final, G. -nis, anglicised -nish: *Ard-tornish*, Thori's cape (G. ard, point, added); *Callernish*, in G. Calanais, uncertain; *Grīminish*, Grím's cape; *Hūnish*, may be húnn-nes, bear cape; *Skipness*

ship cape; *Trotternish*, G. Tron-darnais, Throndarnes, Thrond's cape; *Vaternish*, vatna-nes, water cape (*i.e.* projecting far into the sea); *Dun-staffnage*, fort of staff cape; G. Dun-stafhanais.

óss, river mouth, corresponding to G. inbhear, inver: *Ose*, G. Òs; *Aros*, see *á*.

sker, a skerry, isolated rock in the sea: *Hyskeir*, G. Hei(ll)sgeir, hellu-sker, flat skerry; *Hasker*, G. Haisgeir, hafs-sker, deep sea skerry; *Sùlasgeir*, súla-sker, pillar skerry; cf. *Sūilven* for súl-fjall, pillar fell.

slēttr, smooth: Sléit, *Sleat*; *Slatta-dale*, G. Sléitedal, smooth dale.

staðr, a stead, abode: *Hōsta*, hauga-staðr, howe stead, cairn stead; common terminally as -sta.

stafr, a staff, post: *Staffa*, stafa-ey, pillar isle; *Staffin*, the staff or pillar (here the article is suffixed); *Dunstaffnage*.

staurr, a stake, pillar: *Stòrr*; Bodach Stòrr, "the Old Man of Storr," is a euphemism.

vágr, a bay: *Stornoway*, stjórnar-vágr, rudder bay, steerage bay; common terminally.

vatn, water, lake: common in Lewis as -bhat, -vat; *Sandwood*, G. Sandabhat, sandy water or loch.

vík, creek, small inlet: *Ārasaig*, ár-óss-vík, river's mouth creek; *Càrsaig*, probably kárrs-vík, curl bay, from its arches; *Mallaig*, perhaps mala-vík, pebble creek; *Melvaig*, G. Mealbhaig, mela-vík, bent grass creek; *Ostaig*, east creek; *Shieldaig*, G. Sìldeig, síld-vík, herring bay.

GAELIC

O.G. *abh*, a river; genitive abha: Loch Abha, *Loch Awe*, now Loch Obha. Hence *Loch Abhaich*, L. Avich, loch of river-place; Loch Obhaich, *L. Oich*, is the same. Sc. G.abhainn, a river, is dative of abha, gen. abhann.

allt, primarily a steep height, then a burn : Allt Beithe, *Aultbea*, birch burn. The original meaning is seen in An t-Allt Granda, the ugly precipice, near Novar Station.

àird, a point, promontory : Aird Bhreac, *Ardvreck*, dappled point; Dubhaird, *Duart*, black point; Fionnaird, *Finnart*, white or holy point.

baile, a homestead (primarily a spot) : Baile a' Chladaich, *Balchladdich*, shore stead; Baile Raghnaill, *Balranald*, Raghnall's (Ranald's) stead.

bealach, a pass : Bealach a' Mhorghain, gravel pass; often anglicised *Balloch*.

beann, dat. beinn (used as nom.), a peak, mountain : *Cruachan Beann*, Cruachan (Haunch) of Peaks; it has five peaks; *Bidean nam Beann*, point of peaks (usually given as B. nam Bian, point of the hides, from cattle falling over a precipice there); *Beinn Dobhrain*, Ben Doran, peak of the streamlet, whose mouth is at Inbhir Obhrain, *Inveroran*. Terminally it sometimes replaces N. fjall; see *fjall* : *Roisbheinn*, probably for hross-fjall, horse hills.

bràigh, upper part, upland; gen. bràghad, dat, bràighaid : Bràghaid Albann, *Breadalbane*, upland of Alba (Alba here in a restricted sense); Am Bràigh Mór, *Braemore*, the great upland; so Braemoray, Braemar, &c. Am Bràigh *par excellence* was Brae Lochaber; its men are " fir a' Bhràghad," " the men of the upland."

cairidh, a fish weir : Achadh na Cairidh, *Achnacarry*, field of the weir.

call, older coll, hazel : Callaird, *Callart*, hazel point.

calltuinn, hazel, hazel wood : Barr a' Challtuinn, *Barcaldine*, height of the hazel wood.

camas, a bay, bight : Camas-tearach, *Camusterach*, probably easter bay.

caol, a strait (as adj. narrow, slender) : An Caol, *Kyle*, the strait; Caol Reatha, *Kylerhea* (see text for the legend), perhaps from rìth, gen. reatha, strait of current; Caol-chuirn, *Kilchurn*, strait of the cairn; Caol Acuinn, *Kyleakin*, Hacon's strait.

caolas, a strait : Caolas-port, *Caolisport*, strait-ferry; Baile a' Chaolais, *Ballachulish*, homestead of the strait; *Eddrachilles*, Eadarrachaolas (for eadar dà chaolas), between two straits; An Caolas Cumhang, *Kyles. ku*, the narrow strait.

ceall, dat. cill, now used as nom.; a church (now a graveyard) : Na Cilltean, *Keills*, the churches; Cill Mo-Chumaig, *Kilmahumaig*, church of St. Cummóc. *Loch nan Ceall*, Mull, loch of the churches.

cìoch, a pap : *Sgùrr na Cìche*, peak of the pap.

claon, inclined, bent : *Claonaig*, little bent one—a river; cf. Balbhag the little dumb one, Balquhidder.

cóig, five : A' Chóigeach, *Cóigeach*, the district of fifths.

coire, a kettle, cauldron; hence a corrie : Coire Uisge, *Coruisk*, water cauldron, *i.e.* corrie containing a loch; *Coire Bhreacain*, Breacan's cauldron (see text); *Coire Chatachain*, based on cat, a cat, wild cat.

comraich, a sanctuary, place of refuge: two such in the North; (1) Comraich Bhaile Dhubhthaich, St. Duthac's sanctuary of Tain; (2) A' Chomraich Abrach, Mael-rubha's sanctuary of *Applecross* (Abar-crossan), now simply *A' Chomraich*.

cù, a dog, hound: Conghleann, *Conaglen*, hound glen; so Conghlais, *Kinglas*, hound stream, &c.

cuinneag, a milking pail or stoup: Cuinneag, *Quinag*, from its shape; so Carn Cuinneag, n.e. of Wyvis.

dobhar, water, a stream, Welsh dwfr, Early Celtic dubron: Mórdhobhar, *Morar*, great water; Allar, *Alder*, for all-dobhar, cliff water, rock water, whence *Ben Alder*.

dobhran, stream, streamlet: Inbhir Dhobhrain, *Inveroran*, mouth of streamlet, whence *Beinn Dobhrain, Ben Doran*.

dòrn, a fist; dòrnach, place of fists, *i.e.* of pebbles like fists, or that fill the fist: Dòrnaigh, *Dornie*, place of fist-pebbles. So Dornoch, which is nom., while Dornaigh is dative-locative.

dris, brier, bramble: Tìr nan Dris *Tìrnadris*, land of briers.

drong, a troop, company, dat. druing, fem., but in Sc. G. also nom. droing, masc.: *Lochaidh Druing*, lochlet of (the) troop.

dubh, black: An Dubhlochan, *Dulochan*, the black lochlet.

dùn, a fort: Dùn Domhnaill, *Dundonnell*, Donald's fort; *Dun Add*, fort of the river Add; meaning unknown (not fada, O. Ir. fota, long); *Dun Naomhaig*, fort of (the) small boat, skiff (Ir. naomhóg, not used now in Sc. G.); Dùn Mór, *Dunmore*, great fort;

Dùn Chonaill, Dunconnell, Conall's fort, traditionally connected with Conall Cearnach, the Ulster hero; Dun Sgàthaich, *Dunscaith*, Scàthach's fort (see text); Dùn Treoin, *Duntroon*, Trēn's fort (Trén, gen. Treoin, an ancient proper name); *Dùn Tuilm*, fort of (the) isle.

eala, a swan: Loch nan Eala, *Loch Nell*, loch of the swans.

eas, a waterfall, rapid: Dail an Easa, *Dalness*, dale of the waterfall.

fas, fasadh, a stance, a firm level spot: *Fas na Cloiche*, stance of the stone; Am Fasadh Fearna, *Fassiefern*, the alderwood stance.

fionn, white, secondarily holy, blessed: *Fionnchoire*, white corrie; Fionncharn, *Fincharn*, white cairn; Fionnaird, *Finnart*, white point (probably holy point).

Gàidheal, a Gael: Earra Ghàidheal (for Oirear Ghàidheal), *Argyll*, coastland of the Gael (pl.); Peighinn a' Ghàidheil, *Pennyghael*, penny land of the Gael (sg.).

gàir, a cry, outcry: Loch na Gàire, *Lochnagar*, loch of the outcry (*i.e.* of the wind among the rocks).

gobha, a smith; gen. gobhann: Peighinn a' Ghobhann, *Pennygowan*, pennyland of the smith; Baile nan Gobhann, *Balnagown*, homestead of the smiths.

gorm, green, blue, azure: Carn Gorm, *Cairngorm*, the azure cairn (cairn is not uncommonly applied to a high rocky hill).

hirt, hiort, death: *Hiort* or *Eilean Hirt*, St. Kilda, isle of death, deadly isle; *An Dubh Hirteach*, the black deadly one; hiort is long obsolete.

inbhear, inbhir, a river mouth: Loch an Inbhir, *Loch Inver*, loch of the river mouth; Inver Aora (older Aghra, Adhra), *Inveraray*, mouth of Aray—meaning unknown.

innis, an island, a riverside meadow; often anglicised Inch; Craignis, *Craignish* (by syncope from creag-innis), rock meadow; Aird Mhucnis, *Ardmucknish*, cape of swine meadow.

iubhar, a yew tree: *Creag an Iubhair, Craignure*, rock of the yew; *Gleann Iubhair, Glenure*, glen of (the) yew; *Cill an Iubhair, Kilneuair*, church of the yew; cf. the giant yew at Fortingal Church.

leac, a flagstone; also a hill face, as Leac Ruaidh, *Leckroy*, the hill slope above the river Roy: *Leac na Muidhe*, flagstone or hill face of the churn.

lios, an enclosure, a fort, the enclosure of a monastery: Lios Mór, *Lismore*, great enclosure, *i.e.* Mo Luag's monastery.

lòch, black (now obsolete): Lòchaidh (for Lòch-dea), black goddess, Adamnan's Stagnum Lōchdiae, Nigra Dea), the river of Loch Lōchy; several other rivers Lòchaidh.

machair, a plain, lowland, *e.g.* Machair Rois, Easter Ross; A' Mhachair Ghallda, the lowlands of Scotland: Machair Shanais, *Machriehanish*, plain of "sanas," some kind of plant.

madadh, a dog, hound: Loch nam Madadh, *Lochmaddy*, from three rocks in the bay, called Na Madaidhean, the hounds.

magh, a plain; dat. muigh: A' Mhoigh, *Moy*; Mackintosh is Tighearna na Moighe, lord of Moy.

muc, a pig: *Eilean nam Muc*, Isle of Muck, island of swine; *Aird Mhucnis*, point of swine meadow (see innis).

muir, the sea, in composition mor-: A' Mhorbhairn, *Morvern*, the sea gap (bearn, bearna); A' Mhormhoich, *Morvich* the sea

plain (mor- and magh, plain)—common.

orc, a young boar: Arcaibh, older Orcaib (dative pl.), *Orkney*; lit. "among the young boars," a tribal name. So Cataibh, "among the Cats," Sutherland, strictly south-east Sutherland.

riabhach, brindled: Bràigh Riabhach, *Braeriach*, brindled upland.

rubha, rudha, a cape: *Rudha a' Mhàil*, cape of the rent; probably the ancient Ard Bés, point of taxes; *An Rudha Réidh*, the smooth point.

righe, ruighe, a forearm, a slope: gen. righeadh; Ruighe Cóinnich, *Rhiconich*, mossy slope; very common in northern names. *Portree*, Skye, is regularly Port Righeadh with Gaelic-speaking Skyemen, not Port Rìgh; *i.e.* harbour of (the) slope, not "of the king."

sabhal, a barn: Tom an t-Sabhail, *Tomintoul*, knoll of the barn; so Carntoul, cairn of the barn; *Màm Sabhail*, rounded hill of barns, W. Ross, was noted for its grass.

saill, fatness: Drum Saille, *Drumsallie*, ridge of fatness, *i.e.* of rich grass.

seunta, sianta, holy: *An Loch Sianta*, Holy Loch, Cowal; Na h-Eileanan Sianta, the *Shiant* isles, the holy isles; *Loch Sianta*, Skye, had a holy well (see Martin's *Western Islands*).

slig, a shell: *Sligeachan*, shelly place; so Sligo.

tairbeart, an isthmus: anglicised *Tarbert*, Tarbat.

teallach, a forge: *An Teallach*, W. Ross.

tiompan, a buttock, rounded hillock or point: Rudha an Tiompain, *Tiompan Head*, cape of the buttock.

toll, a hole: *Clach Toll*, stone of

holes; Tollard, *Toward* in Cowal, hole point, from the holes in the limestone of which it is composed; Tollaigh, Tolly, *Towie*, a hollow place—several. *Bidean a' Ghlastuill*, peak of the green hollow.

tòrr, a heap, rounded hill: Tòrr Loisgte, *Torloisk*, burnt hillock.

tioram, dry: *Eilean Tioram*, the general G. term for an island which is accessible on foot at low tide; hence *Caisteal Tioram* on Eilean Tioram.

tràigh, a beach: Ceann Tràighe, *Kintrae*, head of beach; *An Tràigh Bàn*, the fair beach, Colonsay (here tràigh retains its old neuter gender).

INDEX

Note.—The page numbers in italics refer to the Glossary; the stress accent is indicated by a dot placed *before* the stressed syllable.

A

A' ·CHAILLEACH, 3, *323*
Achaius, 146
Ach·aracle, 168, 170, 246, 247
Ach·arn, 210
Achen·bracke, 148
Achda·lieu, 146, 149
Achilti·buie, 23
Achna·carry, 127, 130, 134, 138, *411*
Achna·con, 213
Achna·craig, 271
Achna·sheen, 61
A' ·Chomraich, 50, *412*
·Adamnan, Abbot of Iona, 67, 171, 175, 248, 319, 320, 324, 343, 347, 348
·Aengus, King of Picts, 334
·Ailech, graves of, 321
  holy rocks of, 323
  monastery of, 319, 320, 322
·Ailort, *410*
Ailsa Craig, 370
·Airidh na ·Sliseig, 284
Alan MacRuairidh, 169
·Alba, 221, 288
Alexander II, 230
  charter by, 330
Alexander III, 327, 348
Allan Breac, 211
Allan Mór of Moidart, 172
All Saints Church, Inveraray, 359
Allt a' ·Mhuilinn, 6
Alt·greshan, 36
Am ·Bodach, 3
Am ·Buachaille, 3, 4, 5
Am ·Fasadh ·Fearna, 150
A' ·Mhorbhairn, 238
Amhuinn Shlatach, 153
Anderson, Doctor Joseph, 297
An ·Ealadh, 293
Angel's Knoll, 295
An Gobha Mór, 123
Angus Mór of Stron·tian, 247
Angus of the Isles, 282
Angus, Prince of Ireland, 221
Annals of the Four Masters, 49
Annals of Ulster, 227, 300
An Stac, 21
An ·Teallach, 23, 25, 27–30, 38, 41, *413*
An Tigh ·Dige (Flowerdale House), 34
an t-Sáil Liath, 29
An Uaimh ·Shianta, 58

·Aonach ·Dubh, 198
·Aonaidh nam ·Muc, 304
Apor·crossan, 51
·Appin, 211, 212, 224
·Applecross, 44, 48–52, 54, 55, 119, 123, 125, 159, *412*
  Bay, 55
  churchyard, 42
  Red Priest of, 50
  Sanctuary of, 50, 51
·Arcuill, 12
Ard·alanish Point, 298
·Ard Bheinn, 367
Ard·chattan Priory, 225
Ard·fenaig, 257, 260
Ard·gour, 173, 212, 221, 240
  hills of, 267, 322
Ard·kinglas, 361, *412*
Ard·meanach, 159, 259
Ard·more, 99, 101
Ard·mucknish, *413*
Ardna·murchan, 70, 76, 129, 161, 168, 180, 221, 243–246
·Ardnish, 158
Ard·rishaig, 343
Ard·sheal, 210, 211, 213
Ard·toe, 247
Ard·tornish, 404, *410*
  castle, 239
Ard·vasar, 72
Ard·vreck Castle, 16, 17, *411*
Ar·gyll, 147, 153, 197, 209, 312, 316, 357, *412*
  Archibald, Earl of, 397
  burial-place of, 394
  Colin, Earl of, 392
  Dukes of, 250, 260
  Earls of, 196, 206, 226, 267, 309, 314, 362
  family, 324
  MacCailein, Duke of, 359
  name of, 332
  Regiment of, 201, 202, 205
·Arisaig, 74, 154, 160, 174, *410*
·Arkaig River, 132, 133
·Armadale, 156, 266, *409*
  Castle, 72, 73, 74, 82, 129
·Arnisdale, 129, *409*
·Aros, Castle of, 265, 266, *409*
·Arran, 344, 367–389, 404
  Cock of, 369
  Earl of, 346
Artbranan, 67
Art·chain, 249